POETRY, ENCLOSURE, AND THE VERNACULAR LANDSCAPE, 1700–1830

Rachel Crawford examines the intriguing, often problematic, relationship between poetry and landscape in eighteenth- and early nineteenth-century Britain. Crawford focuses on the gradual change during this period from the British taste for open space to a preference for confined space, so that by the beginning of the Regency period contained sites, both topographical and poetic, were perceived to express authentic English qualities. In this context, Crawford discusses the highly fraught parliamentary enclosure movement which closed off the last of England's open fields between 1760 and 1815. She takes enclosure as a prevailing metaphor for a reconceptualization of the aesthetics of space in which enclosed and confined sites became associated with productivity; and sets explicit images, such as the apple, the iron industry, and the kitchen garden within the context of georgic and minor lyric poetry.

RACHEL CRAWFORD is Associate Professor in the Department of English at the University of San Francisco. She has published articles in *Studies in Romanticism*, *ELH*, *Romanticism*, and *European Romantic Review*.

POETRY, ENCLOSURE, AND THE VERNACULAR LANDSCAPE, 1700–1830

RACHEL CRAWFORD

CAMBRIDGE
UNIVERSITY PRESS

PUBLISHED BY THE PRESS SYNDICATE OF THE UNIVERSITY OF CAMBRIDGE
The Pitt Building, Trumpington Street, Cambridge, United Kingdom

CAMBRIDGE UNIVERSITY PRESS
The Edinburgh Building, Cambridge CB2 2RU, UK
40 West 20th Street, New York, NY 10011-4211, USA
477 Williamstown Road, Port Melbourne, VIC 3207, Australia
Ruiz de Alarcón 13, 28014 Madrid, Spain
Dock House, The Waterfront, Cape Town 8001, South Africa

http://www.cambridge.org

First published 2002

Printed in the United Kingdom at the University Press, Cambridge

Typeface Baskerville Monotype 11/12.5 pt   *System* LATEX 2ε [TB]

A catalogue record for this book is available from the British Library

ISBN 0 521 81531 2 hardback

For Tami
metta

Contents

Illustrations

Preface

Coleridge is only one of many figures in this study who inhabit the long eighteenth century, yet his presence everywhere informs it. Though he once lightly described his own kinetic mind as "unfortunately little more than a far-stretched Series of Et Ceteras" (*Notebooks*, 3: 4250), his was more accurately, in his own neologism, esemplastic. Though his curiosity ranged over interests as disparate as the Prometheus of Aeschylus and the novels of Ann Radcliffe, landscape aesthetics and a nascent industrial canal system, spiritual purity and recipes for vegetables, his habit was to draw alien things together in reshaping moments of surprise, wit, and affection – a habit he once referred to as a penchant toward "fantastic analogue & similitude" (*Notebooks*, 1: 277). All who have read Coleridge's notebooks and letters are familiar with his protean mind, yet his own best gift was one he attributed to William Cowper as "divine Chit chat" (*Letters*, 1: 164). This quality of Coleridge's perhaps more than any other – his genius, his humility, his profound sense of his own psychic depth and loneliness, or his warm humor – has motivated my own work. Coleridge's familiarization of the divine as chit chat, his habitual tendency to regard the high in terms of the low has helped me to see the alteration of notions of English space in the long eighteenth century in a particular light; for while he may abstract jasmine and myrtle as emblems of innocence and love, it was the potato blossom that appeared to his eye as "the loveliest & richest flower of Gardens" (*Notebooks*, 1: 1476). Referring to Sir Walter Raleigh and "Speculative men," only Coleridge could conclude, "Good Heavens! Let me never eat a roasted Potatoe without dwelling on it and detailing its train of consequences" (*Notebooks*, 3: 2488). When contemplating heated responses generated by personal disagreement, only he would couch a self-recommendation for preemptive action in terms of the cooling palliative of a plate of cucumbers:

– in all these cases, write your Letter, *vent, & ease yourself,* and when you have done it – even as when you have pared, sliced, vinegared, oiled, peppered & salted your plate of Cucumber you are directed to smell to it – & then throw it out of the window – so, dear friend! vinegar, pepper, & salt your Letter, cucumber argument – i.e. cool reasoning – previously sauced with passion & sharpness – then read it – eat it, drink it, smell it, with eyes & ears – (a small catachresis, but never mind) – & then throw it into the fire – (*Notebooks,* 2: 2379)

Coleridge draws here on a long tradition of folk custom rooted in the Galenic theory of humors and grounded in associations between a common salad vegetable and homeopathic remedy. Coleridge's eye for the ordinary, for the similitude that reduces abstraction to humble experience even as his mind ceaselessly converted lived experience into abstruse thought, grounds this study. Without presuming to Coleridge's habit of thought, I also seek the ordinary in lived experience, even as I abstract from the ordinary to define the path that charted English revaluations of space in the long eighteenth century. From kitchen gardeners, coal miners, and ciderists to georgic poets and writers of lyric verse, this study looks to vernacular sites in the eighteenth century as forms which define English prospects – forms which allow us to consider different materials (words and space) in terms of shared social proportion and weight, and to locate changes in the concept of social space in the interstices of topographies and literature.

My guides on this path have been the people in my life who constitute my most ordinary friendships and who keep me tethered to the realities of lived experience. In Coleridge's own best words, "Like the Gossamer Spider, we may float upon air and seem to fly in mid heaven, but we have spun the slender Thread out of our ~~fane~~ own fancies, & it is always fastened to something below" (*Notebooks,* 2: 2166). Whether that something below be the domestic requirements of the home or the privilege of friendship, my best understanding of the texts I read has always arisen out of the everyday – the chance conversation, the serendipitous remark, the ordinary affections of life. Chief of these ordinary affections is Tami Spector, and second only to her is Rose Zimbardo, my genial authority, irascible muse, and faithful mentor. Tim Fulford has been friend, critic, and reader, guide to Herefordshire and jazz, benefactor of time, and more valued than an acknowledgment can express. Added to these are my friends – Susan, Carmen, Eileen, Marg and Coll, Nikki and Liz, Marty and Derek, Rick and Terry, Alan and Paddy, Peter and Rebecca. Our shared meals and cynicisms gave me the balance which only humor can provide. I have been shadowed by my best and most demanding teachers – Mary Nicoll, Ann Paton, Mona Modiano, and Hazard Adams. Nat, Nell, and Elwyn, who remain bemused by my academic labor and firmly attached to my more local priorities, have kept my affections moored. And of course there is Percy, whose mealtimes require regularity and whose enthusiasm for his humans knows no bounds. The University of San Francisco Faculty Development Fund provided the seed money that made this project possible. I want to thank the members of this committee, and especially John Pinelli, for stretching institutional resources to meet my research needs. His rationality and generosity confound common notions of academic administrators. Finally, Linda Bree has been a responsive and humane editor who shepherded me through the review process and always answered e-mail.

I have a debt, both institutional and fond, to the Huntington Library, which supported this study with two grants, a Meyer Fellowship in the Summer of 1996 and a Barbara Thom Fellowship for 1997–1998. The elegant environment of the Huntington Library provided not only space and time for reading and research and for daily retreats into its rose, Japanese, cactus, and tropical gardens, but for the friendship of academics who in ways subtle and otherwise influenced my thought. Judith Jackson Fossett and Erika Bsumek were faithful lunch and walking companions; John Steadman, also lunch-date extraordinaire, proved a steady source of materials which were always enriching and almost always relevant. His knowledge of Milton and emblems improved my understanding well beyond the purview of this book. Finally, most important of my Huntington debts is Roy Ritchie, Director of Research, superintendent of the many fellows who move through its halls, and inhabiting spirit whose genial presence can be felt throughout that splendid institution.

Portions of this book have been previously published. Chapter 4 appeared as "English Georgic and British Nationhood" *ELH* 65 (1998): 123–58 reprinted by permission of Johns Hopkins University Press. Portions of Chapter 9 were reprinted from "Troping the Subject: Behn, Smith, Hemans and the Poetics of the Bower," *Studies in Romanticism* 38.2 (1999): 249–79 by permission of Boston University.

PART ONE

Representational spaces

CHAPTER I

Introduction: expansion and contraction

I have upwards of thirty Years been placed near *London*, on a Spot
of Ground, where I have raised several thousand Plants, both from
foreign Countries, and of the *English* Growth; and in that Time,
and from the Observations I have made in the *London* Practice of
Gardening, I find that every thing will not prosper in London; either
because the Smoke of the Sea-Coal does hurt to some Plants, or
else because those People, who have little Gardens in *London*, do not
know how to manage their Plants when they have got them: And
yet I find, that almost every Body, whose Business requires them to
be constantly in Town, will have something of a Garden at any rate.

Thomas Fairchild, Gardener of Hoxton
The City Gardener (1722)

Containment is not the first thing to come to mind when reading histories of Great Britain's eighteenth century. Not only did England enlarge
and codify its native borders through the Act of Union with Scotland
in 1707, it also expanded its imperial drive through its colonial interests
in the Americas, solidified its trading networks in south and southeast
Asia, and laid the groundwork for a second empire which would emerge
in the following century.[1] Expansion was underscored by an intensifying national belief in a uniquely British form of liberty conducive to
productivity in all areas: increased revenues and raw goods from colonial acquisitions, increased exports of woolen, cotton, and linen goods,
of iron, brass, and all manner of small manufactures from egg cups to
garden rakes. Increased production and diversification of food at home
matched growth in exports.[2] A thriving kitchen-garden industry supplied
London and the provincial cities year round with fresh vegetables and
fruits such as artichokes and cucumbers, peaches and oranges, which a
century before had been deemed "curious" and difficult to grow. Experiments in farming and husbandry increased yields of grain and diversified
breeds of sheep and cattle. Perhaps most significantly, after the loss of the
American War in 1783 the nation did not founder but rose to create a

3

new, global ascendancy based on trade between the metropole and a vast periphery of colonial holdings. By the end of the Regency period in 1820 the peoples of Great Britain and her dominions represented more than a quarter of the world population. In order to manage these holdings and to extend British order and virtue into all areas of the world, investments in military strength were substantially increased and the numbers of the armed forces were tripled between 1793 and 1815; military investment in turn assisted the enforcement of the economic doctrine of free trade abroad.[3] At home, especially in the wake of the French Revolution and the execution of Louis XVI in January 1793, ritual displays of monarchy intensified and proliferated, while the scale of civic buildings increased dramatically.[4] As C. A. Bayly has shown, even the hiatus between the first period of empire ending in 1783 and the second, beginning about 1830, was a time of "massive expansion of British dominion, of techniques of governance and exploitation." Ironically, as Bayly elaborates, these developments accompanied (may even have been driven by) distresses at home and abroad which brought with them a sense of national vulnerability. Defeat in North America, the threat represented by revolutionary France, and domestic disorder intensified the drive toward expansion.[5]

During this entire century trade, liberty, and empire apotheosized the increasing reach of Britain's arm and fabricated an image of a small nation defined on all sides by the sea which formed a vital core of centrifugal power, a vigorous heart pumping lifeblood outward into the extremities of a Britannizable world.[6] Even during times of foreign threat that produced sentiments of strident isolationism, expansion remained the key discourse. Landscape treatises popular among those with large estates were vital distributors of this ideal, for the espousal of an unrestrained prospect was consistent with expansionist fervor. As Stephen Switzer commented in his landmark *Ichnographia Rustica* (1715), "This Natural and Rural way of Gardening will appear of more Use, when we consider the Natural Frame and Temper of Mankind; for as the Imagination is continually taken up, and pleas'd with new Objects, and roves through the vast Fields of Nature uncontroul'd, nothing will fully satisfy it, but Immensity . . ."[7] Preoccupation with an unbounded view in the best-known landscaping treatises, however, conceals the presence of sites that cannot so usefully be characterized as representational. Contained, vernacular spaces such as town and kitchen gardens, which did not assist in the conceptualization of England's national agenda, were part of a more muted conversation conducted among a thriftier audience. These spaces form a bedrock that was jolted to the surface by a seismic shift in public perception that took place during the final quarter of the century. In this shift, contained spaces geared toward productivity, usually (although not uniformly) of smaller dimension, took hold of the English imagination. As Stephen Daniels comments, although parkland actually increased in acreage through the Victorian period, "the landed estate loosened its grip on the political imagination."[8] Contained spaces began to receive the attention of the architects of space: building designers, gardeners and agriculturists, even poets.

Such a shift alerts us to the structure of representation inherent in the symbolic content of space in eighteenth-century England. This period opened with the imperative of expanding national boundaries, first through the Act of Union, which confirmed an already existent commercial, political, and geographical relationship with Scotland; and, second, through the Treaty of Utrecht in 1713, which legitimated England's imperial endeavors. Political expansionism was paralleled in landscaping treatises by the celebration of unrestricted views in the vast parks of the gentry and in popular literature by the elevation of the sprawling form of English georgic poetry. Events leading up to the loss of the North American empire, by contrast, were accompanied by a fascination with the constitution and nature of boundaries. After the Regency, in an era when British imperial fortunes once again seemed boundless, a new sense of the kinds of spaces productive of Englishness profoundly different from that which followed the Act of Union emerged. These were the common spaces of the cottage garden, the homes and hearths of ordinary people, and, in literature, the minor lyric, which reemerged after a century of neglect in dizzying numbers as a vernacular form in magazines, correspondence, and parlor games. Susan Stewart suggests, "we can posit an isomorphism between changes in genre and changes in other modes of production."[9] The congruencies Stewart postulates – relationships between things drawn by virtue of their forms – may be better understood in terms of isomerism. Unlike isomorphism, which foregrounds the similarity of forms, isomerism allows us to consider different materials (for example, words and space) in terms of shared social proportion and weight, despite the fact that they may display different properties. The isomeric relations of words and space are revealed in eighteenth-century texts that situate changes in the concept of social space in the interstices of topographies and literature. Indeed, although Stewart cautions that "historical and generic conventions cannot be mapped upon the real," the authors of eighteenth-century treatises which mediate the "real" practices of gardening or farming and poetic composition pilfer from each other's disciplines as they work to build consensus and authority for their respective trades. They readily negate material differences between words and space in order to privilege social and theoretical congruencies. In their minds, it would seem, although the boundaries between the landscape and literature may be posted, they are negotiable by the hucksters of language.

Poets, critics, and garden-manual writers of the eighteenth century and after reveal important assumptions concerning the congruence of topographical and poetic forms brought under the social and artistic requirements of containment. Among the most insightful of these is Regency critic, Leigh Hunt, a prolific writer who lived a long life and who provides a critique of contained forms that is distinguished because, perhaps naively, he is never vexed by the stigma of small or defined spaces. Some of his observations, such as those in *The Book of the Sonnet*, published posthumously in 1867, provide a retrospective lens, having been made well after the change in public approbation for the contained space had taken place – indeed, at a time when the value of containment had become so pronounced that gardeners touted the ultimate abstraction of the greenhouse in the Wardian case and the diminution of the flower garden in the portable potted plant. Hunt's comments on lyric form remain remarkably consistent over these years, beginning with the Regency decade when the authority of extension for its own sake had given way to an acceptance of containment as a positive domestic good. Although his rococo poetic sensibility has not been highly valued, it gave him a fundamental insight into the nature of confinement and the peculiar requirements of contained space, evidenced by his equal enthusiasm for the sonnet and his own suburban garden. His writing consistently reveals crossings between lyric and topographical spaces. His Introductory Letter to *The Book of the Sonnet* opens typically:

I cannot help looking upon myself, in this matter, as a kind of horticulturist who has brought a stock of flowers with him from Italy and England, for the purpose of diffusing their seeds and off-sets, wherever the soil can be found congenial; and therefore, with your leave, and with the privilege of free-speaking which is conceded to guests and graybeards, I hereby give notice, that if in the course of a few years from the date of this intimation a good crop of Sonnets, of all hues and varieties, does not start up throughout the said quarters, like a new flush of beauty to your meadows, or song to your groves, (for birds and flowers grow ripe together), I shall be inclined to ask my American cousins what right they possess not only to the wit and the poetry that already flourish among them, but to the more than Italian sun that warms so much of their territory, and to that extraordinary feathered songster, the Mocking-Bird, which is the only imitator in the world that beats what it imitates.[10]

Hunt's conceit illustrates the porous boundaries between poetry and horticulture by inverting a well-established convention in garden treatises of presenting garden design in literary terms. Addison had famously remarked in *The Spectator* 477 (1712),

I think there are as many Kinds of Gardening, as of Poetry; Your Makers of Parterres and Flower-Gardens, are Epigrammatists and Sonneteers in this Art. Contrivers of Bowers and Grotto's, Treillages and Cascades, are Romance Writers. *Wise* and *London* are our Heroick Poets... As for my self, you will find, by the Account which I have already given you, that my Compositions in Gardening are altogether after the *Pindarick* manner, and run into the beautiful Wildness of Nature, without affecting the nicer Elegancies of Art.[11]

Sir William Chambers demonstrates the continuity of this tradition when he notes in 1772 that "[t]he scenery of a garden should differ as much from common nature as an heroic poem doth from a prose relation; and Gardeners, like poets, should give a loose to their imagination, and even fly beyond the bounds of truth, whenever, it is necessary to elevate, to embellish, to enliven, or to add novelty to their subject."[12] William Marshall, best known as an agriculturist, follows suit when he urges that the landscape garden be continuous with the country round it: "A true Landscape makes but a small part, is but a speck, in the face of a country; a mere episode of the general scene: and it were folly indeed, to mar the poem to make the episode; to sacrifice the whole to perhaps a comparatively insignificant part."[13]

Even when they do not make direct analogies between landscape and poetry, literary critics, for their part, commonly stipulate rules for the small or narrow compass of the lyric poem that can as easily apply to the garden. Literary critics of the later eighteenth century make the congruence so readily that it infiltrates virtually every preface or introduction to a collection of poetry. John Ogilvie, for example, in "An Essay on the Lyric Poetry of the Ancients," written during the height of the greenhouse craze, writes,

the simple beauties of the Eclogue would appear in the same light, when transposed to the Epopee, as plants brought to forced vegetation in a Green-house must do to those who have seen them flourishing in their native soil, and ripened by the benignity of an happier climate. In the one case they are considered as unnatural productions, whose beauty is surpassed by the Natives of the soil; in the other they are regarded as just and decent ornaments, whose real excellence is properly estimated.[14]

Referring to conventions of garden manuals, John Aikin, brother to Anna Laetitia Barbauld and a respected critic in his own right, writes concerning epic and dramatic poetry, "some of the most excellent productions in the former have been the spontaneous growth of a rude and uncultivated soil, whereas the latter have never flourished without acquired richness in the soil and the fostering hand of art."[15]

Poets are equally likely to cross boundaries between the culture of literature and culture of the soil. So Wordsworth alludes to the sonnet in "Nun's Fret Not in their Solitary Cells" as a "a scanty plot of ground" and Keats affixes an epigraph from Hunt's *Story of Rimini*, "Places of nestling green for poets made," to his poem, "I stood tip-toe upon a little hill." Coleridge, in a notebook entry of 1816, writes,

Reflections on my four gaudy Flower-pots, compared with the former Flower-poems – After a certain period, crowded with Poetry-counterfeiters, and illustrious with true Poets, there is formed for common use a vast *garden* of Language – all the shewy, and all the odorous Words, and Clusters of Words, are brought together – and to be plucked by mere mechanic and passive Memory – . . . we carry our judgements of Times & Circumstances, into our Pleasures – a Flower-Pot which would have inchanted us before Flower-gardens were common, for the very beauty of the component Flowers, will be rightly condemned as *common-place out of place* – (for such is a common-place *Poet* – it involves a contradiction but in Terms & Thought –).[16]

Coleridge's comment not only presses the conceit in which horticulture and poetry become equivalent, but also documents the fashion for herbaceous gardening that had grown into a national pastime between the American War and the Regency period. It is small wonder that Regency poets wandered so effortlessly back and forth between these domains. Hunt's metaphors make the aesthetic continuities between literature and landscape especially clear, since he consistently confuses the boundaries between the two. Indeed, he seems to experience landscape *as* literature and literature as a landscape. Thus he notes in *Bacchus in Tuscany* (1825), "In going through the green lands and vineyards, you go through the Georgics. You lounge with Horace under his vine, and see him helping his labourers. Here comes a passage in the shape of a yoke of oxen; – there runs a verse up the wall, – a lizard; – the *cicadæ* ring lyrics at you from the trees."[17]

These examples manifest a tendency, rampant during this period, to equilibrate the intellectual systems of poetry (words) and topography (space). Such overt congruencies provide a point of entry into ways that social forms, whether literary or topographical, generate representational and nonrepresentational spaces. In this book I show how representational conceptions of space intersect with representational forms in literature – from georgic poetry, which dominated the collective imagination from the Act of Union until the reign of George III, to lesser lyric forms, especially the sonnet and minor ode, which caught the imagination of the romantic generations as they had not done since the seventeenth century. In the first part of this book I discuss the construction of English space in the twin movements of park building and parliamentary enclosure. The treatises that document these movements are increasingly concerned over the course of the eighteenth century with the relationship between space and productivity and are correspondingly increasingly anxious about the nature of boundaries. The parliamentary enclosures, especially, reflected assumptions about the relation between containment and productivity and unleashed anxieties about boundaries. Heated arguments, which may support or contest the plight of the disenfranchised, the requirements of the prosperous tenant farmer, or the natural rights of the gentry, suggest that enclosures of wasteland, commons, and common fields became the most visible metaphor for concerns over national identity and imperial prospects. These treatises overlook or obfuscate, however, the vernacular prospects of ordinary life, those prospects that were in fact idealized within the framework of English georgic poetry. In part two, therefore, I examine georgic poetry, paying special attention to two poems which critics have tacitly used to mark the beginning and end of the georgic decades, but which have been rarely examined: John Philips's *Cyder* and Richard Jago's *Edge-Hill*. These poems allow me to explore the role the apple played in creating a sense of English space and to consider the provincial metals industry of Birmingham in "toys" – small iron and brass (and later steel) objects ranging from hinges and castors to garden and farming tools. The significant characteristic of these toys is their embodiment of an association between size, ingenuity, and contrivance. Toys produced by the farmer-smith, the small shopkeeper, or the artisan in the larger factory become emblematic of containment as it was expressed across the spectrum of poetry, the vernacular landscape, and industry. They suggest the role of contrivance in the field of enclosure (to use a loaded phrase) and embody the interrelation between two competing notions: industry, usually

characterized as "laboriousness," and ingenuity. It was not until new
conceptions of genius took hold later in the century that "laboriousness"
would be devalued and lose its artisanal meanings. In the earlier part of
the century it was often used in addition as an honorific term when applied to the farmer, careful kitchen gardener, and poet (although writers
of garden treatises and literary critics distinguish between purely manual
labor and that associated with artistry). When Philip Miller prefaces his
first edition of *The Gardeners Dictionary* with an approbation of the gentlemen who have "generously given Encouragement to Artists to *labour* to
trace Nature more closely in the Propagation of Vegetables" (my emphasis), his use of the word is, without irony, linked to his notion of artistic
invention in gardening.[18] Like the gardener, the poet is an ingenious,
skillful, and "laborious" artist and, as in the case of the gardener, his
labor is distinguished from purely manual toil. Joseph Warton testifies to
this conventional wisdom that linked labor and art. Referring his readers
to Aristotle, he reminds them that "no writer should ever forget, – that
diction ought most to be laboured in the unactive, that is, the descriptive
parts of a poem, in which the opinions manners and passions of men
are not represented"; he cements the association of labor with artifice
when (following Aristotle) he applauds Empedocles' style for being "well
laboured, and full of metaphors."[19] As the century closes into its final
quarter, by contrast, literary critics speak increasingly of indolence as
the state most closely associated with imaginative effort. Laboriousness
becomes an increasingly divided term, as likely to be associated with
pompous, uninventive poets who tire the reader by being, to use Anna
Seward's phrase, "finicaly laboured" as to suggest the role of contrivance
in the manufacture of art.[20] The artist is better, in Keats's remarkable
oxymoron, to practice a "delicious, diligent Indolence."[21]

The Birmingham toy, a product of diligence, ingenuity, and contrivance, feeds into the nexus of meanings that are brought together
in the honorific use of "labor" which enjoyed such currency in garden
manuals and critical essays in the first three-quarters of the century. In
shops and factories these terms intertwine even as they harden into their
modern meanings: the labor of the artisan in Matthew Boulton's Soho
factory or the small shopkeeper producing a myriad of brass cocks is
part and parcel with ingenuity. The toy forms not merely a connection
between the fruits of the soil and the fruits of industry, however, but a dramatic instance of the role of diminution in the aesthetic of forms and the
meanings which accrued to smaller, contained objects and topographical sites. The Birmingham toy thus provides a transition to the subject

of the third part of this book: the reemergence of minor lyric forms, the characteristics of which I apply both to poetry and the landscape, especially the sonnet and kitchen garden. In the last three decades of the century, renewed enthusiasm for the sonnet betrays the labor and ingenuity of the author. The urbane, restrained tones of park-design treatises provide a striking contrast to the enthusiasm, the sublime extravagance toward which kitchen-garden manuals tend while ever expatiating on the boundaries and limitations of their humble subject. In the kitchen garden, the gardener provides a vivid image of an artist who labors to trace the lines of Nature (in Philip Miller's words) "both for Profit and Pleasure, for Use and Ornament."[22] Like the writer of the sonnet or lesser ode in the last quarter of the century, the gardener is a judicious practitioner of a curious and useful art. Within the enclosed space, labor, artistry, and craftsmanship knit notions of creativity and contrivance with notions of class in the terrain and poetic forms of nationhood. It is in the nexus of these ideas, in the ingenuity of the spaces they both produce and inhabit, that new qualities of Englishness were fostered and domesticated as ancient, persistent, and unique.

STRUCTURING ENCLOSURE

Attention devoted to the contraction of space received its most visible expression in the latter part of the eighteenth century in debates over the enclosure of common fields and wastes. In contrast to kitchen gardens, which formed part of a muted discourse, one that has been all but silenced by the passage of time, farms were the center of a loud and bitter polemic. From 1760 to 1780 and from 1790 until 1815 the two great waves of parliamentary enclosure fenced off the last of the open fields and, during the latter period especially, brought into cultivation vast stretches of what was thought of as wasteland or wilderness. Changing notions of form revealed by an increasing appreciation for the contained sites of town and kitchen gardens were subordinate to enclosure debates, but found their most direct expression in them. My own argument is less concerned with the validity of the points raised by defenders and opponents of enclosure than it is with relocating the debates themselves into conversations conducted in agricultural and horticultural treatises and changing assumptions concerning georgic and lyric forms in poetry. The complex, contingent, and plural effects of the single policy of parliamentary enclosure, which has until very recently received the lion's share of the blame for changing social conditions in England after the 1760s, appear quite differently when seen through the lens of these discursive practices and within the broader epistemological context of the evolution of forms in the eighteenth century. Although disputants in these debates may never find resolution, the debates themselves illuminate the symbolic power of cultivated landscapes in the eighteenth century and the forms of containment they produced – aesthetic forms that include those of poetic practice. Indirectly the debates reveal the mechanisms by which nostalgia for an older, simpler England occupied by a "bold peasantry" naturalized and shaped an English sensibility and extended beyond immediate polemical concerns.[23]

Because this polemic has situated a modern, commercially oriented Britain against the nostalgic space of Old England, the cultivated landscape, whether garden or farm, has been reduced to an economic space. And here again, parliamentary enclosure assumes a central position as both metaphor and visual practice. If enclosure entered the British national consciousness as one highly visible aspect of an emerging nexus of nation-identifying and authenticating practices, it did so primarily because of the visual and epistemological relationship it had with the open-field system, in which land was overseen by a paternalistic lord, farmed in common by holders of unfenced strips of field, and governed under a system of customary practices and rituals. Indeed, enclosure could neither have been understood nor have achieved its cultural force apart from the *idea* of the open fields. As I will show in the next chapter, enclosure was both a feature and an effect of the open-field system. In the production of representative English space, both the open- and enclosed-field systems mirror a sense of Englishness in the eighteenth century, depending on one's perspective. While both perspectives link the idea of Englishness to the soil, one views England through the filter of history and memory, through beef, beer, and wheaten bread, and a system of idealized relations centering on the soil in which the laborer is "independent" of the owner of the great country house; the other views England through a progressive future, in which each acre of land produces grain and fruit to its full potential, and in which England becomes a system of enclosed, productive plots. England's soil was the symbolic center of these conflicting yet dependent views: whether it became the natural link to an older, rapidly receding world – one that perhaps never existed as imagined – or as the fertile ground of a new agricultural productivity and prosperity – which perhaps would never be realized.

The polemic that emerged from these opposed visions, which has in large part shaped eighteenth-century landscape arguments, has fundamentally to do with the nature of space itself: what is the nature of space, how does visible space become social space, and how should space be historicized?[24] The debate moves back and forth between reified space and epistemological space, space that is the result of social practice and space which is the naturalized and invisible medium of human behavior. The image of the open fields is crucial, in this respect, for understanding the medium in which notions of space in the eighteenth century were circulated. Because they are unfenced and therefore appear unmarred by boundaries associated with private property, the open-field system can be viewed as the visual correlative of empty space, which provides the canvas, or natural ground that a more acquisitive culture will both mark and scar. The open fields, to which we have only indirect access, thus provide the idea of an innocent space that is later cut up and parceled off. In this sense, the open fields achieve a logical priority epistemologically, morally, and historically. They provide validity, an authority *per se*, as space which has been contaminated and forever diminished. Such a space becomes associated with one's youth, with Eden, with England's Golden Age, and with a paternalistic monarchy.[25] Primordial and natural, this space is also associated with the generative and fruitful earth, a naturally productive world in which the "wastes" are not wasteful at all, but provide the subsistent elements of the noble laborer's board. Even labor is Edenic, since, in a primordial land-sharing system, laborers plough shoulder to shoulder with neighbors, dispute their grievances in a just system of communal rights, and graze a cow on the commons outside the cottage door. The unmarked earth thus confers its innocence on the laborer, who will later be dispossessed, disenfranchised, and propelled into the sinister economy of wage labor. The natural or real space of the land is therefore conflated with the social space of idealized labor relations, masking the fact that laborers under the open-field system were, in fact, disenfranchised and dependent on the good will of post-feudal, paternalistic relations and a year without famine. The open-field system conveniently provides an intellectual site against which the disenchantment of production and accumulation can be proved. It is the visual extension of the idealized laborer, in the same way that hedgerows became the visual extension of the landowner's acquisition of land, labor, and profits (and in the 1990s the nostalgic symbols of a pre-Fordian age).

The visuality of this scene is fundamental to an understanding of the power of the final conversion from the open- to the enclosed-field system after 1760, especially since the aggressive marking and remapping of the landscape which enclosure presupposed repressed the open-field system into a collective imagination. In pitting these systems against each other, therefore, we should be suspicious of the too convenient binary relationship that they construct, especially after the initiation of parliamentary enclosure. The open and enclosed systems always refer to each other: the open fields are associated not only with unimpeded space and communal labor (natural exchange), but also with unwritten agreements; while parliamentary enclosures are associated with hedgerows, wage labor (monetary exchange), and written contracts. The fact that parliamentary enclosure represents a written system suggests that the landscape has lost a certain fluidity. It has been "grasped": not only acquired or engrossed, but rationalized and imbued with a power that it did not have Before or Then; it has been "contracted," not only divided into smaller, well-demarcated, privately owned plots, but also codified as a legislative practice. The enclosed landscape can thus be "read," while the open-field system can merely be nostalgically recollected. The residue of the open fields so often called up in literature comes to constitute our understanding of the enclosed system: it inhabits us as a memory and a loss. It persists as the Real substrata of Old England, still there if only in an effaced form.

The nostalgia that infiltrates the agricultural system at the historical moment when shifting frames of reference are visualized through parliamentary enclosure spills over into all landscapes. It can be detected in an effort in the early and middle eighteenth century to minimize boundaries between the garden or park and surrounding fields grazed by cows and sheep. The unimpeded view, which was the ideal of this landscape, captures the sense of open fields radiating outward from human habitation, while ironically securing a new order of privately controlled and cultivated gardens. It thus mediated between two traditional English scenes: the open-field system and old enclosures. As Christopher Hussey points out, "the enclosed landscape came before long to appear an extension of the park positively demanding views of its beauty to be admitted. And the 'amiable simplicity' produced in it by a combination of precise and empirical methods led to a similar synthesis being applied to creating ideal scenery."[26] In the first decade of the nineteenth century, Humphry Repton describes the effort to achieve a boundless view within circumscribed properties as the central fallacy of garden codes which dominated the first sixty years of Hanoverian rule. Such a park, he reproves, "required UNCONFINED EXTENT WITHIN ITSELF, AND ABSOLUTE EXCLUSION FROM ALL WITHOUT."[27] Repton charged the widespread misuse of the haha, a wall sunk into the ground with a ditch on the outer side, with sustaining the fallacy.[28] By means of the haha, the world could be appropriated as an extension of the landowner's property and a purchase on a view become the gentleman's mark. Thus, a simple ditch provided a provisional (and often unsightly) solution to the problem of how to appropriate the view, harnessing illusion in the service of proprietary status. The haha served an ephemeral yet vastly powerful ideal of landownership which dominated a few decades of British history, from the Act of Union with Scotland in 1707 until nearly the last quarter of the century. During this time, the unbounded prospect, with its nostalgic visual links to the open fields and a passing paternalistic economy, was transformed into a moral and political quality of the man of property. According to John Barrell, the gentleman's unconstricted views became a metaphor for his ability to act disinterestedly for his nation: "the ideal of the universal observer who 'superior to the little Fray' of competing interests, understands the relations among them all." As Barrell suggests, the unobstructed view even provides the gentleman with a kind of omniscience, "a high degree of compatibility . . . with God's vision of the world."[29] Thus, by metonymy, the haha became an overdetermined sign of property ownership, moral purpose, and aesthetic ideality.

The illusion of connection from a particular viewpoint that the haha preserved, an enchantment whereby the world beyond the division becomes a part of the garden, is a fitting metaphor for ways garden and agricultural treatises of the era verbalize the landscape. With the exception of the *ferme ornée* and rhetorical strategies for organizing descriptions of the countryside, farm treatises tend to avoid the language of landscape architects. Garden treatises, by contrast, incorporate the farm into the text, in the early part of the century by naturalizing it as part of the view and a century later by transforming the vocabulary of agriculture into gardening metaphor. Gardenists thus leap or scramble over the linguistic fence to bring the farm into the garden, appropriating key terms of the agricultural debates as metaphors for gardening practice. The most resounding of these terms after 1760, during rapidly intensifying debates over land use and distribution, are those of enclosure. While references to the historical practice of enclosure (as distinct from parliamentary enclosure) are common early in the century, the nature and quality of these references change as the debates intensify. The choice of the word "enclosure" over other words for expressing containment within the landscaped garden or park achieves a soundly political resonance. While early treatises may simply include enclosed fields within the

angle of vision, later treatises incorporate key polemical words of the parliamentary movement into the discourse of gardening, sometimes with
positive and sometimes with negative valences. A common may become
a disparaging term for a lawn or enclosure a positive way of demarcating
a garden.

Whether explicitly opposed to or favoring parliamentary enclosure,
landscape writers link it with a nexus of ill-defined concerns which may
appear completely unrelated to the debate. Taken together, these concerns can be generalized as an increasing preoccupation with the relationship between space and productivity, whether that refers to the
formal space of literary modes, the political space of foreign policy, the
pictorial space of the landscape, the social and architectural space of
the home, the personal space of the human subject, or the cultivated
space of farm or garden. Contained landscape space, whether agricultural or horticultural, provides insight into the acrimony of parliamentary
enclosure debates and reveals links between that polemic and a transformation of the collective "common sense" about the nature of space
itself. The centrality of the debate to widely disparate social and political
developments in the latter half of the century is well illustrated in the
discursive shift from the predilection for an unobstructed view characteristic of early eighteenth-century locodescriptive poetry to that of the
confined garden, which finds literary expression in the renewed interest
in the lesser ode, sonnet and proliferation of bower poems after 1770. In
the first part of the century, georgic poetry in particular embodied the
enthusiasm for unimpeded vision in a well-managed dialectic with the
hidden recesses which the unobstructed landscape both contained and
subsumed. The "georgic century," as the decades from 1708 to about
1770 have been called, was a period dominated by an enthusiasm for
agricultural progress and horticultural improvement. This enthusiasm
laid the groundwork for debates about the merits of enclosure. Whether
supporting or opposing the official policy, however, those engaging in
the debate reveal an increasingly insistent appreciation for the enclosed
place which will produce an Eden of a different sort than that celebrated
in locodescriptive verse in the first decades of the century, and which
provides continuity between the troubles of the present and the values
of England's ancient past. The debates reveal a shifting epistemology
which came to grant authority to the contained space even before the
ideal of the unbounded prospect would be relinquished, and looked to
the vernacular sites of ordinary people as a source for the delineation of
English character.

ACQUISITION AND EMULATION

Altered conceptions of representational space which affected public reception of both property and literary forms were driven in part by the evolution of class structure in England. Increasingly powerful commercial classes contributed to, and were produced by, Britain's expansionist efforts. Indeed, as both the engines and beneficiaries of Britain's increasing prosperity from trade and commercial enterprise, ordinary people increased their average annual incomes from 40 to 400 pounds by the 1760s.[30] The number of banks increased appropriately, private banks in London doubling their number between 1760 and 1800, while provincial banks grew at almost the same pace.[31] During this time provincial presses also grew by three-fold, indicating an expanding literate audience with pocket money to spend on daily, weekly, and monthly publications.[32] Evidence of a growing reading public is underscored by the propagation of circulating libraries, library subscription societies, book clubs, and school libraries which, for a range of fees, distributed serious and popular literature: travels, histories, sermons, and antiquarian studies as well as novels and natural histories.[33] Other kinds of subscription clubs and organizations indicate the vitality of the intermediate classes, their zeal for self-improvement, their forward-looking efforts to protect their new economic power, and sometimes simply their desire to socialize. Box clubs which generated insurance policies and mutual funds, scientific societies, dance clubs, and coffee houses often served both sexes, and had fees ranging from the prohibitive to within reach for even the less affluent. The coalminers had especially strong clubs, most importantly Friendly Societies that provided for widows in the case of catastrophic accidents.[34] The fact that similar clubs also proliferated in laborer communities suggests the pervasive sense of economic mobility that could be more easily achieved when people banded together.

The increasingly capacious pockets of ordinary people made possible the acquisition of comforts once restricted to gentry and aristocrats. This was a target of anti-luxury critics who characterized the acquisition of goods and services by the "lesser" and "middling" sorts as attempts to emulate their social betters. However, there is no surer indication that newly acquired comforts accrued a symbolic meaning far beyond mere emulation of the upper classes than the fact that their acquisition by other folk fostered changes in the structure of representation itself. This phenomenon is important for understanding vernacular landscapes such as the kitchen and town garden, since a changing structure of representation had direct consequences for the interpretation of contained properties. Representational structure is equally significant for understanding the reception of literary forms which during the eighteenth century had been relegated to the lower rungs of poetic hierarchy, emerging to prominence first in the popular press. During the American crisis, reception of the sonnet by critics was inflected by a prejudice against contained forms, which were associated with lesser intellectual and financial consequence. As the structure of representation changed, however, such forms became invested with new social significance. Changes in the structure of representation that provided these forms with respectability can be detected in the explosion in the number of people adopting the title of gentleman or madam – Mr., Mrs., or Esquire. As Paul Langford points out, "This debasement of gentility is one of the clearest signs of social change in the eighteenth century, the mark of a fundamental transformation. Paradoxically, its significance was masked by the concern of those who counterfeited the currency of class to have it pass for sound coin."[35] From another point of view, the "debasement of gentility" is simply a sign of a changing representational structure that generated altered assumptions concerning social space. Thus William Cobbett's familiar example of the Charingtons situates changes in social representation, which he resists, within the indigenous architectural space of the English farmhouse. He charges that the farm they are quitting epitomizes changes that he has observed in the country at large:

Every thing about this farm-house was formerly the scene of *plain manners* and *plentiful living*. Oak clothes-chests, oak bed-steads, oak chest of drawers, and oak tables to eat on, long, strong, and well supplied with joint stools. Some of the things were many hundreds of years old. But all appeared to be in a state of decay and nearly of *disuse*. There appeared to have been hardly any *family* in that house, where formerly there were, in all probability, from ten to fifteen men, boys, and maids: and, which was the worst of all, there was a *parlour*! Aye, and a *carpet* and *bell-pull* too! One end of the front of this once plain and substantial house had been moulded into a "*parlour*;" and there was the mahogany table, and the fine chairs, and the fine glass, and all as bare-faced upstart as any stock-jobber in the kingdom can boast of. And, there were the decanters, the glasses, the "dinner-set" of crockery ware, and all just in the true stock-jobber style. And I dare say it has been 'Squire Charington and the *Miss* Charingtons; and not plain Master Charington, and his son Hodge, and his daughter Betty transmuted into a species of mock gentlefolks, while it has ground the labourers down into real slaves.[36]

Cobbett manipulates two cultural images to raise the anxieties and the hackles of his audience.[37] First, acquisition of the *titles* of landed gentry by the farmer metonymizes all ills which have dogged the laborer in the wake of the French Revolution. Second, acquired titles stand in contrast to the solid English oak of no-longer-valued furniture. In Cobbett's portrait, the new prosperity of a family of tenant farmers, a devalued currency in titles, and a freshly decorated portion of the home symbolize the gilding over of solid English values with cheap social display.

Cobbett's well-choreographed scene reaches a crescendo in his dismay over the Charington's redecoration of a portion of their home, the only social offense in his reprimand that merits exclamation points. That a minor act of interior decoration should require such a level of censure reveals the symbolic power of even small transformations. The parlor was a powerful architectural symbol of retirement, a room where a prosperous English farmer might be waited on by his servants or daughters whose sole task was to produce, in Thorstein Veblen's classic phrase, "vicarious leisure" – the production of a superfluous level of comfort rather than a material product.[38] This is the core of Cobbett's modulated outrage. Taken with his contempt at the Charington's adoption of titles, his scorn for the parlor hearkens back to attitudes preserved in seventeenth-century sumptuary legislation and other such laws regulating class behavior which remained in force through the middle of the eighteenth century, and retained their effects far longer.[39] The long tradition of such regulation in England provided a framework for moral judgment against those who, while improving their fortunes, were unable to advance into a new social register. There are direct implications for the landscape, especially during an era when new fortunes were enabling families who plied their living by trade to buy estates. In 1722, in his handbook for city gardeners, Thomas Fairchild benevolently assumed that successful tradesmen would acquire estates as soon as their financial prospects made it possible. He indicated that in his experience, "true Care and Industry will make [tradesmen's] Gardens larger, as the same Care will increase their Fortunes."[40] Cobbett, writing a century later, however, had a more complex view of social mobility. His opinions are similar to those of landscape architect Humphry Repton, who championed social distinctions while simultaneously producing innovations in garden design adaptable to the restricted prospects of ordinary people. As Patrick Goode observes of Repton, Cobbett "is concerned to establish or safeguard the *social character*" of Old England.[41]

To imitate the manners of the upper classes, in Cobbett's view, was a sign not only of moral decrepitude but also of ridiculous display, the silly intrusion of urban manners into the propriety of rural life. Acid-tongued contemporary critics believed that upon achieving buying power, ordinary people sought to imitate the lives of their social superiors. Whether buying country villas and the services of landscape architects, or dining at eight and drinking saucers of tea with sugar, such social displays were interpreted as tactics to bring the newly affluent into either symbolic or physical contact with the upper class. Equally important, such displays served to generate internal distinctions within classes and engender troubling new social delineations based less on landed wealth than on the portable property of cash and monetary investment. These refined internal distinctions were likely to generate friction not between traditional classes (yeomen versus the landed wealthy), but between increasingly finely constituted modulations within these classes, as Cobbett's opposition between farmer and laborer illustrates. Rather than the local hereditary gentry, the Charingtons with their social pretensions are the source of the ire that suits Cobbett's rhetorical purposes in this passage.

In speaking of these changes, one runs the risk of falling into the same contemptuous language for the newly affluent that characterizes much social discourse of the eighteenth century. This has been the substance of recent attacks on Veblen's theory of leisure. While Veblen himself would be startled at the level of animosity he arouses among students of culture, the basis of the modern attack stems from Veblen's still provocative theory of imitation. In his words,

members of each stratum accept as their ideal of decency the scheme of life in vogue in the next higher stratum, and bend their energies to live up to that ideal. On pain of forfeiting their good name and their self-respect in case of failure, they must conform to the accepted code, at least in appearance . . . No class of society, not even the most abjectly poor, foregoes all customary conspicuous consumption.[42]

The missing perspective in Veblen's thesis is that of ordinary people – the views of those who carried on their lives outside the portentous games of civility practiced by gentry. Despite trenchant comments on the bizarre social arrangements of civilized societies, Veblen's theory of emulation implicitly situates upper-class acquisition as normative. The social experience of most of us teaches that while Veblen's dissection of the hypocrisies of "conspicuous consumption" is apt, his focus on the logic of power and display misinterprets as emulation the complex negotiations and satisfactions of everyday life. A focus on the microcommunities of ordinary people allows a different perspective. For instance, the tactics of gold- and silversmiths in provincial Birmingham over the course of the eighteenth century ingeniously subverted the rules of production laid down by their more respected counterparts in London: they redefined notions of skill, creativity, and fashion according to standards of plate rather than solid metals, inferior rather than precious metals, and paste over "genuine" materials.[43] Their insolence, their "esthetics of 'tricks'" frustrated industry standards formulated on the polarization of true from false, solid from plate, precious from functional, and genuine from artificial.[44] Plate silver goods were not an imitation of solid silver goods, but undermined and redefined notions of what constitutes the genuine. As W. H. B. Court recounts, the reaction of centrally located, powerful London competitors was one of "bewilderment . . . in the face of what were in effect new products but which seemed scandalous and cheating copies to conscientious and conservative craftsmen."[45] The local example of Birmingham, with its reinvention of notions of fashion and use, had implications that were both permanent and national. The same can be said of the kitchen garden. Like the Birmingham shop or factory, the kitchen garden was a vernacular site within which the dominant aesthetic of eighteenth-century landscape design was undermined and reinvented. Within its strict enclosures, the sublime and the sensuous could take root, subverting from within notions of what constituted representative English space. The kitchen garden became the space of Everyman, especially the ordinary professional wage earner or housewife. Within its boundaries craftsmanship, ingenuity, and contrivance produced a vernacular space that was construed as both new and old, the seminary of the English cottage garden and true English virtue. Writers of kitchen-garden treatises explicitly sought *not* to imitate the parks and vistas of the gentry (within which the kitchen garden was often concealed), but to identify an aesthetic with ancient roots that could bring forth new social meanings. They found within the confines of the garden wall a sublime expanse within which time, and especially leisure, could be redeemed.

Given these circumstances, it is not surprising that the complexity of luxury increased over the course of the eighteenth century, pamphleteers citing luxury as a prime factor of social entropy responsible for scarcity and high prices during times of stress.[46] Gardens and farms, like other signs of possession, are dealt with in treatises within the terms of the luxury debate. Thus, one of the qualities of aristocratic gardens in England in contrast to those on the continent was the oft-cited idea that their design was "cheap." Luxury's virtuous counterpart, frugality, is also repeatedly invoked as a conventional component of the management of the lordly estate. Accusations of luxury provided a convenient and familiar set of conventions easily absorbed by the reading public. Aristotle provided the framework for the debate, which was filled out by biblical exegesis: the frugal, virtuous state was built on a foundation of morality, paternalism, and agrarianism.[47] One component of this convention was the trajectory defined by influential classical writers who saw in progressive agricultural methods and the origins of private property an inevitable declension to the marking of boundaries, urbanization, deterioration of a paternalistic social structure, and devolution of moral behavior. This trajectory would be identified in England after 1760 as the shift from an open-field system of farming to the enclosed fields of a purportedly progressive, increasingly commercial agricultural practice. Well before the eighteenth century in England, however, a similar, nonspecific set of linked events provided cultural intelligibility for the well-received notion that a nation's agriculture, and therefore its landed aristocracy, is the foundation of its virtue. The national priority of agriculture endowed with this moral and economic status was reified in the Royal Society of Arts, whose most significant committee for decades was the Georgical Committee. A broad common sense sustained the link between agrarianism and frugality as the stabilizing force of hierarchy, and identified the acquisition of goods and services previously beyond the means of ordinary people as a new and dangerous threat to morality and national security.

The discourse that pitted social display against a theory of customary practice rooted in agrarian ideals was not simple, however, and became increasingly ambiguous in the eighteenth century with the introduction of alternative ways of viewing luxury. Counter-arguments responding favorably to the increased buying power of ordinary people defended consumer culture. David Hume, Adam Smith, and other intellectual luminaries saw in the accumulation of goods evidence of an economic and imperial vitality fed by the ingenuity of a new entrepreneurial class.[48] Their arguments replace the assumption that the relationship between wealth and hierarchical rank is natural with the assumption that the relationship is conventional – having explanatory power, but subject to revision. Cultural meaning, in this view, may be realigned across the social spectrum and those who make their living from commerce revalued as assisting in the advancement of the nation. Hume stood out on the issue of luxury, voicing the alternative possibility decades before it was given credence by even so unlikely a proponent as Samuel Johnson, a powerful spokesperson for conservative Tory values. Hume was in fact a moderate on the issue who believed that luxury "may be innocent or blamable, according to the age, or country, or condition of the person."[49] On the whole, however, he believed that the pursuit of luxury was a national good in that it encouraged a people to be industrious:

The encrease and consumption of all the commodities, which serve to the ornament and pleasure of life, are advantageous to society; because, at the same time that they multiply those innocent gratifications to individuals, they are a kind of *storehouse* of labour, which, in the exigencies of state, may be turned to public service. In a nation, where there is no demand for such superfluities, men sink into indolence, lose all enjoyment of life, and are useless to the public, which cannot maintain or support its fleets and armies, from the industry of such slothful members.[50]

Hume rejects agrarian arguments that typically identify the moment when a people leaves its primary attachment to the soil for commerce and industry as the first step onto a slippery slope leading to urbanization, feminization, infiltration by foreign powers, and the decline and fall of the nation. Indeed, a proper attention to agrarian matters, in his view, brings agriculture under the purview of commerce, for "where luxury nourishes commerce and industry, the peasants, by a proper cultivation of the land, become rich and independent; while the tradesmen and merchants acquire a share of the property, and draw authority and consideration to that middling rank of men, who are the best and firmest basis of public liberty."[51] Contrary to Cobbett's view, luxury assists in the expansion of trading interest and the stabilization of ordinary people.

Hume's argument opened the door for a displacement of the object of luxury attacks from the intermediate classes, the engines of commercial expansion, to aristocrats, who were eventually viewed as effeminized parasites battening off the industry of their social inferiors.[52] Hume also made possible explanations other than that of emulation for the motivations of moderately affluent people. He implies that acquisition of wealth may be viewed as a good in itself since it encourages the corollary virtues of industry, independence, and property ownership, which are meaningful when detached from the trappings of hereditary wealth. There is indeed reason to believe that for the vast majority of English people, the acquisition of marks of social respectability and property was not necessarily seen as a rung to higher rank so much as a right to be appropriated by anyone possessing industry and skill. Repton gives credence to this notion of appropriation when he claims that the desire to own one's own home is a universal human longing which can be satisfied

in the smallest of properties. Sidney Mintz's study of sugar and the stim-
ulant beverages tea, coffee, and cocoa supports Repton's observation.
As Mintz shows, luxuries such as tea and sugar once restricted to aristocrats and the wealthy "were re-employed by poor people in new ways,
on new occasions and under different circumstances."[53] Mintz names
this effect "extensification" and distinguishes it from "intensification,"
which includes emulation. Unlike intensification, extensifcation shifted
luxury items to new contexts and thus endowed them with different social
meanings.[54] In effect, the form, whether of tea or of property, is emptied
of its original social meaning and reinvested with meanings peculiar to
new class-driven usages – meanings which are both practical and imaginative. To pursue Mintz's example, tea drinking by the lower classes
began not as sign of respectability, which implies the motive of emulation, but comfort: tea was a commodity which had the power to turn a
workplace lunch of bread and cheese into a hot meal.[55] Cowper's cherished synecdoche for tea as "the cups / That cheer but not inebriate"[56]
owes more to the symbolic comfort it provided than to the mark of fashion or respectability it conferred upon gentry – an apt instance of a
change in the structure of representation generated when less affluent
people use a commodity in socially specific ways. In this case, as in many
others, the vernacular use of a commodity irrevocably alters its social
meanings. Repton's example of the appropriation of a place one can call
one's own offers a similar transformation of property's symbolic value
from a sign of privilege to a sign of home and ordinary values, paving the
way for the national ideal of the English cottage and its small attached
garden. The cottage garden was not a smaller, more frugal imitation
of the park and vast country house, but a site designed with a unique
set of aesthetic guidelines and invested with a wholly different social
meaning.

THE EXAMPLE OF ENGLISH GEORGIC

We can better understand the social content of space if we examine the
authority associated with English georgic in the eighteenth century. This
is the burden of the second portion of this book, in which I examine
circumstances surrounding the emergence and decline of the georgic
form. Its emergence in 1708 as an authoritative verse form was directly
connected to a national impulse to celebrate England's soil. Based on a
Virgilian model but reshaped by Miltonic poetics, the hybrid form referred to as English georgic expressed the particular aims of a peculiar

people. The production of English space central to an understanding of what constituted British space thus began with a resolute attachment to the idea of England as an agrarian nation of down-to-earth citizens who, despite class difference, shared in the intellectual and material labor of shaping the heartland of an empire. The poetry which represented this endeavor, though it purported to be primarily practical (in that it was overtly didactic in form), was in fact profoundly conceptual (elaborating a less overt notion of Englishness). By means of English georgic, a single center of the world could be represented and nationalized. The English view in these poems becomes the invisible ideological point of view. Others have called attention to the aristocratic biases of this view, yet the class assumptions of English georgic were sufficiently muted that a wide spectrum of English folk could believe in the justice, pleasure, and power of the representation and, by purchasing, reading, and quoting this literature, assist in the production of English space.[57] Although laboring poets such as Stephen Duck and Mary Collier may have contested its claims, English georgic provided a vision from its single perspective which was powerful because of its homogeneity and which promulgated a conception of English centrality and British potentiality that could be grasped by a heterogeneous population.

This was possible in part because georgic poetry yoked two powerful artistic strategies. First, it offered a *visual* image of the world that issued from a single English center. This image is painterly in its use of perspective and vanishing point, but poetic in its organization of degrees of subordination which nevertheless maintain steady reference to the location of the speaker.[58] It provides the illusion of an infinitely expanding space through which the mind darts in an exercise of subjective freedom. By means of this strategy mental space forms an isomeric relationship with visual space. Mental space also colludes, however, in the presentation of history. The visual center of the point of view is also a temporal center – a present which expands backward into an archaic British past in order to authenticate an English present, and which simultaneously presumes the eschaton of a British future. Englishness thus becomes a means of locating the heart of a present moment which is both geographical and temporal and which is unified by an invisible point of view. The second strategy is *aural*, the construction of a patient, paternalistic and pedagogical voice which speaks directly to the reader as listener and learner, but which implies the existence of a wider audience – a schoolroom of readers – with whom the listener has a shared heritage. The second person plural accompanies as an echo the homonymic second person singular which is central to this strategy, providing the illusion that the internal distinctions of the schoolroom have been leveled and that the audience is unified in its goals. The invisible point of view is translated into an equally fixed and invisible vocal presence, with the difference that whereas we see *with* the eye of the speaker, we hear at the feet of the schoolmaster. The illusion of subjective freedom provided by the ever-expanding visual world of the poem is thus riven by the controlling and correcting voice of instruction.

This patient, instructional voice does not restrict the expansion of space represented by English georgic. It provides it rather with an omniscient authority, which simultaneously directs the reader's view and authorizes the reader to participate in the nationalistic project that it extols. It represents the space of liberty and directs the reader's footsteps in that space. It casts a nostalgic eye over the reaches of English history and an acquisitive one over the possibilities of a Britannizable world. It reproduces a British past and produces a British future out of the present tense of a fixed point of view. It represents the space of England at the same time that it produces English space. If we were to borrow Henri Lefebvre's terms we could describe the producing and produced space of English georgic as both a representation of space and a representational space.[59] This space presumes a viewpoint from which the viewer is provided with an unrestrained prospect. Built into this concept is, of course, the *double entendre* of the word "prospect," in which the viewer's apprehension of space presupposes an analogue in the viewer's expectations or fortune. However, English georgic is also a representational space in that the capacious form of the poetry epitomizes the prospect it represents. Its sprawling form has as much to do with its prosody as with its physical extent. It is not accidental that the poems considered to be the most prominent English georgics (with the exception of Gay's *Rural Sports*) are couched in blank verse, a meter employed by Milton that was perceived as fundamentally English not merely because of its high poetic lineage but because it accommodated the rhyme-poor English language. In addition, iambic pentameter was believed of all meters to approximate most closely the indigenous rhythm of the language, while the unrhymed line endings provided a verse equivalent of unfettered feet redolent of English liberty and sinuous paths of the new, anti-French landscape aesthetic.

The vistas which English georgic celebrates take for granted the primacy in landscape of the "ancient seats" of landed gentry, a tradition which permeates locodescription of all sorts in the English literary tradition – from poetry celebrating the country house in the seventeenth century to picturesque descriptions which conduct the reader's mental gaze from landed estate to landed estate in the latter part of the eighteenth century. Over the course of the century, many of these seats, in turn, were redesigned to fulfill the expectations of the concept of which they were in part constitutive, their high-walled gardens transformed into open parks with unrestrained prospects and their physical dimensions into representational sites. These unimpeded spaces obfuscate the importance and meaning of smaller contained spaces that had little representational value in an expansionist discourse. Throughout the century such clandestine spaces took the forms of the kitchen garden, the horticultural "cabinet" set within the broad vistas of landed gentry, and the pocket handkerchief back yards of town gardens. Obscured by the *furor hortensis* which opened the horizons of the wealthy, these spaces were lost to view in the discursive although not the lived tradition of the culture. Prominent gardeners required that the kitchen garden be removed from the visual field of the great house (although their objections were not necessarily heeded), while the continuous tradition of the town garden is preserved in the central decades of the century solely in the records of nurserymen and occasional observers. Only the kitchen garden sustained a thriving record throughout the century in a proliferation of manuals and calendars devoted to growing vegetables, herbs, fruit, and flowers. This vernacular prospect, as J. C. Loudon would point out in the nineteenth century, was one of the commonest English sites: "Of private British gardens, the most numerous class of gardens, and those the most regularly distributed over the British Isles, are those of the country labourer, or what are usually denominated cottage-gardens."[60] It was the humble kitchen garden, not the great parks of the gentry, that would establish the norm and ideal of Englishness over the course of the nineteenth century that remains powerful even today.

Although vernacular sites were instrumental in altering the sense of representational space in England toward the end of the eighteenth century, such changes are recorded only indirectly in treatises that recommend designs for the parks and gardens of the landed gentry. Nevertheless, even treatises devoted to park design disclose a shift from the apotheosis of the view to the celebration of the contained garden. Similarly, the vernacular tradition of kitchen-garden manuals and agricultural treatises map such sites as representative of the nation's aims. Manuals written by agriculturists, gardeners and botanists inevitably draw on historically specific notions of space and national sentiment. Through a focus on specific products of the field and garden – in the case of this book, the apple and the cucumber – I trace the changes that produce representational notions of space. For instance, the apple, the subject of John Philips's *Cyder*, is nationalized in garden manuals as the distinctively English fruit. England can thus be situated as a new Eden, the site of fruit that brings life rather than death. The apple becomes a magnet for writers whose primary goal is to define the English character against that of foreigners, especially the French. These turn the eating of apples and drinking of cider into a patriotic, quasi-sacramental act of national faith. As the subject of the poem that opened the way for the georgic celebration of English soil, the apple also becomes the symbol of the well-delineated and protected island of Britain, which opens out upon the world of trade and colonial acquisition. For this poem celebrates not so much the open vista, as later georgics would, but the sheltered English orchard, the close, protected airs of which are healing and laden with the scent of blossoms and fruit. *Cyder*, and by implication the apple, inhabits the borders between the open view of the farm or park and the enclosed site of the garden. The cucumber, by contrast, exhibits the governance and artifice of the gardener who becomes a figure for the pragmatic and artful leader of state. In contrast to the apple, the cucumber, as I show in the third part of this book, becomes a magnet for a sexualized discourse in the enclosed kitchen garden, reflecting advances in breeding plants and new methods of botanical classification. The apple and the cucumber exhibit in miniature the tendencies of the discourses which they emblematize, the apple opening outward as a symbol of England itself, the cucumber turning inward toward a contained and productive space riven with the language of class and sexuality.

URBAN AND SUBURBAN NATURE: THE TOWN GARDEN

The town garden is a valuable indicator of the evaporation of enclosed spaces from discussions of the open prospect in the eighteenth century. Although contained spaces represented the privacy and therefore privilege of aristocracy in earlier centuries, the advent of the landscaped park relegated the well-framed, contained space to the more confined prospects of urban dwellers. Occupying the periphery in cadastral maps and treatises devoted to great estates, the town garden disappeared from discussions of garden design. In actuality, however, the town garden developed steadily over the course of the eighteenth century under circumstances that required close dimensions and enclosed sites. Todd Longstaffe-Gowan has pointed out that "[t]he small urban garden figured preeminently among the elements which elevated the average household from a level of subsistence to one of comfort and style, and an increasingly commercialized garden industry promoted the activity of gardening as an affordable and viable urban recreation."[61] In the early eighteenth century, botanist Richard Bradley, contemporary with the urban gardenists Batty Langley and Thomas Fairchild, was attuned to the comfort which such small plots could provide, suggesting their possibilities as early as 1726. In a treatise on husbandry and gardening he comments,

A private Gentleman may have Riches enough in a narrow Compass for his use and Satisfaction, as those of the highest Rank can gather from a Multitude of Acres. A single Person in a little Ground, may find as constant Advantage, as one who has an hundred Acres, and a numerous Attendance and Acquaintance to partake with him of his Benefits.[62]

Bradley concurred in this view with Fairchild and Langley, both of whom advised a growing commercial class on the benefits of the small garden. Documenting the difficulties of back yard gardening in contemporary London and its suburbs in 1722, Fairchild defends the prospects of tradesmen: "We may consider," he explains, "that then our judicious Traders in the City have as much Reason to hope for the Enjoyment of the Pleasures of this Life, as the Persons of Quality, which are in the highest Stations; for the Pleasures of Gardening, or country Air, which I speak of, are equally the Right of one and the other."[63] Herbaceous gardening in city and suburban lots, which required inexpensive and, thanks to pervasive coal smoke, hardy plants, was made possible on a wide scale in the third quarter of the century, and this, combined with the increasingly insistent preference among ordinary people for privately owned ground, made the town garden a ubiquitous urban element by the end of the century.[64]

Fairchild's treatise assumes the importance of an active commercial class that forced a new assessment of containment from the vantage point of practicality. Many successful tradesmen were able to parlay their wealth into large country estates, and Fairchild fixes his sights on these. His nascent vision of the intermediate classes and his approval of their limited means were geared toward the eventuality that a successful tradesman would some day accumulate enough wealth to retire to the country. His treatise prepares for future possibilities which are consistent with the ethos of the gentleman in the first decades of the century: "I have therefore advised to give my Thoughts in this Manner, that every one in *London*, or other Cities, where much Sea-Coal is burnt,

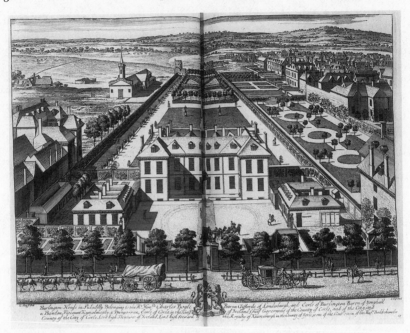

Figure 1 To the right of Burlington House estate the engraving includes views of neighboring town houses with their formal gardens. "Burlington House in Pickadilly," J. Kip and L. Knyff, *Britannia Illustrata* (1714), vol. 1, plate 29, RB 204533.

may delight themselves in Gardening, tho' they have never so little Room, and prepare their Understanding to enjoy the country, when their Trade and Industry has given them Riches enough to retire from Business."[65] Fairchild also inadvertently documents the presence of a thriving interest in urban gardening, given grist by prospering nurseries around London that supplied the demands of small proprietors. By the end of the century a more permanent and contracted notion of ordinary prospects had taken hold, which would in turn generate enthusiasm for the design of contained horticultural spaces. The vast majority of those in the intermediate classes in these decades were more like Leigh Hunt, professionals who were able to buy plots of ground in the bustling suburbs of London or provincial towns. Their plots became the object of "leisure" activity – not the retirement presumed by authors like Fairchild to be cultivated by those of independent wealth, but the relaxation afforded by domestic hours after work. Industrious leisure became a hallmark of the latter decades of the eighteenth century and was interpreted as a moral quality. So pervasive was this notion that prefaces of architectural pattern books, particularly those which fed into a new ideal for building healthful and comfortable laborer's cottages, remonstrate that laborers' "leisure" time must be occupied by productive work in an attached kitchen garden, to the betterment of their morals and impoverishment of the local alehouse.

Hunt's sonnets document this trend particularly well. Writing during the Regency decade, he implicitly calls attention to a rift between notions of nature that dominated romantic ideology and the notion of nature characteristic of the suburbs, for which the suburbs were vilified. Romantic ideology mythologized the sublime, unpeopled landscape, which was most sublime where it was most arduously inaccessible. The alternative that Hunt proposes is part of a different tradition continuous with the idea of nature fostered in garden manuals, which exposes the artifice of the romantic ideal.[66] In a sonnet "To Horatio Smith" published in 1818, the embowered place when dislocated from pastoral verse and English georgic becomes a suburban site which elevates the pleasures of domesticated nature:

> With what a fine unyielding wish to bless,
> Does Nature, Horace, manage to oppose
> The town's encroachments! Vulgar he, who goes
> By suburb gardens which she deigns to dress,
> And does not recognize her green caress
> Reaching back to us in those genial shows
> Of box-encircled flowers and poplar rows,
> Or other nests for evening weariness.
> Then come the squares, with noon-day nymphs about;
> Then vines, and ivy; tree tops that look out
> Over back walls; green in the windows too; –
> And even where gain huddles it's noisiest rout,
> The smile of her sweet wisdom will break through,
> For there, dear Horace, has she planted you.[67]

The indolent Horace, implanted like box-hedges and vines, yet hardly so active as they, is a shrewd extraction from the pastoral tradition of the figure of an indolent, reclining poet, here brought to rest in the suburbs of Hampstead. Relocated, this figure problematizes traditional barriers between country and city, indoors and outdoors, nature and artifice, landscape and vernacular gardening by creating a third space that subsists in its own right as neither the city nor the country. Artifice in this space is the source of nature's beauties, that which nature must imitate in order to achieve human proportion. Hunt's depiction of nature favors the domestic comforts greeting the working professional after a day

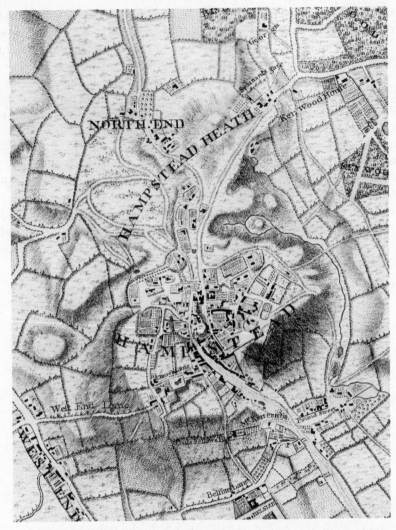

Figure 2 Rocque's map depicts gardens around houses in Hampstead in the middle of the century, many of which would have been kitchen gardens. Hampstead, J. Rocque, *Survey of London* (1746), plate 12, RB 315661.

at the office over the mists and fells cherished by the lonely hiker in the Lake District or the unbounded view from the country house. Nature in a world where leisure is the dialectical counterpart of professional labor is associated with the extremities of the working day. It must be assisted by the gardener's carefully tended parterres, the landscape architect's deliberately designed city squares, and the housewife's potted plants which mock the boundaries between home and garden. The garden, in turn, mimics the architectural symmetries of family rooms. In this space, leisure differs from retirement, which is supported by independent wealth and assumes a counterpart in the world of public service; by contrast, leisure is industrious, filling the spaces between night and day enjoyed by the man who must earn his own way. Inspiration is kidnapped from rural nature and reestablished in a space produced by artifice. Nature is not for Hunt a "detached symbol."[68] Houseplants in windows and parterres in carefully designed squares *are* nature – not pitiful reminders of real nature cherished by people without the resources or taste to experience nature in the raw. Furthermore, the suburban ideal of nature draws on a long, authenticating tradition of drawing greenery in around homes under conditions of high artifice. Nature and artifice belie structural

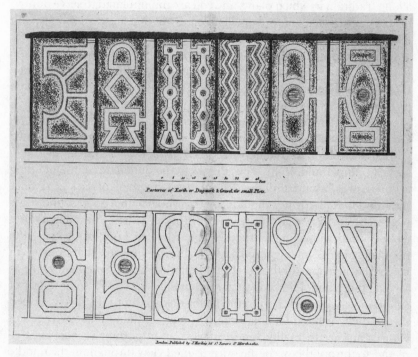

Figure 3 A series of formal designs for small, decorative gardens which indicate ways gardens could mirror the public rooms of a home. "Parterres of Earth or Dugwork & Gravel for Small Plots," J. C. London, *Hints on the Formation of Gardens* (1812), plate 2, RB 385679.

opposition in this view since they are inextricable from each other and a legitimate English history.

Nature during this time period was thus as likely to be determined by gardening tradition and literary topoi as by the aesthetic category of the sublime. As Edmund Bartell put it in 1804 in a rejoinder to the ideal of nature espoused by proponents of the sublime,

Thus, if we take nature in a general sense, we may be allowed to include such objects as by long knowledge become naturalized to the soil upon which they stand. In this point of view, the baronial castle, the ruined abbey, or the humble cottage, by carrying us back to times past, or being combined as objects in a scene, become as much a part of nature, as the soil itself, the trees, and the grass which adorn it, the horse, the cow, or, in short, as any other object animate or inanimate.[69]

Like Hunt's idyllic suburb, Bartell's concept of the natural is drawn from a long tradition in which plants and soil are manipulated to serve human need. Artifice makes nature intelligible by bringing it into proximity with human habitation.

Hunt's writings illuminate a gathering approbation for confined spaces in poetry and topography and attest to aesthetic convergences between these forms. The town garden, whether suburban or urban, reveals these convergences in wonderful ways; however, it constitutes only one historical precursor of the hallowed English cottage garden promoted by Gertrude Jekyll and the British tourist industry. Highly formal, the town garden was often, as Isaac Ware's *A Complete Body of Architecture* (1756) suggests, unplanted. In his view, thanks to the difficulties of maintaining a garden in London's smoke and the close confinement of back yard walls, the London homeowner should "lay the whole with a good sound stone pavement" with perhaps an alcove on the far side.[70] Although Ware's gloomy predictions for the success of gardens in London obscures the popularity of the town garden and the nursery industry that grew up in its service, he captures the accepted design of such a contained space as formal and plain. The kitchen garden, which combined an aesthetic of exuberance with high requirements for design, more decisively shaped the aesthetic criteria for the English cottage garden. The town garden with its austere formality is nevertheless an important vernacular corrective to the apotheosis of the unrestrained view throughout the middle decades of the century. In the vestiges it has left to history we can detect a space which, in containment and dimension, would represent a new ideal of Englishness in the coming century.

Figure 4 Frontispiece, Thomas Fairchild, *The City Gardener* (1722), RB 350037.

As the phenomenon of the town garden suggests, indications of expansion everywhere present in the discourses of the eighteenth century
conceal a paradox: the sense of exuberance and power of the age, which
both contemporaries and historians document, is countered throughout
the century by a demand for contraction, diminution, in a word, *enclosure*.
Nascent empire building is accompanied by an awareness of the danger which expansion presents. The imperial body is different from the
well-defined national corpus, which, after the Union, was an especially

beautiful, visual insular image, one which reminded georgic poets of the contained garden of Eden, complete with the apples of Herefordshire. In its drive to annex other nations, Britain threatened its own idyllic space with foreign contagion. The language of contraction or containment which fills architectural pattern books and garden treatises reflects or parallels the vocabulary of parliamentary enclosure debates, which were especially heated between 1760 and 1815. Enclosure had national ramifications for Great Britain as a symbol, not simply as a practice. It achieved its symbolic status not primarily because of its direct effects, but because it fed into a growing national sense that, willy-nilly, expansion made possible by trade and commerce, which provided a market bursting with marvelous goods and consumable wonders, was stretching the epidermis of the nation, making it thinner and more porous, more susceptible to infection from without. An increasing concern with definition thus accompanied the demand for containment, and with containment, contraction. Forms of containment gave visible shape to national anxieties, and, whether or not they ameliorated them, these forms were promulgated within the context of a growing need for a definition of Englishness. In an expanding empire the self-containment of true Englishness became an expression of enclosure in its human form which was tested by the category of Britishness fabricated through the incorporation of colonial bodies, foreign goods, and heterogeneous exotic forms.

CHAPTER 2

Codifying containment: the parliamentary enclosures

> Ere this, no peasant vexed the peaceful ground,
> Which only turfs and greens for altars, found:
> No fences parted fields, nor marks nor bounds
> Distinguished acres of litigious grounds;
> But all was common, and the fruitful earth
> Was free to give her unexacted birth.
>
> Dryden's Virgil
The Georgics (1697)

In 1732 an anonymous writer published a pamphlet entitled *The Great Improvement of Commons that are Enclosed for the Advantage of the Lords of Manors, the Poor, and the Publick*. He advocates, among other things, enclosing Bagshot Heath into twenty-acre plots on which could be grown potatoes, turnips, carrots, parsnips, madder, grasses, buckwheat, vines, and hops.[1] Each of these close plots, if realized as imagined, would have brimmed with vegetables, grains, and commercial produce. Over sixty years later another writer contesting the purported worth of monopolizing farms under 100 or 150 acres in the wake of parliamentary enclosure in the Midlands expatiates on the link between productivity and curtailed extent, attributing the increased productivity of the latter to brute necessity:

The wealthy farmer's attention is engrossed by the means of producing the greatest quantity of grain and hay; and, when his harvest is over, to let them lay in store till he can take advantage of the highest market-price. The middling and poor farmer not only attends to the production of grain and hay, but also to the rearing of stock; all of which his needs compel him to carry to market as soon and as often as possible, that he may have wherewithal to pay his rent and taxes as they become due. The rich farmer's wife is above the drudgery of looking after pigs, geese, fowls, &c. The poor farmer's wife thinks these her treasures, nourishes them till they bring fourfold, and then adds their produce to her husband's store.[2]

37

This writer forecasts that a policy promoting small farms will lessen the poor rate, slow the flow of emigration and thus increase rural population, and reduce the price of vegetables in cities.[3]

As these remarkably similar views about the productivity of small spaces suggest, the fantasized correlation between containment and productivity was present well before the end of the century – and could be cherished regardless of the position one took on enclosure. The correlation was, in fact, the genetic offspring of millenarian schemes of levelers and republicans the previous century. By the last quarter of the eighteenth century the anonymous writer's view, an inconsiderable voice in 1732 drowned out by the fervor for large farms, had become widespread and the scheme for intensive small farming had been dubbed the "cottage system."[4] The differing positions pamphlet writers take on enclosure indicate that proposals for the promotion of small farms were not limited to those contesting enclosure. One could oppose the enclosure of arable land, for example, but approve the enclosure of waste and commons into small farms. One could, like Arthur Young, favor large farms yet advocate an allotment of smallholdings to diligent laborers. In general, whether for or against enclosure, those favoring a cottage system believed that the agricultural landscape should be imagined as a judicious mix of farm sizes.[5] Proposals for a vernacular agrarian system that these pamphlet writers promoted were forward looking in their concerns for the welfare of the poor, realistic in terms of the current rationalization of agriculture as an industry, and imaginative in proposing a solution aimed at increasing the productivity of the nation at large. Not least, they reveal a social and political interest in kitchen gardens, which became emblematic of a nostalgic reversion to a legal principle rooted in Tudor rule that was appropriated as solidly English by those on both sides of the argument, especially from the early 1770s on. Under ideal circumstances, according to this principle, every laborer should be given or leased a small portion of land to garden for him or herself. This principle challenged the presumption from the 1730s through the 1760s that increased farm sizes would improve agricultural output. Rising agricultural prices and fears of rural depopulation fueled the idea that increased farm sizes were ruining agricultural productivity of all sorts – from bread corn to butter and eggs.

Arguing against "depopulating" enclosure as an official policy, Unitarian minister and political radical Richard Price proposed a return to Tudor legislation which stipulated that every rural cottage should have land attached to it.[6] Price cites legislation beginning with Henry VII that recommended "making farms and houses of husbandry of a standard;

that is, maintained with such a proportion of land to them, as may breed a subject in convenient plenty and no servile condition, and to keep the plough in the hands of the *owners* and not *hirelings*."[7] He traces acts supporting such measures back to Rome, a rhetorical strategy used by radicals and conservatives in the intensive eighteenth-century effort to provide a sound ancient history for English social policy.[8] His proposal is reinforced by strong sentiment throughout the eighteenth century that England is a latter-day Rome – with all her strengths and liable to a similar fate if the principles of English liberty are not maintained. Having established a conventional historical origin, Price recasts the principle as distinctively English by tracing it through the reigns of Henry VIII, Elizabeth I, Charles I, and Cromwell, the last stipulating that "no new house was to be built within ten miles of LONDON, unless there were four acres of land occupied by the tenant."[9]

This ideal was not confined to radicals, but was part of widespread conviction that, properly managed, whether through rent remission, outright gifts of land, or encouragement to farm wastes, England was better imagined as a series of contained plots, or as an agreeable mix of small, middling, and large farms. Arthur Young, who argued tirelessly in favor of enclosure of all lands for most of his life, similarly believed in the principle that each man should have a piece of ground to till and found a model for such a policy in the American colonies. He expostulates in 1784 that given land, even an "idle Irishman" would be spurred to diligence: "All arising from the single principle, one of the most powerful that actuates the human bosom, that if you give property in land you will create the industry that shall improve it. It is this only that spread America with cultivation, and filled her woods with people."[10] In 1798, a correspondent to the *Annals of Agriculture* relates the supposed words of a poor man who was given land rent free by his landlord because of the neatness of his cottage. Conveniently, like Young, he reveals the paternalism of his assumptions: "Now, Sir," the old man is recorded as saying,

you have a pleasure in seeing my cottage and garden neat; and why should not other squires have the same pleasure in seeing the cottages and gardens as nice about them? The poor would then be happy; and would love them, and the place where they lived: but now every little nook of land is to be let to the great farmers, and nothing left for the poor, but to go to the parish.[11]

Conservative narratives thus presume that a gentleman's prospects are as improved by the cottager's neat garden as are the tourist's by the gentleman's country park.

As these examples suggest, moral, aesthetic, and commercial bias toward enclosed space could be defended as a return to truly English values rooted in the authenticity of an agrarian Gothic past and owning a precedent in Roman law. The recovery of this British past responded to a sense of the indelicacy of displays of privilege during the revolutionary 1790s, and was consistent with the increasingly important interest of ordinary people. It was, however, no simple astronomical revolution. "Reversion" from the open prospect revealed a desire to locate tradition within events that signaled radical change and to discover predictability in the face of new economic and class uncertainty. Goldsmith catches the tenor of the response in his much-cited poem, "The Deserted Village," which became a touchstone in late eighteenth-century enclosure debates, and has remained so. I discuss it here because it articulates and perpetuates conventions of an idealized English landscape, joins England's economic and moral prospects to her rural prospects, and exemplifies a reversion in the discursive tradition from the open to the enclosed prospect, especially as it idealizes the cottage system.

The village economy that Goldsmith describes in "The Deserted Village" opposes the new commercial economy through recourse to the ideals of pastoral conventions. In the first verse paragraph alone, Goldsmith creates an image of a nucleated village with its green, "the cultivated farm, / The never failing brook, the busy mill," and the "decent church." In the village's imagined ethos, the narrator celebrates toil, but stresses the absence of regulated labor: blooms are "lingering" and "delayed," bowers are characterized by "innocence and ease," and the speaker remembers having "loitered o'er thy green" (lines 1–12). Within this space remitted toil gives way to play and gregarious voices suggest real rather than mediated relationships in a benevolent social structure. The babble of human tones mingles "in sweet confusion" with those of cows, geese, and watchdog in a world where each living thing is a beneficiary of the common grace of rural virtue (lines 113–24).

But the agricultural system to which Goldsmith alludes is not the scene of pastoral idealism but a cottage system. Six of the most frequently repeated lines in the poem recall Roman, Tudor, and Stuart measures that, if enforced, would have made this possible:

> A time there was, ere England's griefs began,
> When every rood of ground maintained its man;
> For him light labour spread her wholesome store,

Just gave what life required, but gave no more:
His best companions, innocence and health;
And his best riches, ignorance of wealth.

(lines 57–62)

Goldsmith inverts this scene in his essay, "The Revolution of Low Life," where he turns a convention of eighteenth-century garden treatises upside down – that if each plot of ground were beautifully landscaped England would become the Garden of the World. History, he counters, teaches us that such a prospect is inevitably the result of the contagion of public morals produced by commerce.

I shall conclude this paper with a picture of Italy just before its conquest, by Theodoric the Ostrogoth. "The whole country was at that time (says the Historian) one garden of pleasure; the seats of the great men of Rome covered the face of the whole kingdom; and even their villas were supplied with provisions not of their own growth, but produced in distant countries, where they were more industrious. But in proportion as Italy was then beautiful, and its possessors rich, it was also weak and defenceless. The rough peasant and hardy husbandman had been long obliged to seek for liberty and subsistence in Britain or Gaul; and, by leaving their native country, brought with them all the strength of the nation. There was none now to resist an invading army, but the slaves of the nobility or the effeminate citizens of Rome, the one without motive, the other without strength to make any opposition. They were easily, therefore, overcome, by a people more savage indeed, but far more brave than they."[12]

The Eden that Goldsmith invokes in "The Deserted Village" disintegrates because wealthy citizens forcefully appropriate it for their own pleasure. The land-use system it represents can be supported only when national boundaries remain uncontaminated by commerce, since commerce inevitably leads to invasion by foreign armies. In his parable of Rome, Goldsmith provides an instructive history for nations which value expansion and foreign policy over contraction and domestic concerns: England's free and hardy peoples had, like those of her American colonies, originated in those who fled the oppressions of a luxurious empire in the last stages of its decline. The national organism left behind had sacrificed self-definition to commerce, and, thus effeminized, had given way before the incursions of a savage and implicitly masculine people, a version of Rome's earlier and more virtuous inhabitants.

For Goldsmith, a utopic cottage system provides the nostalgic affect normally reserved for descriptions of open fields. As he would have been well aware, even the open-field system had its portion of the entirely dispossessed – squatters relegated to the margins who were granted not even common grazing rights in meadows and fallows – and Goldsmith's poem is far more radical in its stipulation of what constitutes a just system of land disbursement. Like those who grieved for the open-field system, Goldsmith envisions blithe and deeply contented peasants who live frugal but full lives. The village common figures prominently in his poem not as a pastoral topos but as the only barrier against starvation, and his utopic vision reveals the precarious status of villagers who are dependent on the ministrations of a benevolent lord. Certainly the idea that people who have little are contented with little was and continues to be a mainstay of defenses of the open fields. J. M. Neeson is perhaps the most passionate modern advocate of this view, maintaining that "[c]ommoners had little but they also wanted less."[13] While sharing a similar view, Goldsmith nevertheless indicates that this village has always been threatened by the flow of people and customs over its insular boundaries: by ambition, desire for luxury, and temptation to move beyond one's place. His history of social decay thus echoes that of Richard Price. In such a chronology, the villagers embody Price's first stage of civilization when "agriculture supplies plenty of the means of subsistence; the blessings of a natural and simple life are enjoyed; property is equally divided; the wants of men are few, and soon satisfied; and families are easily provided for"; the tyrant embodies the last or "refined states of civilization" when

property is engrossed, and the natural equality of men subverted; artificial nec-essaries without number are created; great towns propagate contagion and li-centiousness; luxury and vice prevail; and together with them, disease, poverty, venality, and oppression. And there is a limit at which, when the corruptions of civil society must arrive, all liberty, virtue, and happiness must be lost, and complete ruin follow.[14]

Although the villagers possess a natural virtue that provisionally guards them from the seductions of luxury, they are not immune. Goldsmith depicts the consequences of luxurious impulses in a scene of urban decay, in which a poor village girl, seduced and betrayed, "her virtue fled" (line 331),

> With heavy heart deplores that luckless hour,
> When idly first, ambitious of the town,
> She left her wheel and robes of country brown.
>
> (lines 334–36)

Indeed, Goldsmith's radical vision of an England where "every rood of ground maintained its man" (line 58) closets in the well-versed arguments of luxury debates his belief that laborers should be kept in their place.

Although Goldsmith's lament is specifically aimed at the notoriously predatory practice of imparkment – the enclosure of productive lands, even entire villages, for conversion to a pleasure ground – it has become a touchstone for critics of parliamentary enclosure.[15] It was common, in fact, to address the evils of parliamentary enclosure in terms of the motivations and concerns of this horticultural counterpart. Imparkment represented an extreme manifestation of the social endorsement of contained space after 1770, and represents one factor in a continuum of enclosure practices. It helped to fuel discomfort with the implications of vast extent voiced in landscaping and farming treatises of the 1760s and 1770s. These concerns do not evince simple anti-enclosure sentiments, but a new preoccupation with the contained site and epistemological assumptions on which containment rests. Despite the fact that the links between agriculture and horticulture reveal their common source in changes in social understanding about how space should be represented, there are dramatic differences in the way these practices have been historicized. The parliamentary enclosures triggered an ideological battle more vigorous and more sustained – though not necessarily differently politicized – than those surrounding eighteenth-century gardening practices. The heat that this legal and economic practice generated has blurred aesthetic and philosophical issues that contributed to the practice and epistemology of containment.

Parliamentary enclosures became the epicenter of shifting national attitudes toward containment in part because they were the most profound visual expression of an altered angle of vision. Depending upon one's stance, they represented either a symbolic threat to the Eden represented by Old England or a symbolic promise of a new Eden. Targeted by social critics both contemporary and modern, parliamentary enclosures have been blamed, among other things, for the rising poor rate, increased cost of living, vagrancy, wage labor, loss of a "natural" system of social welfare, and emergence of the picturesque aesthetic.[16] While the misery of rural laborers and small farmers during this period did increase, to culminate in conditions which produced the Captain Swing riots in 1830 and Chartist movement of the 1840s, it is instructive that their plight should so frequently have been attached to a single domestic policy. The pervasiveness of this view has obscured the fact that parliamentary enclosures were part of a long process of land rationalization characteristic not only of England but also of vast reaches of the European and Asian continents. Bayly points out that throughout the Ottoman, Safavid, and Mughul empires which stretched from eastern Russian through Persia and southern China to Bengal, "a discernible shift towards forms of individual and marketable property in land, or its profits, took place between the fifteenth and eighteenth century." As in England, this tendency was "[i]n many areas . . . accompanied by the growth of great private estates or of more complex local forms of commercial profit."[17] Although rationalization of land in the empires of the fifteenth to eighteenth centuries does not justify the effects on the poor of the development of alienable property – land which can be sold because it is owned rather than leased or held by right of copyhold – it does place the process in a larger global context. Significantly, in both cases the process accompanied and supported the growth of intermediate classes involved in commerce and the money trade.[18] The principle of alienable property was vital to the stabilization of a middle class rooted in commercial rather than landed wealth.

The process of land rationalization that had such important implications for ordinary people encouraged critics to pit those in the intermediate classes against the laboring poor, as Cobbett would do prior to the Captain Swing riots. Yet intermediate classes didn't thrive simply by battening on the surplus labor of the rural poor. Scapegoating the ordinary people of these classes has obscured the fact that changes taking place in England at this time were systemic, while parliamentary enclosures were not. Affecting limited regions of England and manifesting an inexact correlation with traumas that accompanied wide-ranging social change, parliamentary enclosures nevertheless became pivotal to debates over social change and policy. They were simultaneously a central symbol of the epistemology of containment and a legal process that had real effect on people's lives. The difficulty is how to situate them as the former without seeming to minimize the latter. In order to unravel the many threads which have been tangled in these debates, one must address parliamentary enclosure both as an agricultural practice most intense from 1760 to 1815, when national legislation codified customary practice, and as a general development over the course of English history; as a movement with real physical consequences, and as an academic product created by scholarly debate; as a field system which generated specific agricultural techniques, and as an intellectually contrived antithesis to the open-field system; as a practice which had epistemological implications, and as a process which produced visible effects on England's agricultural landscape. The regional shift in Midland and adjacent counties of England in the 1760s and 1770s from open to enclosed farms, with more sporadic enclosures in other parts of the country, accompanied and inflected the discursive shift in garden treatises from the open to the contained prospect which is the focus of the next chapter. This occurred during the same years that the urban prospect was changing in response to the development of suburbs, with their own system of enclosed garden plots. The relationship between enclosed- and open-field systems, therefore, has social, material, and epistemological significance.

BEFORE PARLIAMENTARY ENCLOSURE: OPEN- AND ENCLOSED-FIELD SYSTEMS

From the eighteenth century to the present, the idea of open fields has provided a mythic connection with an English past which, having receded, carries implications both spatial and temporal, both social and moral. Economist Joan Thirsk reduces the open (or common) field system to four essential elements: (1) arable (soil tilled for grain) and meadow (soil reserved for grass) divided into scattered strips which individual farmers cultivate; (2) arable and meadow which is pastured in common after harvest and during fallow (when the land is left unplanted for a season); (3) common pasturage and waste where farmers granted common rights of field may graze animals or gather fuel (a privilege referred to as botes or estovers); (4) a decision-making body such as a manorial court or vestry (village meeting) that regulates the use of fields, commons, and wastes.[19] In practice, aggregate farmland was typically divided into either two or three large fields. These were tilled in rotation, with autumn crops sowed on half a field (in the two-field version) and spring crops on the other half while the second field would be left fallow for a season in order to recover its fertility. In the three-field version, fall and spring crops would be sown on two of the fields, with the result that only a third of the arable would be left fallow at any given time. The fields were divided into strips that, in a coarse measurement, could be plowed in a single day by, perhaps, an ox team shared with the entire village. Ideally, in a perfectly communal system, each farmer would have an equal number of strips divided between the two or three great fields and scattered within them. In practice this was not the case. Although allotments of arable were scattered into literally dozens of separate plots in each of the great fields, tenants often consolidated their plots by a variety of means of exchange in order to cultivate a series of contiguous plots. In their classic text, *The Open Fields*, first published in 1938, C. S. and C. S. Orwin show that inequality among strip-holders was in place from the first records of open fields so that over time the system developed a hierarchy of free-holders and sub-manors within manors.[20] This supported the Orwins' argument that the communal social organization of the open-field system "was the consequence rather than the cause of the system of land tenure and cultivation" and that communal farming developed because the open-field system was the most effective system for "the urgent task of wringing a bare subsistence from the land in the face of all the difficulties imposed by their rudimentary technical knowledge and by Nature herself."[21] The Orwins thus separate the practice of open-field farming from the idealized moral base which conventional accounts ascribe to it. The development of a hierarchy of owners, tenants, merchants, and laborers suggests that if the system did in fact begin with a fair share for all, some farmers were able to wrest more lands under their control than a communal allotment would have allowed, while others lost lands. Such practices were not limited to powerful people, although engrossment certainly had an enormous impact in the sixteenth century. There were other ways of acquiring small amounts of land that would enable the crafty and forward looking to raise themselves above subsistence level. Encroachment into wastes and forests was one of these, but others entailed small thefts, such as stealing a furrow from a neighboring furlong.[22]

This account of open fields overlooks crucial visual features that have had a lasting effect on the collective imagination. While open fields were divided into dozens, sometimes hundreds, of separate strips, individual plots in a fully developed system would not be hedged or fenced. Such a system would be characteristically wheel-shaped, with the village at the hub and unhedged fields surrounding the village. Full-fledged open-field systems were usually arable, so the fields were grain bearing and provided a visible social calendar of seedtime and harvest. The pictorial effect was of open expanse and unhindered passage from strip to strip and field to field radiating out from the social center of the village, with work conducted around the Church calendar (as plot designations such as Lammas fields have preserved in their names).

Historians have been unable to determine when the process of enclosure actually began, but it is apparent that open- and enclosed-field systems existed side by side and developed unevenly together over a long period of time. In contrast to the open-field system, the enclosed system was characterized by plots of fenced or hedged lands of various sizes, from less than an acre to many hundreds of acres, which were farmed by peasants or overseen by a tenant farmer or landlord. Lands reallocated in this way were referred to as "severalty," or individually owned plots of arable land that had formerly been tilled in common. Initially enclosure seems to have been promulgated primarily by powerful landowners, but was also often advocated and defended by smaller landholders, including copyholders.[23] By the middle of the sixteenth century the process had shifted from vicious land grabbing by unscrupulous lords and informal hedging-in of plots by smallholders toward enclosure by agreement among a variety of landowners, and proceeded primarily through either piecemeal or general enclosure by agreement until the middle of the eighteenth century.[24] Early enclosures often entailed the transformation of land from arable to pasture as farmers sought to avoid falling grain prices and take advantage of the lucrative husbandry in sheep. In fact, although official Tudor policy did not oppose enclosure itself, it did seek to minimize its perceived effects: dearth resulting from loss of arable and forcible depopulation of rural areas, which resulted in the deserted villages of the fifteenth and early sixteenth centuries. Depopulation was an effect of the transformation of land use from arable to grass, since animal husbandry required far fewer hands than grain cultivation. Its worst effects followed the aggrandizing efforts of landowners that had the power to withdraw land from common cultivation without general agreement. Tudor acts were directed against this sort of practice, and included provisions controlling the conversion of land from tillage to pasture, the engrossment of land by a landlord, and too-rapid increase of the sheep population.[25] Although in critical parlance open fields are commonly depicted as the structural opposite of enclosure, the drift from an open- to enclosed-field system should more accurately be viewed as a gradual transformation of agricultural practice that had implications for land use, ownership and labor, technical method, and the visible form of the cultivated prospect.

Historians argue the causes, effects, and amount of pain involved in enclosure, but they agree on a number of crucial points. It is clear, for example, that the rate of enclosure in specific areas was affected by regional soil differences which influenced the type of farming – whether arable or pasture and depending upon the amount of waste.[26] It is also clear that enclosure was a long historical process that occurred with varying degrees of intensity in specific historical periods from before 1500. By 1550, as most historians now accept, up to 45 percent of England was already enclosed.[27] Archaic agricultural words compose the sediment of this history, recording a process which moved forward sometimes through the petty theft of gnawing away a furrow, sometimes through the power to aggrandize holdings, sometimes by the expediency of bringing a piece of waste under cultivation. Each parcel, no matter how small, had its own peculiar name: assarts and intakes were encroachments into forest and waste land; brecks, temporary enclosures which often became permanent through customary usage; tofts and crofts, closes, and messuages, enclosed land attached to a dwelling, sometimes, as in the latter, for kitchen gardens, and sometimes, as in tofts and crofts, for arable.[28] The evolution of the agricultural system occurred not simply by depredation from upper levels of the landed social hierarchy, but by a thousand small acts of self-preservation.

Over the course of the sixteenth century, enclosure advanced more slowly so that by 1600 England was at most 47 percent enclosed. By 1760, however, on the brink of the first wave of parliamentary enclosure, 75 percent had been enclosed. Thus, contrary to what is widely imagined, parliamentary enclosures were not responsible for the enclosure of most of English land or for the majority of depopulations. As J. R. Wordie points out, "[c]learly, the 160 years from 1600 to 1760 were the most crucial in the whole of England's enclosure history. It was during the seventeenth century that England swung over from being mainly an open-field country to being a mainly enclosed one."[29] Yet it is surely significant that as large a proportion as 47 percent was enclosed by 1600. The perception that parliamentary enclosures were responsible for the enclosed landscape was encouraged by the fact that the historical process was naturalized over the process of time as hedgerows (and stone walls in the Pennines) became an established feature of the landscape, but also because parliamentary enclosures occurred at a moment in history when containment was in and of itself a volatile national issue.

PARLIAMENTARY ENCLOSURE

Unlike enclosures generally, parliamentary enclosures were enacted through legislation that codified the process, giving it the weight of official approbation. These enclosures account for less than 20 percent of total enclosures, but were concentrated within the sixty-year period of the American War, French Revolutionary War, and Napoleonic wars. Contrary to traditional practices that had been in place for centuries – whether general enclosure by agreement, general enclosure through unity of control, or piecemeal enclosure – parliamentary enclosures were determined by Act of Parliament in a legally stipulated process.[30] This included a nominal attempt to determine and allocate the interest of each parishioner in land allotments by a group of commissioners, who were typically selected by church, manor lord, and freeholders. It was required that those controlling two-thirds of parish property approve allocations. Subsequently the land was surveyed and roads, paths, and ridings were laid out. By 1804, the process had become so thoroughly interconnected with larger concerns of commerce, especially transportation of goods, that even the width of roads was stipulated (sixty feet including a verge on either side). Pre-parliamentary enclosures were by comparison unsystematic. Parliamentary enclosure therefore fed into a national spirit in which science was prized both as a realm of knowledge and as an empirical practice, and systemization was perceived as key to its practice.

The two great waves of parliamentary enclosure constituted 80 percent of all such enclosures. The first wave, responding in part to falling grain prices, focused primarily on converting land from arable to pasture. It was in this wave that the full-fledged open-field system of arable farming in England's heartland was converted to pasture through enclosure. The second wave, during the French Revolution and Napoleonic wars, took advantage of inflated wartime grain prices and aimed primarily at reclaiming untilled lands such as wastes and commons (as distinguished from common fields) for arable.[31] Parliamentary enclosures had multiple and varying significance depending on the region in which they were enacted, the transformation in land use they aimed to bring about, and the concentration of lands that were enclosed. For example, the conversion from arable to grass characteristic of the 1760s and 1770s had important implications for ownership and labor, since the consolidation of ownership accompanied accelerating wage labor, a process already of more than a century's duration.[32] This wave fueled fears of rural depopulation because animal husbandry required fewer hands than arable farming. By contrast, the reclamations of the 1790s had greater consequence for cottagers and squatters – people who had no land rights even under the open-field system and made their living on marginal lands in marginalized ways.[33]

Perhaps the most forceful symbolic consequence of enclosure was its visible effect on the Midlands, as recently enclosed fields were embossed with hedges, fences, and walls. It is frequently implied that this was an issue only for fields enclosed primarily between 1760 and 1815, and the Midland counties in which the parliamentary enclosures predominated are indeed characterized by more geometrically regular fields. However, the whole face of England changed over the course of centuries as a result of the enclosure process. In time, the hedges and walls of "old" enclosures became naturalized, absorbed into the idea of Old England. Wordsworth's reference in *Tintern Abbey* to "little lines / Of sportive wood run wild" idealizes old enclosed lands of Herefordshire, thus indicating the power of time to generate structural oppositions to the realities of the present moment. As if to lay bare such naturalizing tendencies, the cold, heavy clays of fields most enclosed during the 1760s and 1770s, those of Oxfordshire and Northamptonshire, retained as a signature the impress of the ancient ridge and furrow of open arable fields when they passed into grass. The visual effect of enclosure in Midland counties was crucial to the conventional wisdom that parliamentary enclosure, and not enclosure in general, changed the face of England. These counties, which had retained an open-field system longer than those of England's extremities, were in some cases more than 50 percent enclosed in the first intense wave of parliamentary enclosures. Seven counties were more than 40 percent enclosed by legislation during this time period, and all were in the heavier-soiled Midland and adjacent counties. These were Leicestershire, at 42 percent, Bedfordshire, at 49 percent, Cambridgeshire at 53 percent, Oxfordshire at 54 percent, Huntingdonshire at 50 percent, Northamptonshire at 53 percent, and Rutland at 45 percent.[34] These were also the counties, as Thirsk points out, which had fully developed open-field systems. The transformation to an enclosed landscape was thus starker and more dramatic than it would have been in a more rudimentary stage when open and enclosed fields existed side by side. Because these enclosures had been surveyed, they were more geometrical in appearance. They also tended to be smaller in size, often fewer than ten acres.[35] In addition, the newer and therefore less naturalized boundaries conferred upon them a more artificial appearance. Finally, land use in these counties was transformed since the clays were put down to grass. Thus the entire appearance of the counties, which, with their full-fledged open-field systems would become a symbol of Old England, was altered in the space of twenty years.

There is much speculation about the timing of parliamentary enclosure, which, although first enacted in 1604, became the primary means of enclosure during the reign of George III.[36] Certainly, as the notion of containment itself became more tightly linked to productivity it was associated with "improvement," a talismanic word for agricultural change that grew in fantastic significance as well as common usage from the sixteenth century on.[37] Eighteenth-century critics and later scholars variously represented improvement from the extremes of landowner greed for profits to disinterested desire to boost national productivity. Although accounts of motivation provide conflicting interpretations of history, both are founded on the idea that enclosure produced profits *de facto* and are informed by the assumption that the enclosure process was a necessary antecedent to more productive agricultural methods. Both, therefore, feed into the fascination during the latter half of the eighteenth century with the relationship between containment and productivity. A shift from the practice of fallowing to a regular cycle of crop rotations which allowed all fields to remain in production throughout the year, technological innovations such as horse-drawn hoeing and more efficient plows, increased varieties of crops including turnips and the so-called artificial grasses, and experimental breeds of sheep and cows – all such "improvements" reshaped the way agricultural enterprise was imagined over the course of the seventeenth and eighteenth centuries. Yet enclosure and improvement are not necessarily corollary: the enclosure of an open field did not necessarily presume the adoption of improved methods of agriculture; methods of agriculture assumed to be progressive did not necessarily boost production over the traditional methods of the open fields; and new crops such as the turnip may have helped to produce poster sheep, but they did not therefore improve either their wool or meat. As a land agent commented in 1811, "though the common field husbandry doesn't make land better, it keeps it from becoming worse . . . severalty makes a good farmer better, and a bad one worse."[38]

The sense of cultural consequence attending parliamentary enclosure probably has less to do with actual material effects than the fact that these enclosures codified an agricultural practice at a particular moment in history when many other unsettling transformations were taking place. Enclosure was only one of the causes assigned to social and economic malaise by pamphleteers during these years. Others included poor harvests, rising population, war, national debt, and middlemen. The latter were targets of the most intense ire on the part of common folk, expressed in destructive riots, for middlemen were believed to be the prime culprits in the high cost of bread corn, especially during lean years.[39] Nevertheless, parliamentary enclosure provides a focal point for debates, both contemporary and modern, about this changing culture. A parallel can be drawn with the natural phenomenon of the thermocline, an apt heuristic for explaining the sense that parliamentary enclosure inhabits a time and space that is radically separate from previous English agricultural history.[40] The thermocline is a phenomenon most of us have experienced when swimming in the spring: a cold layer of water somewhere around our calves feels distinctly divided from warmer water above it. Although this phenomenon is produced by temporal rates of flow in a body of water, the water is perceived as consisting of two separate spaces divided by a surface – the line between the warm and cold portions. Such a surface is formed by a "significant gradient," in this case a localized concentration of energy. Such surfaces may also form, however, in the presence of concentrations of information or matter of many different kinds. In the absence of such a surface, changes or differences within a space occupy a gradual and continuous scale of distribution. The surface forms when differences, rather than being spread out, are attracted to a narrow band of the gradient. Once this happens, differences may be clearly distinguished since they intensify at a specific gradient. The spaces on either side of the surface thus formed appear to be separate, self-consistent systems even though they are the single product of temporal phenomena, such as rates of flow.

The example of the thermocline provides a heuristic that illuminates why, if parliamentary enclosures were not responsible historically for either the vast majority of enclosures or the preponderance of agricultural and social change in the eighteenth century, they should appear to many observers as the source of social entropy. Because (as Acts of Parliament) they were different in character from the vast majority of enclosures, because they occurred in high concentrations at a specific time when many other less visible changes were occurring, and because areas on which they had the greatest impact were those with the most fully developed open-field systems, parliamentary enclosures constitute a significant gradient. Although they cannot easily be interpreted in terms of the continuous gradient they form with earlier enclosures, they make a great deal of sense in the temporal and social space they share with other parliamentary enclosures. As in the pond, the significant gradient produces two self-reflexive and apparently distinct spaces. Similarly, we view the social disturbances associated with parliamentary enclosure not in terms of economic changes occurring over time and vast regions of the world, but in terms of economic changes occurring within the surface formed by this localized concentration of acts. The rate of exchange *within* the temporal and spatial surface that the parliamentary enclosures provide (between 1760 and 1815) is different from that we perceive *beyond* that surface. The surface so formed is therefore critical, the point at which change can most clearly be observed and therefore the point most likely to attract attention.

Parliamentary enclosures produced an affective concentration that divided this period from the prelapsarian era of the open fields. They are one expression of a growing sentiment in the latter part of the century about the role of contained sites. The emergence of authority for contained sites, while less clearly delimited, must also be viewed within the concentration of events and information marked off by the parliamentary enclosure period. For instance, writers of architectural pattern books during this period make containment synonymous with taste and true Englishness. By contracting himself in the true English style, the gentleman defines himself in contrast to the opulence of Oriental potentates. In the new cottage architecture, humility becomes the characteristic mark that brings a man into correct alignment with English values. Enclosure into domestic bliss, like enclosure of commons and wastes, is associated with productivity. The family contracted into itself correspondingly produces true English values. One of the goals common among authors of such treatises, whether they promote or oppose the official policy of enclosure, is to advocate giving or renting land to laborers who can make it productive. The small parcel of land attached to a cottage is perceived to be more productive per acre than lands of large estates (whether or not this is indeed the case). Gardenists, architects, and agriculturists almost uniformly suggest that Eden will be the product of a widespread *system* of contained cottage plots. "The cottage system," says Edmund Bartell,

I am persuaded, need only be carried to its extent to render England indeed a paradise . . . I am convinced that the scheme is not a visionary one; and the man of fortune who would put it in execution, and promote it with his full interest, would be more than entitled to the praise which Virgil bestowed upon Augustus for the restoration of his farm.[41]

This belief accompanied the idealization of America as the colony in which each man can be his own freeholder. A widespread system of enclosures (parliamentary or otherwise) takes into account the nature of the home occupying a plot of ground, the vegetables it produces, and even the vines that grow over it. For the majority of these writers, whose views hearken back to the millenarian vision of the Civil War period, England will be a fully productive Eden when enclosure is fully democratized, whether through a system of leases or of grants to diligent laborers. The notion of Eden thus becomes identified with a system of vernacular enclosures rather than the open prospect of the country gentleman.

IDEOLOGY, CONVENTION, AND NOSTALGIA

In the foreshortened account of parliamentary enclosure provided here, I have avoided addressing directly the ideological factors which made the movement loom so large both in the events of the eighteenth century and as a product of continuing scholarly polemic. Because of its symbolic weight, the eighteenth-century enclosure movement cannot be assessed simply as one response to the increasing fascination with contained spaces over the course of the eighteenth century. What is remarkable for the purposes of this study, however, is the extent to which reading in and about agricultural tracts and materials drains parliamentary enclosure of its spectacular effect and provides us with a glimpse of the disparity between historical circumstance and symbolic representation. It becomes clear that the symbolic power of enclosure far exceeds either its positive effects for agriculture or its negative effects on the poor or landscape. Enclosure alone cannot account for economic, social, and technological changes which accompanied the transformation from an open- to an enclosed-field system.

Early in the twentieth century a fault line was established between agricultural historians who emphasized the economic gains of enclosure and social historians who examined its human cost. Initially this debate divided apologists for the movement, who presumed that parliamentary enclosure was a progressive agricultural practice, from critics of the movement, who responded that productivity was bought at a dear price, the dispossession of the rural poor.[42] Among agricultural historians, however, this fault line has become increasingly less easily definable in terms of ideological position. Studies of the laborer and grain production which have driven much research have resulted in a kind of murkiness as historians across the ideological spectrum grapple with the fact that either view reduces a complex historical process to a single social or economic effect, whether the dispossession of the poor, a process which must concern us all, or increased agricultural productivity, which was essential to a rapidly growing population. Scholarship in the twentieth century has moved in the direction of micro-economic studies of individual parishes and counties in Great Britain. The examination of particular historical records has called into question conclusions concerning the direct effects of parliamentary enclosure and indicates the patchwork effects of agricultural practices on both landowners and workers. Despite the fact that parliamentary enclosure has been a convenient scapegoat for social disease of the eighteenth century, it was only the most visible aspect of a confluence of social, legal, and political events and practices that altered not only the English landscape but even common-sensical notions about the distribution of space.

Enclosure studies rarely distinguish between historical events and the conventions employed to articulate such events, which are drawn from long traditions of social, legal, and literary history. Alistair Duckworth warns, "what might seem then to be a considered personal response to a specific historical stimulus may often be a coded structure better related to previous literature or the structure of language itself."[43] Description relies upon convention. Although, as he cautions, we need to be careful not to reduce description to mere convention, it is important to be able to identify the presence and persistence of conventions in descriptions that purport to be empirical. Description relies upon convention, especially when the author seeks to tap into shared cultural meanings. Furthermore, interpretation of past practices relies on shared meanings in order to present credible representations of those practices to an audience schooled in the commonplaces of convention and that requires convention in order to preserve the intelligibility of cultural practice. In fact, several kinds of conventions have helped to shape our understanding of the transformation of landscape in eighteenth-century England. These include conventions governing notions of social decay and disorder as well as those of descriptive language drawn from pastoral and locodescriptive poetry that spilled into polemical tracts of the eighteenth century. Analysis of the import of these conventions must begin with those that are most invisible to the twentieth-century eye, those of criticism itself. In particular, I want to return to the representation of space, which is central to an understanding of the epistemological net in which literary, horticultural, and agricultural practices of the eighteenth century were caught. The practice of representing space is common to the disparate discourses that this book brings together, from practical manuals of gardeners and polemical tracts on land use to contemporary poetry, which also represented the soil, its products, and its national interest. Earlier, I proposed that the two field systems commonly referred to as open and enclosed have been constituted through critical discourse as a single binary system. This means that rather than one replacing the other on an historical trajectory the two systems form a nexus at which a variety of discourses intersect. It is therefore more useful to view the field systems as occupying one spatial system and as having been produced by the same temporal forces. This view of the English field systems is reinforced by an observation made by agricultural historian J. A. Yelling in 1977:

the "complex distributional changes" associated with the agricultural revolution "might be seen to form part of one fundamental process of economic rationalisation and social change: in effect the emergence of a new economic and social order."[44] Yelling's observation has additional implications. As Lefebvre, drawing on the writings of Paul Klee, remarks, space is not shown but created.[45] In this case, the representation of the open fields is very much the product of the fears and desires of a nation in the midst of a changing economy and world status, a receptacle for a nation's idealized image of itself. This has radical implications not only for agriculture but also for how ordinary tradesmen or housewives viewed their own small gardens, since the idea of the open fields has more to do with the social organization of space than with the cultivation of crops; for while the receptacle of representational practice retains a conventional and therefore easily recognizable form, it can be filled with the changing contents of an evolving social practice.

The binary system in which the open and enclosed fields are caught can be visualized if we construct a list of the conventional attributes of each. In the following simple chart I deliberately list attributes of parliamentary enclosures first in order to suggest that the qualities that idealize the open-field system reflect those which derogate the enclosed system:

Enclosed field	Open field
Great Britain	Old England
hedge-rows or fences	unimpeded view
owner/employer	benevolent paternalism
individuated labor	communal labor
wage labor	wage-in-kind
contracts	customary agreements
machinery	handiwork
artificial grasses	indigenous crops
urban markets	village economy
dispersion, mobility	self-contained circumference
market demand	seasonal calendar
secularization (endless uniformity)	ritual (identity in difference)
poor rate/vagrancy	parish benevolence
time supervision	otium/independence

While the listing on the right represents a qualitatively different lifestyle than that on the left, including more benign economic expectations, less regulated management of lives, and a sacramentalized daily and yearly rhythm, it also repeats the qualities on the left – in a repetition that produces and controls its difference from those qualities so that difference simultaneously represents an alternate *and* a quite familiar reality. We are haunted by the sense that we are intimate with this alternate reality at the same time that it seems forever lost to us. Commenting on the illusions of the mirror that such relationships express, Lefebvre points out, "Here what is identical is at the same time radically other, radically different – and transparency is equivalent to opacity."[46] The question is not whether difference exists – certainly it does, although the degree of difference may not be so polar as the conventions of a binary system suggest. Rather, the question is to what extent the kinds of difference projected by the comparison are "imaginary with respect to origin and separation."[47] Here Yelling's observations are of acute importance, since he indicates that the "origin and separation" which has formed the etiology of the open and enclosed fields has become a highly conventional aspect of an imagined cultural heritage.

The structural oppositions which open- and closed-field systems exhibit would have neither their persistency nor urgency did they not draw on other deeply entrenched conventions. One is fear of social disorder such as was rampant during the period that parliamentary enclosures were at their height: the era of the Seven Years War, Gordon Riots, American War, French Revolution, and Napoleonic wars. Fear of social entropy found an outlet in arguments opposing the accumulation of luxuries by ordinary people, which I outlined in the first chapter. The vocabulary of the luxury arguments also informed both sides of the debate over parliamentary enclosure. In either case, the social mobility of less affluent people was often viewed as an expression of social entropy, although views of laborers are tellingly bifurcated. Many proponents of enclosure, for example – evangelical reformers such as John Wesley, influential political figures such as Edmund Burke, and certain architects proposing innovations for laborers' homes – depict laborers as vicious, lazy, sexually depraved creatures who cause social chaos as they drag themselves up the social ladder or sink into further depravity. Would-be social reformers believed that laborers could be controlled only through hard work.[48] On the other hand, laborers could be seen by georgic poets, many architects, and even some modern critics through a more Horatian lens as the expression of the *beatus ille*: unlike other human beings, they are happy with just enough, living from day to day and from hand to mouth. Social order is still at risk if laborers move up the ladder, because social mobility is the product of a modern system of commodity exchange that has extinguished customary, hierarchical relationships; laborers can be truly happy only in a paternalistic system unmediated by wages, which permits them to live their happy, simple lives. This paternalistic system was idealized as a moral foundation by both those that opposed parliamentary enclosure or supported it with the condition that poor families be provided with cottages and gardens. In their view, the peasant has a natural dignity that has been marred by social practice. Quartered in a comfortable home furnished with the conveniences necessary to the modern family (especially separate bedrooms for parents and children), the "patriarch peasant," in Edmund Bartell's words, who once "was no uncommon character among the English peasantry" would once again thrive as "a striking and happy feature in English scenery."[49] William Atkinson, like many improvers, similarly believed that building and keeping cottages

in good repair, are objects of the first national importance; as it is from the active exertions of the industrious labourers, that the other classes derive the greater part of those benefits which they enjoy. Justice, requires that every thing should be done to encourage cleanliness among them, and to add to their comfort and convenience, which will not fail to have a salutary effect on their conduct and character, and tend, in an essential manner, to render them much more useful in their respective stations.[50]

Only in rare and refreshing cases is the laborer presented as a human being possessed of a full range of human emotion and capacity, strengths and foibles. As in any depiction of an exotic, the laborer is invested with either an absolute natural virtue or an equally absolute natural depravity. Typically, however, the position a social moralist takes on the laborer cannot be correlated with a particular view on enclosure.

The conventions of declensionist theories of history and morals provide the form for arguments both for and against enclosure. These differ primarily in locating the source and temporal trajectory of social entropy. Those in favor of enclosure find the source of present evils in scarcity of grain, overpopulation, war, and a recalcitrant labor force. Those opposing enclosure locate the source in a new economy of commodity relations, including speculation in currency, wage labor, and middlemen (speculation in commodities). In the former, nostalgia is suppressed in favor of forward-looking methods for ameliorating the pace of social entropy, which to the modern reader seem crass. In the latter, nostalgia is the central affect of a conventional lexicon of loss and national decay; yet nostalgia also supplies a desire to contract into English values associated with domestic rather than foreign trade and with the ancient Briton rather than heterogeneous peoples being brought under the umbrella of Britishness. One can therefore anticipate that nostalgia would inform much of the scholarship on changing conditions in the cultivated landscape of the eighteenth century and the social effects of those changes. The role of nostalgia in these critiques is important for understanding landscapes since one of the most perplexing aspects of cultivated land, from a scholarly view, is its proclivity toward change and loss. Not only are the products of the cultivated landscape organic and therefore consigned to constant cycles of growth, maturation, and decay, but fashions of cultivation, whether in the service of utility or pleasure, inevitably obliterate earlier fashions. Thus in *Mansfield Park*, Fanny mourns the noble alleys of fine trees sacrificed to the vagaries of fashion – a conventional lament expressed in literature at least as early as Michael Drayton's *Poly-Olbion* and reiterated by Switzer: "Thus do we often see many a noble Oak, or sometimes whole Lines of these and other umbragious Trees, fell'd, to humour the regular and delusive Schemes of some Paper Engineers... "[51] By placing a conventional elegy in Fanny's mouth, Austen makes an instantaneous association for her readers: despite the fact that Fanny possesses social mobility and is thus a modern individual, as a *reluctant* social climber she gives voice to customary practice and a rapidly fading culture. She thus exemplifies the conventional affect of nostalgia.

Nostalgia has been extensively analyzed in recent years, to a better understanding of the structural oppositions that inform England's historic agricultural systems. Susan Stewart finds in it a search for a past that

has never existed except as narrative, and hence, always absent, the past continually threatens to reproduce itself as a felt lack. Hostile to history and its invisible origins and yet longing for an impossibly pure context of lived experience at a place of origin, nostalgia wears a distinctly utopian face, a face that turns toward a future-past, a past which has only ideological reality.[52]

If we unfold Stewart's reflection we can locate the components from which nostalgia is composed: a declensionist theory of history, an entropic theory of ethics, the sacrifice of real (that is, direct) relationships for wage-mediated relationships, and loss of national authenticity which had been bound to the simple values of agrarian life.[53] The declensionist theory of history with its biblical resonance of the Fall, presumed by the first two elements, is central in the Christian West, yet the moment of fall is relocated to the most recent point in history at which a significant gradient can be detected. By contrast, the desire for authenticity that characterizes the third and fourth elements reaches backward to a great original agrarian form of culture that has been lost. The provisional means for recovering such loss is to etch onto a collective national memory the place and time which it enshrines – most likely a place and time when memory was unmediated by the printed word and embodied instead in the liturgy of everyday life. Stewart suggests that hostility for the present is a component of the teleology which nostalgia constructs and points out that, in its interpretation of the past, its "prevailing motif... is the erasure of the gap between nature and culture."[54] It thus shares in convictions motivating sumptuary legislation which, in seeking to erase the gap between substance and appearance, heredity and social display, caters to a longing for visible and unequivocal forms of status. In contrast to sumptuary legislation, which promotes the entitlement of wealth by limiting the choices of ordinary people, nostalgia for past landscapes idealizes the life of subsistence labor and a system dependent on the good graces of the landlord, the caprice of weather, and the social welfare of the village common.

J. M. Neeson exemplifies the role declensionist theories of history and nostalgia play in conventions informing the anti-enclosure literature of the twentieth century. She opens her scholarly study of commoners with a rhetorical maneuver that implicitly positions any critique of the argument as a rejection of the shared values of a national history. She describes her first trip to Laxton, the sole remaining open-field system in England (now protected by the National Trust). I quote at length in order to give a full impression of the sense of virtue, authenticity, and loss, which indicate the author's deep familiarity with the literary conventions that have shaped our collective understanding of the open fields:

When I got to Laxton it was the late afternoon. I was tired because it had taken a long time to get there. But when the road dipped down under the railway bridge on the western side of the parish and came up next to the old common, without doubt it invaded an older world. The description of common fields as *open* fields is entirely appropriate. Distances are shorter when fields are in strips. You can call from one to the next. You can plough them and talk across the backs of the horses at the same time. You can see at a glance whose bit of the hedges or mounds needs fixing, what part of the common ditch is choked with weeds. Standing at the centre of the village feels like standing at the hub of the whole system: the fields spread out around you, the decision to sow one with wheat, another with barley is written on the landscape. For all that individual men and women work their own bits of land, their economy is public and to a large degree still shared.

It was even more so in the eighteenth century, when more of a parish was common than in Laxton now, and when pasture, the central common right, was still shared... The fields were places where people talked while they worked, and they worked together. The countryside was busy not empty. The village pound was a source of constant interest. You could tell the time of day by the regular comings and goings of common flocks and herds along the village roads, and the time of the year by their disposition in the fields and meadows. Fieldsmen, pinders and haywards were often about. Twice a year they made field orders to manage the fields and pastures, and a jury sat to ratify them and to hear complaints. Jurors and fieldsmen met at an inn, in public, with an audience of commoners. They drank together with the rest of the company, or in earshot of them. Then they had the orders cried round the village, before they nailed them to the church door. Once a year the whole parish met together and walked the bounds naming the field marks, remembering the line between what was theirs and what belonged to the parishes around them. Every year after harvest the field officers opened the wheat field to the gleaners and cried the hours of gleaning round the village. Gleaners came in procession, the women and children led by their Queen. After that the herd came into the stubble, followed later by the sheep. And all through harvest and afterwards the pigs and geese picked up fallen grain in the lanes and streets.[55]

In this description, the railway bridge under which the author must proceed in order to encounter the past works as a visual expression of a significant gradient. On either side of that boundary, social systems appear to be self-reflexive and to inhabit different rates of social, agricultural, and economic exchange. Their temporal discontinuities bolster the sense that the hither and nether sides of the railway bridge are detached spaces. Yet the appropriation of Laxton as a National Trust site suggests that the structural oppositions that Neeson observes are not antithetical. In fact, Laxton owes its character to a truly modern notion of preservation that constitutes rather than sustains the past. As David Lowenthal points out,

Every act of recognition alters survivals from the past. Simply to appreciate or protect a relic, let alone to embellish or imitate it, affects its form or our impressions. Just as selective recall skews memory and subjectivity shapes historical insight, so manipulating antiquities refashions their appearance and meaning. Interaction with a heritage continually alters its nature and context, whether by choice or by chance. [56]

The past can never be preserved except through alteration, restoration, denaturalization, and reconstitution. Similarly, Laxton could not operate as it does were it not supported by, and did it not form an integral part with, an economy based on commodity relations and sophisticated systems of exchange – one of which includes the preservation of an open-field "system" as spectacle for tourists who, in traversing the railway bridge, vivify interactions across a temporal surface produced by the invisible economic and social exchanges which unite two worlds.

Neeson's impassioned description of the landscape of loss borrows from a stable of literary conventions that began to house the idea of the open fields well before the eighteenth century. The very term "open," which she links with the sense of possession without ownership, is a conventional metaphor for a way of life that is absolutely shared, in which privacy and, by extension, private or alienable property are inconceivable; in which technology is secondary since distances are short and navigable without machines; and in which the landscape everywhere gives itself up to the laborer's eye. As metaphor, the word "open" also conveys moral connotations of honesty, sincerity, and justice. As a visual image, the open fields surrounding the nucleated village resemble the pre-Copernican universe, with the human figure at the center of an orderly and harmonious system that is naturalized as both surface and code. Communal decision-making becomes merely the logical effect of fields that produce their own syntax, decipherable to those who are a part of the intricate balance of the whole. In the social economy of the village, industry, frugality, and affection correlate with democratic rule and ritual order, and thus the familiar lineaments of the luxury arguments are brought into the orbit of the description. Finally, the subordination of the written to the spoken word asserts the authenticity of communal practice and customary regulation. The immediacy which the spoken word intimates is further reinforced by the image of a deeply symbolic visual calendar which joins the village community to a natural hierarchy, expressed by the conviviality of the gleaning rite led by the Queen of the harvest in microcosm of an orderly universe. Life is thus sacramentalized in rituals that confer the benison of common grace down through a natural order, including, on its bottom rung, even pigs and geese.

Neeson's description typifies the image of the open-field system proffered by critics of the parliamentary enclosure movement. It is powerful not merely because the open fields suggest a simpler time prior to the rigors of free-market competition and wage labor, but because the system has passed, and in passing has been constituted as an irretrievable origin. Such loss is calculated by the Orwins, who call deliberate attention to the idealized representation of the etiology and practice of the open fields which has become a part of the English national heritage. The first page of their book informs us that the transmission of this image has become central to every English child's sense of who he (or presumably she) is as English, since "every schoolboy has been instructed in it."[57] The image that the Orwins call up precedes Neeson's by almost five decades, years which have been filled with intense research into the development and functioning of the open fields and the shift to a market economy. Yet the codes the Orwins question which call up this shared memory continue to control a set of conventions so tenacious that they could well be characterized as a genre of the cultivated landscape.

Indeed, the sense of loss that Neeson so accurately conveys is strengthened when one is exposed to the vibrant vocabulary of Old English field systems (whether these were open or enclosed) and the sense they provide of the richness of a life spent close to the soil at a time when every piece of land had its use. The effect is as odd and compelling as the nomenclature of the subparticles of the atom: balks, ings, wongs and gores, shotts and flatts, oxgangs and virgates, stitches, selions, and assarts – each term thoroughly specific and utterly practical. To augment the sense of lexical riot, individual words, like "selions" (strips dividing the furlongs of the open fields), have distinctive variants in many counties – so that in Cambridgeshire selions are balks, in Westmoreland dales, in Nottinghamshire and Yorkshire lands, in Dorset lawns or loons, in Sussex paulls, in Somerset raps, in Northumberland riggs, and in the southern counties stitches – and the term "balk" itself had as many variations. The ancient practice of land regulation and enforcement produces an equally rich and strange idiom: feet of fines, glebe terriers, extents and surveys, court-leets, stints, merestones, mainports, and frankpledges evoke the mysteries of a way of life lost like the words which served it. These alien words reinforce the sense that the rich diversity of a simpler and more equitable economy has fallen before the homogenizing forces of regulation, monetary exchange, and agribusiness that find their original referent in parliamentary enclosure. The shift from the singular diction of the soil to that of agricultural improvement – the statute acre, hedging and ditching, surveying and political arithmetic – erased the eccentricities and tamed the verbal hodge-podge of the old system. Parliamentary enclosures were thus accompanied by far more than a change in the structure of land use and management and conferred on the open-field system with its lost vocabulary a powerful and persistent mythology. The pair continues to function as a structural opposition in a familiar process whereby the replacement system is perceived by some as the necessary but painful corollary to progress and by others as the decline from an effective economic system which fell prey to the greed of the landed. The two are perceived to be segregated into separate spheres, divided by the impenetrable boundaries of time and spatial practice.

Goldsmith suggests that the heart of the reversion to contained space was a powerfully conservative aesthetic impulse toward forms that evinced an internal harmony and simplicity consistent with the notion of what constituted true Englishness. The open fields were a fitting visualization of such internal harmony, especially when they could only be imagined – and they remain so. The sense of harmony instilled in the idea of the open fields remained a powerful aesthetic consideration in eighteenth-century discussions of field systems. This was produced by the sense of congruence between the ordering of the fields, the church calendar, and the social system; hereditary relations, a reciprocity between those lower and those higher on the social ladder; a calendar characterized by sacred repetition rather than secular linearity; and a system of uniform justice in which each person is thought to reap his or her due. Such a system was, ironically, reinforced by Newton's new cosmology, which presented an absolutely ordered universe. An increasingly powerful ideal emerged, however, in the face of pressing social problems. This one, the enclosed landscape, like the aesthetic that drove the open fields, was also perceived to be truly English. Drawn from the vernacular messuage or kitchen garden – an enclosed area by the house – this space reinterpreted aristocratic enclosures of the Stuart era as an indigenous phenomenon associated with ordinary people who were descendants of the true Britons. Adaptable to the broad market represented by suburban prosperity, the ideal of the messuage permitted a modern notion of private ownership, Lockean in cast, with a national memory of the cottage and its enclosed plot, and a convenient biblical precedent. If England were to become a new Eden, it would be through this model of cultivation, one that was available to ordinary Englishmen who wished to tend their gardens.

CHAPTER 3

Altering the prospects: Switzer, Whately, and Repton

This then is a general View of the Errors and Misapplications of
Mony in a Country Seat, and such they are, that by that Time, a
Gentleman has made a Garden of Ten or Twenty Acres, he is very
often Sick of it, when by a little good Management, and a little
Patience in the bargain, he might have made his whole adjoyning
Estate of 1, 2, 3, nay sometimes 4, 5, or 600 Acres, all appear as
if it was a Garden, and for the same Expence, and I will be bold
to affirm, to 10*l.*, will go as far in this as 50*l.* will in the Methods
commonly taken.

Stephen Switzer
Ichnographia Rustica (1718)

My plan is not to shew all its CAPABILITY, but rather its
FEASIBILITY.

Humphry Repton
The Sherringham Redbook (1812)

On a snowy night deep in the winter of 1811 Humphry Repton's car-
riage overturned on an icy road. His spine was severely damaged in the
accident, leaving him paralyzed for weeks.[1] Confined to a wheelchair for
a good deal of his remaining life, Repton, the most prominent English
landscape architect from 1788 to 1818, devoted part of his final treatise to
making the confined space of the kitchen garden accessible to someone in
a wheelchair.[2] In his final series of designs, for which he proposed no less
than fifteen separate gardens, he comments, "when no longer able to un-
dertake the more extensive plans of *Landscape*, I was glad to contract my
views within the narrow circle of the *Garden*, independent of its accom-
paniment of distant scenery."[3] Repton's focus on the contained site with
its contracted prospect was compelled in part by his personal calamity;
yet his proposal for the enclosed, even monkish, gardens of Ashridge,
styled after "those ancient trim Gardens, which formerly delighted the
venerable inhabitants of this curious spot," was not motivated solely by
his personal history.[4] His experience cannot wholly account for the drift

in gardening from the early Hanoverian predilection for the boundless prospect toward the Regency partiality for the gardenesque – the
contained, decorative, suburban garden style popularized by Repton's
younger rival, J. C. Loudon. Repton was an adolescent and young man
during the first wave of parliamentary enclosures and American War,
began writing during the second wave of parliamentary enclosures and
French Revolution, and continued to publish throughout the Napoleonic
wars. His distrust of absolute extension for its own sake and vexation with
the manner in which gardens should be demarcated is one expression of
a collective discomfort with unbounded space which developed during
the period of the American War. Indeed, the shift in sensibility toward
smaller, more confined gardens expressed contemporary, material realities of the English horticultural landscape. Most importantly, by the
end of the century, a new audience for landscape designs had emerged.
The intermediate classes fused economic means with a desire to fashion
smallholdings and suburban gardens into spaces for pleasure and recreation. Awareness of this target audience appears most dramatically in
J. C. Loudon's *Hints on the Formation of Gardens and Pleasure Grounds* (1812).
Although Loudon's proposals did not immediately appeal to readers,
his attempt to recover the small garden space was directed squarely at
ordinary people. He thus attacks aesthetic assumptions that validated
the open prospect. Most conspicuously, he dissociates taste from size and
wealth:

It is natural for a mind unacquainted with the powers of art, to suppose that
professional assistance can effect little in laying out small gardens or places
of a few acres; but this is to infer, that nothing can be beautiful that is not also
extensive. Beauty or expression depend no more on dimension than on expence,
but are the result of a combination of parts forming a whole, calculated by its
fitness and utility to gratify the mind, and by its effect to charm the eye.[5]

Loudon's revaluation of small gardens, like Repton's, subscribes to a
changing sentiment concerning the aesthetic and moral value of the
unbounded prospect. This transformation was brought about in part, as
Stephen Daniels points out, by the alarms of conservative moralists "at
the scale of Brownian parks and their disconnection from the humbler
side of the English countryside";[6] in part simply because landscapers
during the Napoleonic wars were presented with smaller contracts in
general, an economic reality to which Repton and Loudon adapted
with realism and ingenuity. The sea change described in this chapter,
however, reflects less a transformation of the landscape *per se*, than a shift

in toleration and focus. While unimpeded views linked British liberty to independent wealth and the landed elite, containment exemplifed values of productivity and domesticity with which intermediate classes identified.

Switzer's *Ichnographia Rustica* (1715), Thomas Whately's *Observations on Modern Gardening* (1770), and Humphry Repton's *Designs for the Pavillon at Brighton* (1808) document changing gardening strategies in the face of colonial expansion abroad and agricultural and commercial expansion at home. Taken chronologically, these treatises provide a way of understanding the evolution of representational values, inflected in the latter part of the century by reversionary conservatism in the face of violent change abroad. They locate boundaries as the problem at the heart of this evolving view. This mark of proprietorship incises the landscape and renders it intelligible, since at the boundary values associated with proprietorship, politics, and aesthetics converge.

Aesthetics throughout the century was yoked to debates over gardening practice. From Addison's "Pleasures of the Imagination" (1712), which adapted Longinus's rhetorical analysis to the categories of the landscape, to Kames's *Elements of Criticism* (1762), which includes a chapter on gardening and architecture, the English landscape was viewed and evaluated in terms that generated increasing discriminations between the sublime and the beautiful and the refraction of the former in the grotesque, the magnificent, the grand, and of course the picturesque. No aesthetic judgment was as important to the landscape as the sublime – a fact disguised by the furor in the latter part of the century over the picturesque, an aesthetic category that in actuality extends and democratizes the judgment of the sublime by making it available to an ordinary audience of limited means and circumscribed prospects. As England's representative prospect changed over the course of the century, the attachment to the sublime remained intact and the contained vernacular prospect, which should logically fall under the judgment of the beautiful, was drawn, counterintuitively, into the compass of the sublime. This occurred in part because a general trend toward psychological models privileged the agency of the human mind in apprehensions of sublimity over qualities inherent in objects. The psychic potential of the sublime was recognized by readers of Longinus and developed in a rudimentary way by Addison, who, consistent with a hint from Longinus, attached the experience to expansive or mighty vistas. The first highly profiled psychological treatment of the sublime was Burke's, whose otherwise physiological model gave pride of place to an analysis of terror. Indeed, the vocabulary popularly associated with sublimity, whether Longinus's ravishment and transport, Burke's delightful horror, or Adam Smith's wonder and surprise, indicates a subjective response not essentially moored to unrestrained vistas.

The sublime received its most detailed philosophical treatment from Kant, whose third critique (1790) provides an aesthetic model of disinterestedness within which the sublime is realized as an intellection produced by the play of mental faculties; moreover, in his analysis, as in Burke's, the sublime is clearly demarcated from the beautiful. Whately and Repton indicate that they subscribe to a premise similar to Kant's in that, for them as for many British aestheticians, the sublime is properly located not in objects but in the mind. More typically, however, Whately and Repton seize this premise when it promotes a favorite gardening principle. Their inclination is more accurately part of a British tradition exemplified by Kames, who provides a means by which aesthetic judgments may be linked to utility and moral worth, and whose analysis of beauty tends to slide into his analysis of the sublime. As Andrew Ashfield and Peter de Bolla point out, in the British tradition "attention moves away from the obsessive drive to locate the sublime affect and effect towards the construction of a descriptive model which can account for the transactions between inner mental states and the qualities of objects in the world."[7] Although differing in their negotiations between target audiences and ideal prospects, between affect and effect, Switzer, Whately, and Repton each articulate a distinctively British notion of the sublime that is simultaneously subjective and practical, aesthetic and political, psychological and moral. An aesthetic imbued with utilitarian and moral objectives thus provides the theoretical framework for sublime judgment that can be appropriated for confined prospects, and in which beauty is a function of use. Switzer's frugality, Whately's control, and Repton's feasibility contribute to a visualization of landscape in which the soul, in its imaginative flight, is sturdy enough to bear a political and moral charge. Such an aesthetic helps to explain why, after the onslaught of the enclosure debates, the bounds of the garden could be simultaneously viewed as a space of compressed sublimity and of fantasized productivity. Kames provides a theory of utility which accounts for the pleasure such spaces provide. Although sometimes couched in the vocabulary of beauty, its principles in an era when aesthetic terms remained fluid could be applied to the category of the sublime. "Relative beauty," distinguished from "intrinsic beauty" because it is "founded on the relation of objects," admits pleasure as a result of use, and "[w]hen these two beauties concur in any object, it appears delightful."[8] Even the kitchen garden, that most utilititarian of sites, was "susceptible of intrinsic beauty" if it was disposed so as to "contribute to the beauty of the whole."[9] The pleasure Kames takes in utility indicates the direction sublimity could take in the circumscribed garden as the requirements for the beautiful are infused with the affect of the sublime. Despite Kames's latent prejudice toward small spaces, the intervention of utility in the aesthetics of space made possible the democratization of sublimity and associated it with domestic ideals of hearth, home, and industry. Ashfield and de Bolla make this point in their analysis of the classed relation between the picturesque and the sublime: "The domestication of the landscape is a cover for an attempt at dismantling the culture of land ownership but, and this is the point, the sublime reappears in the picturesque, which should be seen as a tropological transformation of the discourse of the sublime . . . "[10] The treatises I examine here trace an alteration in assumptions about the relationship between space and aesthetics, beginning with the emblematic linkage between the unbounded view and English liberty, but ending in the possibilities of containment, condensation, and contrivance as a national ideal.

"THE PLEASURES OF A COUNTRY LIFE": STEPHEN SWITZER

Switzer began his career as an independent gardener in 1710. From this time, he practiced the design principles laid out in *Ichnographia Rustica*, first published in 1715 as *The Nobleman, Gentleman, and Gardener's Recreation*. In this treatise, Switzer stages the fashion for the unbounded prospect as a rejection of the taste for high-walled aristocratic gardens privileged by Elizabethan and Stuart monarchs. He gives vivid expression to the expansive view that formed a central principle of English georgic poetry. Although his rhetoric echoes Addison's fusion of Lockean politics and Longinian taste in "The Pleasures of the Imagination," Addison actually drew on ideas in garden design that were already gaining acceptance by the time the series was published. In this, as in the entire gardening movement of the eighteenth century, the timing of Switzer's treatise on gardening was crucial. Switzer could demand consensus on his designs in a public forum in 1715 because they gave visual expression to Whig ideals, which gained ground after George I's accession in 1714:

and since all agree, that the Pleasures of a Country Life cann't [sic] possibly be contained within the narrow Limits of the greatest Garden; Woods, Fields, and distant Inclosures should have the Care of the industrious and laborious Planter: Neither would I . . . advise the immuring, or, as it were, the imprisoning by Walls, (however expensive they are in making) too much us'd of late; but where-ever Liberty will allow, would throw my Garden open to all View to the unbounded Felicities of distant Prospect, and the expansive Volumes of Nature herself.[11]

Switzer detaches the pleasure of the prospect from the demarcation of property, which is assigned a negative valence, and reattaches it to the appropriation of a view. This notion of appropriation is curious: unlike the appropriation of farmland more polemically referred to as engrossment, which was accompanied by the creation of hedges or walls, the appropriation of a view is fundamentally meaningful when marks of ownership – boundaries – have been perforated so that the viewer can gaze out into the wide landscape. The landowner's property thus becomes a right-of-way to the prospect. The viewpoint from the fixed location of the country house provides owners with an expanded proprietorship when they dismantle the conspicuous barriers which testify to their wealth, while nevertheless separating their property from the less cultivated lands beyond the pale. The dissolution of conspicuous boundaries makes possible an amalgamation of private property, necessarily bounded, and prospect, necessarily unbounded, in a visual oxymoron of proprietorship. The person who controls wealth also controls the view through a trick of good fencing and concealed borders.

Switzer's apostrophes to the expansive prospect seem to contest his visual designs, which reveal clearly visible property boundaries as well as internal divisions between gardens devoted to different styles within the park. Orange trees in their pots are set apart from evergreens in the portion allotted to "greens," and these areas are divided from parterres devoted to flowers or grass. While for the modern reader expansionist discourse conjures the open prospect of Capability Brown's grassy parks, Switzer's notion of expansion is actually quite different, obtained by means of a view through a gap in the wall or a walk extended into the neighboring pasture. Expansion is thus intimately connected with demarcation, confinement, and utility as Switzer's reference to "distant enclosures" suggests. Progressive agricultural practice (Switzer was a proponent of enclosure) is a feature of the view. Switzer does not merely recommend including enclosures as a portion of the view, however, but draws them into the compass of the garden itself as a constitutive element of the design. Hedges within the park serve as mystifying devices – ambiguous internal markers which may conceal "Cabinets of Retirement" or, just as easily, a plot of land usefully reserved for corn or grazing.[12]

The avowed purpose of his plan is to recommend a "frugal" approach to gardening which makes extension possible without alienating land from the plough.[13]

Such a system, which incorporates farm into garden, or utility into beauty, was endorsed by Addison, who asked rhetorically, "But why may not a whole estate be thrown into a kind of garden by frequent plantations, that may turn as much to the profit as the pleasure of the owner?"[14] Switzer draws on the old-enclosed landscape of Yorkshire to suggest the indigenously English possibilities of such a view. He explains that some of the Yorkshire enclosures are "for their Shape and Smallness ... call'd Shoulders of Mutton; notwithstanding, the Irregularity of which Shape they plow and sow them, as truly as any other regular Pieces whatsoever." He uses this quintessentially English farmland to answer the objection "that this rural Way will (by its Serpentine Lines) cut all the fields of an Estate into irregular Shapes and circular Turns, and, consequently, spoil an Estate in Relation to Tillage."[15] The garden expanded into the country makes no attempt to disguise the agricultural landscape, not because Switzer imagines a more benevolent relationship between proprietors and their laborers but because the single most important quality of this landscape is expansiveness. The expanses that permit the soul to take flight, however, are also frugal since they are not bought at the expense of utility. Sublimity is everywhere linked to reminders of industry in the form of enclosures. It is simultaneously reinforced by the presence of the "laborious Planter," who, like God in *Paradise Lost*, is a maker of intricate designs, but also labors to bring the fruits of the soil into being.

This expansive yet frugal prospect is mirrored within the park by "Cabinets of Retirement." Switzer grants these enclosed sites epistemological significance that helped to shape the evolution of the ideal of containment during the georgic decades. "In the mean time," he comments, "I preserve some private Walks and Cabinets of Retirement, some select Places of Recess for Reading and Contemplation, where the Mind may privately exult and breathe out those Seraphick Thoughts and Strains, by which Man is known and distinguish'd as an Intelligent Being, and elevated above the common Level of Irrational Creatures."[16] Unlike agricultural enclosures, which aid frugal management of the prospect, Switzer's horticultural cabinets are a necessary adjunct to the gentleman's public task of cultivation, governance, and commercial enterprise as suggested by Locke. Such secluded spots gained increasingly moral associations over the course of the century, since spaces for retirement were viewed as auxiliary to the exercise of judgment. Thus a political environment that supported the concept of the unbounded prospect also put in place claims for retirement that justified the creation of enclosed gardens. Emblematic of reflection, introspection, and righteous government, the precedent for these cabinets lay in the *hortus conclusus*, the walled garden that allegorized the inviolate body of the Virgin Mary. Cowper exemplifies this persistent motif in his paean to his garden in the third book of *The Task*: it is in the enclosed garden that the "self-sequestered man" pauses to reflect on his condition (iii. 385). George III's personal physician, J. G. Zimmermann, echoed these sentiments in a popular text of the 1780s and 1790s, advising, "The wise man, in the midst of the most tumultuous pleasures, frequently retires within himself, and silently compares what he might do with what he is doing . . . The silent retreat of the mind within itself has more than once given birth to enterprizes of the greatest importance and utility."[17] The unimpeded view is incomplete without contained spaces that make retreat into subjectivity possible, and neither of these is possible without the resource of property. Imbued with the virtue of restraint, concealed spaces are the birthplaces of judicious action, moral rectitude, and frugal management. Switzer's justification for contained gardens is nevertheless subordinate to his enthusiasm for the unbounded prospect and is accompanied by a vocabulary that links the idea of containment to a set of conflicting traits. Although a garden recess to which one retires in order to become a politic man is requisite, the very idea of confinement is "mean-spirited" and causes the eye to be "bounded to it's discontent."[18] The open prospect, by contrast, is aimed toward the dominant principle that "[t]he Eye is covetous of Extent."[19] Although frugal management puts into play a dialectic between the open prospect and contained space, the prospect at the beginning of the century is a privileged symbol of liberty and social consequence.

CONSTRAINING THE EYE: THOMAS WHATELY

By 1770 the easy, illusionary principle governing the interplay between private property and the unbounded prospect had disappeared and the prospect had become correspondingly fraught with conflicting meanings. With its various scenes, unimpeded views, and serpentine paths symbolic of mixed government, imperial prospects, gentlemanly disinterest, and English freedoms, the open prospect had been viewed as an exemplum of the principles of English liberty rooted in Locke's political philosophy; yet, subsequent to increasing censure of engrossment and imparkment, the same prospect could be viewed as a symbol of tyranny

and the vulgar taste of acquired wealth. This was especially true after the
1760s, a decade during which political radical John Wilkes reshaped per-
ceptions of ordinary people. Wilkes's political agitation helped to realign
the conception of the "True Briton" from landowner to sturdy tradesman
and to pit the liberty and customary rights of the intermediate classes
against the arbitrary power of the current administration centered in
George III.[20] The Wilkes decade generated a rhetoric increasingly hostile to acquired wealth, directed especially against those that realized
vast sums through commerce and subsequently improved their acquired
estates on the latest Brownian principles. Owners of estates that had been
redesigned to emblematize Locke's political virtues were suspected of
having been corrupted by a continental form of tyranny and foreign
aristocratic ambitions. In the wake of Wilkes's libertarian politics, suspicion of polluting sources which might compromise the truly English
character took root.[21] The threat of pollution from without, whether
Scottish, American, or East Indian, forced a sentimentalized return to
images of the true Briton. Thus, foreign pollution suggested ways the
eighteenth-century Englishman could be defined. To be British was to
benefit from England's acquisitive imperial policy; to be English was to
have a birthright.[22] At the same time, "Briton" was also the term used
for the primeval ancestor of the English. Britishness was thereby given
a kind of historical validity that emanated outward from an insular and
well-defined center while it simultaneously, as a heterogeneous category,
delineated the benefits of being parochially English.

Whately's treatise appears at the cusp of this debate, when extension
was no longer valued as a good in and of itself and the first British
Empire was experiencing the pains that would bring it to an end. Although his principles for park design are indebted to Kames, his approbation for parks nostalgically associated with vernacular English scenes
is also shaped by the conflict generated by the political phenomena of
Wilkes and the American crisis. Whately thus reveals ways that Kames's
utilitarian and moral aesthetic could, when applied to the landscape,
epitomize political policy. His treatise is informed by a tension between
the need to gratify owners of large estates for whom he writes and his
own self-consciousness about the emblematic implications of large parks.
He attempts to resolve this tension by lading the aesthetics of park design
with the very emblems that figured the emerging sense of political worth
expressed by urban tradesmen, newly anointed as the descendants of
British yeomen who shaped and were shaped by Saxon freedoms. As
in the argument expressed by Goldsmith in his essay, "The Revolution

in Low Life," traits of the Goths who helped people ancient Britain – boldness, virtue, and virility – persist in their descendants.[23] The land-scape aesthetic consistent with this view gathered its misgivings at the focal point of boundaries. Boundaries of estate parks marked both containment and exclusion. Distinctions of ownership that were magically erased to create the illusion of absolute extension from within were fully visible to those who lived and worked beyond the pale.

Whately addresses the relationship between extension and containment within this context. Although he endorses the open prospect, he indicates a critical dilemma in his directives concerning property lines. Switzer's imperative to enlarge the view for its own sake no longer prevails as a simple concept in his treatise. The crisis over boundaries reveals itself first as a discomfort with one of the effects of the haha: by concealing the boundary between the landowner's property and adjacent countryside, the haha risks confusing boundaries between social classes as well as between lands owned by different gentlemen: "The use of a fosse [haha] is merely to provide a fence, without obstructing the view. To blend the garden with the country is no part of the idea: the cattle, the objects, the culture, without [outside] the sunk fence, are discordant to all within, and keep up the division."[24] Whately's primary concern is to provide an unimpeded prospect; nevertheless, the implication of joining the prospect onto the park troubles him, since, with or without barriers, differing kinds of ground make the "point of separation" obvious.[25] His solution is to concentrate on the boundary, in this case the illusionary aspect of the haha. In so doing he indicates how far gardening practice had deviated from Switzer's early principles. He is averse to the idea that owners should admit views for the sole sake of expanding the view. In the case cited above, the owner should not admit ground into the view that by the nature of its use is discordant with the whole. Furthermore, it is not enough to conceal a boundary by sinking the fence; one must also conceal the concealment.

Whately repeatedly emphasizes the point that "[t]he manner of concealing the separation should itself be disguised."[26] Kames provides a rationale for this strategy in his stipulation that "in such works of Art as imitate Nature," in which gardening is included, "the great art is to hide every appearance of art."[27] This recurrent theme in Whately's treatise, which focuses attention on illusion, suggests that the working relationship between possession and appropriation had become a troubling problem in overall design. The universe of the proprietor no longer involved a simple relationship between centers and circumferences, with a fixed viewpoint from the house and increasingly distanced prospects providing eccentric circles of vision. The necessity of concealing boundaries brought with it the problem of demarcating property and distinguishing it from sights which "are discordant to all within." Much of Whately's treatise is a technical manual for dealing with these twin problems, since, as he explains,

The relation of all the parts to the whole, when clearly marked, facilitates their junction with each other; for the common bond of union is then perceived, before there has been time to examine the subordinate connections; and if these should be deficient in some niceties, the defect is lost in the general impression. But any part which is at variance with the rest, is not barely a blemish in itself: it spreads disorder as far as its influence extends; and the confusion is in proportion as the other parts are more or less adapted, to point out any *particular direction*, or to mark any *peculiar character* in the ground.[28]

In this passage, the illusion that there is no boundary becomes itself a kind of intellectual marking of property, since unity of parts is the result of active perception. While picturesque theorists would as a matter of course stipulate the importance of variety, Whately reveals that heterogeneity in the well-designed landscape is really only a form of homogeneity. Decades later, J. C. Loudon would underscore this awareness in his treatise on greenhouses: "The object of this mixture," he acknowledges, "is to produce variety; but a little reflection will convince any one, that instead of variety it produces a sameness of mixture exactly the reverse."[29] The picturesque produces an *affect* of difference that is successful in taming fears about boundaries only because difference is brought under the rule of the same. "Unity" becomes a code for an illusion which rather than tricking viewers into overlooking the "subordinate connections" of otherwise disparate parts, as Whately suggests, persuades them that heterogeneity is harmless. Thus, the effect of the haha (or other such devices that conceal the bounds) fills in for the device itself, which must be concealed if variety within sameness is to be preserved. Visual control (which has its counterpart in the agricultural practice of enclosure) leaps the technical devices that make its illusions possible.

Concealment of the device that was itself invented to conceal the bounds, a technique used to maximum effect by Capability Brown, had far-reaching implications. It demonstrated, for one thing, that the illusion at the heart of the relation between possession and appropriation functions effectively only when it is itself occulted. Such illusion within illusion would be imported into interior design in the first decades of the nineteenth century by means of mirrors. In 1770, however, when Whately's treatise was first published, the technique's implications had a resonance as political as it did horticultural. For example, his comments on the management of far-flung views parallel contemporary Whig arguments about the management of colonies, and he utters them in the vocabulary of foreign policy. His treatise absorbs and reflects the instability associated with extension of the British empire while simultaneously exuding confidence in being English. Treatises on parks were exceptionally well positioned to encode such contradictions since the country estate had become an emblem of empire. The house that lay at the epistemological center of this emblem was enfolded by its well-tended gardens and radiated power through its unrestrained prospects. As Stephen Bending points out, "alterations in the physical estate reflect, indeed are inseparable from, alterations in the political estate and vice versa."[30] Cowper underscores this point when he figures the world of policy and governance as a topographical map. "'Tis pleasant through the loop-holes of retreat," he says, "To peep at such a world" (*The Task*, IV. 88–89). Throughout garden and agricultural texts, writers who are manifestly concerned with prevailing aesthetic criteria make metaphoric and direct connections with contemporary political policies. Marshall, for instance, in a treatise published shortly after the loss of the American colonies, makes a series of statements about fences and hedges that initially seem innocent of political import. "The value of an estate," he observes, "is heightened or depreciated by the good or bad state of its fences; which, it is well known, are expensive to raise, and, when once let down, are difficult to get up again." His vocabulary, however, becomes strangely militaristic as he discusses the composition of hedge-rows: "We declare ourselves enemies to Pollards; . . . they encumber and destroy the hedge they stand in, . . . and occupy spaces which might in general be better filled by timber-trees." His recommendations finally metamorphose into a critique of the integrity of England's borders: "For, although Great Britain is at present mistress of her own coast, what man is rash enough to say, that, amidst the revolutions in human affairs, she will always remain so? She *once* was mistress of the sea at large!"[31] The indifferent condition of an estate's fences discloses the shortcomings of foreign policy. Arthur Young expresses a similar response to the loss of the American War: "Our view therefore ought not to be increase but PRESERVATION."[32]

Over the course of the century, a steady conversation about the sublime accumulated a ready theoretical vocabulary for dealing with boundaries, whether physical or visual, social or epistemological. The onset of the American crisis, which was accompanied by concerns about trade with India and the governance of the East India Company, gave this vocabulary a particular resonance since an unimpeded view became not merely an occasion for a sublime experience, but also for a sense of a disorienting loss of cohesion. Whately recasts this ambivalence in Kames's aesthetic terms and applies it to the structure of the prospect. He waivers between his admiration for the now distinctive English style of gardening with its natural contours and wide views and the political and aesthetic dilemmas which such a prospect entails, especially dilemmas created by boundaries. His observations on boundaries are ineluctably drawn to problems created when distinctions between *classes* are not carefully enough exposed, and he thus participates in the process through which principles associated with the sublime aesthetic were first attached to boundaries and then refracted into an array of social concerns. He was not alone. Austen's fickle Maria Bertram in *Mansfield Park* illustrates the way concerns about boundaries were conflated with moral questions when, confronted with the haha at her stolid fiancé's estate, she feels its "restraint and hardship" – and scrambles over it to achieve the dubious freedom of the wilderness beyond.[33]

Like Austen, Whately suggests that the open prospect represents a dubious freedom. He exposes the dilemma introduced when space is defined only by extent – the lynchpin of Switzer's prospect. In the process, he charts the path by which the demarcation of the beautiful may be invested with the apprehension of sublimity. In this he follows Kames, who believed that limitation was essential to the sublime: "within certain limits, they [grandeur and sublimity] produce their strongest effects, which lessen by excess as well as by defect."[34] Whately is thus vexed by two kinds of natural scenes: those that are exceptionally far-flung and those that include large expanses of water. Of the former he observes, "As scenes encrease in extent, they become more impatient of controul: they are not only less manageable, but ought to be less restrained; they require more variety and contrast."[35] The aesthetic principle of visual control is central to understanding the different tolerations of wide and contained spaces. It also marks a moment of disorientation in the reversion from the authority of unimpeded prospects to that of enclosed gardens more characteristic of English gardens historically. Unbounded space permits neglect, demands leniency; the contained space closer to home requires greater care, compulsion, and severity. Farflung space is associated with nature; that closer to home with art.

Precisely because far-flung prospects permit neglect, the essential principle of unity in their design requires more ingenuity. As Whately points out, extension is risky "where the several parts often lie in several directions; and if they are thereby too strongly contrasted, or led towards points too widely asunder, every art should be exerted to bring them nearer together, to assimilate, and to connect them."[36] Widely flung views necessitate the "art" of imposing unity on the view, but connection can only be achieved by means of the proprietor's gaze. The assimilating function of the viewpoint, aided by judicious control over the view provided by carefully placed apertures, devices of concealment, and a variety of illusionary contrivances, is a fundamental requirement of the principle of unity. This, in turn, is crucial to imaginative freedom. The intellectual liberty thus afforded depends only secondarily on unboundedness and primarily on the principle of unity.

Expanses of water introduce a different aspect of the problem of extension. In his strictures on the role of water in the landscape, Whately makes plain that while space ordered by the unified view makes itself available as a subject of internal contemplation, unformed space is unproductive and even exhausting: if the eye is not checked, the mind will not be satisfied. Kames's notion that limitation is an essential component of sublimity was part of growing attention to a technology devoted to the process of apprehending sublimity. This would be defined most precisely by Kant as a mental breach which occurs when the resistance of the mind to the sublime object leads us to acknowledge the mind's power, "in comparison with which everything else is small."[37] The technical apparatus of mental checks that make subjective freedom possible finds a visual correlative in Whately's landscapes, which contest the principle, best represented by Burke, that formlessness, vastness, or infinity are essential to the sublime. By contrast, Whately, like Kames, warns of the pernicious effects of formless space especially when water is used in the landscape:

Space is essential to a lake; it may spread to any extent; and the mind, always pleased to expand itself on great ideas, delights even in its vastness. A lake cannot be too large as a subject of description, or of contemplation: but the eye receives little satisfaction when it has not a form on which to rest: the ocean itself hardly atones by all its grandeur for its infinity; and a prospect of it is, therefore, always most agreeable, when in some part, at no great distance, a reach of shore, a promontory, or an island, reduces the immensity into shape. If the most extensive view which can be the object of vision, must be restrained, in order to be pleasing; if the noblest ideas which the creation can suggest, must be checked in their career, before they can be accommodated to the principles of beauty; an offence against those principles, a transgression of that restraint, will not easily be forgiven on a subject less than indefinite: a lake whose bounds are out of sight, is circumscribed in reality, not in appearance; at the same time that it disappoints the eye, it confines the imagination; it is but a waste of waters, neither interesting nor agreeable.[38]

Here, Whately converts the goal of visual extension, a God-like appropriation of views, into the equally God-like impulse to impose form on chaos. His description of water recalls two biblical scenes: the expanse prior to Creation when "the earth was without form, and void," which God demarcated by "dividing the waters from the waters"; and the account of Noah's first attempt to release a dove upon the surface of the deep, which culminated in the bird's return when, in that vast waste of waters, it could find no place to rest.[39] In Whately's version, the waters must be divided from the waters if they are to satisfy vision; the eye, like the dove, requires a form on which it may rest. The terms Whately uses to warn against expanse without form give his pronouncements moral weight: mere expanse without form is "an offence," a "transgression" which "will not easily be forgiven." He thus conflates moral and aesthetic judgments.

Interaction between forms of containment and extension informs Whately's judgments concerning the nature of space. But while unlimited space may transgress only against imagination, there is a distinct allusion in this passage to the foreign and domestic policies under greatest contemporary debate: management of the American colonies and parliamentary enclosure. Clearly, space is chaotic only when it is unmarked by the specific forms that make it intelligible to the viewer. Similarly, both the unbounded prospect of the American colonies and contained fields of the domestic enclosure system produce positive and negative content depending upon how well they conform to aesthetic, commercial, and political concepts which were considered quintessentially English. Following Kames, Whately counsels that intelligible form can be successfully imposed only closer to home in spaces that can be successfully contained, and only if they are successfully contained will these spaces be lent "ideal extent" by the imagination.[40] Extension, on the other hand, may be inimical to the impress of these forms and thus resist the controlling hand of distant governance. We can surmise that a policy of salutary neglect – the colonial policy of Robert Walpole abandoned by George III soon after his accession – has the greatest potential to provide control over distant prospects without jeopardizing extent.

Containment defined by rigorous control should thus be reserved for the prospect beneath one's very gaze, and is associated with the virtues of industry, productivity, frugality, and judicious restraint.

We can see clearly here the slippage by which "ideal extent" becomes a quality imposed by the mind rather than an attribute of the landscape. The soul, which is filled and transported by the contemplation of intelligible forms, ultimately becomes the subject of its own contemplation. It is possible, then, to acknowledge that objects that lack great size – for example, in a garden – may also provide forms for such a purpose. Whately makes just such a maneuver, arguing that sublimity in the garden cannot be achieved merely by imitating the sublimities of nature, but may be disguised as singularity and surprise:

> Singularity causes at least surprise, and surprise is allied to astonishment. These effects are not, however, attached merely to objects of enormous size; they frequently are produced by a greatness of style and character, within such an extent as ordinary labour may modify, and the compass of a garden include.[41]

That which is sublime in the vastness of nature is merely grotesque within the compass of the garden. By referring to the effects of the sublime, Whately brings the concept into the familiar terms of garden design. Style and character count more than an enlarged view and within the "narrow bounds" of the garden ordinary labor produces sublime singularity similar to that which nature produces in "scenes licentiously wild."[42] The "Ha! Ha!" of the viewer on being halted by a barrier where no fence appeared to be produces the psychological disruption necessary for apprehending the domestic sublime, different in kind but not inferior to the savage contrarieties and forces in the vastness of nature.

Though it would be inaccurate to imply that Whately's treatise marks a decisive cultural break with the fashion for extension, its preoccupation with boundaries reveals changing attitudes toward the representation of space in England which have political, social, and aesthetic significance. The difference between the sublime of vastness and profundity and that adopted by landscapers who domesticated it is clear when we compare Wordsworth's famous response to crossing the Simplon Pass to Whately's account of astonishment experienced in the garden. The difference helps to account for presentations of sublimity in the work of those romantic poets who did not adopt Kant's critique. Wordsworth, who like others received Kant's analytic of the sublime through Coleridge, captured its essential character in his recollection of crossing the Alps in *The Prelude*:

Halted without a struggle to break through;
And now recovering, to my Soul I say
'I recognise thy glory'. In such strength
Of usurpation, in such visiting
Of awful promise, when the light of sense
Goes out in flashes that have shewn to us
The invisible world, doth Greatness make abode,
There harbours whether we be young or old.
Our destiny, our nature, and our home,
Is with infinitude, and only there;
With hope it is, hope that can never die,
Effort, and expectation, and desire,
And something evermore about to be.[43]

In these lines, Wordsworth lays out the most recognizable version of the romantic sublime: the recognition of human greatness out of loss, the verticality of sublime forms, the connection between sublime experience and psychological crisis, the affect of infinitude, and the ideal of eternal process. By contrast, poetry such as Keats's seems little inclined toward sublimity precisely because boundaries persistently intervene as problematic sites in the representation of spatial concepts. Yet Keats's poems, like garden treatises after the American War, express a less alienated and more accessible version of the sublime which forms around the site of boundaries – a version which emphasizes compression over infinitude and surprise over psychological crisis. Such an expression of sublimity is caught quite clearly in Blake's illustration for Milton's "Il Penseroso," "The Peaceful Hermitage." Although the title suggests a quiet, domestic scene, the engraving itself depicts sublimity compressed into a narrow, well-demarcated space. The prophet, his hands thrust out toward the walls of his cell gazes upward at the roof of his enclosure, but seems to see beyond it the infinitude of the starry night sky and tangled forms of passion and desire. The inscription reads, "Milton in his Old Age sitting in his 'Mossy Cell,' Contemplating the Constellations, surrounded by the Spirits of the Herbs & Flowers, bursts forth into a rapturous Prophetic Strain."[44] Here, infinitude finds its expression within confinement. The inexorable movement toward containment, which was inseparable from the professionalization of gardening, gave control over the landscape a new valence, which enabled the less affluent and less mobile to assist in the production of a new vision of England as an Eden of sublime, albeit enclosed, spaces.

"SOMETHING WE CAN CALL OUR OWN" : HUMPHRY REPTON

By the end of his career, Repton had transformed the direction of land-scape design by diminishing the importance of the unimpeded view, championing visible demarcations, advancing the role of artifice in areas adjacent to the house, emphasizing convenience, and redefining utilitarian portions of the park (such as paths or the kitchen garden) to assist aesthetic pleasure.[45] With the publication of his *Designs for the Pavillon at Brighton*, unrealized plans for a comparatively circumscribed property belonging to the Prince of Wales on the edge of the resort town of Brighton, Repton proposed a new direction for landscape gardening which abandoned the illusion of boundlessness and appropriated, rather than excluded, the urban setting.[46] The Pavilion at Brighton (more familiarly known as the Marine Pavilion) may have dwarfed a town garden; nevertheless, the text of Repton's proposed renovation suggests principles for more modest domestic sites. Although the Prince did not adopt his designs, they are important since in them Repton complicates the boundary as the location of division between proprietor and tourist, yet as the point of an idealized social reciprocity. In his etiology, the boundary originated in the feudal necessity of defense, and was only afterward transformed into a mark of social distinction.[47] Although the boundary continues to mediate between social classes, proprietors should ideally permit it to function as a portal for the gaze of those outside the pale. It thus makes legible the operation of a benevolent, natural hierarchy.

Repton's designs for the Marine Pavilion are also important because they appropriate the notion of taste associated with landed proprietors for an urban site, and he develops those principles in ensuing treatises. Consequently, one of his central concerns after the publication of the *Designs* was to reestablish two English landscapes: the "ancient style," associated with a monarchic and paternalistic system of landownership, and the *jardin ornée*, or decorative kitchen garden, which he believed was indigenously English. In exploring the possibilities of the kitchen garden, Repton, solidly in the tradition of Kames, draws attention to the importance of a functional, vernacular landscape for producing astonishment, productivity, and national values. Despite his devotion to landed wealth, Repton's strong sense of human proportion, his regard for utility, and his insistence on accessible views shifted the focus of garden design toward the potential of contained urban or suburban plots – a transformation exemplified by the fact that the primary audience for Repton's collected works, brought out by Loudon in 1840, was the middle class.[48] Even when designing parks for the affluent, Repton's focus on accessible space suggests that his attention to demarcation and function secured a vision of the landscaped garden that linked it to a vernacular idiom. Although his social views were conservative, his theory of landscape design could be appropriated by ordinary people for spaces they called their own.

Repton endowed the concept of appropriation with meaning quite different from the mere capacity to purchase a view that we find in Switzer. In Repton's works the association between the boundary and appropriation implies an entirely new notion of ownership. At its simplest he reduces the word appropriation to "something we can call our own."[49] Despite the homely implications of Repton's transliteration of the Latin, recent landscape historians and art critics have focused on his use of the idea primarily for its negative connotations.[50] This is largely because the concept of appropriation has a theoretical history that makes its direct application to Repton's use of the term problematic. Introduced into political discourse by Marx and into art history via Marxist hermeneutics, appropriation, as Robert S. Nelson points out, is "the equivalent in the cultural sphere of capitalist expropriation of labor in the economic sphere."[51] Repton's candid use of the term invites modern critics to load it with Marxist freight, with the result that his own evolving sense of its meaning and social significance is distorted. Nelson makes a fitting comment: "Because appropriations, like jokes, are contextual and historical, they do not travel well, being suppressed or altered by new contexts and histories."[52] The result of the alteration of contexts in this case has been to exclude Repton's positive application of appropriation for property ownership by ordinary people. For example, Stephen Daniels misleadingly applies a crucial comment on appropriation in the *Fragments* to his discussion of Repton's commission for the trade-wealthy clothier, Gott. Daniels states, "The mill at Armley was the only one Gott owned outright and Repton wanted him to look upon it with undivided pride of possession, incorporating it in an idea of landscape whose basis was 'appropriation', 'the *exclusive right* of enjoyment with the power of refusing that others should share our pleasure.'"[53] In fact, Repton did not condone this "human propensity,"[54] and on the page following this quotation reflects

This propensity for appropriation and exclusive enjoyment is so prevalent, that in my various intercourse with proprietors of land, I have rarely met with those who agreed with me in preferring the sight of mankind to that of herds of cattle, or the moving objects in a public road to the dull monotony of lawns and woods . . . For the honour of the Country, let the Parks and Pleasure-grounds of

England be ever open, to cheer the hearts and delight the eyes of all, who have taste to enjoy the beauties of Nature.[55]

David Worrall's discussion of the term demonstrates more justly the inconsistent ways that Repton used the term, including his strictures against property owners who set spring guns and mantraps to maim or even kill trespassers. Worrall maintains the pejorative view, however, that Repton's use of the term is apolitical.[56] Modern judgments of appropriation as a concept fail to represent the power of Repton's notion of appropriation for describing the desire of ordinary people to own homes within which domesticity fostered by representations of English values could be secured. Indeed, exclusively negative readings run the risk of implying that property ownership is itself an evil.

Taken as a whole, Repton's understanding of appropriation is complex and inexact, positive and negative. For instance, in the preface to his proposal for the Marine Pavilion, he castigates appropriation as an unfitting use of property that results from combining great extent with exclusive enjoyment. This outworking of appropriation, he believed, confuses extent with beauty and endangers the vision of England as the Garden of Europe. After his spinal injury, however, when much of his time was spent in a wheelchair, he redefined appropriation as the most domestic of all desires: "And after all," he concludes, "the most romantic spot, the most picturesque situations, and the most delightful assemblage of Nature's choicest materials, will not long engage our interest, without some appropriation; something we can call our own; and if not our own property, at least it may be endeared to us by calling it *our own Home.*"[57] Here he speaks from the vantage point of his own home which lay on a straightened property at the busy intersection of the main village streets in full view of a butcher.[58] This domestic version of appropriation, consistent with contemporary views on the size of farms, implies a system of homes which people of every rank can call their own. In this ideal of England, the nation is not one large garden but a gathering of gardens, owned, bounded, and differentiated in terms of social hierarchy, but open to "that constant moving scene" of humanity beyond the pale. "I have also lived to reach that period," he concludes, "when the improvement of Houses and Gardens is more delightful to me, than that of Parks or Forests, Landscapes, or distant prospects."[59]

Seen in this context, Repton's sense of appropriation addresses the crisis of the boundary by destroying illusions designed to conceal the concealment. He derides much of the technical apparatus developed for naturalizing boundaries, from new invisible fences which he refers to as "that *wire-bird-cage* expedient," to the widespread misuse of the haha.[60] He believed that the haha remained a crisis point not primarily because of its use as an external boundary, but because it had been misapplied in the garden. He explains that a garden, as opposed to a park, forest, or riding, is by its very nature fenced off, defended, in a word, walled. It manifests the essence of appropriation, since it should be designed for the "use and pleasure of man: it is, or ought to be, cultivated and enriched by art with such products as are not natural to this country, and consequently it must be artificial in its treatment, and may, without impropriety, be so in its appearance."[61] Like the gardens of romance epic, Repton's garden is a curiosity cabinet filled with wonders, demarcated as the place of artfulness. In his severest stricture against the haha Repton deplores the fact that "where ground is subdivided by sunk fences, imaginary freedom is dearly purchased at the expence of actual confinement."[62] Imaginary freedom, in his view, is more likely to be found within the visual boundaries of a well-demarcated spot. Repton thus finds the concealed boundary to be both visually and morally dubious.

Repton's solution is not simply to make boundaries visual. In a foreshortened version of the garden the boundary is relocated between the garden and the world outside it or between the home and garden, which becomes the home's architectural extension. When continuity between the architecture of the home and the landscape becomes instrumental, illusory devices are transferred from the outer vista to the home itself. The domestic version of the haha is the mirror, which, by disguising internal boundaries at the ends of hallways or between home and conservatory, suspends disbelief in its own fictions and recreates the surprise of finding a checking point where none appeared to be. Repton's anecdote of encountering a mirror in a home for which he had designed a greenhouse is similar to older accounts of first stumbling on a haha: "Having directed a Conservatory to be built along a south wall, in a house near Bristol, I was surprized," he exclaims,

to find that its whole length appeared from the end of the passage in a very different position to that I had proposed: but on examination I found that a large looking glass, intended for the salon . . . had been accidentally placed in the green-house, at an angle of forty-five degrees, shewing the conservatory in this manner: and I have since made occasional use of mirrors so placed to introduce views of scenery which could not otherwise be visible from a particular point of view.[63]

A similar connection is provided by architectural mirroring between house and garden, wherein "artificial decorations of Architecture and Sculpture are softened down by natural accompaniments of vegetation."[64] While conservatories bring vegetation into the house with the aid of the mirror's illusions, formal landscape designs extend the architecture of the house into the garden.

Keats provides a dramatic example of Repton's devices for expanding the interior space of the home and diminishing the importance of the bounding line of the house in the illusory palace that Lamia rears in Corinth. Lamia's banquet hall plays out the duplications and reflections of art that, in mirroring nature, emphasizes its own artifice:

> Fresh carved cedar, mimicking a glade
> Of palm and plantain, met from either side,
> High in the midst, in honour of the bride;
> Two palms and then two plantains, and so on,
> From either side their stems branch'd one to one
> All down the aisled place; and beneath all
> There ran a stream of lamps straight on from wall to wall.[65]

Like the Marine Pavilion, Lamia's urban palace suggests that the display of nature in the city requires high artifice. Although the attempt to bring nature into suburbs and cities was ridiculed by many, Repton found the exigencies of designing a town site to be beneficial, for in such sites the garden is permitted to display its artifice. "Fortunately," he says,

the sunk fence cannot be applied to the Gardens of the Pavillon; we cannot blend the surface of the grass with adjoining streets and parades; we cannot give great ideal extent by concealing the actual boundary; we cannot lay open the foreground of the scene to admit distant views of sea or land, while impeded by intervening houses . . . [66]

Fortuitously, the confinement of such a scene produces its own sublime pleasure. As in Blake's depiction of the prophet in his cave, the contemplation of internal space yields the oxymoron of compressed magnitude. Like Whately, Repton rejects the conventional corollary between grandeur and the sublime. Similarly, when he implicitly contests Burke's notion that the experience of sublimity is a necessary exercise of mental alertness, he does not reject the sublime but reapplies its central principle of psychological disjuncture to the surprising and yet familiar site of the garden, which expands as one contemplates it from within. Contained within its boundaries, the sublime may be contracted in scope but it has not thereby lost its power. The rift which lies at the heart of the sublime experience is transmogrified from Burke's terror into "surprise"; "vast extent" is detached from the sublimities of the Alps; and, in the last analysis, beauty, and not "boundless range," reveals the landscape's "character of greatness and importance." The psychological response that provokes the sublime experience is released by qualities more strictly associated in aesthetic arguments with the judgment of the beautiful.

The alteration described in this chapter accompanied a shift in predilection from extensive to intensive, from nature to artifice, and from instruction to sensibility. Adaptations of popular aesthetic ideals led the way to defining the essential attributes of contained space and following on the heels of the georgic decades such spaces were found in lyric poetry and the kitchen garden. As a visual concept, however, georgic forged a powerful metaphoric association between nation and soil that remained intact when its authority foundered in the last quarter of the century. The delineation of English race and its connection to English soil, the central theme of John Philips's *Cyder*, continued to govern poetic and topographical space even when the contours of an expansive national topography had been radically altered.

PART TWO

The poetry of earth

CHAPTER 4

English georgic and British nationhood

If Virgil really designed to instruct the farmer by his Georgics, he
might have done it much more effectually in plain prose.

John Aikin
An Essay on the Application of Natural History to Poetry (1777)

In the spring of 1788, the manufacturers of Bury burnt Arthur Young
in effigy in response to his opposition to the Wool Bill, a position that
supported landowners against the interests of trade. One of Young's
admirers responded with a letter in which he proposed

doing you honour in effigy in order to make up to you in some measure the disgrace
you have undergone (as is creditably reported about town) of being burnt in
effigy by the wool manufacturers at Bury. My brother is for procuring your
effigy, and after having crowned it with a wreath composed of turnip roots,
cabbage leaves, potato-apples, wheat-ears, oats, straws, &c., and tied with a
band of wool thinks it ought to be placed upon its pedestal (being the volume
of Virgil's "Georgics") to be worshipped by the real patriots . . . [1]

This "very lively letter" (in Young's words) suggests an idealized link between Old England and Great Britain, between traditional husbandry
and the new commercialism, between the poetry of earth and the science of agriculture. The composition of produce heaps the crops of
time immemorial – wheat, oats, straw, and cabbages – with the radical
crops of the present: turnips and potatoes. Pitting the pastoral world of
English sheep herding against the self-interested world of commerce, it
undergirds the whole with Virgil's great green poem, "the best poem,"
in Dryden's words, "of the best poet."[2] And it links all to the politics of
patriotism and the land. Progressive, Whig, and literary, the effigy centers fruits of the soil popularized in the eighteenth century in a tradition
both founded by and superseding Virgil's *Georgics,* and is a monument to
a failed farmer paradoxically acknowledged from Russia to Italy as the
greatest agricultural expert of his era.[3]

The proposed effigy thus wittily suggests ways in which British agriculture was popularly imagined in the eighteenth century. Clever as the effigy is, however, it cannot articulate the interconnections in the eighteenth century between the literary form of English georgic, its popular approval, practices of reading, and cultural authority. For instance, in appealing to a patriotic spirit, the effigy does not reveal the essential Britishness of the agricultural project; by evoking Virgil, it idealizes the prosiness of the project so properly exemplified by the agricultural essayist to whom it is dedicated; and while extolling the land, it occludes the most potent and contested landed prospect for Britons in the eighteenth century – the idea of America. These subjects lead me to examine the circumstances which first fed and then undermined the phenomenon from 1708 to 1767 which we describe as "English georgic," circumstances which began by reinforcing the authority of the open prospect and closed with a fascination for confined forms.

I begin with Anthony Low's working definition of georgic poetry: "that georgic is a mode that stresses the value of intensive and persistent labor against hardships and difficulties; that it differs from pastoral because it emphasizes work instead of ease; that it differs from epic because it emphasizes planting and building instead of killing and destruction; and that it is preeminently the mode suited to the establishment of civilization and the founding of nations."[4] My argument is premised on the notion that English georgic poetry did not, as is sometimes supposed, disappear during the 1760s, especially after the publication of Richard Jago's *Edge-Hill* in 1767.[5] Rather, I suggest that it is more accurate to characterize the historically specific phenomenon of English georgic as an essentializing of georgic's more characteristic manifestation, that of mode. In response to georgic's potential for giving shape to new and indispensable notions of national productivity, the eight or so poems generally considered to be "true" georgics achieved the authority of genre between 1708 and 1767.[6] If this is the case, the true problem for the critic is not to explain English georgic's demise, but the reasons for its loss of authority.

I propose three historical contingencies for the efflorescence and deflorescence of this generic authority. First, while the vitality of public approval for the form may appear to date from Dryden's translation of Virgil's *Georgics*, published in 1697, its popularity was in fact more closely associated with the Act of Union with Scotland in 1707, which realized the notion of Great Britain.[7] I see Dryden's translation as a fortuitous antecedent to this political event, the popularity of which was ensured by other cultural forces including new patterns of reading. Second, attention for the national and moral agenda accompanying georgic was deflected from poetry into prose over the course of the century as science in general, not merely agricultural science, went through a period of unprecedented popularity and as new predilections in reading affected the commerce in books. Third, the loss of the American War, which began with George III's disastrous attention to the colonies in 1763, diverted the association in the public imagination between political leadership and agrarian ideals from the Hanovers to the newly constituted United States of America, from George III, the Farmer King, to George Washington, the Cincinnatus of his race. That crisis, in fact, drew attention to progressive elements not embodied in the English georgics, making them an improbable form for the imaginative articulation of the national agenda.

THE ACT OF UNION, 1707

In the tradition established by Virgil's *Georgics*, the connection between nation-building and the poetic mode that celebrates labor is intimate, and it is commonly understood that the emergence of georgic as an authoritative form coincides with a pronounced period of nation-building in Great Britain; however, the connection between georgic and nation-building is not as straightforward as the coincidence between the elevation of georgic and the growth of British nationalism in the eighteenth century would seem to suggest. Classical epic was the premier form associated with nation-building. Certainly, the fact that literary critics normally identify the catalyst for the phenomenon of nation-building as the Civil War in the previous century would seem to provide as logical a rationale for the repute of epic as for georgic forms, and the *Aeneid*, popularized like the *Georgics* by Dryden's translation in 1697, is particularly congenial to the ideal of a nation reborn out of the ashes of its former self. The propensity for foreign wars during this period would also seem to encourage an epic rather than georgic sensibility. Great Britain was at war for the whole of the century and beyond. The War of the Spanish Succession from 1702–13, which culminated in the Treaty of Utrecht, the War of the Austrian Succession from 1743–48, the Seven Years War from 1756–63, the French Revolutionary War, engaging Britain from 1793 to 1802, and the Napoleonic Wars from 1803 to 1815 were all conflicts that enhanced Britain's nationalistic sense.

Why then did epic not emerge as the popular civic form in the eighteenth century? It is not sufficient to argue that Milton operated as a bogey who prevented poets from exploring the long form of epic.[8] As

Low has shown, Milton's positive influence over georgic poetry was singularly encouraging for later poets. It is not the association between nation-building and war that generated cultural authority for literary form in the eighteenth century, but rather the particular connection established between nation-building and the soil. The shaping event of the georgic century was a political event that defined new parameters of nationhood and simultaneously suppressed the memory of internal war and redirected native sensibilities to the land: the Act of Union with Scotland in 1707 which created Great Britain, bounded now on all sides by the ocean, rising like Botticelli's Venus out of the foam, and making possible the sense, pervasive by the middle of the century, that to be British was to belong to a heterogeneous category.[9] James Thomson, who wrote the most popular georgic poem of the century and perhaps the most fundamental English georgic of all time, exemplifies this sensibility. Not English, but Scottish, Thomson celebrates the virtues associated with the new sense of Britishness. The idea of Britishness would not have been possible without the sense of nationhood produced by the Union, and Scotland played a profound role not only in making such a notion possible, but in establishing connections between Britishness, commerce, agriculture, and science that had significant effects first on the reception of georgic poetry and then on the demise of its authority as a form. English prejudice against the Scots and the concomitant Scottish feeling of inferiority, recorded so poignantly by James Boswell, who like David Hume and other Scottish luminaries was plagued throughout his life by his ambivalence toward his own country, is actually consistent with the new sensibility.[10] English prejudice was a product of the need to define Englishness against and by means of Scottishness, much as English Protestantism was defined against and through Roman Catholicism. Common sense as well as history indicates that prejudice against Scotland was fueled in part by English insecurity about the increasingly important role of Scotland in Great Britain's intellectual life, including its school reform, scientific advancement, extraordinary involvement in Britain's imperial policies, and, not least, establishment of agriculture as a necessary subject of advanced study and research.

At the same time, the Lowland Scottish drive to approximate Englishness was heightened by the Act of Union and gave an edge to attempts toward improvement which led to a Scottish enlightenment far more potent, and more famous on the continent, than England's. Scotland, indeed, supplied much of the intellectual and cultural power that forced georgic into its brief literary prominence. This was true not only on the level of individual genius, but in a larger cultural context. Innovations, propelled by the strong Scottish interest in making education in Scotland serve the practical needs of commerce, introduced widespread study of subjects such as mathematics and book-keeping, history, geography, and natural philosophy, outstripping English schools in these areas.[11] Such innovations, like those of Dissenting academies in England, designed to educate the sons of merchants, mechanics, and farmers, were central rather than peripheral to the national project of education.[12] In addition, university training was a far more ubiquitous middle-class tradition for boys in Scotland than in England. An idiosyncratic critique launched by a Scottish pamphleteer in 1704 amusingly illustrates this fact when the author disparages the university system for being too open to "the Mechanicks and poorer sort of People." The author believes that the Scottish university system is simply too inexpensive to keep out undesirables. Such a system, in his view, will "unfitt a Scholar for a Gentleman and to render a Gentleman asham'd of being a Scholar ... And till we Reconcile the Gentleman with the Scholar, 'tis impossible Learning should ever flourish. But were this once done, were Learning taken out of the hands of the Vulgar and brought to be as Honourable and Fashionable among the Gentry, as 'tis now contemptible, I think it would be indeed in a fair way of prospering."[13] The Scottish University system had, of course, an effect opposite to the one the writer envisioned, and, in particular, created an atmosphere congenial to the professionalization of agriculture.

The image of a productive nation that sounded this keynote in education and which is central to much English georgic found another correlative in Britain's expanding commerce, the importation of exotic foods, raw materials for textiles, and, most potently, the acquisition through the Treaty of Utrecht of a monopoly in the slave trade, a subject that directly or by inference was incorporated into all the English georgics after 1713. But productivity was even more powerfully linked in the public imagination with Britain's own ability to produce food, to its agriculture. Thomson's apt allusion in his anthem "Rule Britannia" to Britain's "rural reign" and his development of that theme in *The Seasons* is an expression of, and testimony to, the new commerce in agriculture. Thus although many historians of agriculture now agree that the agricultural "revolution" did not occur in the eighteenth century at all, that its revolutionary aspects occurred much earlier and that it saw unprecedented development in the nineteenth rather than the eighteenth century, the perception among the British who lived in the middle years between revolutionary developments and the practical expression of those developments was certainly that something new and of great importance was happening in the very soil of Britain. For the first time agriculture, not merely sheep herding, figured in a burgeoning national ideology of Britishness. Profits achieved from the soil were seen directly to affect the fortunes of the country, and the personal prosperity of the landed proprietor was supposed to forward the more general prosperity of the nation. The tendency of georgic poets to organize their landscapes in terms of the locations of aristocratic country houses is significant in this regard. This tendency does not conflict with the idea, driven by Scotland's remarkably populist educational system, of accessible higher education for the intermediate classes: country houses, like the growth of hedgerows throughout the course of the century, became deeply symbolic of the link between the soil and rapidly accelerating nationalism under the banner of Britishness. The Scottish intelligentsia, despite its predominantly middle-class roots, tended to seek identification with the landed classes and ancient aristocratic families. Unlike their French counterparts, they were not given to "social and political iconoclasm."[14] Attitudes toward agriculture in the early and middle parts of the century were aristocratic in their biases, and, supported by Virgil's *Georgics* and the classical agricultural treatises, or *Scriptores rei rusticae*, this bias became integral in the English georgic poem.

The vision of Britain laboring in order to establish itself as a productive nation had tremendous popular appeal for an increasingly literate people. The dramatic intensification of georgic poetry from mode into genre was not the only response to this idealized notion of Great Britain, since agricultural societies and prose treatises on husbandry and the soil grew correspondingly. The literary form became a metaphor for Britain laboring which supplied a national and aristocratic imaginative ideal of Great Britain as a newly created georgic Eden. Agricultural societies and prose accounts, by contrast, promoted a different ideal, that of the progressive farmer diligently conducting experiments on turnips, manure, and course rotations, a plain preacher rather than a singer of the landscape, driven by profit rather than the muses and improvement rather than art.

SCIENTIFIC SOCIETIES AND PROSE TREATISES

In *The Georgic Revolution*, Anthony Low locates a tradition of growing approbation for the arts of agriculture, beginning with Francis Bacon and continuing through Milton, which paved the way for the uncommon cultural authority and civic approval attached to georgic poetry in the eighteenth century. Clearly influenced by agricultural historian Eric Kerridge's 1968 thesis which argued that the agricultural revolution occurred not in the eighteenth, but in the seventeenth century or even earlier, Low argues that contrary to popular perception "the georgic revolution took place in England between about 1590 and 1700."[15] He illuminates a shift in national attitude during the Interregnum that granted new moral authority to labor, and stresses the relationships between a revolutionizing agricultural science and the rise of georgic poetry. In the process, he indicates the powerful role not of successful farmers, but of institutions like the Royal Society, founded in 1662, which had both official backing and a core membership of gentlemen powerfully interested in agricultural reform.[16] Faced with the concatenation of forces that transformed public perception of this poetry, the curious inference one must make is that the factors which led to georgic's improved status are identical with those which led to the decline of its authority: the linking of scientific method with agriculture, the growth of societies that supported this endeavor, growing numbers of agricultural treatises, and new attitudes toward the relationship between gentlemen and labor.

Interestingly, English georgics do not on the whole reflect the new attitudes that Low describes. Indeed, part of their imaginative appeal was surely the form's aristocratic bias, its gentrification rather than accurate portrayal of labor. Addison's frequently quoted description of Virgil in his anonymous introduction to Dryden's translation of the *Georgics* as the poet who, in spite of his rustic subject matter, "delivers the meanest of his precepts with a kind of grandeur," and who "breaks the clods and tosses the dung about with an air of gracefulness" exemplifies this interpretation of labor in English georgic poetry.[17] This has implications for the authority invested in a poetic form charged with forging the link between Great Britain and the soil, since georgic poems maintain a covert distinction between those who work in the fields and those who have the leisure to read didactic agricultural texts. While Virgil makes a parallel between writer and laborer, as would georgic poets of the eighteenth century, the distinction between reader and laborer is in both cases kept intact.

The division also haunts the pages of agricultural treatises and responses by readers to this increasingly popular prose form. In 1786, Charles Burney would whimsically respond to Arthur Young's *Annals* by asking,

What have I without an inch of land to do with farming? Is it the subject or manner of treating it, or both that fascinated me, when you first were so kind, my dear friend, as to send me some of your "Annals of Agriculture"? I was in the midst of my winter's hurricane and immersed in other pursuits, but now, having conversed with some of your correspondents, seen your farm, and rubbed up my old rusticity, all my love for country matters returns, and I sincerely wish myself a villager. You seem to have worked yourself up to a true pitch of patriotism, and I think, besides the instructions the essays convey, that your knowledge on the subject, and animated reasoning, and admonitions, must have a national effect. Your book fastened on me so much on the road that I hardly looked on anything else.[18]

Burney's enthusiasm is typical of an increasing audience of readers for didactic prose texts over the course of the century, and, fanciful as his response may seem, gets to the heart of the role played by them as they imagine Britain laboring. As Burney's response astutely suggests, the prose treatise is invested with the authority of a nationalistic agenda, a function ably borrowed from English georgic. But Burney also records the gripping effect of the treatise. Young similarly captures the extraordinary imaginative force provided by agriculture in the eighteenth century when describing the need for a renewed agricultural endeavor following the loss of the American War:

Whatever may be those consequences [of the loss of the war], of this we can entertain no doubt, that they call for the combined exertion of all the wisdom and talents in the nation to draw into activity every latent resource, and to create new ones equal to the new burthens that are experienced in the present period, and dreaded in the future.[19]

These responses suggest the imaginative power of the tie between a nation and its soil which agricultural treatises were able to generate. In particular, Burney's response indicates the excitement prose accounts of agriculture fostered in the general reading public by the last quarter of the century. While the prose treatise often had little more to do with actual labor than georgic poetry, it succeeded in shifting the authority for shaping Britain's imaginative vision of labor from poet to progressive farmer.

Diversion of imaginative interest from georgic poetry into prose treatises parallels a more general and well-documented tendency in the eighteenth century toward increased readership of various kinds of prose from encyclopedias to the novel. Significantly, it can also be seen in a temporary mid-century shift from a preference for poetic translations of the classics (Dryden's *Virgil* and Pope's *Homer*) to prose.[20] In the case of georgic poetry, the stimulus for draining poetry into prose was even more forceful, since prose came to represent science in a way that poetry could not, and agricultural writings incorporated many aspects of the georgic agenda, particularly its rampant nationalism. Thus while scientizing agriculture in the seventeenth and early eighteenth centuries may have contributed to the interest in the poetry of agriculture, it eventually displaced georgic ideals from poetry into treatises and common discourse toward the last quarter of the eighteenth century.

Kurt Heinzelman justifiably counters this notion when he observes that while georgic is perceived to have disappeared by around 1770, the upsurge of agricultural treatises developed during the last quarter of the century, thus producing a time lag between the demise of the poetic form and the emergence of the treatise.[21] This is true. In fact, although the romantic period saw a rush of regional agricultural societies and journals, the first British academic chair in agriculture, and the creation of a major national organization (the Board of Agriculture, founded in 1793), exclusively agricultural journals did not have their greatest increase in number and circulation until the last half of the nineteenth century. In addition, although Arthur Young began to publish his own *Annals of Agriculture* in 1784, they clearly postdate the literary period often used to circumscribe English georgic. Nevertheless, the many publications devoted to scientific and experimental method from the 1730s on indicate that enthusiasm for finding a solid scientific footing for agricultural method began much earlier in the century. This is evidenced by several short lived journals which preceded Young's *Annals*, including the *Musaeum Rusticum et Commerciale*, first published in 1763 as the unofficial organ of the Society of Arts. A more important gauge of enthusiasm for a newly scientific art of agriculture, however, were articles published in different contexts. *The Gentleman's Magazine*, the first widely circulated monthly periodical, for example, included articles on agricultural subjects, as did numerous provincial periodicals, pamphlets, and more esoteric journals.[22] Indeed, what is significant here is not how early these articles and pamphlets began appearing, but that they begin to appear at precisely the same time that newspapers and other periodicals were themselves in their infancy. The incorporation of agricultural subjects with those of science, politics, literature, and the polite arts had greater force in gentrifying the subject for a wide audience than did journals devoted exclusively to agriculture. Young's highly touted *Annals* had a circulation of only 350 to 500. Despite the fact that the number of readers would have greatly exceeded circulation figures (Young complains that reprinting the *Annals* cost him his profits, but he was excessively proud of the fact that the king took two copies, loaning one to the celebrated farmer, Mr. Ducket) readership of the *Annals* cannot account for the general public enthusiasm for agricultural matters. *The Gentleman's Magazine* had a circulation of ten thousand by the end of the century.[23]

Popular fascination with the natural world was also reflected in the emergence of scientific and agricultural societies. These sprang up throughout Great Britain in the course of the century. Like the Royal Society of Arts founded the previous century, whose core membership consisted of a group of men interested in agricultural improvement, the names of these societies do not necessarily contain references to agriculture (which was variously construed as either art or science).[24] They nevertheless provided a venue for progressive farmers to meet and discuss their interests with scientists and other intellectuals who linked agricultural endeavor with the most recent scientific findings. Well before the full-fledged emergence of the agricultural treatise, the new prosy voice of agriculture was being shaped by scientific societies that provided an oral culture for the transmission of agricultural ideals. As Sarah Wilmot points out, "the appeal and influence" of science, as it was understood through these societies, did not rest in the growth of "formal participation in scientific culture." Rather, the "power of science . . . lay in its emblematic uses as a symbol of progress, in its ability to symbolise change in general, not in its membership."[25]

This was especially true in Scotland, where, according to Wilmot, at least fourteen regional agricultural societies were formed between 1723 and 1784.[26] At least seventy scientific societies sprang up in the British Isles between 1660 and 1793, including the Royal Dublin Society (1731), whose special focus was on growing flax. The best known, the Society for the Encouragement of Arts, Manufactures, and Commerce, founded in 1754 (the Society of Arts) assisted the emergence of agriculture as above all a scientific endeavor that required a thorough knowledge of the chemistry of soils, the physiology of animals, the biology of plants, and their relation to both the soil and the air. The importance of early Scottish societies in promoting the agenda at first associated with English georgic may have been overlooked in studies of georgic in part because of the American and English tendency to disregard the importance of Scotland in escalating notions of Britishness in the eighteenth century. The societies as a whole have received little attention, however, because of the tremendous importance accorded to the writings of Arthur Young, who did not begin his popularization of new agricultural techniques until

1767, nor his *Annals of Agriculture* until 1784. Nevertheless, the societies are a barometer of a rare public fascination with science in general and with its implications for Britain's productivity.[27] As the full title of the Society of Arts suggests, these societies were interested in the imbrication of agriculture and commerce, agricultural advancement and technology.

Scientific and agricultural societies made possible an environment in which progressive farmers could freely exchange ideas. Throughout the eighteenth century, the effort to scientize agricultural knowledge succeeded in removing it from its traditional bases in the *Scriptores rei rusticae* and relocating it in journals and in the contributions of farmers to the animated sphere of public discussion so characteristic of the eighteenth century. This new environment for the transmission of knowledge of husbandry and the soil helped to undermine English georgic's authority to envision Great Britain as the new georgic Eden. Its authority was undermined even further by Britain's increasing difficulty in the final decades of the century to produce sufficient wheat for her growing population. The georgic celebration of a traditional scheme that equates happy labor with the soil could not ameliorate the hunger of the poor. Dyer's mid-century poem, *The Fleece*, which extols the role of the state in policing the poor into industry as a solution to inadequate supplies of bread, is a perfect example of georgic's failure: the poet teeters between his celebration of the new world of commerce founded on progressive farming methods and his yearning for a traditional paternalistic structure, figured by the image of the king as a faithful shepherd. The return to this traditional social order recast in the celebrated terms of commerce is realized both in the workhouse and rosy future of successful tradesmen. The workhouse paternalistically reshapes the recalcitrant poor into the "happy swain" central in the georgic vision of labor that prevailed earlier in the century, and becomes, in the process, a macabre version of the aristocratic country house:

> O when, through ev'ry province, shall be rais'd
> Houses of labor, seats of kind constraint,
> For those, who now delight in fruitless sports,
> More than in chearful works of virtuous trade,
> Which honest wealth would yield, and portion due
> Of public welfare? . . .
> Ye children of affliction, be compell'd
> To happiness: the long-wish'd day-light dawns,
> When charitable rigor shall detain
> Your step-bruised feet. Ev'n now the sons of trade,

Where-e'er their cultivated hamlets smile,
Erect the mansion: here soft fleeces shine;
The card awaits you, and the comb, and wheel;
Here shroud you from the thunder of the storm;
No rain shall wet your pillow: here abounds
Pure bevrage; here your viands are prepar'd;
To heal each sickness the physician waits,
And priest entreats to give your MAKER praise.[28]

The heavily-weighted phrase "fruitless sports" applies a Miltonic pun to Philips's *Cyder*, which recasts Britain as the Eden whose fruit brings life rather than death, and to Gay's *Rural Sports*, which reshapes Virgil's images of labor into the traditional aristocratic sports of hunting, birding, and fishing. In Dyer's version, the "sports" of the poor reflect their idleness, their fallen natures. They will be redeemed by trade, which tricks out the pre-commercial georgic vision in more fashionable dress.

THE IDEA OF AMERICA

Dyer's attempt to celebrate the new realities of trade within the traditional terms of the genre articulates the complexity of English georgic's resistance to a new commercial culture. Resistance is most clearly evident in the georgic response to America. Georgic poets persist in representing the American colonies as providers of exotic materials, rather than, as agriculturists were increasingly aware, competitors with the mother land. In the relationship between Great Britain and the colonies during the georgic century, however, few things are more intriguing than the historical coincidence between the names of the foremost military and political leader in the colonies and the sovereign of Great Britain. Indeed, one of the oddest aspects of the rise of georgic poetry is that it so neatly coincides with the reigns of the first three Georges. This coincidence reaches its most suggestive extreme, of course, in the reign of George III, popularly known as the Farmer King. Heinzelman asserts a fully authoritative moment arising from the coincidence, claiming that "[t]he ascent of George III not merely to the throne (in 1760) but to the full referential burden of his name in becoming the kind of progressive farmer applauded by the agricultural improvers coincided almost exactly with the disappearance of georgic as an acknowledged literary form in English letters, a departure so abrupt and documentable that if anything fits Foucault's definition of the fissure or disjunction that marks a changed *episteme* this must be it." The result of this moment, Heinzelman proposes, is that "Georgic, which even in Virgil's original had been problematically referential, is undermined by an unexpected and relentlessly singular referentiality." It thus "vanished as a *named* genre . . . largely because of the political burden of georgic reference."²⁹

This hypothesis rests upon two problematic historical notions: first, that agricultural progressiveness is central to English georgic, and second, that George III held a high status among agriculturists as an improver in the scientific mode which coincided with the disappearance of georgic. English georgic and history suggest otherwise. First, as *The Fleece* demonstrates, even when English georgic incorporates agricultural innovations and the celebration of trade, its traditionalist structure is far stronger than the new subject matter it contains. The gentrification of labor, in particular, demonstrates georgic's anti-progressive impulse. Based on a paternalistic system of landed inheritance, the English georgics tend to celebrate the leisurely "rural sports" and the euphemistically "happy swain" or his industrial counterpart. Even commerce with the colonies is celebrated in a backward-looking vision familiar from Jonson's "Penshurst," whose "ripe daughters" "bear / An emblem of themselves in plum or pear" to the lord and lady of the demesne.³⁰ Similarly, the American colonies, typically personified as female, are represented as bearing to Great Britain an exotic natural produce. The reality by the last quarter of the century was a different, more competitive commercialism, in which American exports replicated those of the mother country and filled in for her insufficiency. The entrenched traditionalism of the English georgics was therefore deeply assaulted by the American War and its consequences.

Second, it is not accurate to describe George III's status among agriculturists as a "potentially transcendent" British image of the georgic ideal.³¹ George III's agricultural status is, in fact, difficult to separate from official compliments he would have received regardless of how agriculturists viewed his work as an improver. In this regard, the paucity of commentary from agriculturists upon the king's record is instructive.³² Furthermore, his nickname, Farmer George, did not become popular until well after the publication of the last "true" eighteenth-century georgic, Jago's *Edge-Hill* in 1767. It was not until after 1790 that the nickname really took hold, and did so then in response to changing public sentiment toward the king, not for his farming efforts, but because irritation over the American War and compassion for his mental instability had turned public sympathy toward him. The nickname thus represents an affectionate and comic response to George III's infirmities and failures.

Such an image is consistent neither with that of the ideal georgic hero, Cincinnatus, nor with the late eighteenth-century progressive agriculturist. The former, a victorious General, was, according to legend, discovered in his fields at his plough by the embassy from Rome who sought him for their Dictator; the latter is a forward-looking, commercially oriented improver. The nickname Farmer King, by contrast, documents neither George III's engagement in war and cultivation, in public service and retirement, nor his reputation as an agricultural improver. It defines instead the reaction of an imagination looking backward through the American War with nostalgia for the role of the traditional paternalistic gentleman or country-house lord. Anecdotes depict just such a figure in the person of the king benevolently dispensing pocket money and advice to the rustic workers on his Windsor estates. Unlike George III, George Washington was repeatedly hailed in the popular press as a latter-day Cincinnatus, successful in the field of battle, retired into the cultivation of his land and intellect, and reluctantly returned to the political arena in response to the demands of his people. There could not exist a more direct contrast to George III: signateur of his people not by the new democratic principle of election but by the older one of inheritance, viewed less as a progressive agriculturist than as a figurehead, and tortured by madness.

Recollections and early loyal histories of George III do not include informative narratives of his agricultural efforts; rather, they connect the king's agricultural interest with his benevolent role as paterfamilias of his country. The Scot, John Galt, for example, publishing a history that is riddled with inaccuracies after George III's death, fashions a mythology around the king's nickname which persists to the present day. He opens his account with the claim that it is to "his fondness for agriculture" that "much of our present prosperity may be attributed; for he brought it into fashion: and to his praiseworthy example we are in a great measure indebted for the exertions of our most celebrated agriculturists, and for the widely-diffused benefits both of their theories and practice."[33] Contrary to Galt's depiction of George III's agricultural influence, the king could more accurately be described as following the fashion for agriculture than setting it; nevertheless, he gauges the profoundly symbolic importance of garnering royal validation for the practice of agriculture from the first Hanover born on English soil, and helps to account for eulogies to his "practical" farming skills.

Young, a more reliable source of information about the king's influence on farming than Galt, follows a similar eulogic pattern. In lieu of

describing the king's efforts, a marked departure from his normal practice after visiting large farms, he produces an encomium on the king's
example which serves as a reprimand to the government at large for not
adopting requisite "public measures." Young's most extended affirma-
tion of the king's national influence celebrates the king's gift of a merino
ram in 1791, and is, of course, infected by Young's need to advertise
himself as a special recipient of royal favor:

How many millions of men are there that would smile if I were to mention the
Sovereign of a great Empire giving a ram to a farmer as an event that merited
the attention of mankind! The world is full of those who consider military glory
as the proper object of the ambition of monarchs; who measure regal merit by
the millions that are slaughtered; by the public robbery and plunder that are
dignified by the titles of dignity and conquest, and who look down on every
exertion of peace and tranquillity as unbecoming those who aim at the epithet
great, and unworthy the aim of men that are born the masters of the globe.
    My ideas are cast in a very different mould, and I believe the period is
advancing with accelerated pace that shall exhibit characters in a light totally
new, and shall rather brand than exalt the virtues hitherto admired; that shall
place in full blaze of meridian lustre actions lost on the mass of mankind; that
shall pay more homage to the memory of a Prince that gave a ram to a farmer
than for wielding the sceptre obeyed alike on the Ganges and on the Thames.
    I shall presume to offer but one other general observation. When we see his
Majesty practising husbandry with that warmth that marks a favourite pursuit,
and taking such steps to diffuse a foreign breed of sheep well calculated to
improve those of his kingdoms; when we see the Royal pursuits take such a
direction, we may safely conclude that the public measures which, in certain
instances, have been so hostile to the agriculture of this country, have nothing
in common with the opinions of our gracious Sovereign; such measures are the
work of men, who never felt for husbandry; who never practised it; who never
loved it; it is not such men that give rams to farmers.[34]

Young's encomium is significant since, contrary to the georgic tradition,
it separates imperial politics and military success from the notion of the
leader as farmer, indeed represents imperial politics as somehow inimical
to domestic agriculture. Young suggests a portrait of the king not as a political leader but as a benevolent, paternalistic landowner experimenting
with sheepbreeding. Behind the rhetoric which links George III's reign
with newly acquired holdings in India lies the absence of any mention of
America, the arena of Britain's single military defeat in the eighteenth
century. Young divorces the notion of military greatness from the georgic ideal in a way that exonerates the king for that military loss. Unlike
Cincinnatus, whose georgic character is the mythologized encounter of

public virtue with retirement and of greatness in military affairs with expertise with the plough, the king is presented as the friendly country squire who knows his tenants by name.

This portrait is not truly inconsistent with the one developed by Galt over the whole of his two-volume panegyric history. In Galt's version, the infant king, in the tradition of legend, is nursed by "the fine, healthy, fresh-coloured wife of a gardener, probably the head gardener of one of the palaces." When this nurse is informed that

according to the court etiquette, the Royal infant could not be allowed to sleep with her – from an etiquette so cold, and, in the present case, so likely, in her opinion, to prove prejudicial, she instantly revolted, and, in terms both warm and blunt, thus expressed herself: – "Not sleep with me! then you may nurse the boy yourselves."

The royals, in true fairy tale tradition, are depicted as giving in to her rustic wisdom, and Galt editorializes:

To this conscientious obstinacy on her part, it is more than probable that the nation owes the blessing it has for so many years enjoyed, of being governed by one of the best of men, and of kings, that ever united in himself the virtues which grace both characters.[35]

The king's identification as a virtuous farmer finds legendary roots in the bed of a gardener's wife, a relationship whose later extraordinary correlative is his faithful, domestic spousal with the homely and fecund Queen Charlotte. The couple produced thirteen children and an image that became cemented in the nascent ideology of the fireside: "In fact, patriotism was so fixed upon a sure foundation. He who could depend upon the truth of his partner – he who could round his *fireside*, and call every thing there *his own*, could not fail to love the country which contained such blessings."[36]

Galt's anecdotes of the Farmer King are intimately attached to this association between rustic virtue, fireside, family, and property ownership. They grow out of a rich tradition in popular legend of kings like Alfred, who travel unrecognized into the fields and very homes of their subjects. In one such instance, the king, separated from his attendants, is "overtaken by a violent storm of rain." Taking shelter in a cottage, he finds a girl, who does not recognize him, turning a goose on a spit. He volunteers to turn the spit if she will take care of his horse, which she does. While she is out, the farmer returns, "and felt much astonished to see his Sovereign, whom he knew by sight, thus domestically employed." The king, meanwhile, converses "with his usual good-nature on this mode of cookery and the advantages of a jack." After he rides away, the farmer spies "a paper on the shelf, and having opened it, found in it five guineas, with these words written in pencil, 'To buy a jack.'"[37] On another occasion, the king

passed a field where only one woman was at work. His Majesty asked her where the rest of her companions were. The woman answered, they were gone to see the King. 'And why did you not go with them?' rejoined His Majesty. 'The fools,' replied the woman, 'that are gone to town, will lose a day's work by it, and that is more than I can afford to do. I have five children to work for.' 'Well, then,' said his Majesty, putting some money into her hands, 'you may tell your companions who are gone to see the King, that the King came to see you.'[38]

Galt's messianic tone as he relates these events loyally redirects George III's energies from military exploit abroad and the specter of revolutionary democratizing forces into peaceful domestic inquiry and traditional rural paternalism. The aggregate power of the anecdotes lies in Galt's reconstruction of the king's character from a georgic hero modeled on the Virgilian ideal into a gentleman farmer. Big-shouldered rustic greatness is pared down and gentrified as the king makes his rounds incognito, riding his lands and dispersing his blessings in order to be among his people. His famous indifference to the court and to contemporary culture, the appalling boredom expressed by peers and others commanded to attend him and his queen, is reinterpreted as an engaging attentiveness to rural affairs that censors unsuccessful military engagement in America; the Virgilian representation of a national hero longing for retirement in the face of pressing political engagement is replaced by the view of a monarch perpetually engaged in the activities of retirement.

The anecdotal reconstitution of George III's character as the Farmer King that developed during the long years of his decline and after his death is far more compelling than actual accounts of his farming efforts. Fundamentally, it was not George III's progressive example that popularized him as Farmer George, but his absorption into the stereotype of the traditional landowner whose best manure was the mark of his footsteps on the soil. His nickname appeals not to a progressive agricultural future, but to nostalgia for a past in which paternalism represented a compelling contrast to the new commercial sense of agriculture and property, with its attendant republican resonance. The development of this ideology of nostalgia parallels increasing attacks, after the conclusion of the unsuccessful American War in 1783 on the notion of America as an agrarian paradise. Advertisements of land by American land agents had nurtured a sense that the colonies represented an agrarian site of infinite potentiality. Popularly characterized as a freeholder's dream, land holdings from Kentucky to New York were advertised by hucksters as inexpensive and requiring minimal labor, presumptions which would be central to such schemes as Coleridge's and Southey's Pantisocracy in the mid 1790s.[39] Even in the 1780s, however, such schemes were exposed as fraudulent, and descriptions of the newly formed republic by British (primarily English) loyalists derided the American agrarian dream.[40] Nevertheless, even Sir John Sinclair contemplated a scheme of emigration in 1795,[41] and Arthur Young, despite his vigorously loyalist politics, betrays a fascination for America as a unique and fortunate idea. Critics of the American dream of agrarian prosperity and protectors of that dream sought either to expose the tricks of land agents or to perpetuate the notion of America as a freeholder's georgic paradise.

It was the latter, however, whose notions of America most aptly caught the effect that the nascent republic exerted on the British georgic imagination. Clearly, their version of America was not drawn from fact. As recent studies have shown, workers of the American soil were not primarily freeholders but tenant farmers who were unable to progress beyond subsistence farming. In addition, many of the freeholders themselves never rose above subsistence levels, and vast percentages of the populations of southern states were enslaved.[42] The agrarian dream, nevertheless, had great force for reasons similar to those attending the Act of Union in 1707 – because of the powerful association it made between America and the land. In the case of America, however, the link between land and space, or, in contrast to Britain, the sense that external limits did not exist, was particularly powerful. Enclosure of the wilderness by second-wave settlers was different symbolically from parliamentary enclosures in Britain: rather than being popularly viewed as a fall from a previous era of agricultural innocence, these enclosures were the *fiat lux* that transformed inchoate wilderness into another Eden.[43] As Myra Jehlen argues, "The prior vacancy of the continent was [the] crucial founding fiction" that Europeans clung to in their settlement of America.[44] The fiction generated correlative fictions, that limitless space was inherent in the character of Americanization and that "any man could afford to own property."[45] Regardless of transatlantic reports of boorish society, poor agricultural technique, lazy laborers, an erratic climate, and shallow, infertile soil, the sense of space associated with America made possible an ideal within which the American could be mythologized, in Jehlen's words, as "ideally self-reliant and self-sufficient."[46]

The myth of America as a land of freeholders with small but independent properties, rooted in naturally productive soil, by contrast to
Britain's increasing difficulties in feeding a population almost double
what it had been eighty years before, was powerful. Even more compelling was the changing nature of American exports to Great Britain.
America had begun by supplying its mother country with exotic raw
materials such as cotton, tobacco, and cane sugar. While these imports
were gradually transformed from novelties to necessities, they did not
duplicate Britain's own produce. Increasingly after the war, however,
America exported foods which were *like* those produced in Britain, but
which Britain was finding increasingly difficult to grow in adequate quan-
tities, especially wheat.[47] In spite of the fact that the new nation doubled
its population in the first twenty-three years of nationhood, it still produced an excess. As Joyce Appleby points out, "After 1755 the terms of
trade between grain and all other commodities turned decisively in favor
of the grains and stayed that way until the third decade of the nineteenth
century." American farmers, quick to realize this advantage, converted
tobacco fields into wheat. In the years of dearth in Great Britain, particularly 1788–89 and 1794–96, American exports of wheat were crucial,
although Britain was forced to import wheat for twenty-seven of the
thirty years following the war.[48] All of George III's efforts to provide a
benevolent example by forcing his Windsor laborers to eat brown and
potato breads, all of Arthur Young's scolding the poor into contentment,
could not efface the fact that America's assistance in the form of wheat
exports was necessary to feed the British people.

Although the idea of America initially emerged as a variant on the
theme of Great Britain, it became through the catalyst of the American
War an innovation on the idea of nationhood.[49] Early tracts suggest that
America's farmers would help to realize Britain's eighteenth-century
georgic dream by enclosing the wild and unproductive wilderness into
productive tracts of land which were imaginative extensions of the
mother country and equally imaginative innovations on parliamentary
enclosures. The American War, however, served as a lens through which
the vision of America not only became focused, but, in a striking parallel of the optical process, inverted. The imagined relationship between
space and time central to the idea of the so-called new world was pivotal
to this inversion, and had consequences for the imagining of agricultural
space. The European concept of space, and certainly of Great Britain
as well, was that of limitation. But whereas spaces were small in the Old
World, the historical continuum was enormous, providing a history that

went back for generations, even beyond record. This sense was reversed in America, since the war produced a new nation whose history broke sharply with its ancient parent's. In this new land, time was contracted, enclosed within the cataclysmic events of modern history, whereas space was conceived as limitless. Agricultural matters were correspondingly inverted. In Great Britain, a progressive agricultural practice was proudly seen as one of its greatest successes, especially as that practice was linked to an official policy of enclosure. America could be said to replicate that process, since the transformation of wilderness into georgic landscape also followed a process of enclosure. Oddly, however, the process was not viewed imaginatively in the same way. Notwithstanding the enclosure of the wilderness, the American dream continued to be the dream of limitless agricultural space, of an infinite number of such sites for those who chose to renovate them. The idea of enclosure in America was thus inverted and given a different valence associated not with contraction but with expansion.

The letters of George Washington to Arthur Young and Sir John Sinclair express the reality that agricultural practice in America was not progressive. On the one hand, Washington appeals to Young's agricultural expertise precisely because of his sense that "the system of agriculture (if the epithet of system can be applied to it,) which is in use in this part of the U.S., is as unproductive to the practitioners as it is ruinous to the land-holders";[50] on the other, he suggests that America is productive *in spite* of resistance to technical progress. In a series of letters, Young responds to the enigma of American farming practice and productivity: "Your information has thrown me afloat on the *high seas*. To analyze your husbandry, has the *difficulty of a problem*. Is it possible, that the inhabitants of a great Continent, &c. can carry on farming as a business, and yet never calculate profit by per centage on capital?" In his response, Washington extends Young's nautical metaphor, conducting him into America's "safe harbour," which "will enable him to arrive on a shore, pleasant in its prospects, and abundant in its resources; not so much indebted to Art as to Nature, for its beauties and conveniencies."[51] Washington then indulges in a peroration on the ills to which America is immune: self-indulgent princes, ecclesiastical drones, and high taxes, but most pertinent to his conversation with Young, expensive land. America emerges as the agricultural site which is to Europe as Nature is to Art, and specifically in this ratio, Nature is georgic nature and art, the arts of agriculture. The notion of American productivity inverts Great Britain's:

whereas in the mother country, productivity is associated with progressive ideas, in America it is rooted in the soil itself.

George Washington comes to represent this dream of nature, mythologically uniting rootedness in the soil with progressive practice, military success with a farmer's homely interests. Essayists occupying widely opposed political views during the 1790s saw in Washington the personification of this vision of America. One might predict that Coleridge would hold such a view, who in *The Morning Post* in 1799 described America as a land "where the great mass of the people possess property, and where, by the exertion of industry, any man may possess it in its most permanent form" in contrast to "old and populous countries, in which land is of high value, and where the produce of individual labour can hardly be large enough to admit of considerable accumulation." Even when Coleridge later became disaffected with American politics, he retained his fantasy of America's first President as "her own spotless Washington."[52] Likewise, Arthur Young projects this image of Washington upon America's farming spaces both before and after his conversion to an aggressively conservative politics.[53] In the *Annals* of 1792, published a year before his political sharp right turn, Young includes an extensive account of Washington's farming practice at his Mount Vernon estate reported by Brissot de Warville, a member of the French National Assembly and travel writer. Warville carefully notes the General's participation in the work of the estate, and bolsters his reputation as a latter-day Cincinnatus:

The General came home in the evening, fatigued with having been to lay out a new road in some part of his plantations. You have often heard him compared to Cincinnatus; the comparison is doubtless just. This celebrated General is nothing more at present than a GOOD FARMER; constantly occupied in the care of his farm, and the improvement of cultivation.

Warville goes on to document Washington's improvement of a barn based on plans solicited from Young, his extensive holdings ("more than 200,000 acres" in "different parts of the country"), and the propriety of his domestic scene with Mrs. Washington, who "joins to the qualities of an excellent housewife that simple dignity which ought to characterise a woman, whose husband has acted the greatest part on the theatre of human affairs . . ."[54]

Warville's account of his trip to Mount Vernon characterizes Washington both as military leader and as a down-home farmer who can be found at the equivalent of the plough; as the progressive landowner who, rather than riding his lands incognito, labors in the improvement of his prospects; and as the paterfamilias who combines these qualities with domestic virtue. Unlike George III, he does not need a brood of children to realize this ideal, since, precisely because of America's constructed temporal trajectory, he is his country's *Pater Patriae*.[55] George III, by contrast, although eulogized as monarch, cannot fill this Adamic role. Young's assiduous attention to anecdotes of Washington's progressive agricultural attitudes helped to create an imagined view of Washington as a truly georgic leader who, like Cincinnatus, had innately georgic qualities, much as the newly fledged country was the locus of a natural rather than an artisanal productivity. Young solidifies this image by publishing Washington's quintessentially georgic reluctance to be cast in such a public role: "I can only say for myself," Washington discloses in his letters, "that I have endeavoured, in a state of tranquil retirement, to keep myself as much from the eye of the world as I possibly could . . . For I wish most devoutly to glide silently and unnoticed through the remainder of my life. Dec. 4, 1788."[56] When, in the conclusion of his edition of Washington's letters to himself and Sinclair, Young memorializes Washington's character, he infuses it with the subtle and various qualities that comprise a georgic figure. He refers, that is to say, to Washington's military talents, his skill as a statesmen and founder of the constitution, his public virtue, his sense of retirement, and his literary endowments.[57] Under Young's scrutiny, and those who likewise helped to promote this exemplary figure, Washington becomes the ideal George, whereas Great Britain's king becomes little more than a shadow of that ideal.

The whimsically coincidental names of George III and George Washington illuminate the imaginative links between labor, statesmanship, and British nationhood in the eighteenth century, a period which has been called the georgic century. Such an unlikely connection between two national figureheads grants an odd entrance into the complex relationship between agriculture and national identity. The public sense in Britain of the importance of the soil in the formation of this identity, in which soil is a metaphor for productivity, independence, and racial identity, was extended and undermined by the idea of America. It was extended so long as America could be imagined as a variation on Great Britain, a natural and primeval space which Britons could feel formed a logical extension of their own history – forward into the increasingly complex politics of commercial trade, but also backward into an archaic Edenic space. In this sense, George Washington, who began his career as a surveyor of the uncharted wilderness, becomes the natural, earthy, and less sophisticated counterpart of George III. The loss of the colonies, which haunted George III in his madness, was accompanied by a loss of the imaginative ideal of America. It was at this historical intersection, America's revolutionary transformation from a variation on the idea of Britain to its innovation as modern state, that English georgic became an improbable form for the expression of the fantasized link between nation and soil.

CHAPTER 5

Philips's Cyder: *Englishing the apple*

There is no kind of Fruit better known in England than the *Apple*, or more generally cultivated. It is of that Use, that I hold it almost impossible for the *English* to live without it, whether it be employed for that excellent Drink we call *Cyder*, or for the many Dainties which are made of it in the Kitchen. In short, were all other Fruits wanting to us, *Apples* would make us amends.

Richard Bradley
New Improvements of Planting and Gardening (1731)

In 1929 a crusty British patriot by the name of E. A. Bunyard could say, "No fruit is more to our English taste than the Apple. Let the Frenchman have his Pear, the Italian his Fig, the Jamaican may retain his farinaceous Banana, and the Malay his Durian, but for us the Apple."[1] Bunyard's comment may be abrasively jingoistic, but the association of the apple with England is not a point most of us would challenge. More recently, Richard Sax, in a magnificent dessert cookbook, notes, it is "funny that along with Mom and the flag, apple pie has come to represent the quintessential American spirit because apple pie was brought over from England. The English love their apples," he comments before turning his attention to other pies, and notes that "[i]n virtually every English and American cookbook from the mid-17th century on, apple pie is the first fruit pie mentioned."[2] Sax's deeply appreciative comments, while contrasting with Bunyard's in tone, likewise link a nation with a particular fruit in a way that appears common-sensical. His engaging introduction to fruit pies suggests how deeply and invisibly a part of Anglo-American culture the association between the apple and England has become. Moreover, Sax suggests an historical trajectory for this connection, locating the precise decades in which the connection was being formed. That recipe collections dating from the latter half of the seventeenth century should begin to reveal a preference for the apple is not historical accident, but a piece of the puzzle which provides a more complete

114

picture of English georgic poetry and the process of nationalism in which it participated. Affirming the accuracy of Sax's observation, garden treatises before 1657 give the apple no special privilege in terms of order or commentary, while during and after the 1660s the apple is featured in treatise after treatise as a peculiarly English fruit. By the nineteenth century spurious etymologies invented by interpreters of British antiquities yoked the apple to the origins of Britain itself. In the words of George Johnson, author of *A History of English Gardening* (1829),

That the Apple was known and cultivated by the Britons before the arrival of the Romans, we are warranted in believing by the etymology of the name. In the Welch, Cornish, Armorican and Irish languages or dialects, it is denominated the Avall or Aball. The Hoedui, who dwelt in the modern Somersetshire, appear particularly to have cultivated this fruit, and their town which stood upon the scite [sic] of the present Glastonbury, was known when the Romans first visited it, by the name of Avallonia (Apple Orchard).[3]

Philips's *Cyder* (1708) was a landmark in the historical progression sketched here, contributing decisively to the mythology of origins that had grown up around the apple in the decades before the composition of his poem. Just as scientific societies and treatises helped establish English georgic's power to infuse a sense of national purpose after the Act of Union, so political factors, the details of which we have since forgotten, helped to shape the authority that accrued to the form in the decades between 1708 and 1770.

Cyder was especially important in configuring English georgic because it provided an ur-narrative that idealized native English character as issuing from the sheltering apple orchards of Herefordshire in England's hinterlands. The declension from Philips's sheltered orchards into the world of trade depicted in *The Fleece* recapitulates the essential georgic theme elaborated by Virgil and Milton: painful labor is the consequence of expulsion from a garden – specifically a fruit garden – an ejection from a benign world in which labor is sweet delight.[4]

CELEBRATING THE SOIL: PHILIPS, HEREFORDSHIRE,
AND THE SOUTHWEST MIDLANDS

Philips's genius lay in his ability to conceptualize a British application for georgic poetry. In revisualizing the Virgilian form, he places celebration of the soil in the foreground of his tribute to the union of the three lands out of which Britain was born. He begins with this earthy theme:

Figure 5 Laborers plant, dig, and graft in an orchard with a design like that of a park. Frontispiece, John Philips, *Cyder* (1708), RB 147217.

> What Soil the Apple loves, what Care is due
> To Orchats, timeliest when to press the Fruits,
> Thy Gift, *Pomona*, in *Miltonian* Verse
> Adventrous I presume to sing; of Verse
> Nor skill'd, nor studious: But my Native Soil
> Invites me, and the Theme as yet unsung.[5]

The chiasmic positioning of "soil" in this initial verse paragraph resituates the subject of the first lines of *Paradise Lost* in the framework of

Virgilian georgic. Like Virgil, Philips states the theme of his poem in the first lines of the first book; like Virgil, he takes credit, if modestly, for his own song. Unlike Virgil his subject matter is limited to two elements of a single horticultural endeavor: the care of apple orchards and cider brewing. Furthermore, he identifies his poetic forbear not as Virgil, but Milton, adapting the central horticultural feature of Milton's theme, the fruit garden, to georgic (and implicitly comic) purposes. Where Milton places "the Fruit / Of that Forbidden Tree" within a theodicy, Philips specifies that fruit as the apple and relocates it in the world of gardening;[6] where Milton invokes the "Heav'nly Muse" (*Paradise Lost* 1: 6), Philips invokes the Greek goddess of orchards, Pomona; where Milton outlines a theater of cosmic proportions, Philips restricts himself to his own "Native Soil," suggesting the movement of his plot between the soil's role as an essential component for growing trees and its wider symbolic status as the ground out of which the nation rises. The opening of *Cyder* comically recasts *Paradise Lost* in terms of its latent georgic possibilities at the same time that it suggests the serious intention of extolling English soil for nationalistic purposes.

The collusion of subject matter with poetic form in *Cyder* thus constructs a recognizably English space. Once an identification between soil and nation had been made, the georgic form could be attached to other English subjects, thereby perpetuating and widening the terms within which that space could be understood. Philips celebrates a local site for the purpose of constructing a national history. In so doing, he draws on a precedent of Silurian literature – literature specifically evoking the shifting boundaries of the southwest Midlands and adjacent Welsh counties.[7] The general outline of this topography appears in histories of the region. Brayley and the aptly named Britton's *Beauties of England and Wales*, for example, defines the parameters of the region while etymologically linking the name to qualities of landscape most admired by 1805 when their panoramic survey of England and Wales was concluded:

At the period of the Roman Invasion, HEREFORDSHIRE was inhabited by the SILURES, who also occupied the adjacent counties of Radnor, Monmouth, and Glamorgan, together with that part of Glocestershire which lies westward from the Severn. In the British language, this district was called indifferently, by the nearly synonimous names of *Esyllwg* and *Gwent*; words implying an open country of downs, abounding with prospects: hence its inhabitants were denominated *Gwr Esyllwg*, *Gwr Essyllyr*, &c. and from their derivatives, SYLLYRWYS.[8]

Such histories helped generate a mythography which traced in the landscape the legendary bravery of the Silurian people, who although defeated by the Romans are typically cited as the last bulwark of British resistance. Silurian literature perpetuated the idea that England's mythic heart lay in the southwest Midlands.

The southwest Midland counties, which provide the settings for *Cyder*, *The Fleece*, and *Edge-Hill*, share a similar political and economic history. Relatively isolated before the outbreak of the Civil War, the region as a whole was deeply affected by that event. The first battle of the war, the historical occasion for Jago's poem, took place near the foot of the Edge Hill headland in southeast Warwickshire. One of the most contested regions of England, these counties were the scene of constant occupation by soldiers. Households, by-and-large Royalist in Herefordshire and Parliamentarian in Warwickshire, were forced to contribute to both sides of the cause.[9] The memory of the Civil War surfaces in the expressly Royalist sympathies of Philips and Jago, while both poets use Milton's angelic battle as an allegorical set piece through which the war is replayed. The Civil War is an especially important event for Philips's poem, since soldiers from throughout England who occupied this region spread the fame and popularity of its cider beyond its boundaries.

In addition to a common political history, southwest Midland counties shared similar agricultural patterns. Farmers in the region were profoundly interested in horticulture, which influenced their agricultural protocols, including small farms, a penchant for applying to agriculture labor-intensive gardening practices such as spading and dibbling, and a vibrant kitchen-garden culture which underwrote the market for fruits and vegetables. As Thirsk remarks, "It is significant that . . . the horticultural interests of gentlemen, clergymen, and foreigners meet with an existing tradition of gardening among the local population."[10] Herefordshire, in particular, was known as a county of smallholders where, even as late as 1866, properties were typically smaller than fifty acres. In this county enclosure practices tended to be benign, in part because of the large proportion of free- and copyholders.[11]

Though the region was distinguished as having diverse resources – including rich cornlands, hop gardens, cheese, salmon, and iron – it was especially famous for its fruit. Residents and tourists describe the region as filled with trees grown not only formally in orchards, but also along highways and byways, in hedgerows and in corn fields. In 1696 Celia Fiennes comments in her diary that Herefordshire "appears Like a Country off Gardens and Orchards the whole Country being very full of fruite trees &c. it lookes like nothing else – the apple and pear trees &c. are so thick even in their corn fields and hedgerows."[12] The signal treatise on the subject, *Hereford Orchards, a Pattern for All England* (1657) written by John Beale, a correspondent of Samuel Hartlib and future fellow of the Royal Society, convinced John Evelyn of the salutary effects and patriotic benefits of eating apples and drinking cider. Evelyn added an appendix to his *Sylva* entitled *Pomona* that supplements his own observations on *"Fruit-Trees"* in relation to CIDER" with a digest of eight short treatises, including one by Beale. In Beale's and Evelyn's treatises Herefordshire is described as having become, under the instigation of "publick spirited Gentlemen, . . . but one intire Orchard."[13] Beale comments,

I need not tell you how all our Villages and generally all our Highways (all our Vales being thick set with Rows of Villages) are in the Spring-time sweetned, and beautified with the bloomed Trees, which continue their changeable Varieties of Ornament, 'till (in the End of Autumn) they fill our Garners with pleasant Fruit, and our Cellars with rich and winy Liquors. Few Cotagers, yea very few of our wealthiest Yeomen, do taste any other Drink in the Family, except at some special Festivals, twice or thrice in the Year, and that for Variety rather than with Choice.[14]

Even in later decades, when the primacy of Herefordshire as the apple county came into dispute, arguments against its reputation paradoxically cement the general conviction of its special status. Marshall would admit that "HEREFORDSHIRE has ever borne the *name* of the first cider county" even while suggesting an alternative view: "GLOCESTERSHIRE, however, claims a preference in the two most celebrated fruit liquors the district affords: – WORCESTERSHIRE, and MONMOUTHSHIRE have their claims of excellency."[15]

One of the reasons for Herefordshire's legendary status was undoubtedly that travelers considered it an English Eden. An almost circular landlocked county composed of an alluvial plain edged by hills, it is affirmed even by the dry William Marshall as "without flattery, to be altogether beautiful."[16] John Clark, in his report to the Board of Agriculture in 1794, couples Herefordshire's beauty with its reputed healthfulness. The atmosphere of the plain, he claims, "is so loaded with the riches which it collects from the sweet scented herbs around, that the inhailed air gives a glow of health and vigour to the surrounding vegetables on which it breathes; hence the ancients, with much propriety, complimented this favourable district with the appellation of the GARDEN OF ENGLAND."[17] Herefordshire's soil was believed to be the foundation of its loveliness, including its unusually temperate climate. John Clark accepts the connection as a given. Describing the climate as "remarkably mild," he explains

This is partly owing to the soil, partly to the situation. The soil of the hills (which have always an influence on the climate of the districts that surround them) is here a light kindly *sandy mould*. This kind of earth readily admits the entrance of the sun and air, by which means the cold superabundant moisture of winter is soon exhaled, and the earth, by that means, enabled to admit the *operation of vegetation* more early in the spring than other places lying in the same latitude, that have the soil of a more retentive nature. Stiff clays, by shutting out these *friendly guests*, and by their strong attachment to moisture, require a more increased degree of heat in the sun to drive from their brows the surly frown of a winter.[18]

Clark's assessment of Herefordshire's soil echoes Galen's theory of humors, in which the masculine qualities of hot and dry, unless overbalanced, are considered more healthful than the feminine qualities of cold and wet. In fact, Herefordshire soil contains significant amounts of clay in the form of marl, and the band of soil considered especially good for fruit trees is not constrained by the boundaries of the county. According to Loudon in his treatise on agriculture (1825), the best soil for apple orchards lay "on the same stratum of red marl which stretches across the island from Dorsetshire to Yorkshire," spanning several regions of England.[19] The allure of the relationship between Herefordshire's soil, climate, and fruit was deeply influential, however, and the quality of its soil, like its climate, although variously described over the century, is always portrayed as an exemplary matrix for the cultivation of fruit and the ideal English character.

The stridently nationalistic quotation with which I opened this chapter attests the enduring power of the idea that the character of a people and the fruit of their land are products of the soil. Philips uses an epic simile which conflates these associations with instructions on planting:

> The miry Fields,
> Rejoycing in rich Mold, most ample Fruit
> Of beauteous Form produce; pleasing to Sight,
> But to the Tongue inelegant and flat.
> So Nature has decreed; so, oft we see
> Men passing fair, in outward Lineaments
> Elaborate; less, inwardly, exact.
> Nor from the sable Ground expect Success,
> Nor from cretaceous, stubborn and jejune:
> The Must, of pallid Hue, declares the Soil

Devoid of Spirit; wretched He, that quaffs
Such wheyish Liquors; oft with Colic Pangs,
With pungent Colic Pangs distress'd, he'll roar,
And toss, and turn, and curse th' unwholsome Draught.
But, Farmer, look, where full-ear'd Sheaves of Rye
Grow wavy on the Tilth, that Soil select
For Apples; thence thy Industry shall gain
Ten-fold Reward; thy Garners, thence with Store
Surcharg'd, shall burst; thy Press with purest Juice
Shall flow, which, in revolving Years, may try
Thy feeble Feet, and bind thy fault'ring Tongue.

(*Cyder*, I. 46–66)

The idea that a rich prospect (whether in soil or human beings) does not necessarily indicate a fine product was, of course, ancient and hence easily absorbed by Philips's readers. More pertinently, although the production process more likely causes the colicky effect that Philips ascribes to chalky soils, he assumes that the soil itself is intangibly present in the cider. Thomas Andrew Knight, first president of the Royal Horticultural Society, brother to Richard Payne Knight, and native to Herefordshire, takes note in 1797 of the entrenched conviction of the residual power of the soil in cider even as he disputes it:

The fruit liquors, for which the county of Hereford has long been celebrated, have always been supposed to derive their excellence from some peculiar quality in the soil which produces them; but a preference has been given to soils of opposite kinds by the planters of different ages. Those of the last century uniformly contended in favour of a light sandy loam, and on this their finest ciders were made: at present a soil of a diametrically opposite quality, a strong red clay, is generally preferred ... But the strongest, and most highly flavoured liquor, which has hitherto been obtained from the apple, is produced by a soil, which differs from any of those above mentioned, the shallow loam on limestone basis of the Forest of Dean. Hence it is evident that those qualities of soil, on which the strength and flavour of the liquor are supposed to depend, either are not discoverable from external appearances, or that liquors of nearly equal excellence may be obtained from soils essentially different.[20]

The soil that Philips celebrates as the finest for growing apples is precisely the sort that Knight describes as favored in the earlier part of the century: a soil suited to arable farming. In Herefordshire, which was also famous for its corn, conventional wisdom ordained that farmland should combine arable and orchard. Toward this end, agricultural writers recommended growing apple trees in cornfields, spacing them far enough apart that the grain would receive sufficient air and sunlight and reapers

Figure 6 Farmhouse with Orchard, Thomas Hale (pseud. for Hill), *A Compleat Body of Husbandry* (1756), between pages 612/613, RB 370028.

could move easily between the trees. Such a scene is recorded in G. R. Lewis's well-known painting of Herefordshire reapers drinking their cider in a cornfield against the backdrop of an orchard.[21] The practice is also illustrated in John Hill's *A Compleat Body of Husbandry*.[22] Although Clark alludes to this unique practice, like Knight he disputes the received wisdom concerning the soil supposedly typical of Herefordshire: "Some of the most valuable apples, such as the stive, hagly crab, and golden pippin, are said to be fond of a light sandy soil. The best orchards, however, are on a strong clayey soil."[23] By the time Clark was recording his observations of Herefordshire, science had gained a significant purchase on the received wisdom of cider production; nevertheless, even though his own project helped scientize the agricultural industry, he perpetuates the notion that there is a direct relation between the qualities of soil and those inherent in fruit: "It seems to be admitted," he concludes, "that the cider from trees in clay, is stronger in the body, and will keep better than cider made from trees that are on a sandy soil."[24]

CELEBRATING THE SOIL: ENGLISH RACE

The physical relationship between soil and fruit is not scientific in the way these writers indicate, although soil certainly influences the quality of its products. The parallel was primarily metaphoric: soil shapes the people that live on it. Hence, there is an inevitable connection between the national temperament of a race and the type of soil on which they make their living – the stereotype of the rugged Scot is a case in point, or, in an example from Philips, the "hardy Men" of the rocky Plinlimmon (*Cyder*, I. III). In eighteenth-century horticultural terminology the word *race* indicates an unmediated relationship between soil and fruit – literally the flavor of the soil in the fruit. In his edition of *Cyder* (1791), Charles Dunster notes Philips's use of the phrase "racy Wine" (I. 497): "Dr. Johnson, speaking of Thomson's Poems, after they were altered and enlarged by subsequent revisals, says, 'They are, I think, improved in general; yet I know not whether they have not lost part of what Temple calls their *race*; a word, which applied to wines, in its primitive sense, means the flavor of the soil.'"[25] Used as a modifier, the word "racy" seems more closely related to liveliness: the sudden rush of flavor in a fruit, the shock and delight imparted by a compactly built phrase, or even behavioral license, as when we say that someone is "fast." In fact, "race" as used by horticulturists in the eighteenth century is more closely related to meanings assembled around the concept of generation, which links it to groups of people.[26] The relationship between soil and fruit is connected metaphorically and etymologically with qualities that link people to the land they inhabit. This connection is encouraged by deep-seated metaphors in our language that associate human development with plant growth. Children are the fruit of marriage as well as the seeds of a new generation, they are kept in nurseries, can be shaped when young as twigs can be bent, and will reap what they sow. Coleridge, ineluctably drawn to such analogies, captures the intersection of metaphors that link the soil to its dwellers in a notebook entry written during his voyage to Malta in 1804:

– I have many thoughts, many images; large Stores of the unwrought materials; scarcely a day passes but something new in fact or in illustration, ~~occur~~ rises up in me, like Herbs and Flowers in a Garden in early Spring; but the combining Power, the power to do, the manly effective *Will*, that is dead or slumbers most diseasedly – Well, I will pray for the Hour when I "may quit the tiresome Sea & dwell on Shore; If not a Settler on the Soil, at least To drink wild wine and to pluck green Herbs, And gather fruits fresh from their native Tree."[27]

Recording this entry, Coleridge teetered for a moment on the word *occurs*, a verb that charts events in terms of causation. He abandoned this ratiocinative line of thought, however, for a series of metaphors founded on organic connections. The initial simile likening the activity of the fancy to the growth of herbs and flowers yields a parallel between human conceptual activity and plant growth. It gives way in Coleridge's reflection, however, to two images borrowed from Wordsworth: the disciplined settler, a cultivator who forces the soil to produce according to his dictates, and the "natural" man who lives off the land. The unforced and unprocessed fruits of the soil become, in this metaphor, an image of innocence, liberty, and natural profusion. The image is undergirded, however, by an assumption that the natural man, wild wine, green herbs, and fruits from a "native" tree are all products of the same soil. Common metaphors in eighteenth-century garden treatises similarly suggest that the settler participates in the natural economy of the soil, a disciplined master who brings fruits, whether native or exotic, to their fullest potential. Authors of garden treatises describe the garden as a microcosm of the state or family in which the gardener acts as governor or caretaker, someone who, especially in the case of the hothouse, faithfully nurtures and protects plants which must be gently forced to do his bidding. Exotic fruits bear the "race" of the new soil in which they are grown, and the English gardener's art improves the healthful qualities of fruits native to less civilized soils in foreign lands.

The discursive connection between a race of people and the land they inhabit enables Philips to present the county of Hereford as the site on which the character of the English people is nurtured and proved. In the following passage he cloaks concerns central to the luxury debates in advice against fertilizing fruit trees. Dressing the ground with exotic manures reflects the vocabulary of the critics of luxury and, as in the tradition that had developed since Evelyn's *Pomona*, produces sentiments tinged with suspicion of foreign influence.

> There are, who, fondly studious of Increase,
> Rich Foreign Mold on their ill-natur'd Land
> Induce laborious, and with fatning Muck
> Besmear the Roots; in vain! the nurseling Grove
> Seems fair awhile, cherish'd with foster Earth:
> But, when the alien Compost is exhaust,
> It's native Poverty again prevails.   (I. 119–25)

The concern in this passage is not whether or not to manure the soil. Philips later argues in exact reverse that the soil "with fit Manure, / Will largest Usury repay" (I. 543–44).[28] Here, by contrast, soil provides a rhetorical occasion for delineating the English character. Native soil rather than rich but superficial dressings will ultimately determine the quality of fruit. Philips completes the connection between a people and their soil by showing that the blood of ancient Britons has manured Herefordshire's apple trees. Appropriately for his narrative of origins, his theme is a *felix culpa*. Ariconium, the most ancient seat of Britons, was one of the last English cities to fall to the Romans, proving the resiliency and native strength of the Silurian people, who were as "uncontroul'd, and free" (I. 179) as their remote region. According to legend, however, the city itself was not at that time destroyed. Ariconium was more grievously ruined by an earthquake that swallowed the city and its inhabitants:

> with swift Descent
> Old *Ariconium* sinks, and all her Tribes,
> Heroes, and Senators, down to the Realms
> Of endless Night. (I. 228–31)

The Ariconium episode in *Cyder* counters the tradition of interpreting natural catastrophe as divine retribution for national sin, as in the account of Sodom and Gomorra. Philips suggests instead that the effect of this apocalyptic event was to preserve the stalwart Silurian character in Herefordshire's soil. Drawing from a passage in Virgil's *Georgics* which became a topos of the georgic tradition, he notes that vestiges of that ancient race remain in the soil, turned up by the ploughman in coins, urns, and "huge unweildy bones" (I. 239). Its lasting memorial, the apple tree, is a product of that mould. Philips deepens the notion of race by suggesting that eating apples and drinking cider is a national sacrament in which the English eat the body and blood of their most redoubtable ancestors. Lest the reader miss the point, he incorporates the argument of fervently patriotic treatise writers that the vintage of the apple is to true Englishness what the vintage of the grape is to foreignness. In his apostrophe to the Hereford redstreak, Philips sets a comparison that informs the rest of the poem:

> why, in quest
> Of Foreign Vintage, insincere, and mixt,
> Traverse th' extreamest World? Why tempt the Rage
> Of the rough Ocean? when our native Glebe
> Imparts, from bounteous Womb, annual Recruits
> Of Wine delectable, that far surmounts
> *Gallic*, or *Latin* Grapes, or those that see
> The setting Sun near *Calpe*'s towring Height.
>
> (I. 530–37)

As his paean to Queen Anne at the close of the poem emphasizes, national allegiance demonstrated by fidelity to English cider expresses conservative and monarchical political ideals. The apple and Englishness are as inseparable as the monarchy and Britishness.

THE ROYALIST NARRATIVE

Philips's history of England reinterprets great events of English history by situating the royal line in terms of the soil, rooted like the apple tree in the nation's heritage. The Stuarts are the centerpieces of this history, which marches toward the eschaton of union with Scotland. James, "first *Britannic* King" (II. 631), presages the rule of Anne, author of the new dispensation of union with Scotland. Throughout the poem the local image of Herefordshire and labor in the apple orchard is presented as an epitome of the nation. Grafting, for example – the gardener's essential mechanism for propagating new trees – symbolizes the process of nation-building that the Union assumed. Calling into play the heavily freighted technical word "union" to describe this practice, Philips cannot help but turn his readers' minds to the grafting of first Wales and now Scotland onto sturdy English stock, and foreshadows imperial aspirations:

> Some think, the *Quince* and *Apple* wou'd combine
> In happy Union; Others fitter deem
> The *Sloe*-Stem bearing *Sylvan* Plums austere.
> Who knows but Both may thrive? Howe'er, what loss
> To try the Pow'rs of Both, and search how far
> Two different Natures may concur to mix
> In close Embraces, and strange Off-spring bear?
> Thou'lt find that Plants will frequent Changes try,
> Undamag'd, and their marriageable Arms
> Conjoin with others. So *Silurian* Plants
> Admit the *Peache's* odoriferous Globe,
> And *Pears* of sundry Forms; at diff'rent times
> Adopted *Plums* will aliene Branches grace;
> And Men have gather'd from the *Hawthorn's* Branch
> Large *Medlars*, imitating regal Crowns.   (I. 297–311)

That Philips borrows thoughts on grafting from an already disproved Virgilian tradition suggests not merely the conservative force of convention in didactic texts, but also the usefulness of convention for smuggling political metaphors into moments of instruction. The final allusion in this passage to the crown telescopes the overall progress of the poem, which concludes with an apostrophe to Queen Anne and the Union's political confirmation of the Stuarts as the first British monarchs. Just as the pip of the apple may be perceived through the microscope to bear within itself the elements of an entire orchard (1. 350–58), so Hereford-shire is the pip of England: a remote county which contains the essential elements of true Englishness and true patriotism. It is an emblem of the isle of Britain, "sever'd from the World / By Nature's wise Indulgence" (II. 532–33).

Cyder was a landmark in the history of the nationalizing process, in part because Philips imitates Milton in order to suggest a narrative that distills the possibilities of *Paradise Lost*, one in which England, and espe-cially Herefordshire, provides the landscape for a history that undoes the effects of the Civil War. In representing the war as the chaos out of which Britain emerged in the Act of Union, Philips foreshortens and trans-poses the viewpoint of Milton's narrator. Philips's history is the story of the redemption of England rather than the redemption of mankind; the struggle between Cromwell and Charles I humanizes Milton's cosmic forces; Milton himself is revealed as that great poet who, unhappily, was faithless to England's ancient monarchy. Appropriately for the subject of the second book, cider brewing, the battle is staged as a misuse of liquor, a fall into drunkenness that strongly echoes *Paradise Lost*:

> Can we forget, how the mad, headstrong Rout
> Defy'd their Prince to Arms, nor made account
> Of Faith, or Duty, or Allegiance sworn?
> Apostate, Atheist Rebells! bent to Ill,
> With seeming Sanctity, and cover'd Fraud,
> Instill'd by him, who first presum'd t' oppose
> Omnipotence; alike their Crime, th' Event
> Was not alike; these triumph'd, and in height
> Of barbarous Malice, and insulting Pride,
> Abstain'd not from imperial Bloud. O Fact
> Unparallel'd! O *Charles*! O Best of Kings!
>
> (II. 498–508)

Closely following Milton's war in Heaven, Philips's melee casts Parlia-mentary forces as apostate angels and Herefordshire as the portion of England "unstain'd with Guilt" (II. 514). Charles, the innocent, merciful, supreme figure, is slain by the "inglorious Hands" of Cromwell's armies (II. 511), but contrary to the conclusion of the redemption story, the forces of evil win. Using phrases from *Paradise Lost* while drawing on Royalist

narratives that referred to Charles as the royal martyr and associated his
execution with the crucifixion, Philips writes

> The Cyder-Land, obsequious still to Thrones,
> Abhorr'd such base, disloyal Deeds, and all
> Her Pruning-hooks extended into Swords,
> Undaunted, to assert the trampled Rights
> Of Monarchy; but, ah! successless She
> However faithful!   (II. 515–20)

Philips's account is a lookingglass version of those offered by Protestant
reformers during Protectorate rule. Theirs foretell a future of peace from
civil strife that will eventuate in union with Scotland. In the words of a
preface attributed to Samuel Hartlib,

when God shall have furnished this Wise and Noble Nation with all these and
many other means of Plenty we shall then be all inclined to beat our swords
into Plough-shares, and our spears into pruning-hooks, and that by a happy
Union of *England* and *Scotland*, and the peaceable settlement of the affections of
all people under the present Government, we shall live as Brethren, and study
by the wayes of Common Industry to strengthen the hands of those that bear
Rule over us, and are set for our defence.[29]

Philips views the story through a Royalist lens and from the hindsight of
the Restoration. While, as Hartlib foresaw, expectations of union with
Scotland had been achieved, they have ironically been realized by the
return of Stuarts to the throne. Anne's Act of Union produces a new
nation, which, like the apple tree, is stronger for having grafted the
scion onto the stock. The graft brings about an eschaton of military and
commercial power:

> And now thus leagu'd by an eternal Bond,
> What shall retard the *Britons'* bold Designs,
> Or who sustain their Force; in Union knit,
> Sufficient to withstand the Pow'rs combin'd
> Of all this Globe? At this important Act
> The *Mauritanian* and *Cathaian* Kings
> Already tremble, and th' unbaptiz'd *Turk*
> Dreads War from utmost *Thule*; uncontrol'd
> The *British* Navy thro' the Ocean vast
> Shall wave her double Cross, t' extreamest Climes
> Terrific, and return with odorous Spoils
> Of *Araby* well fraught, or *Indus'* Wealth,
> Pearl, and Barbaric Gold.   (II. 645–57)

In this narrative, to reverse the consequences of the Fall means to reverse the political effects of the Civil War and usher in a millennial age of British imperial success abroad and peace at home, centered around the apple industry. The latter is figured by swains peacefully reaping apples which provide a salubrious liquid that will blend with Britain's streams: a utopia in which the entire nation is infused with cider, signal of an era of peace and prosperity:

> mean while the Swains
> Shall unmolested reap, what Plenty strows
> From well stor'd Horn, rich Grain, and timely Fruits.
> The elder Year, *Pomona*, pleas'd, shall deck
> With ruby-tinctur'd Births, whose liquid Store
> Abundant, flowing in well blended Streams,
> The Natives shall applaud; while glad they talk
> Of baleful Ills, caus'd by *Bellona*'s Wrath
> In other Realms.   (ii. 657–65)

In this picture, English dominance will proceed through the peaceful flow of cider. In the eschatological conclusion of Philips's poem, the imperial success of the Union confirms Herefordshire's emblematic status in the spread of cider around the world:

> where-e'er the *British* spread
> Triumphant Banners, or their Fame has reach'd
> Diffusive, to the utmost Bounds of this
> Wide Universe, *Silurian* Cyder borne
> Shall please all Tasts, and triumph o'er the Vine.
>   (ii. 665–69)

Philips certainly meant this flourish to be humorous, and he draws on his own substantial talents as a burlesque satirist in passages such as these. Nevertheless, his humor conveys a sincere message from the citizen of Herefordshire concerning Britain's imperial aspirations: her rewards are to be found not only in the importation of exotic foreign products into Britain, but in the exportation of *English* spirits; infused with cider, other races become British.

REVERSING THE FALL

Philips's selection of the apple as the object of horticultural and patriotic instruction was neither serendipitous nor indebted solely to Milton's epic. The appropriation of the apple as a symbol redolent of English

nationhood was a process already begun by the authors of cider treatises in the previous century. In addition, mythologies sprang up around
the apple that contributed to its singular status and continued to con-
solidate its power as the symbolic fruit of England long after Philips
died.

The word "apple" has traditionally been used both to name a specific fruit and as a term for fruit in general. Thus any fruit – edible or
otherwise, from cucumbers and pomegranates to gall apples and may
apples – has from earliest times been referred to under the designation.
Similarly, the fruit in the Garden of Eden, unidentified by the writers
of Genesis, could be referred to as an apple yet stamped as this specific fruit. The coincidence is documented by the OED as early as 1000
when Caedmon assumed that the apple was the fruit of the Tree of the
Knowledge of Good and Evil. The association is complicated, however,
by a grammatical coincidence between the Latin word for the apple, the
accented "mālum," and the word for evil, the non-accented "malum,"
which provides an intriguing semantic connection.[30] Despite the paucity
of official commentary on the subject, Thomas Browne, who rejected
the semantic connection in his *Enquiries into Vulgar and Common Errors*,
indicates that there existed a popular tradition connecting the fruit of
the Knowledge of Good and Evil with the apple. His energetic opening
sally challenges the entire corpus of error: "That the Forbidden fruit of
Paradise was an Apple, is commonly believed, confirmed by Tradition,
perpetuated by Writings, Verses, Pictures; and some have been so bad
Prosodians, as from thence to derive the Latine word malum, because
that fruit was the first occasion of evil."[31] Milton himself, in a momen-
tous precedent for the eighteenth century, acknowledged the semantic
connection twice, both times in the words of his epic punster, Satan. In
the temptation scene, Satan, unlike Adam and Eve, God, or Raphael,
identifies the fruit as an apple. "To satisfy the sharp desire I had / Of
tasting those fair Apples," he tells Eve, "I resolv'd / Not to defer" (*Paradise
Lost*, IX. 584–86). Later, when he recounts the success of his adventure
to his fellow demons, he contemptuously points out that the catalyst of
this primal catastrophe was a common fruit:

> Him by fraud I have seduc'd
> From his Creator, and the more to increase
> Your wonder, with an Apple; he thereat
> Offended, worth your laughter, hath giv'n up
> Both his beloved Man and all his World,
> To Sin and Death a prey . . .   (x. 485–90)

For the apple to become England's representative fruit, however, its symbolism had to be reversed.[32] In staking England's claim to the apple, Philips draws on patristic and medieval biblical typologies to reverse images of the Fall in the redemption story. Typologically, Mary is the second Eve, Jesus the second Adam, the fatal tree the salvific cross, and so forth. This possibility was already latent in apple treatises. Authors such as Ralph Austen, John Beale, and Evelyn had heralded the apple and cider as a means of resisting incursions of foreign trade and adulterated liquors such as wine; producing a wholesome and natural drink which was the basis of health and longevity; preventing the diseases of the sedentary life; providing a staple food for the poor and the economic maintenance of families; bequeathing the incidental benefits of orchards which purify the air and provide beauty; and not least, turning England into a garden and from thence into a place of prelapsarian social harmony. In Philips's celebration of Herefordshire the apple most likely to reverse the effects of the Fall was a cultivar that some early treatise writers believed was indigenous to England: the Hereford redstreak. Philips's admonition to "Let every Tree in every Garden own / The *Red-streak* as supream" (I. 512–13) skillfully manipulates biblical typology while remaining consistent with contemporary garden lore. This apple, originally a hedgerow tree, was regarded as the preeminent cider apple not only because of the high quality of its pressed juice but also because of its reputation as a prolific fruiter. Despite the fact that ciderists from other counties would later dispute the redstreak's preeminence, it retained its status until after the middle of the eighteenth century. It was doubly useful for the history that Philips constructs. Streaked with red as its name indicates, its coloring suggested the presence within it of the blood of the ancient Silurians. Also, and conveniently for a redemptive typology, Satan, in *Paradise Lost*, describes the fruit of the Tree of the Knowledge of Good and Evil as uncannily similar to the redstreak: a prolific fruiter and "of fairest colours mixt, / Ruddy & Gold" (IX. 577–78).

The apple was not, however, the only hedgerow fruit with an ancient presence in English orchards. The pear, useful in making perry, a drink similar to cider, was also grown widely in England. The pear is not, however, as symbolically fraught, and this may have contributed to the growing preference over the latter half of the seventeenth century for the apple over the pear. For instance, although like most ciderists Beale treats pear trees and perry making, it is clear that for him the apple is England's representative fruit and the orchards he describes are dominated by its many varieties. Beyond this, he exhibits an actual prejudice against the pear, an attitude which would become more pronounced in English treatises leading up to the Act of Union, and would thereafter be assumed even when not stridently invoked. Conjuring the fruit that enriched his native Herefordshire, he claims that

From the greatest Persons to the poorest Cottager, all habitations are encompassed with orchards and Gardens; and in most Places our Hedges are inriched with Rows of Fruit-Trees, Pears, or Apples, Gennet-Moyles [a variety of cider apple], or Crab-Trees. Of these, the Pears make a weak Drink fit for our *Hines*, and is generally refused by our Gentry, as breeding Wind in the Stomach.[33]

There is no reason to believe Beale's claim that perry is an inferior drink to cider. Some ciderists, in fact, cite the pear as producing a drink superior to cider, one so like fine champagne that strangers could not tell the difference. Charles Dunster comments that Teinton Squash perry was "considered as equal, if not superior, to the best Cider. The Teinton Squash Perry is a liquor most highly prized, and sells for more, upon the spot where it is made, than almost any wine whatever."[34] Beale's comments about the pear suggest, rather, the process by which the apple became instrumental in the production of English space. Only a few years before in 1653, eminent horticulturist Ralph Austen had not discriminated between these fruits. In his treatise, the cultivation of a great variety of fruit trees is proffered as a means of ushering in a millennial age in which the poor would prosper in a system of smallholdings and England would become the new Jerusalem:

An eminent person once said of *this Nation*, that it is *a very Garden of delights*, and *a Well that cannot be exhausted*: What then would it be, did it abound with *goodly Fruit-trees*, and other *Profits*, where now are *barren Wasts*: Might it not then be called another *Canaan, flowing with Milke and hony*, of which it is recorded, that there were *Fruit-trees in abundance. Nehem.* 9. 25.[35]

All fruits, foreign or domestic, contribute to this vision, and, as Austen makes plain in *The Spirituall Use of an Orchard*, teach us about God.[36] Although Austen consistently treats the apple first, a practice followed by most other English horticulturists (although not by the French), the overall tenor of his treatise is to persuade his readers that fruits of all kinds are the source both of use and delight. Repeatedly he makes reference to the apple and the pear. Although he abbreviates his discussion of the pear, claiming that "*Galen* saies they have like properties with *Apples*, and what is said of *Apples*, if we attribute the same to *Peares*, there needs nothing anew to be said of them," he also includes the observation that

Avicenna found them more nourishing than apples.[37] He prefers either cider or perry to wine made from grapes, but for reasons of thrift and health rather than politics.

Austen's treatise was widely admired as the first extended scientific treatment of cider and perry making; nevertheless, its neutrality was followed shortly by pronounced nationalizing tendencies. Beale's assumption that the apple is superior to the pear found a ready audience in Evelyn, who in the 1670s pushed the claims of the apple even further, alleging that the apple is to England not only what the pear but also the grape is to France. The shift in these treatises from viewing the apple as another of God's fruits, and a useful rather than a purely pleasurable one, to viewing the apple as England's particular fruit parallels a documented change in public opinion of foreign affairs. Stephen Pincus traces this shift in public opinion to the early 1670s when the English veered from the belief that the Dutch were attempting to assert "universal dominion" over the rest of Europe to the fear that there was a French plot afoot to revive the throne of Charlemagne.[38] While he locates a shift in public opinion during the early 1670s, he notes that anti-French sentiment had long been a hobbyhorse of Protestant radicals who feared a return of French popery. These are the voices that we find emerging in fruit treatises of the earlier decades. John Beale's extravagant conclusion to his treatise, while not specifically aimed at French popery, marries Protestant conviction with economic sentiments likely inspired by Raleigh's much-quoted portent, "Whosoever commands the sea, commands the trade, whosoever commands the trade of the world commands the riches of the world and consequently the world itself."[39] Beale's stridently Protestant revision of this sentiment concludes that successful trade is the sign of God's blessing, for "daily Experience sheweth, that where any Trade of Manufacture is driven on, there the Word of God bears a Price: Where Trade thrives not, there the Word of God is, at the best but a pleasant Song."[40] Beale's correlation of Protestantism and economic expansion with the fruit trade helped prepare the way for the apple. As with public hostility toward France, however, the feeling that the apple was English and the pear French reached a pitch during the 1670s. John Evelyn, who lent his voice to the debates over universal monarchy, was passionate about the Englishness of the apple.[41] In what would become part of the tradition surrounding the apple, he inflects his comments with biblical assumptions, launching an attack not only on the pear but the grape, both of which came to be viewed first as foreign and then as specifically French.

Although the pear was no more biblical a fruit than the apple, the grape had the distinction of being viewed as the source of a second lapse in biblical history. After the cleansing waters of the flood had dried up and Noah and his family emerged from the ark, Noah's first act was to plant a vineyard. He made wine from his grapes, drank it, and, to his shame, was discovered naked in a drunken stupor by his son, Ham, who mocked him and was subsequently cursed for filial disrespect. The story repeats the themes of the Fall: the consumption of fruit leads to a disgrace in which nakedness, shame, filial disrespect, and a curse play prominent roles. As in his repudiation of the semantic link between the Latin words for apple and evil, Thomas Browne indicates the tenacity of the link between drunkenness and the grape by rejecting it. "Thus," he says, "whereas in the brief narration of Moses there is no record of wine before the flood, we cannot satisfactorily conclude that Noah was the first that ever tasted thereof."[42] Evelyn, by contrast, picks up on the nationalizing potential of this biblical anecdote in a testy synopsis of oenologically inspired peccadilloes:

To sum up all: If *Health* be more precious than *Opinion*, I wish our Admirers of Wines, to the prejudice of *Cider*, beheld but the *Cheat* themselves; the *Sophistications, Transformations, Transmutations, Adulterations, Bastardizings, Brewings, Trickings*, not to say, even *Arsenical Compassings* of this sophisticated *God* they adore; and that they had as true an *Inspection* into those *Arcana Lucifera*, which the Priests of his Temples (our Vintners in their Taverns) do practise; and then let them drink freely that will . . . : − Give me good Cider.[43]

Evelyn's diatribe vividly illustrates the inverse proportion in English treatises between the magnitude of the consequences of the first Fall, which brought sin and death into the world, and the enthusiasm with which the apple was embraced as England's representational fruit. The Englishness of the apple, which by the eighteenth century was a matter of general consensus, set the stage for a wider mythology in which the apple was counterpoised against the pear and grape to the advantage of the former.[44] Like other nationalistic writers, Philips absorbs this view in his poem, first marking the common belief that while apples required at least a moderately fertile soil, the pear can grow anywhere:

> But if (for Nature doth not share alike
> Her Gifts) an happy Soil shou'd be with-held;
> If a penurious Clay shou'd be thy Lot,
> Or rough unweildy Earth, nor to the Plough,
> Nor to the Cattle kind, with sandy Stones
> And Gravel o'er-abounding, think it not

Beneath thy Toil; the sturdy Pear-tree here
Will rise luxuriant, and with toughest Root
Pierce the obstructing Grit, and restive Marle.

(1. 89–97)

While this passage may seem simply to recommend good husbandry
of poor soil, the idea that the pear could grow anywhere, like a weed,
was part of the prejudice against it. Latent assumptions feed into the
association between soil and fruit. The pear is thus often invoked during these years in negative terms. Quoting copiously from *Cyder*, the
Reverend George Turner resolves concerning the Fall (1756), "Suppos-
ing therefore that the Mischief did lie in the Fruit itself, I should be
inclined, from those ill Properties of it, to conclude, that the Grape, and
not my favourite Apple, was the very Fruit forbidden. For it was the
Juice of the Grape which gave the first occasion to Drunkenness, that
we read of."[45] His views incorporate Evelyn's and transform them into
a caricature of the assumptions that had accrued around the apple well
after the political history that formed the idea was forgotten. During
the period of military tension with France just before the Seven Years
War, it must have seemed natural to include within the orbit of the apple all the evils of French culture, to assume that "this little Treatise on
Cyder [will be] acceptable to some others of my judicious Friends, as
well as to the Gentlemen above: for as their Hearts are entirely English:
so they would no more consent that the Health of their Countrymen
should be impaired by *French* Liquors, than that their Understandings
should be subjected to a *French* Religion."[46] The connection of the apple
with Englishness was deepened by the tradition that Evelyn helped to
launch, in which the fruit not only recast England typologically as the
new Eden, but could be conveniently poised against the French grape
or pear.

AVALON

In 1835, J. C. Loudon would say of the apple in his *Encyclopaedia of
Gardening*, "Of all the different fruits which are produced in Britain, none
can be brought to so high a degree of perfection, with so little trouble; and
of no other are there so many excellent varieties in general cultivation,
calculated for almost every soil, situation, and climate, which our island
affords."[47] His observation, on the face of it so practical, is bolstered by
the mythmaking of poets like Philips and ciderists before him – a process

that put national energy behind the production and distribution of the apple, even as the nationalistic discourse surrounding apples helped to generate the industry. The mythical association between the apple and England was bolstered by a new academic business in British antiquities, which was bent on excavating England's ancient past. Particularly important to this line of study was the *Cronica* of John of Glastonbury, first edited in 1726 by Thomas Hearne. John's history located Glastonbury Abbey as one of the most ancient and revered sites in the British Isles, and most importantly for this discussion, the Isle of Avalon as having existed in the marshes at that site. The *Cronica* is a pastiche of historical sources and spurious etymologies that helped to generate the island's mythic associations. In John's account, the island "is called Avalon either from the British 'aval', which means apple (since the place abounds in apples and orchards), or from Avallo, once a lord of that territory."[48] The isle, known in Wales as the Isle of the Dead, was mythicized through etymological confusion as the place of the dead which was filled with apple orchards. It provided an indigenously British paradise to supplement and anglicize the Hebrew garden of our First Parents. Apples are thus planted on either side of the continuum of British history, flanking both origins and mythic destination, accommodating both biblical and pagan histories. John's account does justice to the apple's paradisal associations, helping to root them for unseen generations in the soil of England's own West Country – not far from the more recently mythicized Herefordshire orchards. Conveniently, as in Virgil's fourth *Eclogue*, the myth of the Isle of Avalon conjectures a golden age before the pain of labor when earth brought forth fruit of her own accord, and melds that history with a Christian eschaton. Quoting from Geoffrey of Monmouth's *Life of Merlin*, John records that

The island of apples, which is called fortunate, is truly named, for it brings forth all things of its own accord. It needs no farmers to till the fields, and there is no cultivation save that which nature provides. It freely brings forth fertile stalks and grapes, and apples born of precious seed in its forests. The earth nourishes all things, as bounteous as tended land; one lives there a hundred years or more. This was the new Jerusalem, the faith's refinement, a holy hill, celebrated as the ladder of heaven. He scarcely pays the penalties of hell who lies buried here.[49]

Somewhat more than a century after Philips's celebration of the apple a mythology had been woven around it which made it symbolic of English nationality and British endeavor. Keats's "To Autumn," written in 1820, captures this mythology in its portrayal of an English rural prospect shot through with images already rendered nostalgic and nationalistic. The "moss'd cottage trees" bending with their store of apples are interlaced with images redolent less of an actual harvest than an English space produced by means of myth, poetry, and popular painting: fruitful vines, hazelnuts, and beehives give way to the granary, the "half-reap'd furrow," and, not least, a cider press, with the spirit of Autumn gazing patiently at the "last oozings hours by hours." Among these images, the apple orchard set in an arable landscape stirs a recollection of the farming practices of Herefordshire and, linked to these practices, mythologies that reach beneath the historical past to tap a reservoir of myth and faith. Hanging on ancient cottage trees, apples evoke the easeful fruition of Eden and Avalon – and a Fall; for pressed into cider they yield a sacramental image in which the body of the apple gives itself up into the vinous spirits of true Englishness. As in contemporary treatises that document the decline of the Hereford redstreak, Keats's tone is elegiac, yet finds in the dying sounds of the season a *felix culpa* borne on autumn's own music and the quiet recompense of the English croft – the cottage garden which only over the course of recent years had come to symbolize the true Englishman: his diligent leisure, his welfare, his independence, and his attachment to the soil.

CHAPTER 6

Jago's Edge-Hill: *simulation and representation*

In the manufactures of Birmingham alone, the quantity of gold
and silver annually employed in gilding and plating, and thereby
disqualified from ever afterwards appearing in the shape of those
metals, is said to amount to more than fifty thousand pounds sterling.

Adam Smith
An Inquiry into the Nature and Causes of the Wealth of Nations (1776)

When Richard Jago published *Edge-Hill* in 1767, the fortunes of English
georgic poetry had already declined.[1] Samuel Johnson's trenchant criti-
cisms of Somervile's *The Chace* and Dyer's *The Fleece*, published more than
a decade after Jago's poem, granted critical authority to the decline, especially since he leveled his most disparaging comments at georgic's technical component. Yet critics immediately following Johnson felt that his
criticism, particularly of Dyer, was unjust. As Nathan Drake put it, "This
beautiful, but too much neglected poem, had ere this attracted the admiration it so justly merits, had not the stern critique of Dr. Johnson inter-
vened to blast its rising fame."[2] Even when they react most defensively
against Johnson, however, these critics indicate that they are aware of the
inverse fortunes of didactic poetry and prose treatises. John Aikin says so
plainly when he defends *The Seasons*: "If Virgil really designed to instruct
the farmer by his Georgics, he might have done it much more effectually
in plain prose."[3] Although since ancient times some critics had elevated
the utility of prose treatises over didactic poetry, Aikin's comment reveals
a prevailing modern reading sensibility less inclined to be diverted by
poetry, very likely, in fact, to be entertained by prose. Aikin's confidence
in the explanatory value of prose contrasts with Joseph Warton's equal
confidence in poetry, expressed in "Reflections on Didactic Poetry" published a mere quarter of a century earlier. Warton maintains that "[t]o
render instruction amiable, to soften the severity of science, and to give
virtue and knowledge a captivating and engaging air, is the great privilege of the didactic muse."[4] The difference between Warton and Aikin

is primarily in emphasis. Aikin attempts to elevate didactic poetry by emphasizing the importance of extended description over every other aspect of the form. In comments directed at an older school of critical opinion, he says concerning Thomson's descriptive technique,

the merited success of this piece has proved a refutation of those critics who deny that description can properly be the sole object of a poem, and would only admit of its occasional introduction as part of a narrative, didactic, or moral design. Why, indeed, it might have been asked, should poetry be clogged with matter so unfavourable to her exertions, as historicall relations, philosophicall systems, or the rules of an art? Why not allow her the same privilege as her Sister-Muse, who is at liberty to employ her pencil on what parts of nature she most delights in, and may exhibit the rural landskip, without encumbering herself with the mechanism of a plough, or the oeconomy of the husbandman?[5]

Aikin's rhetorical questions express the revaluation of English georgic that was set in motion by Thomson's poem. *The Seasons* came to be considered the greatest of English georgics, in part because in it Thomson emphasizes extended description over the versification of a technological manual or scientific treatise, or ekphrasis at the expense of metaphrasis. This had a deep effect on georgic poets who followed him. When James Grainger, author of *The Sugar-Cane* (1764), wrote that he "preferred the way of description, wherever that could be done without hurting the subject," he was marking the influence of Thomson over the form.[6]

In using ekphrasis in this way I return to an earlier, broader understanding of the term. As used since the nineteenth century, ekphrasis is a practice confined to poetic descriptions of the visual arts – as in Spenser's masque of Busyrane, Coleridge's "The Garden of Boccaccio," or, most celebrated, Homer's description of Achilles' shield. Although it was certainly used in this way in the eighteenth century, descriptions of landscape also fell under its purview, in part because landscape was often described as though it were a work of art. As John Barrell has shown, locodescriptive poetry in the eighteenth century closely followed Claude's and Poussin's compositional techniques in painting.[7] Poets who took landscape as their subject did not copy nature in the raw, but composed verbal translations of visual compositional structures. Most importantly, however, as Murray Krieger explains in an apt discussion for georgic poetry, the precedent for expanding the notion of ekphrasis beyond its modern restriction exists from ancient times when "ekphrasis, as extended description, was called upon to intrude upon the flow of discourse and, for its duration, to suspend the argument of the rhetor or the action of the poet; to rivet our attention upon a visual object to be described, which it was to elaborate in rich and vivid detail."[8] In the eighteenth century we can detect an ambiguity in the exact relation between poetry and painting and between poetry and landscape because art and nature, as Krieger points out, could be "conceived as substitutes – mutually reflecting signs – for one another . . . "[9] Extended description could be identified as ekphrastic because it utilized the compositional techniques of painting and thus blurred the boundary between art and nature. As Barrell reminds us, the painterly technique of eighteenth-century locodescriptive poets indicates "a very different attitude to nature from, say, Ruskin's, who, a century later, advised whoever wanted to look at or to paint a landscape to lie down and start with the blades of grass in front of his face."[10]

Ekphrasis is an especially useful term for understanding English georgic poetry since it helps to explain the changing relation between extended description and versification of prose treatises (or metaphrasis) over the course of the century. In earlier decades of the eighteenth century, metaphrasis was viewed as a rhetorical device essential in georgic poetry: not the most important component, but one piece in the diverse elements which were elegantly brought together to comprise the whole. Relieved by ekphrasis and narrative digression, metaphrasis was the heart of the poem's instruction. It was in metaphrasis that less competent poets revealed their ungainliness and skilled poets their grace. In his preface to Ovid's *Epistles* (1680), Dryden defined the kind of translation that involved the least invention as "metaphrase." Yet when skilled poets employed metaphrasis, the effect was far closer to Dryden's second order of translation, or paraphrase. This, said Dryden, is "Translation with Latitude, where the Authour is kept in view by the Translator, so as never to be lost, but his words are not so strictly follow'd as his sense, and that too is admitted to be amplified, but not alter'd."[11] Metaphrasis, ekphrasis, and narrative digression were kept in balance, each contributing to the vital purpose of didactic poetry: to instruct by engaging the imagination of the reader.

The shift in weight toward ekphrasis in georgic poetry provides the occasion for examining the relation between imitation and representation in these poems. English georgic poetry is the product of a variety of well-contrived imitations – of Virgil, Milton, Philips, and prose treatises. Ingeniously, although georgic is a highly conventional and self-referential literary form, it purports to be descriptive, its reference directed outward toward the natural world and technical processes of agriculture (or any of a variety of other pursuits, such as hunting, fishing, or the practice of medicine). At its very heart, English georgic simulates and dissimulates, practices various orders of imitation and presents those imitations as references to an observable reality. Over the course of the eighteenth century, orders of imitation in the genre became more complex, interinvolved, and cloaked even as metaphrasis was increasingly devalued by critics as mere versification.

It was a critical commonplace that, unadorned or unrelieved by digression, metaphrasis is unpalatable. Joseph Warton spoke for most when he admitted that "the reader will soon be disgusted with a continued series of instruction, if his mind be not relieved at proper intervals by pleasing digressions of various kinds, naturally arising from the main subject, and closely connected with it."[12] By the 1780s, critical elevation of description at the expense of metaphrasis prevailed. John Aikin expresses the altered balance when he extols the descriptive power of *The Seasons* while verging on a depreciation of Virgil:

if it was his [Virgil's] purpose to inspire a true relish for the beauties of nature, to write an original poem of a higher cast than the confined plan of pastorall would allow, we may lament that he pursued a plan that necessarily threw so much of his work into details which even his versification cannot render pleasing. I mean not here to enter at large into a disquisition concerning didactic poetry; but only to suggest a comparison between the result of Thomson's unconfind plan, scarcely less extensive than nature itself, and that of some other writers, not inferior in genius, who thought it necessary to shackle themseles [sic] with teaching an art, or inculcating a system.[13]

Aikin indicates not so much the role of metaphrasis in georgic poetry as the altered relation between reference and description. He points out two kinds of didactic poems: "Those to which the term is more properly applied, are such as directly profess to teach some art or science. The other species consists of those which, taking up some speculative topic, establish a theory concerning it by argument and illustration."[14] Given that didactic poetry was presumed to include versification of prose accounts, Aikin's first category is metaphrastic while his second provides the occasion for ekphrasis, including extended landscape description. As his reflections on didactic poetry make clear, Aikin places Thomson in the descriptive tradition while he implicitly places authors such as Dyer (whom he nevertheless admired) in the tradition of the metaphrasts. Similarly Hugh Blair places Thomson in the descriptive category. In his view, "Description is the great test of a Poet's imagination; and always distinguishes an original from a second-rate Genius."[15] Consistent with this view, Blair argues that "the principle beauties of Virgil's Georgics lie in digressions of this kind, in which the Author has exerted all the force of his genius."[16]

Earlier critics also extol digression in georgic poetry, but consider it as
one piece in a mosaic of diverting elements. They correspondingly value
it for the grace with which the poet returns to the instructive heart of
the poem, not as a separate element. Clearly, the view that ekphrasis is
more important to poetic material than metaphrasis elevates a lyric over
a didactic sensibility. While locodescriptive poetry is not lyrical in form,
it helped to usher in the great turn toward lyric, construed as a *sensibility*.
The inducement descriptive passages provided for emotional and moral
response to the landscape took precedence over instruction.

My discussion of *Edge-Hill* centers on the georgic technique of metaphrasis and its relation to the poem's descriptive passages. In Jago's
poem, metaphrasis is raised to the level of a problematic. Jago's simulation of the technique demonstrates how metaphrasis interacts with
ekphrasis to cloak the complex relation between a georgic poem and
the prose source it translates. In order to examine Jago's manipulation
of these techniques, I venture onto what may appear to be decidedly
non-georgic terrain: the coal mines, iron forges, and smithies of the west
Midlands.[17] Yet, as Jago's poem makes clear, these sites were intimately
connected in the west Midland imagination with georgic endeavor. It was
from iron, through the intervention of coal's fierce heats, that ploughs,
hoes, scythes, pruning hooks, and other georgic tools were fashioned; and
molds of smelted iron were referred to (depending on their size) as pigs
and sows. The connection went beyond tools and metaphor, however,
to lifestyle, for in the Midlands the separation between agriculture and
industry was subtle. The figure of the farmer-smith, the tenant farmer
who worked the iron forges in winter and plough and rake during growing season and harvest, stitches together two landscapes. As T. S. Ashton
points out, the iron industry "was intimately dependent on the land for
its raw material in the form of ore, limestone, and charcoal; and it was
the demand of the landed classes for the implements of agriculture and
war that constituted the main reason for its existence."[18] Edge Hill, the
location of the first battle between Parliamentarians and Royalists in the
Civil War, reveals the intimate, real connection among war, agriculture,
and the land that in English georgic poetry often proves metaphoric or
intellectual.

Manufactures form a center of energy in *Edge-Hill*. By means of
"active industry," Jago redirects English georgic from unrestricted space
to the small, well-delineated quarters of the industrial shop and from
the unbounded prospects of gentry to the ingenuity of tradesmen. In the
"peopled streets" (ii. 350) of Coventry, youth are counseled to

> . . . learn,
> With sidelong Glance, and nimble Stroke, to ply
> The flitting Shuttle, while their active Feet,
> In mystic Movements, press the subtle Stops
> Of the Loom's complicated Frame . . .
>
> (II. 397–401)

Birmingham's metals manufactures, however, with their attendant coal and iron industries, are the object of Jago's greatest enthusiasm. The manufacture of tools redirects georgic from the soil to the ingenuity that makes tillage possible; yet tools form only part of an industry of "toys" for which Birmingham is famous. In Birmingham's small shops, and the coal mines, iron forges, and fineries surrounding it, "Invention is ever at work."[19] As Jago admiringly observes,

> How the coarse Metal brightens into Fame,
> Shap'd by their plastic Hands! what Ornament!
> What various Use!   (*Edge-Hill*, III. 548–50)

In one of the georgic metaphors that punctuate histories of the coal and iron industries, William Hutton, who published the first history of Birmingham in 1781, attributes invention to the profit motive: "It is easy to give instances of people whose distinguishing characteristic was idleness, but when they breathed the air of Birmingham, diligence became the predominant feature. The view of profit, like the view of corn to the hungry horse, excites to action."[20] Diligence and invention defined an industry that prospered on novelty and technological innovation. The picture of Birmingham provided by all of its historians from Jago and Hutton to the present provides an image of the body politic similar to Virgil's bees in the fourth Georgic: one that compresses industry and activity within a circumscribed space. For Jago, as for Hutton, the industrious citizens of Birmingham are the epitome of Englishness; yet he sets Birmingham industry within the context of a highly traditional georgic convention, a survey of the landed estates of Warwickshire. The hive of industry and ingenuity which exhibits the productivity of the intermediate classes is nestled within extended descriptions which validate patterns of conservative landownership. The poem thus positions metaphrasis, the versification of instructions for mining, iron smelting, and refining (which appears progressive), within ekphrasis, the wide view of the landscape (which is fundamentally traditionalist). Within this structure, simulation and dissimulation are ever at work.

EKPHRASIS: THE ESTATE

From its beginnings in *Cyder*, English georgic had a propensity for merging georgic description with that of the landed estate, thus betraying its intimate connection with one of its antecedents, country-house poetry. The country house was a metonym of the landed gentry and troped the assumption that gentry preserved core English values. In English georgic poetry the house itself evaporates while the estate, though sometimes represented by its dual landscapes of farm and park, is more often than not registered as a place or family name. The pivotal characteristics of the country-house poem, however, remain: reciprocity between classes based on a social system of natural hierarchy and an economic system of natural exchange; mystification of labor, which includes its redistribution from laborer to poet; a system of values based on traditional ways of living; and belief in the civilizing influence of local gentry.[21] Philips initiates the transference from the country-house poem to georgic in his roll-call of the great families of Herefordshire in Book I of *Cyder*; Chandos, Cecil, Beaufort, and Weymouth exemplify the virtuous, generous, and patriotic gentry of Hereford.[22] The panegyric to Weymouth most closely calls up the image of the master of the country house,

> whose hospitable Gate,
> Unbarr'd to All, invites a numerous Train
> Of daily Guests; whose board, with Plenty crown'd,
> Revives the Feast-rites old: Mean while his Care
> Forgets not the afflicted, but content
> In Acts of secret Goodness, shuns the Praise,
> That sure attends.   (*Cyder*, I. 643–49)

The country-house poem provided a ready set of values that could be transferred to a celebration of the soil in English georgic poems by the simple elimination or abbreviation of the estate description. The tendency to order the local countryside of a particular county or region by estates is part of the convention of a morning or evening ascent to a hilltop from which these estates may be viewed. In drawing on such a familiar topos, the georgic poet could reduce conventions associated with the country-house poem to a mere residue and yet retain the powerful resonance of a fractal order in the body politic. Thus, when George III is hailed in *The Fleece* as chief shepherd of his people, the image is not merely biblical (though it is that); nor is it merely pastoral (though it is that also): the image deepens an order in which the shepherd caring for his sheep is an iteration of the lord managing his demesne, who is, in

turn, an iteration of the king ruling his people. This traditionalist structure organizes the progressive elements of English georgic, including its
exaltation of trade and industry.

The ordering of the countryside by landed estates reaches its most
abstract form in Jago's *Edge-Hill*, which ricochets across the surface of
Warwickshire like a stone skipping over water. In contrast to the concern
with national boundaries in Thomson's rendition of Great Britain, Jago
is captivated by Warwickshire's internal delineations. The conventions
of the country-house poem are turned inside out: a system of estates,
rather than providing the inner strength and political meaning of a georgic landscape, become its scaffolding – an external support which is
purely organizational. Jago's geographical survey of Warwickshire produces the image of a county that is literally the sum of its parts, where
those parts are comprised of its landed estates. There are no images
in this poem, as in those of Philips, Smart, or Dyer, of a laborer bent
to agricultural tasks. Neither do we find the more pictorial scenes that
punctuate Thomson's visual recalibration of that image – the swain coming home to his simple cottage, engaged in his earthy tasks, or wrestling
with the indifferent forces of nature. As if in deference to the increasingly
authoritative status of prose agricultural treatises, Jago removes agriculture from the celebration of English soil and substitutes landed estates
and the legends attached to them – legends that depict the soil not as
the source of food but as a topography engraved with the memorials of
kings, lords, and gentry. As he instructs the reader in Book I, "Thus, from
the rural Landscape, learn to know / The various Characters of Time
and Place" (1. 414–15). The topography is marked by "paternal Worth, /
No less than lineal Claim" (1. 219–20), and Jago rewrites local lore to underscore his theme. The Roll-Rich Stones, for example, a modest circle
of standing stones, are construed by "vulgar Fame" as ancient warriors
"transform'd to Stone" (1. 531 and 530). Jago's wiser lore reveals a

> Fabric monumental, rais'd
> By *Saxon* Hands, or by that *Danish* Chief
> ROLLO! the Builder in the Name imply'd.
> (1. 535–37)

The colloquial name preserves a narrative that unfolds from the builder
of the artifact, thus inscribing Warwickshire soil with the text of its ancient history: conquerors who through time become absorbed into an
indigenous Warwickshire patrilineage. Similarly, the great horse cut in
the sod that denominates the Vale of Red Horse inscribes the history of

conquest out of which the British peoples were formed. The horse is only one among many such ciphers, "the Mark of her new Lords / Frequent exhibiting" (1. 628–29). These encoded histories of conquest and seizure are transformed through the blazon of a contemporary lord and yearly folk ritual into a benevolent sign of traditional social bonds:

> . . . the pictur'd Horse!
> Carv'd on the yielding Turf – th' armorial Sign
> On HENGIST's Standard blazon'd erst, as now
> On thine, accomplish'd BRUNSWICK! BRITAIN's Pride!
> And, with her Lyon match'd, for martial Fame,
> And far-extended Empire, ROME's fam'd Bird
> Outrivalling. They, studious to preserve
> The fav'rite Form, their vassal Tenants bind
> Its fading Figure yearly to renew,
> And to the neighb'ring Vale impart its Name.
>
> (1. 633–42)

Events that contribute to a pattern of conquest and progressive civilization form a notational system that makes the topography of civility in Warwickshire legible. History is recorded in these impressions, and one of the purposes of Jago's poem is to decode marks the soil has preserved.

The landed estates that form a litany of place names in the first, second, and fourth books are essential to this project, since in them the record of patrilinear possession is sustained. Individually, each of the estates encrypts an aspect of Warwickshire history; together they form a pattern of history which is geographically, historically, and philosophically central to the distinctive character of English liberty. As emblems of national history, estates mark the surface of the soil as much by their design as by their histories. Early in the poem, Jago urges landowners to consult the genius of the place. In a set of conventional instructions, owners are counseled to

> Improve, not alter. Art with Art conceal.
> Let no strait terrac'd Lines your Slopes deform.
> No barb'rous Walls restrain the bounded Sight.
> With better Skill your chaste Designs display;
> And to the distant Fields the closer Scene
> Connect. The spacious Lawn with scatter'd Trees
> Irregular, in beauteous Negligence,
> Clothe bountiful. Your unimprison'd Eye,
> With pleasing Freedom, thro' the lofty Maze
> Shall rove, and find no dull Satiety.
> The winding Stream with stiffen'd Line avoid

To torture, nor prefer the long Canal,
Or labour'd Fount to Nature's easy Flow,
And artless Fall. Your grav'lly winding Paths
Now to fresh'ning Breeze, or sunny Gleam
Directed, now with high embow'ring Trees,
Or fragrant Shrubs conceal'd, with frequent Seat,
And rural Structure deck. Their pleasing Form
To Fancy's Eye suggests Inhabitants
Of more than mortal Make, and their cool Shade,
And friendly Shelter to Refreshment sweet,
And wholesome Meditation shall invite.

(1. 448–69)

Though Jago provides no full description of individual estates, each of those selected for abbreviated description contains some element of the wholesale requirements outlined in this passage. The concealment of art, winding line of liberty, melding of offscape with foreground, unbounded view, groves for retirement, and various scenes compose not a georgical landscape exactly, but a portrait of Warwickshire that builds by accretion through the whole of the poem. When we compare this treatment of park design with Whately's *Observations on Modern Gardening* (published a mere three years later), however, we see an invisible element of Jago's manipulation of georgic strategies. Although Jago's poem was written within four years after the end of the Seven Years War, in the middle of rising tensions over the American policy, and at the height of the Wilkes decade, the image of Warwickshire in the greater part of the poem remains detached from foreign policy and domestic unrest. The one exception is the treatment of Coventry and Birmingham. The image of the landlocked, heartland county of Warwick serves rather as an exemplar of a traditional England which is confirmed in the survey of landed estates. These estates are depicted as responding to no external circumstances, as whole in and of themselves, and as producing nothing tangible – certainly no agricultural produce. Their harvest is more potent: a system of natural values, a history in which civilization and hence civility are achieved through a series of national conquests and subsequent absorption of foreigners into the English line, and a topography on which this history may be read.

The ironic history in which stages of invasion and assimilation inexorably produce an evolved civil order is contrasted in the final book of the poem with the horror of civil war. The title of the poem invokes the first battle of the Civil War, fought at the town of Kineton at the foot of the

Edge Hill headland on the southeast border of the county. Yet the battle
is not mentioned until the final pages of the poem, where it is depicted
as an almost mythic event. Philips too invoked the Civil War in *Cyder*,
in an implied comparison between a drunken brawl and Milton's heav-
enly battle. In Philips's version, we may recall, Charles I is a vanquished
Christ-figure, Cromwell a victorious Satan; nevertheless, the Glorious
Revolution rights this evil turn of events and finds its ultimate expression
in the Act of Union under the Stuart queen, Anne. Jago's version of the
conflict is more ambiguous. Rather than make a direct contrast between
the antagonists of the Civil War, he makes an indirect contrast between
the history encrypted in Warwickshire's topography and the evil of civil
war.

Edge Hill was an especially useful battle upon which to center these
images, both topographically and strategically. Royalist forces who occupied the headland swept down onto the plain below like a band of heav-
enly angels; yet the outcome of the battle was indecisive, notable mainly
for ghastly losses on both sides. Since it was rumored that Cromwell had
been within hearing distance of the battle but had been too faint hearted
to reinforce his own troops, an image of the Protector as crafty but cow-
ardly could be drawn from the initial conflict. The battle provided Jago
with an extended metaphor that, though weighted toward the Royalist
side, enabled him to focus attention on the evils of civil war itself. The
following passage illustrates the ambiguity that arises when English folk
war against each other:

> Mean while, below,
> Another Band, diff'ring in Sentiment,
> But not in Blood, jealous of Kingly Pow'r,
> Of Popular Rights tenacious, boast no less
> Intrepid Courage, from a Source as fair
> Deriv'd, the sacred Love of Liberty.
>
> (IV. 404–09)

In a series of negatives in the subsequent passage, Jago turns the problem toward the destructive consequences of civil war: "No Romans" had
imperial designs on the land; "No ... Danes" were looting its wealthy
towns; "Nor Scot, nor Pict, / Nor Gallic Foes" were invading the island;
"No ... Vandal" was seeking the land for his own (IV. 422–27): no
invaders who could be naturalized into the English race were responsible for this internecine war. The consequence of civil war is to draw
arms against "Members of one social Family" (IV. 433) – to destroy the

fabric of a civil society knit together by the confluence of invasion and the civilizing arts.

The interpretation of the soil in Jago's poem finds its source in its object of versification. Rather than selecting a scientific treatise for his purpose, Jago chose the 1730 edition of Sir William Dugdale's *The Antiquities of Warwickshire* (first published in 1656). Dugdale's book is a celebration of Warwickshire organized as a review of the estates, towns, and rivers of the county's four hundreds, Knightlow, Kineton, Barlichway, and Hemlingford. The account relies heavily on the Domesday Survey ordered by William the Conqueror shortly after his accession to the English throne. Dugdale focuses on landed estates and, where they exist, the legends that attach to them. With the exception of Coventry and Birmingham, he pays scant attention to cities, though he does record their mayoral histories in fine print. By contrast, he assiduously documents estates, their churches or cathedrals, and the burial places and relics of landed gentry. He omits the importance of agricultural industries, especially cheese, that made the county notable outside its own boundaries. His history is not, after all, a county history, but a documentation of the lineages and properties of the ruling class that arose in Warwickshire after the Norman invasion.

Significantly, although Warwickshire as a whole was Parliamentarian during the Civil War, Dugdale, who held the post of garter knight-at-arms under Charles I, was loyal to the king. Despite the fact that Coventry went down in English history for refusing entrance to Charles I in 1642 and Birmingham was notorious for supplying Parliamentarian troops with guns, Dugdale sprinkles his estate histories with narratives of loyal gentry who were martyred or punished for serving the Royalist cause – and otherwise omits their role in the civil war. He is also preoccupied with finding the Saxon or Roman sources of the English people, usually in the roots of place-names that predate the Domesday Survey. One of the objects of the *Antiquities* is thus to connect England to its ancient roots, while another is to provide a revisionist narrative of Warwickshire's allegiance during the Civil War. In a typical pattern Dugdale argues that the name "Coventre" derives from the words "coven" and "tre": a coven of religious folk prefixed to the ancient British word for house.[23] The history of the city of Coventry is traced back beyond its rude reception of Charles I to its legendary origin as a monastery built from the beneficence of Leofrik, husband of Godiva, during the reign of Edward the Confessor. Dugdale's chronology buries Coventry's disloyalty during the Civil War in the minutiae of mayoral history.

Jago probably found Dugdale's *Antiquities of Warwickshire* adaptable to
his purpose for a combination of reasons. First, it was the only local history of Warwickshire available at the time he wrote his poem. Second, its
Royalist narrative satisfied the traditionalist tendency of the genre. Third,
it accommodated the need to trace the English people back to the original
Britons and provided grist for the popular parallel between contemporary Britain and ancient Rome. Finally, it provided a connection with
English georgic's indigenous roots in Michael Drayton's "Chorographicall Description of Great Britain," *The Poly-Olbion* (1622). This version
of georgic is more travelogue or atlas than versified manual, as Jago's
preface suggests when he classifies the poem with topographical works
rather than Virgilian georgic. He planned, he says, to reveal the "natural
Beauty, and historical Importance" of Warwickshire,

by considering the Character, Natural History, and other Circumstances of such
Places as were most likely to afford Matter for Ornament, or Instruction of this
Kind; forming from the Whole, by an imaginary Line, a Number of distinct
Scenes, placed in the most advantageous Light, and corresponding with the
different Times of the Day; each exhibiting an entire Picture, and containing
its due Proportion of Objects, and Colouring.[24]

As Jago's goal to produce a series of pictures suggests, his poem may depend upon the silent versification of Dugdale's *Antiquities*, but his strategy
is to produce an ekphrastic effect. Ironically, rather than an instructional
manual, he selected a descriptive and historical treatise as the basis of
metaphrasis. Jago's georgic celebration of Britannia is, as it should be,
rooted in English soil, but its focus is not on soil as the foundation of
agricultural production but as a familiar and local topography striated
with signs that encode its history. Jago's redistribution of subject matter
from nature to topography, from the dearest freshness of deep down
things to an encoded surface provides a metaphor for the shift in the
perspective of georgic from depths to surfaces: from viewing the form as
the noblest means of celebrating national unity, character, and productivity in the most pleasing form, to viewing it as an ornamental surface of a
solider substance.

METAPHRASIS: THE ARTS OF COAL AND IRON

It is hardly surprising that Matthew Boulton, famous for his partnership
with James Watt, subscribed to six copies of *Edge-Hill*. His great Soho
factory lay a mere two miles from Birmingham, and although strictly

speaking it was located in Staffordshire it was linked with Birmingham by association. Boulton's inventiveness was seen as an outgrowth of the energy and resourcefulness of Birmingham, which Arthur Young described as "the first manufacturing town in the world."[25] In addition to the manufacture of the steam engine (and, incidentally, the world's first iron bridge, built to span the Severn in 1779), Soho was celebrated for the vast number and variety of its "toys" – an astonishing array of small objects from clocks and dinner trays to buckles and buttons made from a variety of materials. A contemporary *Birmingham Directory*, in a description of the founding of Boulton's factory, draws on agricultural conventions similar to those that punctuate Arthur Young's population-conscious accounts in the *Annals of Agriculture*. Like Young, Myles Swinney offers an account of a waste transformed into populous, productive country:

> The environs of this building was Seven Years ago a barren, uncultivated Heath; tho' it now contains many Houses, and wears the appearance of a populous country: And notwithstanding the number of People in that Parish is double what they were a few Years since, yet the Poor's Rates are diminished, which is a very striking instance of the good effects of Industry.[26]

This description of the lands on which Soho was established in 1764 uses a formula also used in *Edge-Hill* to relocate georgic values. In Jago's words,

> What? tho' no Grain,
> Or Herbage sweet, or waving Woods adorn
> Its dreary Surface, yet it bears, within,
> A richer Treasury.   (III. 401–04)

In the case of Soho, the dreary surface concealed a lively site of production famed both for its modern manufacturing methods and the encouragement it extended to workers to exercise their artistry and ingenuity. Georgic labor, the labor of hands and body, was reinvented in Soho as modern industry. In contrast to the nightmarish spectacle of Manchester's textile factories that Engels would put forward as the norm of the industrial "revolution" and class differentiation, the Soho factory (and Birmingham industries in general) presented a more benign formula by contemporary standards, steeped in a centuries-long tradition of manufactures that encouraged resourcefulness.[27] Consistent with this local view of manufactures, Jago associates "active Industry" with "peopled Streets" – with urban rather than rural enterprise.

Birmingham's reputation as an industrial city that founded its prosperity on metal wares goes back to the earliest descriptions of the region.

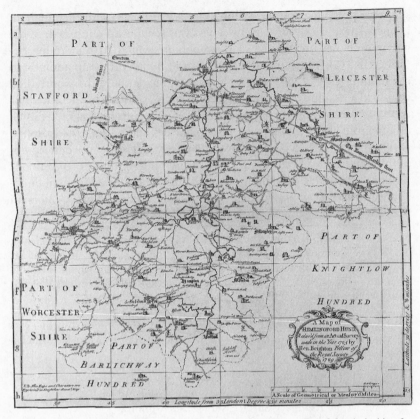

Figure 7 Hemlingford Hundred, Warwickshire, Sir William Dugdale, *Antiquities of Warwickshire* (1730), vol. II, between pages 868/869, RB 81078. Birmingham is located at E3 on the peninsula between Worcestershire and Staffordshire.

Leland, Camden, and Speed all refer to Birmingham's iron industry. The city was especially famous in their time for cutlery, nails, and mixed leather and iron products such as bridles. Hutton believed that the metals industry was already in place before colonization by the Romans, though the evidence is sketchy at best, and his effort to trace the town's skill with metals to the Saxons and Britons is integral with his purpose of making Birmingham the centerpiece of English history. It was popularly believed that the people of Birmingham were born with a skill for metalworking that enabled them to adapt quickly to the introduction of alloys such as brass and innovative industrial processes such as plating. This notion continued well into the nineteenth century, when William West asserts,

It is a happy circumstance for the artisans of Birmingham, that when one species of employment ceases, they can direct their attention to others, from the universal talent they possess in the metallic arts; and their employers, whether they turn their thoughts to iron, brass, copper, or any other material, may be termed alchemists in a certain degree, for they appear to possess the power of converting each and all of them into gold.[28]

Like the apple, whose "racy delicious gust" retains the traces of English soil in its flavor, Birmingham's "black soil" delivers the very Englishness of the English in a sooty inheritance from father to son, and in the case especially of naylors, from mother to daughter, from the dawn of English civilization.

As Hutton's and Swinney's accounts suggest, Jago was not the only writer to cast Birmingham's industries within a georgic ethos. In the case of Birmingham and its environs, writers capitalize on the link between the soil and the production of English values, especially the value of labor. Hutton's description of the soil in which Birmingham took root, for example, assumes that human industry and the nurturing soil are the bases of Birmingham's produce. The black soil's richness marks not its fertility, however, but its use for manufacturing "the instruments of war and of husbandry, furniture for the kitchen, and tools for the whole system of carpentry."[29] Thus, although Jago's poem ignores the agricultural arts for which Warwickshire was famous – its cheeses, its meats, its corn – it incorporates technical aspects of coal mining, iron smelting, refining, and smithying into a typically georgic format. His georgic endeavor to supply the nation with an indigenous history linked to its natural produce takes precedence, however, over technical accuracy. This is not unusual in georgic poetry. When Philips seems to reject amending the soil under apple trees in the first book of *Cyder* only to recommend it in the second he reveals that georgic "instruction" often cloaks a social principle; when he espouses Virgil's erroneous instructions for grafting, he does so primarily for mythographical and political reasons. Similarly, Dyer's exacting description of Silurian sheep in *The Fleece* skews representation in favor of mythicized national ideals.[30] Despite the satisfying appearance of technical precision, carefully contrived errors may be incorporated into the verse. Error may therefore be viewed as a convention of English georgic poetry when it serves a larger moral or political purpose, as a discerning reader would have recognized. Jago pushes this convention to a limit, however, which allows us to examine the tenuous balance between ekphrasis and metaphrasis in georgic instruction, or between imitation and reference. For while *Edge-Hill* appears, like any English georgic poem, to balance ekphrasis, metaphrasis, and narrative digression – even practicing Virgilian misinformation – it actually reverses the first two categories. As we have seen, Jago's metaphrastic description of the Warwickshire hundreds masquerades as ekphrasis. Perhaps it is to be expected, then, that passages which form the metaphrastic heart of the poem's instruction – the technical processes of coal mining and iron refining – turn out to be ungrounded in prose instructional manuals.

Jago introduces two different kinds of misinformation into his poem, neither of which is foreign to the genre. First, he permits ambiguities concerning the historic role of mineral coal in the iron-founding process.[31] This enables him to construct a local history of Birmingham's citizens that is proudly linked to an ancient and indigenous British industry. Second, he purveys technical information of a gentlemanly rather than a scientific sort – the kind that would have circulated in newspapers and coffee houses rather than in instructional manuals. He is less informed about technicalities of coal mining and iron refining, and better informed about new, and hence newsworthy, technologies. The "metaphrastic" portions of the poem thus offer the *kind* of information that would have appealed to an audience readily diverted by prose accounts of modern innovations, although the information is faulty. There is a good reason for this: no coal treatises were published in English between 1708 (which predates technology that dramatically altered the relationship between the coal and iron industries) and 1797, well after Jago's death.[32]

Jago's description of local coal as a general fuel for the several stages of iron production exemplifies the strategic use of georgic misinformation. In his poem, misinformation creates an organic image of Birmingham as a primeval English city, grown out of the west Midlands black soil, and nurtured by the twin minerals of coal and iron. This is in keeping with the very earliest records of the southwest Midlands, which associate Birmingham with mineral coal and iron products consumed for the most part by adjacent communities. It is also supported by Birmingham's first historian, Hutton, whose history (1781) presumes that Birmingham's prosperity was due to the confluence in its soil of coal and iron stone (or iron ore):

The minute sprig of Birmingham, no doubt first took root in this black soil, which, in a succession of ages, has grown to its present oppulence. At what time this prosperous plant was set, is very uncertain, perhaps as long before the days of Caesar as it is since. Thus the mines of Wednesbury empty their riches into the lap of Birmingham, and thus she draws nurture from the bowels of the earth.[33]

Like Jago, however, by whom he was undoubtedly influenced, Hutton obscures the distinction between coal and charcoal in order to put forward the claims of the west Midlands coal fields. For example, he suggests that Aston, a forge lying near Birmingham, had operated during ancient times as a blast furnace and permits the assumption that iron ore was reduced to unrefined iron at Aston by means of mineral coal. More accurately, bloomeries, the precursors of the blast furnace, existed in England only from 1496 and would have been fueled exclusively by charcoal.[34] Aston, which Jago apostrophizes as "*Queen of the founding Anvil!*" (*Edge-Hill*, III. 493), continued to depend on charcoal well into the 1780s, longer than most forges in the region.[35] Because the chemical properties which coal imparted to iron made it metallurgically unfit for the smithy, charcoal (carbonized wood) was used in blast furnaces and forges until the latter half of the eighteenth century. It became, however, increasingly scarce and expensive.

Jago could not have been ignorant of the fact that Warwickshire's historic forested region, the Arden, had been stripped of its trees, thus producing a critical demand for a fuel which could be used in the blast furnace without compromising the quality of pig iron. Coal in its natural form was unsuited for smelting or refining in part because it was too frangible to bear the weight of the charge (the combination of ore and limestone in the blast furnace), and in part because its high sulphur and carbon content created a reaction which produced a very brittle metal.[36] Coke provided a partial solution to the crisis, and by mid-century the fundamental problems of carbonizing coal had been solved.[37] Coke became vital to the iron industry for several reasons. First, it burned hotter than charcoal thus creating a more fluid metal. Second, it remained solid at extremely high temperatures and could therefore support a greater charge; this in turn provided a greater height down which the molten metal could run, which contributed to greater fluidity. Finally, as coke burned it provided stable passageways within which molten metal could come into contact with gases necessary for the chemical reaction that separated iron from oxide in the ore.[38] Influenced by increasing charcoal-smelting and diminishing coke-smelting costs, the demand for coal by the iron industry after 1750 increased dramatically. Significantly, however, the region around Birmingham produced a form of coal unsuited for coke and thus did not profit from the coke revolution.[39]

Although the development of coke made coal the essential fuel in all stages of the iron-refining process, coal had nevertheless always been closely associated with the final stage. Smithying, the step in which refined iron was transformed into wares, relied upon coal heat and was so important in the Birmingham area that T. S. Ashton records the tradition that "on the coalfields lying within a radius of ten miles of Birmingham, no fewer than 45,000 metal workers, it was said, drew subsistence from the manufacture of iron wares." Yet, in typically georgic language he points out that "[e]ven so fertilised . . . it is clear that the shrivelled seed of English iron could not of itself yield a harvest so rich and varied; and over two-thirds of the bar iron used in the British metal industries was brought in from abroad, principally from Sweden."[40] Naturally Jago makes no reference to England's dependence on foreign bar iron in his apostrophe to the "native British ore!" (*Edge-Hill*, III. 582–646). He does not, in fact, allude to coke at all – neither to the technical process of creating it nor to the final product.

Jago's neglect of the coking process is a startling lacuna even considering his commitment to local patriotism. It is not surprising that his knowledge of coal mining tends to be general, what any newspaper-reading gentleman of the age in that particular region would have known. For example, although he is familiar with the effects of fatal gases known as damps, he is apparently unfamiliar with mining vocabulary for them: choke, suffocating, peaseblossom, or black damp for carbon dioxide which simply snuffed out a miner's life; fire or fulminating damp for flammable methane which could ignite a mine in seconds before the safety lamp was invented. He alludes to the function of the two most familiar categories of miners (hewers and putters) without specifying either their titles or their unique tasks. And he is generally familiar with the most recent safety technology (the ventilator and fire engine). His method is the same when describing the process of smelting and refining iron: although he is vague about traditional methods that survived into the present, he is aware of contemporary innovations. Thus he does not describe the heady atmosphere of the furnace, forgoing what seems the extraordinary georgic opportunity to describe molten ore oozing to the bottom of the furnace where it lay protected by its mothering mantle of slag; he does not differentiate between stages of the refining process in the forge where the metal was brought to increasing malleability; neither does he allude to the vital task of slitting bars of iron into sheets in slitting mills which populated the banks of the Stour. None of these omissions is as startling, however, as that of the coking process, especially since Jago does include a description of the newest technology to enter the fining industry. This was potting, which, because it relied on indirect heat, could use coal rather than coke in the first stage of the refining process that followed the smelting of ore into iron.[41] Even here, however, Jago's description leaves the erroneous impression that potting was used to convert ore into pig iron:

> Now another Process view,
> And to the Furnace the slow Wain attend.
> Here, in huge Cauldrons, the rough Mass they stowe,
> Till, by the potent Heat, the purer Ore
> Is liquified, and leaves the Dross afloat.
> Then, cautious, from the glowing Pond they lead
> The fiery Stream along the channel'd Floor;
> Where, in the mazy Moulds of figur'd Sand,
> Anon it hardens, and, in Ingots rude,
> Is to the Forge convey'd.   (*Edge-Hill*, III. 505–14)

What stands out in this passage is the way metaphrastic effect may be simulated at the expense of accurate information. Jago's gentlemanly information, used in part to provide an illustrious history for Birmingham, brings into focus an issue that had perplexed literary critics over the course of the century: how does the didactic poet manipulate imitation and reference in order to produce the greatest possible delight? Critics throughout the century insist that georgic poetry must weight instruction toward delight. This was especially crucial in the 1760s, when few could have been under the misconception that a georgic poem's actual purpose was practical instruction. The skill of the poet lay in providing an illusion of instruction that bore the more significant social purpose of conveying moral precepts and contributing to a national mythology. Jago, who was no doubt familiar with arguments over the relative merits of imitation and reference, attempts to balance the extensive ekphrastic portions of his poem with intensive metaphrastic interludes. Yet, in the absence of technical manuals on coal and iron, he resorts to a simulation of metaphrasis in order to confer the authoritative voice of science upon his work, while using metaphrastic strategies to enhance his city's reputation.

We might ask why Jago's simulation of metaphrasis is necessary. The answer lies in the broad notoriety that Birmingham had acquired over the course of its emergence as England's first manufacturing city. Contrary to the image of honest urban vitality drawn from the soil that Jago proffers, Birmingham was viewed in the forum of public opinion as the primary locus for the manufacture of counterfeit goods, especially inferior household goods plated with gold, silver, or cheap imitations of precious metals. There is, of course, no direct connection between Jago's simulation of the georgic technique of metaphrasis and the simulation by smiths in Birmingham of precious metals with inferior alloys. The role of simulation in both these practices is a fortuitous event, one that provokes us to examine the presence of simulation at the heart of georgic poetry. Jago's simulation of georgic technique, like his survey of landed estates, calls attention to the surface of the poem rather than its substance. Metaphrastic effect in passages on the coal and iron industries is more important than the substance from which it is drawn. Similarly, the Birmingham smiths' simulation of precious metals, whether by plating or by use of gold- or silver-colored alloys, calls attention to the surface of their wares and divorces surface from the substance within. Ornamentation in this case takes priority over substance. In what follows, I explore the dimensions of "brummagem," a word which entered colloquial speech as a sign of contempt for Birmingham's false wares, which in an unconscious irony Jago celebrates as revealing the basic nature, the substance, of the English people.

SIMULATION: BRUMMAGEM

Hutton's *An History of Birmingham* helps to clarify Jago's enthusiasm for Birmingham's industrial wares. Though Hutton's history postdates Jago's poem, the two authors share a perception of their city that stands in direct contrast to national opinion. Indeed, Hutton's history was an apology designed to reshape public opinion. Jago, who lived in the vicinity of Birmingham, was certainly aware of its notoriety as well as proud of its industrial achievements. His account of its products and Hutton's tribute to its industrious, inventive craftsmen are not merely attempts to redeem the city's tarnished reputation; rather, their accounts indicate an alternate way of viewing Birmingham industry, a view which privileges surfaces and thereby feeds into cultural currents which were producing new valuations of poetry, the arts of ordinary people, and emerging notions of Englishness.

Birmingham was noted by the eighteenth century not only for its counterfeit wares, but its status as an unincorporated city. While this meant it could not return members to Parliament, it also made it a haven for dissenters after the Civil War, ministers excluded from their congregations by the Five-Mile Act, and entrepreneurs who wished to avoid the complications of guild regulation. The historical freedom of the city helped to lay a foundation for radical qualities that many believed accounted for the extraordinary ingenuity and industry of its inhabitants. It could be argued that as a guild-free city it fostered the industry of all kinds of craftsmen, and the demonstration of the argument was the unrestrained ingenuity and inventiveness of its citizenry.[42] A travelogue of England and Wales published in 1805 draws on this traditional account of Birmingham's industrial success:

Little more than a century ago, this "grand toy shop of Europe" was an insignificant market town, that never experienced the emanations of royal favour. – Birmingham, though containing upwards of 70,000 inhabitants, is governed by no other authority than that which regulates the meanest village. She covets not the oppressive honours of a corporation: her free, generous, and active spirit disdains to be shackled even with chains of gold. She throws her arms open to all mankind, inviting strangers of all descriptions into her hospitable bosom: the effect of this liberal system is self-evident.[43]

All early historians, from Hutton to those who contribute to the *Victoria County History*, cite these features in accounting for Birmingham's industry and the unusual number of patents applied for there: ninety by the end of the century in contrast to the next highest patent-seeking city, Manchester, which took out twenty-seven.[44] In buttons alone, of the twenty-one patents granted between 1770 and 1800, nineteen were from Birmingham.[45] As W. H. B. Court points out,

These patents communicate a vivid feeling of activity to our picture of the eighteenth-century town, where the great inventors by no means loomed so largely as they do to us, but were on the contrary almost lost to the sight in the press and throng of many others hoping to do as well, without possessing either their genius or their good fortune.[46]

Court's insight is acute: accounts which focus on the Matthew Boultons and Henry Corts of Birmingham's industrial history distort the every day reality of its bustling, entrepreneurial citizens, the vast majority of whom lived well below financial affluence and well above the conditions of workers in textile cities such as Manchester. Like his contemporaries, Jago captures a sense of bustling, artisanal energy:

> 'Tis Noise, and Hurry all! The thronged Street,
> The close-piled Warehouse, and the busy Shop!
> With nimble Stroke the tinkling Hammers move;
> While slow, and weighty the vast Sledge descends,
> In solemn Base responsive, or apart,
> Or socially conjoin'd in tuneful Peal.
>
> (*Edge-Hill*, III. 539–44)

The noise and hurry that Jago describes is paralleled in language used by historians. From Hutton, who praises Birmingham as the "nursery

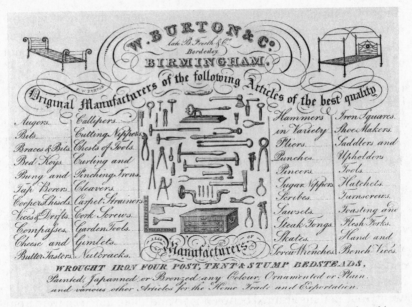

Figure 8 An advertisement that suggests the variety of ironware toys produced in
Birmingham shops. William West, *The History, Topography and Directory of Warwickshire*
(1830), page 317, DA670.W3W5.

of arts" where "invention is ever at work," to Court, who describes its
"general ferment of invention" and "intellectual liveliness," this image of
Birmingham is projected and reinforced.[47] One of the most vigorous is
caught in the *Victoria County History of the County of Warwick*, where graphic
lists of goods and industries, from plating to the recovery of gold, silver,
and brass from "the scraps, dross, filings, sweepings" of jewelers' shops
and smithies, suggest the vitality and ingenuity of its citizenry.[48]

Teeming lists disclose that metal workers were willing to smithy goods
without question – not only manufacturing iron goods for the slave trade,
but also indulging imaginative advances in the technologies of crimes and
punishment. In Hewitt's words,

Curiosities of the Birmingham heavy steel toy trade have been the secret manufacture, by men known to the police, of housebreakers' implements, such as
gouges, ripping chisels, skeleton keys, and pocket jacks; whilst, by way of an
antidote to these, handcuffs, manacles, leg-irons, and chains have also been
provided from the same source; "suits" of chains for Brazilian slave-ships; tom-
ahawks for North American Indians, and a mysterious order, executed as late
as 1849, for two dozen thumb-screws, for some South American state.[49]

Goods produced for purposes ranging from the doubtful to the depraved reinforced a reputation Birmingham had already achieved for its production of counterfeit coinage in the seventeenth century, a reputation which accounts such as Hutton's and Jago's seek to redeem. Although knowledge of Birmingham's contribution to criminal industries may not have been widespread, its reputation for counterfeit was commonplace. In fact, outrage at the goods produced by Birmingham artisans was expressed most keenly by London merchants, who, while typically contemptuous of provincial occupations, actively resented the success Birmingham metal workers achieved in silver plate.[50] Birmingham platers stood in impudent contrast to the silver- and goldsmiths of London, who prided themselves on castwares made from solid metals. Birmingham trickery became even more notorious when metal workers began replacing precious *plate* metals with a variety of nonprecious metals, including tutania (an alloy of tin and antimony) and pinchbeck (an alloy of copper and zinc).

The legacy of this reputation remains in the OED's citations for both "brummagem" and "Birmingham." There we find a continuing record from the last quarter of the seventeenth century, when "Bromicham" (an alternate spelling of Birmingham) is said to be "particularly noted a few years ago, for the counterfeit groats made here, and from hence dispersed all over the Kingdom," to 1843 when Southey invokes "a Brummejam of the coarsest and clumsiest kind." Between these years, Birmingham became noted for a multitude of counterfeit products. These included not only plated flatware, but papier-mâché, japanned and lacquered wares, and jet jewelry made from blackened and polished block paper – all products composed of inferior base materials and coated with ornamental exteriors. The colloquial form of the city's name thus entered the language as a contemptuous epithet. In 1861 the word was used to describe "The vulgar dandy, strutting along, with his Brummajem jewellry"; to "Birminghamize" was "to artificialize."

The extent to which simulation permeated the market structure of Birmingham's industries can be felt in accounts of Birmingham industries edited by Samuel Timmins in 1860. These often unconsciously underscore the simulative bent of Birmingham manufactures. For example, Timmins suggests that when the button industry redounded onto Birmingham after 1778, the chief metals introduced into the industry were tutania and pinchbeck.[51] Soho is described as the temple of the simulative arts, and Matthew Boulton its high priest. His factory became renowned for its production of any object that could be dipped, plated, or

japanned. The arts of simulation spread into a thriving papier-mâché industry, a process patented by Henry Clay in 1772. Papier-mâché became
the basis of a whole line of decorative objects, from jewelry to the ceilings
of coaches, reaching its most fantastic expression in Clay's gift to Queen
Charlotte of a sedan-chair and a set of console tables made entirely of
paper.[52] The entire inclination of the industry was perhaps summed
up by James Watt's introduction of the perfected "copying machine."[53]
Account after account depicts Birmingham as a hotbed of simulation, as
a locus where invention and simulation become indistinguishable. The
preoccupation with distinguishing real or original products from simulated products reflects accusations voiced by proponents of the luxury
argument that ordinary people purchase goods in order to counterfeit a
higher social status. In their desire to imitate the upper classes the less
affluent become themselves a kind of brummagem, counterfeit goods
with a showy exterior, like the vulgar dandy strutting his imitation jewelry.
Such simulation is of course a direct affront to the benevolent natural
relations extolled in georgic rural order, even as it operates on the georgic principle of simulation of a prior text devoted to the substance of the
matter.

The concerns of social critics suggest important questions about the
nature of simulation and what drives it.[54] Typically, contemporary critics
assume that simulation entails imitation in common materials of objects
originally made from rare and expensive materials. This is not necessarily
the case. As the coincidence in Birmingham of simulation and innovation suggests, common materials can create rather than imitate fashion.
Such was the case with jewelry in the eighteenth century. As Timmins
points out in his discussion of Birmingham's toy trade, iron and steel
jewelry was fashionable in its own right. In his words, the "'toy trade'
of that age *represented and anticipated* the extent of the jewelry trades of the
present time" (my emphasis).[55] In this case, the fashion for precious metal
jewelry in the nineteenth century imitated the expansions and variations
on jewelry fashions set by inferior metal products a century earlier. Just
as street fashions in the last half of the twentieth century were imitated
by prestigious couturiers, so iron and steel jewelry produced rather than
imitated fashion possibilities. Imitation and simulation are not, in these
situations, synonymous. Whereas imitation involves the reproduction of
an original object, simulation obfuscates the difference between originals and reproductions. In the case of Birmingham toys, the proliferation of goods is both playful and inventive. The arts of simulation scatter

the memory and even the meaning of any original object, and we find ourselves in a world where originality, though not invention, has been drained of meaning and ingenuity takes precedence over genius. James Watt did not invent the steam engine or copy machine, but perfected them and brought them into use. We find ourselves in a hall of mirrors in which, in multitudinous dispersions, images are caught, reflected, reinvented, and reflected again. The play of images provides further depth to the world of toys which form the basis of Birmingham industries, and which historians of the city so studiously distinguish from children's playthings; for Birmingham's inventors literally toyed with the market, playing out the baffling relationship between imitation and genius, duplication and invention. Ingenuity confers authority on the surface rather than the depth of an object. As in a hall of mirrors, the play of images takes precedence over the point of origin.

Matthew Boulton's response to accusations that Birmingham shops were producing wares which resembled plate but were in actuality "dipped" in inferior metals illuminates local attitudes toward simulation. Boulton addressed the artisans of Birmingham calling on them not to cease dipping, but, in a truly modern moment, to distinguish between plated and dipped goods. In Timmins's account of this event,

[Boulton] denounced the deception of "marking 'gilt' on buttons which were not gilt, and 'plated' on such as were not plated," and added in characteristic style, "As I am an old button maker, allow me to advise my brethren to make excellence rather than cheapness their principle of rivalry; and pardon me if I advise the merchant to be satisfied with buying good commodities at a fair price, to lay aside the arts of reduction, and not to expect to buy his goods cheaper than any other man who has money in his hands."[56]

In Timmins's account, Boulton's censure of merchants who sold dipped goods as plate is significant since he overlooks the distinction between solid metals and plated metals, calling on artisans to distinguish between different orders of simulation. He redistributes the order of value from solid, cast goods to different orders of plated wares, from substance to artifice. He also tacitly turns from distinguishing between the target markets of the upper and lesser classes to ever finer distinctions among ordinary people who choose goods based not on substance (the internal value of the object) but on different orders of plate.

Boulton's canny redistribution of value inevitably draws attention to the simulative character of castwares. It is evident that when we think of these as real or original products, we do so because of their "solid" worth. Indeed, the primary characteristic of such goods, repeatedly cited today, is their solidity – the fact that the outside of the product indicates the composition of the inside. This in turn calls attention to the fact that metal, a ductile product, actually simulates a different point of origin – the non-ductile materials from which flatware and other such goods were made: wood, soft stone, and ivory. The point of origin itself is part of a process of simulation that has regulated the taste for household goods. As Jago and Hutton suggest, brummagem is a sign not of falsity but of native ingenuity.

Thus we return to the question of what the "real" nature of georgic is, especially since English georgic is both a simulation and a reinvention of a Virgilian form, a true indicator of Britishness and a true indicator of English ingenuity. The product of several orders of simulation, English georgic simulates a Virgilian original, itself a poetic simulation of prose treatises. Indeed, one of Virgil's primary sources, Varro's *De re rustica*, is a prose treatise which simulates a dialogue between two people. Thus the regress to originals threatens to become infinite. In like manner, georgic achieves its aims by means of a simulation of Miltonic verse and "our English georgic," Philips's *Cyder*.[57] The fact that Jago handles the form in ways so intentionally imitative of its English manifestation in order to achieve the maximum *effect* of the form mirrors the significance of Boulton's concern with the plate industry. The redistribution of value from solid precious metals to distinctions between kinds of plate recalls Jago's redistribution of value from georgic substance to georgic devices of ornamentation, from georgic consideration of depth to a preoccupation with legible surfaces.

A rare, truly georgic setpiece in *Edge-Hill* casts light on this exchange. Jago uses the topos of the evening walk in order to draw a conventional contrast between fancy and virtue. In the figure of the poet he remonstrates with his companions who prefer

> to wander still along the Plain,
> In Coverts cool, lull'd by the murm'ring Stream,
> And whisp'ring Breeze; while playful Fancy skims,
> With careless Wing, the Surfaces of Things:
> For deep Research too indolent, too light
> For grave Reflection.   (IV. 212–17)

In a familiar comparison, languorous fancy touches only surfaces while Virtue labors in the georgic scene:

O! beware
Of Sloth, envenom'd Weed! and plant betimes
The Seeds of Virtue in the tender Soil.
Rear the just Sentiment, the wise Resolve
Invig'rate, and their infant Blossoms guard:
Then, like a Garden's cultivated Trees,
Their Shoots shall flourish, and the musing Mind
Shall banquet on their Fruits, when Youth is o'er.

(IV. 223–30)

When Jago slips in a reference to a fruit garden, he readjusts the pagan, Virgilian scene of georgic virtue by recollecting Milton's mythic tale of the fall from a dream of innocence. Here, in an image that haunts English georgic poetry, fruit, rather than causing the fall of our youthful first parents, redeems time. Ironically, despite this georgic interpolation, Jago's manifest affections in the poem have unconsciously shifted its burden from the innocent produce of the soil in the happy realm of the rural swain to the productivity of urban industry – a move which replicates the tendency of English georgic poets to dilate the moment in *Paradise Lost* when Adam is told that redemption will shift from the garden to the scene of georgic labor. Jago's simulation of English georgic is not simply a forward-looking adjustment to modern technology and industrialization. Rather, within a traditionalist framework, the object of his inquiry redirects georgic sensibility to a concern with manufactured wares which are products of artifice and which focus attention on exteriority and the nature of imitation – qualities that became integral with an aesthetic that would govern confined topographical and poetic spaces.

PART THREE

Infinitude confined

CHAPTER 7

Lyric art

Nor in this bower,
This little lime-tree bower, have I not mark'd
Much that has sooth'd me. Pale beneath the blaze
Hung the transparent foliage; and I watch'd
Some broad and sunny leaf, and lov'd to see
The shadow of the leaf and stem above
Dappling its sunshine! And that walnut-tree
Was richly ting'd, and a deep radiance lay
Full on the ancient ivy, which usurps
Those fronting elms, and now, with blackest mass
Makes their dark branches gleam a lighter hue
Through the late twilight: and though now the bat
Wheels silent by, and not a swallow twitters,
Yet still the solitary humble-bee
Sings in the bean-flower!

S. T. Coleridge
"This Lime-Tree Bower my Prison" (1797)

In "This Lime-Tree Bower my Prison," Coleridge draws the mind's eye
to the remarkable scenes of the roaring dell and the wide landscape into
which the walkers descend and emerge in the poem's central scenes. The
final, vernacular site of the cottage garden sinks, by contrast, into the
shadows of the poet's reverie as he gazes on the dilated glory of the setting
sun. This is fitting since the concluding portion of the poem returns
the poet to a scene habituated to the average English eye: the kitchen
garden lying, in this case, between Coleridge's own tiny cottage and
Thomas Poole's house. As the poet retreats from his imagined journey
with his friends to this familiar scene he lists evocative fragments of
its contents which serve both use and beauty: a walnut tree, ancient
ivy, sheltering elms, and fragrant beans. He thus records in lyric verse
a domestic site which would, by Gertrude Jekyll's time a few decades
later, be hallowed as the English cottage garden and mythologized as an

ancient and indigenous topography. The cottage garden, with its mixed borders of vegetables and flowers, was a spot in which lavender might grow next to gooseberries and cabbages in among roses. A derivation of the kitchen garden, a term which since Switzer had been used to describe gardens which grew not only vegetables, but fruit, flowers, and herbs, the cottage garden reinterpreted formal principles developed in kitchen-garden manuals in the eighteenth century and idealized the ancient messuage. Thus, in 1835, Loudon would claim that "[o]f private British gardens, the most numerous class of gardens, and those the most regularly distributed over the British Isles, are those of the country labourer, or what are usually denominated cottage gardens."[1] The kitchen-garden aesthetic, in which beauty is a function of use, expressed national aims of productivity that had an indigenous English history not only in the topographical spaces of real gardens, but poetic topoi which reinvented the aesthetic of the garden in metaphorical space.

In these final chapters I focus on the intersections between two discourses implicit in Coleridge's conversational ode which fed notions of containment in the latter decades of the eighteenth century. The first is the critical discourse which raised lyric poetry from the bottom of eighteenth-century poetic taxonomies to the elevated position it still retains and encouraged poets like Coleridge to explore its diverse forms. The second is that of the kitchen-garden manual, which forms part of the evocative machinery of Coleridge's insistently English bower in "This Lime-Tree Bower my Prison." Authors of kitchen-garden manuals had throughout the century extolled the virtues of the enclosed, productive garden. In a counter-current to treatises on the landscaped park, these authors advanced an aesthetic formulated around notions of containment, productivity, and function that was subordinate to the park's aesthetic of disinterest. In the decades between the ascension of George I and the American War, designers of parks recommended that functional sites such as the kitchen garden be screened from view, a point upon which Capability Brown, the premier designer of large estate parks from the 1750s to the 1780s, insisted. Whether or not all owners of estates screened functional sites in practice, the fact remains that in dominant landscaping discourse, the kitchen garden with its confining walls and functional purpose was not construed as a representational site. By the end of the decades during which lyric poetry sprang into prestige on the scale of literary forms, however, kitchen gardens in their new aspect as "cottage" gardens were reconceived as representing true Englishness. An aesthetic of exuberance within confined space and productivity linked to functionality supplanted values emblematized by the great park and established notions of Englishness over the course of the nineteenth century which remain powerful today. The critical discourses that constituted these literary and topographical ideals provided cultural intelligibility for new values of containment and productivity which were inseparable from notions of space, leisure, plenty, taste, and even sexuality.

In the unceasing exchange between garden manuals, literary criticism, and poetry, several congruencies may be documented. These include the formal requirement of a high level of artifice, the affective requirement of sublime power, the synaesthetic effect of temporal diffusion, and an inherited erotic discourse which was habituated to the contained, contrived space. In this chapter I set out the parameters of artifice, sublimity, and temporality within the context of literary critical thought of the period, and show how these parameters are held in place by kitchen-garden manuals and calendars. That contained forms took hold with such celerity in the 1770s and were thoroughly established by the Regency decade is inextricable from emerging notions of productivity which had implications not only for gardening but for poetry, not only for space but for sexuality. I treat both the kitchen garden and minor lyric forms as vernacular sites within which the dominant, expansive aesthetic associated with gentry for most of the eighteenth century was questioned and reinvented. Within the close confinement of these forms, sublimity, sensuality, and utility united to reinvent notions of what constituted representative English space.

LYRIC TURN AND LYRIC CONTINUITY: THE GREAT ODE
AND THE SONNET

No tropes naturalized the connection between topography and poetry more effectively than Addison's brash metaphors. I have already alluded to his famously whimsical comment of 1712:

I think there are as many Kinds of Gardening, as of Poetry; Your Makers of Parterres and Flower-Gardens, are Epigrammatists and Sonneteers in this Art. Contrivers of Bowers and Grotto's, Treillages and Cascades, are Romance Writers. *Wise* and *London* are our Heroick Poets...As for my self, you will find, by the Account which I have already given you, that my Compositions in Gardening are altogether after the *Pindarick* manner, and run into the beautiful Wildness of Nature, without affecting the nicer Elegancies of Art.[2]

Working upward through the valences of poetic hierarchy, Addison reveals in this self-congratulation a prejudice against the radically constricted poetic forms of sonnet and epigram that would become normative in succeeding decades. He smoothly transfers this prejudice to the equally constricted topographical form of the parterre, or small, well-demarcated flower bed. He ranks the fanciful but lengthy romance higher than minor lyric on his list of poetic forms, although he thematizes it in terms of the enclosed confines of the bower. From this erotically charged site, he ascends to the morally purposive heroic poem, while he places the great or Pindaric ode, the lyric equivalent of epic, at the vertex of his list. Following public enthusiasm for Cowley's odes, Pindaric was installed in poetic taxonomies as having epic or near-epic value. Respectably lengthy, powerful in its sentiments, public and occasional in its purpose, and provided with impeccable credentials from the classics and Psalms of David, the great ode, sometimes referred to (mistakenly) as the irregular ode, was elevated by critics.[3] The rhetorical features of Pindaric were reaffirmed by Longinus's treatise, first translated into English in 1652, which provided approbation for lyric form, at least in its most elevated mode.[4] Viewed as biblical in its sublimity and carrying with it the legitimation of a classical precedent, the great ode assisted in constituting a value system, both classed and gendered, which would permit wide admiration for the kind of landscape which Addison promoted.

The essential characteristics of the great ode could easily be taken from the landscape treatises that created, maintained, and superintended public taste from the ascension of George I until the American War. Its qualities included irregularity as a sign of liberty to be distinguished from mere art; imagination permitted jurisdiction over cold judgment; boldness accorded the dignity of an artistic principle; and art occulted to produce the illusion of sublime transport.[5] One can almost hear in these qualities Addison's moral dictum that

a spacious Horison is an Image of Liberty, where the Eye has Room to range abroad, to expatiate at large on the Immensity of its Views, and to lose itself amidst the Variety of Objects that offer themselves to its Observation. Such wide and undetermined Prospects are as pleasing to the Fancy, as the Speculations of Eternity or Infinitude are to the Understanding.[6]

The landscape that Addison saw as defined by his own practice was modeled on the same principles as the great ode. Similarly, the highly emblematic landscapes depicted in Stephen Switzer's designs produced an open prospect composed, like the ode, as a series of strophes marked by resolute turns and abrupt transitions. Thus the new emphasis on natural design through the first part of the century is expressed in sharply differentiated plots of ground often devoted to remarkably homogeneous plantings: sometimes to "rural" gardens, sometimes to parterres (formal flower gardens), sometimes to "greens" (evergreens from conifers to laurels), sometimes to "English parterres" (well-defined plots of grass), sometimes to potted citrus trees. "Wildernesses" were formal plantings of trees, usually set in the quincuncial pattern in which a group of five trees is mortised, Escher-fashion, with groups of trees surrounding it. While it is true that such plantings would have been experienced as more haphazard by the walker in the landscape than plans suggest – and despite Switzer's devotion to sinuous paths – the *idea* of nature as highly designed would have been as powerful for the hypothetical walker as for the person who produced the designs. Not yet fashionable were the loosely formal lines of Brown's parks with their "natural" plantings, exposed surfaces veneered with grass, and continuous transitions between contrasting topographical sites – a landscape that influences so profoundly our notion of what is meant by the open prospect that it is difficult to regain a sense of Switzer's intent. Just as Switzer's designs estrange our sense of what is meant by an open prospect, so the great ode differs from what we recognize as lyric. Like georgic poetry, the ode was lengthy, digressive, and oriented toward a public purpose rather than private emotion.[7] The verse form referred to by all literary critics of the period as "lyric" thus has much to distinguish it from minor lyric forms such as the sonnet that achieved enormous popularity after the 1770s. Nevertheless, despite its overtly public purpose and lofty form, the great ode's lyrical strategies assisted in elevating the claims of the sonnet and other minor lyric forms considered fit vehicles for the expression of private emotion. In these cases, conventions and symbols kidnapped from the literary heritage were pressed into the service of an altered epistemology.

In his critical study of the assumptions within which romanticism has been historicized, Clifford Siskin draws attention to the point at which the "georgic-descriptive hierarchy of forms" gave way to a "lyricized hierarchy."[8] He uses the phrase "lyric turn" to describe a history in which "creative and critical narratives . . . veer from the generic and historical to the natural and transcendent, metamorphosing all analysis into claims for Imaginative vision."[9] Siskin's phrase, "lyric turn," is apt for the topographical and literary developments that I trace over the course of the eighteenth century. His argument pivots on the shift to a poetry that provided new options for the presentation of subjectivity and placed a high value on the immediacy of the relationship between author and poem, poem and reader. The phrase is ironically fitting, too, because it recalls what had come in the wake of public approbation for the great ode to constitute one of the essential features of lyric verse. Edward Young suggested the quality in his preface to "Ocean. An Ode" (1728) when he stipulated, echoing Longinian rhetorical principles, that the "conduct" of the ode "should be rapturous, somewhat abrupt, and immethodical to a vulgar Eye. That apparent order, and connection, which gives form, and life to *some* compositions, takes away the very Soul of *this*."[10] Bold or impetuous transitions that turn abruptly to new images or redirect thought were consistently viewed as essential to the spirit of lyric poetry, and Thomas Gray was seen as having eclipsed even his classical antecedents in this art. Similarly, but in more condensed form, the "legitimate," or Petrarchan, sonnet incorporated such a turn in the volta, usually the ninth line of the verse. At this breaking point the speaker veers from the inquiry and development of the octave to the resolute or compensatory response of the sestet. Significantly, the sestet embodies a special intellection that supersedes that of the octave, a discovery that leads to higher knowledge, or a private resolve to consider alternative possibilities. The semantic structure of the sonnet thus suggests an affirmative narrative (even in the face of irrevocable sorrow and loss) which moves sometimes through reversal, sometimes from a lower to a higher psychological or moral plane, from weakness to resolution, or from constricted to expanded vision. Form and content underscore this progress, since they collude to provide not only a tropological semantics but a tropological structure: apostrophes or adverbial conjunctions formalize the volta's about face, while rhyme regulates the progress of the argument. Form generates meaning – or, in the terms of the kitchen garden, use generates beauty.

Though Siskin's phrase accurately captures a shifting epistemology that began to privilege a lyric sensibility, it overlooks the historical continuity of lyric strategies held in place by the Pindaric ode since the seventeenth century. Thus, the Pindaric ode, while elevated far above minor lyric forms, paved the way for their reception by the final quarter of the eighteenth century. Siskin's argument also overlooks the problematic status that minor lyric forms, especially the sonnet, posed for eighteenth-century critics. As Curran points out, Johnson's definition of the sonnet as "not very suitable to the English language" is repeated not only by virtually every contemporary critic, but also by sonnet writers.[11] Critics remained doubtful of minor lyric forms in general, and the sonnet in at least one taxonomy occupied the bottom rung with the epigram, as a wry verse quoted ironically by Thomas Warton in his *History of English Poetry* (1774–81) reveals:

> Once by mishap two poets fell a squaring,
> The Sonnet and our Epigram comparing.
> And Faustus having long demur'd upon it
> Yet at the last gave sentence for the Sonnet;
> Now, for such censure, this his chiefe defence is,
> Their sugred tast best likes his likrous senses.
> Well, though I grant sugar may please the tast,
> Yet let my verse have salt to make it last.[12]

Sonnet enthusiasts typically sought to provide it with a status separate from that of the ode or other minor lyric forms. Anna Seward, a voluble if eccentric apologist for the sonnet, expresses this critical position when she says, "Petrarch is famed for his sonnets, – I never heard of him as a lyric poet."[13] Critics may have denigrated the sonnet, especially in the sentimental or sugared mood it frequently assumed; nevertheless, they were also drawn by its lyric qualities and formal ingenuity, especially the volta, which compressed and architecturalized the wilder logic of the great ode. Keats exemplifies the ambiguity that followed popular enthusiasm for the sonnet. He entered spiritedly into the commerce in sonnets – exchanging them with friends, engaging in sonnet contests with Leigh Hunt, or using them to jolt himself out of periods of creative lethargy. But while experimenting vigorously with the form, he was dogged by the implications of its breadth, in one instance playfully grouping together "a Sonnet or a Pun or an Acrostic, a Riddle or a Ballad – 'perhaps it may turn out a Sang, and perhaps turn out a Sermon.'"[14] Keats's response to epic reveals his lyric sensibility most clearly. A modern reader, Keats considered epics with a lyric eye, extracting lines and phrases from their narrative contexts and importing them into lyric forms.[15] He shaped his craft through the lyric techniques of syntactical compression and oxymoron, that most condensed locution of the volta. Yet simultaneously he gazed at the unbounded prospect of epic form "like a sick eagle gazing at the sky."[16] In Keats we find a distillation of the new lyric sensibility, with all its yearning for broader vistas.

One can see in retrospect that despite discomfort about the sonnet's status the shift in popularity from long to short forms schematizes a larger literary alteration in which the expansive and somewhat baggy, finger-shaking georgic impulse turned, by means of the great ode, to a different poetic sensibility which privileged compression, intensity, well-defined borders, contrivance, and the dissolution of barriers between subject and object. Poets consider the minor lyric and reconnect it with a serious purpose, turning back to confined forms that poets earlier in the century abandoned.[17] The space of georgic poetry had been identified with expansiveness, volume, and the unhindered view and its poetic boundaries were obscured by a digressive organizational principle. Although the "extraneous" features which fill out its bulk are not incidental but central to its structure, the georgic form produced a sense of open-endedness brought arbitrarily to a close by the four-book Virgilian pattern, or its two-book variation.[18] Furthermore, georgic is mediated by instruction, a technique that is outwardly directed and presumes a distance between the pedagogue and a receptive audience. It lacks the sense of immediacy between poet and poem and between poem and audience which lesser lyric assumes. Similarly, the great ode presumed a public and official relationship between speaker and audience, a fact that prevents a modern audience from recognizing qualities esteemed as lyrical by eighteenth-century readers. The lyric turn signaled not merely a miniaturization of the georgic structure, as Siskin's study underscores, but a changing conception of the work of literature and criticism which continues to govern the reception of poetry. The volta, which presumes a progressive narrative within the sonnet, finds a counterpart in the critical narrative of literary history which devalues georgic garrulousness and pedagogical purpose, and continues to reproduce a progressive history of literary forms that apotheosizes the imaginative vision of lyric.

Siskin's application of a lyric structure to the history of criticism argues that lyricality is not merely a poetic mode but a cultural sensibility. Lyric has, in fact, been notoriously difficult for critics to define. While it is not the place of this discussion to dispute the precise qualifications of this broad cluster of poetic forms, it is instructive that since the romantic period critics have by-and-large chosen to categorize lyric less in terms of form than sensibility. Lyric sensibility is principally defined in terms of the private voice (described by John Stuart Mill as overheard rather than heard),[19] self-consciousness or reflexivity which produces interiority, and spontaneity or immediacy. Coleridge captures the essence of this requirement in a witty marginal comment on a volume of Petrarch's verse: "O that the Pope would take these eternal keys, which so for ever turn the bolts on the finest passages of true passion!"[20] As romanticism deepened, however, finally forming the invisible medium of modern critical assumptions, emphasis was placed not merely on the lyric expression of passion and inwardness, but the lyric externalization of consciousness and psychological depth. Thus a monograph published in 1913 could claim,

the lyric is concerned with the poet, his thoughts, his emotions, his moods, and his passions. In the lyric the individual singer emerges, conspicuous in the potency of his art. We have no longer, as in Homer, a sonorous mouthpiece for the deeds of Achilles or the fated wanderings of Ulysses, but, as in Sappho, the passionate throbbing of a human heart seeking artistic expression. With the lyric subjective poetry begins.[21]

This definition, of course, excludes forms of lyric that were public and occasional in character, even though they too are formed by means of the lyric strategies of impassioned utterance, abrupt transition, strophic dialectic, and syntactic distillation. Meanwhile, the exegetical methods of modern criticism, which simultaneously emphasize difference and subjectivity, have deepened the romantic notion of lyric by shifting the locus of subjectivity from the relationship between the lyric poem and its authorial source – the passionate throbbing of the poet's heart – to differences *within* the subjectivity articulated in the poem. While dedicated to close analyses of texts, these interpretations tend themselves, therefore, to be hermetically sealed. For example, a rigorous, close reading of Shelley's *Prometheus Unbound* is founded on the assumption that "lyric, as a purely subjective form, is marked by the exclusion of the other through which we become aware of the difference of the self from itself."[22] The outcome of this tendency, when ironic subjective illusion is not identified as a highly formal generative device, is that any form can be discovered to possess "lyricality," although lyric *forms*, by implication, do not necessarily do so.[23] Though lyric poetry is certainly characterized by the sensibility described above, it is a mistake to separate its sensibility from its artifice. Artifice produces and rules the subjectivities of the contained poetic space. In Stuart Curran's pithy observation, "All such fixed forms are invested with the logic of their structure" – lyric form generates content.[24] Lyric cannot be characterized as the result of an author's success in "induc[ing] the reader to know, from within, the virtual experience of a more or less particularized consciousness."[25]

This is not to dispute the fact that long forms incorporate lyric moments. One of the attributes of the lyric moment in epic and georgic poetry, however, is its extractability from its contexts, its capacity to exist in isolation from the rest of the text as an antinarrative. Lyric moments in long poems are not necessarily equivalent to lyric forms, either in construction or, especially, in social significance. Lyric moments in long poems are often embowered episodes that deviate from narrative and incorporate the structure of lyric emotion that we have come, since the romantic period, to associate with lyric sensibility. If the cultivated landscape and poetics intersect, it is not merely because they project a similar sensibility, but because the aesthetics of form literally *informs* their disciplines. By the same token, however, to locate the mechanisms by which lyric form generates lyric content requires that the critic step outside the poem's seductive interior world, which is a part of its own self-iterative contrivance, and to interrupt the tautologies of self and otherness so sensuously recounted in Keats's "Ode to Psyche" – to step, as Annabelle Patterson demands, into the relationship between lyric and history, in this case the history and contexts of form.[26]

THE KITCHEN-GARDEN MANUAL

As in the case of lyric poetry, the contained garden exercised a material presence early in the eighteenth century. Visual designs reveal that diverse spatial forms existed side by side in the landscape throughout the century, even though the broad views from a country house may have had disproportional representational power in treatises and literature. Engravings of estates by Kip and Knyff in *Britannia Illustrata* (1714 and 1724) reveal the imbrication of kitchen garden with landed estate and of landed estates neighbored by the homes and gardens of ordinary people, although cottages (presumably with their gardens) were often omitted from estate maps in the mid- and late century.[27] These engravings, published before the *furor hortensis* that would eventuate in Capability Brown's parks had gathered force, suggest that though the kitchen garden may ultimately have been erased from the views and maps of many great houses, it was a common vernacular site in the everyday life of ordinary people. The extraordinary attention paid to the design of kitchen gardens bears out this conclusion. Even though designs for parks may have dictated that kitchen gardens be screened from view, plans for kitchen gardens were highly contrived, even indistinguishable from those for formal parterres beneath the public rooms of a great house. Only captions reveal the differing purposes of these sites. Thus, even when kitchen gardens were concealed from the great house, they were regarded by gardeners as highly designed sites in their own right, their form contributing to their function. Apart from the fact that any member of a gentry household who visited local towns and villages or simply

Figure 9 In addition to gardens that lie between the cathedral and houses in the foreground, numerous gardens can be seen attached to the homes surrounding the cathedral. "The Prospect of Nottingham," J. Kip and L. Knyff, *Britannia Illustrata* (1714), vol. 1, plate 75, RB 204533.

rode into the country would have daily seen kitchen gardens attached to town houses and laborer's cottages, these, and not the open prospect, *were* the customary views of the vast majority of people. Coalminers, laborers, successful artisans – an array of ordinary people – had some kind of garden, whether rented or owned, which they filled with vegetables, flowers, herbs, and fruit. As Loudon would later point out, these gardens were not necessarily places for keeping a pig or growing a few cabbages, but sites within which the ordinary person had "an opportunity of displaying his taste in its cultivation."[28] The kitchen garden, sometimes with its attendant greenhouse or stove, preserved a sense of the bounded, domestic space, even when landscape treatises applauded extension as the emblematic British prospect.

Throughout the eighteenth century, authors of both garden manuals and landscape treatises maintained that contained space requires its own set of aesthetic guidelines – it could not without absurdity simply miniaturize larger forms. Small proprietors who telescoped the serpentine

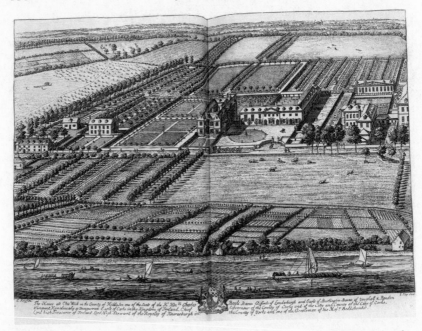

Figure 10 This estate view features the Thames in the immediate foreground and kitchen gardens between the river and the estate. Chiswick House, Middlesex, J. Kip and L. Knyff, *Britannia Illustrata* (1714), vol. 1, plate 30, RB 204533.

walks, wilderness, and lawns of the great park into a constricted space came in for a good deal of ridicule. Even botanist Richard Bradley, a contemporary of Switzer, found it "disagreeable, to see Works of the highest Grandeur, which ought only to appear in Gardens of the greatest Extent, attempted in a small Garden" in which it will "lose its Beauty."[29] George Mason proved more acerbic on this point, commenting in 1770, "From a general view of our present gardens in populous districts, a stranger might imagine they were calculated for a race of LILLIPUTIONS. Are their *shade*, their *ponds*, or their *islands* proportionable to common mortals? Their winding walks – such as no human footstep (except a reeling drunkard's) could have traced."[30] We may infer that the unique requirements of contained space remained an ongoing topic of consideration and discussion well before such space achieved representational status. The kitchen garden, which forms so essential a part of the aesthetic of contained space, was carefully documented in treatises which span the hiatus between Fairchild's and Langley's plans for urban gardens and Loudon's for suburban gardens. These projected an aesthetic

Figure 11 Upper left center depicts the garden district lining the Thames at Chelsea. The Neathouse Gardens, where Switzer and many other received their first training as gardeners, are located at upper right center. Chelsea and the Neathouse Gardens, J. Rocque, *Survey of London* (1746), plates 10 and 7, RB 315661.

characterized by compression and delineation fitted to the demands of a site which, designed to be useful, was nonetheless enthusiastically acclaimed for its beauty.

By the second decade of the nineteenth century, the suspicion attending contained sites had altered so radically that treatise writers could acclaim their virtues. From the beginning of renewed attention to smaller gardens, the histories and fortunes of the pleasure garden and kitchen garden are linked. For example, abandoning Brown's principle of screening functional sites from view, Repton would, in 1816, advocate the kitchen garden as a good in and of itself. He urges,

let us now consider the Garden for Use, rather than for Beauty, and we shall find that these two objects are by no means incompatible. The walks of a Kitchen Garden are apt to be uncomfortably exposed to the sun's heat during the summer and autumn: this may be corrected by training the fruit trees of espaliers on hoops over the walks, to make shaded alleys; or covered *berceaux*, from whence the apples, pears, and plums, are seen hanging within our reach; and grapes so trained, will sometimes ripen without artificial heat. These trellis arcades may be straight or curved, and the walks may be of gravel or grass, surrounding and enclosing those quarters for garden crops, which, if well managed, will be scarcely visible from the walks; and a skreen of gooseberries, currants, raspberries, and asparagus beds surrounding these, will make a cheerful blind during a great part of the summer months.[31]

As this observation suggests, Repton espoused the view of functional beauty geared toward productivity which designers of kitchen gardens had pressed for the entire century. Enthusiastic about the recreative prospects of this small space, authors of kitchen-garden manuals found precedent in the bowers of Milton's Eden and Spenser's *Fairie Queene* and ostentatiously borrowed their vocabulary from lyric passages in the fertile tradition of English poetry. It is hardly odd, therefore, that descriptions in manuals and calendars of gardens brimming with fruits, vegetables, flowers, and herbs should exhibit techniques of lyric form, while employing strategies that are didactic *and* lyrical. Manuals provide a singular continuity between those decades delighted by English georgic poetry and post-American War fascination with lyric forms. Unlike georgic poetry, in which the embowered space is hidden within expansive prospects and subsumed by purposive instruction, kitchen-garden manuals extract the small enclosed space from the larger text of the landscape, and in so doing unite didactic purpose with lyrical technique, *utile* with *dulce*. Treatises on the kitchen garden contributed to both georgic and lyric impulses, conforming to the profitability, industry, and occasion for instruction required by the former and to the artifice and sublime immediacy of the latter. Through them we glimpse a capacious public mentality that valued both the curious and the visceral, both instruction and profligacy. In the continuous tradition of the kitchen-garden manual we watch the aesthetic for contained topographical space taking shape and discern a convergence between topographical and literary form. A growing interest in the healthful qualities of vegetables, "physical" properties of herbs, and commercial possibilities of flowers combined with new enthusiasm for dietary variation was already well established early in the century. In addition, as the long tradition of labor-intensive farming in the southwest Midlands proved, the methods practiced in the kitchen garden were believed to have profound implications for the practice of agriculture, providing methods for growing food that could boost the productivity of farmlands. Richard Weston and Humphry Repton were only two of many gardeners who advocated transferring methods from kitchen gardening to farming. In the words of the former:

Every one who is a lover of agriculture and gardening, and has once observed the manner in which the grounds around London are cultivated and cropped, cannot but wish to see similar methods more practised in the interior parts of the kingdom; as they are attended with so many advantages to the cultivator, making the same ground produce double or treble the quantity of vegetables which it would otherwise do, and where land is scarce, as in the neighbourhood of all large towns, are of great national utility, especially as, from this practice, the country farmer would by degrees begin to see the great difference in value of grounds which have drilled crops, and are hand or horse hoed: his land being more benefited by a drilled crop than by a fallow, and yet he receives profit that very year.[32]

Weston's comments feed into a growing sense that containment is a precondition for productivity, and, like those on both sides of the parliamentary enclosure debate, link containment to a national purpose. Writers of many of these manuals are also convinced that a properly managed kitchen garden provides pleasure and beauty. Unlike Weston, who calculated the profit in roses, peppermint, and poppies and recommended planting onions around the base of fruit trees since they guarantee income their first year, others marveled openly at the beauties of this vernacular space. The numerous manuals devoted to garden practice and design reveal that because beauty in the kitchen garden was viewed as an effect of its function, these gardens provided a way of defining the elements of form for a contained space quite distinct from those of the landscaped park. The functional aesthetic, obscured by the passion for the "natural" contours of the English landscape garden, was brought by means of the kitchen garden into the domain of pleasure.

The convergence of artifice, sublimity, and temporal diffusion in the discourses surrounding kitchen gardens and minor lyric forms is expressed most clearly in prefaces and essays on lyric poetry which began to proliferate during the 1780s. Literary critics and poets often take their cue from Edward Young and adapt his principles to lesser lyric forms. In addressing minor lyrics such as the Horatian ode and sonnet as serious poetic forms, literary critics formulate aesthetic principles that parallel stipulations of garden manuals. This visible transversion underscores the fact that, beyond expressing a subjective sensibility, minor lyric was perceived as a formal *space* that generates content. Its brevity, indeed, as W. R. Johnson points out, was not simply viewed as beautiful, but became the standard for beauty – and a fitting receptacle for the sublime.[33] Literary critics and authors of garden manuals share assumptions concerning artifice, sublimity, and temporal diffusion that are historically specific and socially weighted. In particular, despite the fact that lyric is a self-reflexive form while garden manuals are instructive, both fabricate the idea of a self-enclosed world in which the speaker whispers poetry's secrets into her own ear. In kitchen-garden manuals the self-enclosed world is, like Milton's Eden, a horticultural plenum filled with diverse fruits and vegetables from the four corners of a Britannizable world. Most strikingly, lyric's self-reflexivity, its self-proclaimed enunciation of private emotion, is ironically designed for a highly public purpose. Inversely, as a didactic text the kitchen-garden manual opens with the assumption that the speaker occupies a public forum; yet it presumes, as the etymology of the word "garden" suggests, a guarded and secluded space, one which is shielded from the eye of the passerby and which shuts out the external prospect. As readers of the kitchen-garden manual we peer through the chink in the wall or the break in the hedge into our neighbor's yard. The allure in each case, so unlike the indifferent gaze over the wide prospect presumed by the aesthetic of the landscaped park or open forms of georgic and the great ode, is the allure of the bounded, the excluded, the voyeuristic gaze.

ARTIFICE

Critical esteem for confined forms is determined in large part by the kind of value placed on artifice, considered here as the presentation of formal strategies in the art object in such a way that art stands in for nature – for artifice, which places art higher in the system of values than nature, is the hallmark of confined forms. Under the restriction of space concealment of design is not the object. Design forthrightly calls attention to itself and asserts itself *as* nature. This principle may seem indistinguishable from that of the Brown landscape which, although an object of contrivance, asserted itself as natural. Eighteenth-century garden manuals, however, locate a structural opposition less between nature and culture than between two categories of nature – cultivated nature and neglected nature – both of which are presumed to be natural.[34] Cultivated nature, in this instance, is akin to Sidney's notion of art, which requires the creation of a different world, a golden world or second nature that the observer can enter by a willing suspension of disbelief. William Marshall astutely observes that what we often refer to as "nature" is always in some measure a human construction. He argues,

there is not a tree, perhaps not a stick, now standing upon the face of the country which owes its identical state of existence to Nature alone. Wherever cultivation has set its foot, – wherever the plow and spade have laid fallow the soil, – Nature is become extinct . . . Therefore our idea of *natural* is not confined to *neglected* nature, but extends to *cultivated nature* – to nature *touched* by art, and rendered intelligible to human perception.[35]

Marshall here proposes that the term "nature" include *human* nature since nature must be organized through familiar cultural categories if it is to be "rendered intelligible." As an advocate for the English landscape garden, Marshall had a low opinion of artifice, which he equated with undisguised labor,[36] yet even his conventional stricture against artifice exposes the other side of the argument, which poises artifice against unimpeded vistas, economic privilege, even the ideal of English manliness. The state of artifice is akin to Tasso's bower of Armida, a garden that "seemed to be the art of Nature herself; as though, in a fit of playfulness, she had imitated her imitator."[37] In Armida's garden, as in Spenser's Bower of Bliss, the posture art displays toward nature is impudent, although artifice more accurately creates a productive confusion of *origins* between art and nature even as it privileges surfaces over substance. This very confusion serves to make artifice suspect. Disguising the bounds between design and the natural world, the artist seizes nature in order to transform it into art's own highly ordered world.

By this account, artifice results from an appropriation of nature so profound that nature becomes art. Hunt clarifies this point with regard to minor lyric when discussing Raleigh's sonnet on Spenser's *Faerie Queene*: "You see in this one little sonnet, what possession he takes of the whole poetical world, in favor of the sovereignty of his friend Spenser. He was not exactly in the right; but when did conquerors consider the right?"[38] Hunt's comment presupposes that artifice is achieved through an act of artistic appropriation, here intensified because in this instance the sonnet appropriates the "world" of another poem, which then substitutes for "nature." Hunt exposes the eighteenth-century fallacy that minor lyrics are innocent – sugary verses about love or pleasure, songs written by troubadours or pub-crawlers. Not incidentally, he makes possible a higher status for the contained space, and thus his comment has ramifications for the kitchen garden and its hothouse, which are repeatedly depicted as worlds unto themselves created through just such an act of appropriation. The poet's and gardener's acts of possession presuppose that an entire world (rather than merely a view) can be absorbed within the contained space, and in the process not merely miniaturize but transform that world through a highly artificial staging of its qualities.

Such acts of possession bring space under the rule of artifice and stage the profligacy of highly designed, contained forms.

Literary critics considering the merits of minor lyric reveal such a principle: the smaller the space of the literary form the more artful it should appear. In her preface to the first collected edition of Collins's poetry, Anna Laetitia Barbauld observes that a minor ode, "like a delicate piece of silver filligree, receives in a manner all its value from the art and curiosity of the workmanship. Hence Lyric Poetry will very seldom bear translation, which is a kind of melting down of a Poem, and reducing it to the sterling value of the matter contained in it."[39] For Barbauld, the "sterling value of the matter" constitutes the intrinsic value of the epic. In lyric poetry, by contrast, value shifts from substance to surface, from matter to manner. She elaborates,

> The *substratum*, if I may so express myself, or subject matter, which every composition must have, is, in a Poem of this kind, so extremely slender, that it requires not only art, but a certain artifice of construction, to work it up into a beautiful piece; and to judge of or relish such a composition requires a practised ear, and a taste formed by elegant reading.[40]

Barbauld distinguishes between epic and lyric in order to defend a form of poetry that she suspects her audience is not yet properly schooled to appreciate. She thus opens a vista onto an historical moment when reading patterns are shifting from one sensibility to another. She exemplifies this point in her posture toward Collins's poems, for though reluctant to fully endorse artifice, her criticism is serious and sincere. Congruent with the testimony of a variety of critics, she demonstrates that lyric forms require not only a different reader sensibility than long poems, but recognition of the formal strategies which distinguish them from traditionally more prestigious forms.

SUBLIMITY

As we have seen, critical approbation for the great ode eventually made it possible to view even lesser lyric forms as vessels of sublimity. Figures of containment are potentially unlinked from figures of mental limitation, so that even within the narrow compass of the sonnet sublime power can be held under compression. Thus, while small size could still be mustered as part of an attack on the limitations of a poet's capacity and survive in landscape treatises as a class-coded dismissal of the acquisitive sorts, it nevertheless accrued combustive affective possibilities. As notions about the relationship between size and sublimity change, the containment of form is dealt with not by arguing that containment *per se* is beneficial, but by transforming containment into a sign of vastness and power. Not least, lyric space becomes associated with vatic space – the vastness and power of the poet.[41] In consequence, appreciation for classical poets considered masters of minor lyric, especially Anacreon, Sappho, and Horace, increased. Taking advantage of this incipient trend, John Aikin could expostulate in the preface to his anthology of songs,

But to those who are enamoured with that sacred art, which beyond every other elevates and refines the soul, to whom the sprightly lyre of Horace and Anacreon, and the melting music of Sappho still sound, though ages have passed since they vibrated on the ear, I will venture to promise a source of enjoyment, from the works of those great masters whose names adorn this collection.[42]

Barbauld, more cautious in her approval of minor lyric forms, takes a similar position in her preface to Collins's works. Still clinging to the superior merit of epic, she nevertheless claims that

Collins, amongst our English Authors, has cultivated the Lyric Muse with peculiar felicity; his works are small in bulk, but highly finished; and have deservedly gained him a respectable rank amongst our minor Poets. His characteristics are tenderness, tinged with melancholy, beautiful imagery, a fondness for allegory and abstract ideas, purity and chasteness of sentiment, and an exquisite ear for harmony. In his endeavours to embody the fleeting forms of mind, and clothe them with correspondent imagery, he is not unfrequently obscure; but even when obscure, the reader who possesses congenial feelings is not ill pleased to find his faculties put upon the stretch in the search of those sublime ideas which are apt, from their shadowy nature, to elude the grasp of the mind.[43]

Observations such as these facilitated an inversion of the conventional wisdom that extended dimension reflects the capacity for genius. Despite Barbauld's reservations, she finds in the quality of obscurity a source of the sublime: Collins's verse stretches the faculties beyond their limits in the intellection of noumenal ideas.

Hunt captures the inversion of dimension and capacity when he remarks, "A perfect sonnet is a beautiful thing, and shuts up the ear in a 'measureless content.'"[44] The word *content*, depending upon emphasis, plays out the nuances of satisfaction and constituent parts: satisfaction because its contents are profligate; profligate because it is formally contained and defined, under pressure, concentrated, intense. To use Sharon Cameron's suggestive phrase, the lyric object "compress[es] space in its

own restorative design . . . "[45] The "measureless content" which closes
one in on oneself, as the image of the reader's stopped ear suggests, also
creates the illusion of an unmediated connection between artifact and
audience – the conundrum of the lyrical relationship. Like the speaker,
who in Keats's "Ode to Psyche" "begs pardon" that he whispers Psyche's
secrets into her "own soft-conched ear," Hunt suggests that lyric dissolves
the boundaries between subject and object, adding a new dimension to
the sonnet's sublime potentiality. Sublimity is possible not merely because
immensity has been contracted and compressed, but because sublimity
sets the conditions under which the dissolution of boundaries between
subject and object are fantasized, where the world of In Here becomes
a world unto itself.

The formal requirements of the great ode provided the criteria for
a poetics of the sublime which critics in the last quarter of the century
applied to far more compressed forms, within which concentration, intensity, and immediacy could find as great a power. One strategy for
producing this effect is to relieve images from their strict connections to
each other by introducing bold transitions. The sonnet's volta is a version
of this poetic device, as are Keats's oxymorons, which distill transitions
into their most rarified essence. The central strategy in these instances is
to expunge words that hold merely syntactical places. The great ode was
the model for these techniques, as Young had shown. Recognizing and
censuring lyric strategies, Samuel Johnson insightfully if disapprovingly
commented: "Independent and unconnected sentiments flashing upon
the mind in quick succession, may, for a time, delight by their novelty, but
they differ from systematical reasoning, as single notes from harmony,
as glances of lightening from the radiance of the sun."[46] It was precisely
this quality, so Longinian in its sensibility, that nurtured the turn to the
lyric sensibility. For if lightning could intermittently glance on the long
reaches of epic and georgic poetry or in the strophic turns of a great ode,
how much more sublime if those glances could be isolated, extracted,
and made the substance of one brief but radiant verse. It was almost
inevitable, therefore, that critics should increasingly apply such techniques to minor lyric forms. John Ogilvie observed that lyric diction is
"adapted with great accuracy to the sentiment, as it is generally concise,
forcible, and expressive. Brevity of language ought indeed particularly to
characterise this species of the Ode, in which the Poet writes from immediate feeling, and is intensely animated by his subject."[47] Exemplifying
an increasing tendency to blur distinctions between the great ode and

minor lyric forms, John Pinkerton falls into vocabulary usually reserved for the former when discussing the poetics of the latter:

Above all, uncommon elegance in turns of language, and in transition, are so vital to this kind of lyric poetry in particular, that I will venture to say they constitute its very soul; a particular that none of our lyric writers, before Gray, at all attended to. His mode of expression is truly lyrical; and has a classic brevity and terseness, formerly unknown in English, save to Milton alone.[48]

Pinkerton's examples reveal the synaesthetic effect when phrases such as "liquid air of noon" are compressed to "liquid noon."

Hunt concludes his preface to *Bacchus in Tuscany* in the same vein: "out of one glass [the poet] can fetch as much treasure and surprize, as the Arabian did out of his nutshell that contained a tent for a[n] army."[49] He catches the idea more provocatively, however, in an addendum on the evils of opium in which he recollects an account

of the famous Old Man of the Mountain, or Chief of the people called Assassins, who used to intoxicate his followers with opium, and then transport them into a garden full of luxuries and beautiful women, where they thought they had been enjoying the Prophet's Paradise. But the old gentleman was superfluous; for the drug and a wooden bench are all that is necessary to supply a *bang-eater* in the streets of Constantinople with his paradise for the evening.[50]

Here, just as in poetry, the removal of every extraneous feature finds its impulse in the desire to produce intensity. The embowered paradise, that enclosed garden which is the prospect of Hunt's most precious lyrical moments, is achieved not in the transitive powers of an extraneous actor, but in heaped images produced variably in the space of a poem or opium dream.

TEMPORALITY

Johnson censures the practice of "heaping together" images among his strictures against writing in general, objecting that heaped images lack logical connection. As he recognized, however, heaped images are central to lyric technique, and he describes the "lightness and agility" of the ancients, who "passed from one sentiment to another without expressing the intermediate ideas." He insinuates that moderns, who ignore the constraints of ancient poetry, tread heavily where the ancients' "footsteps are scarcely to be traced."[51] The effect of heaped images is central to the presentation of temporality within lyric's narrow compass, as Keats's playful poem, "Fancy," indicates. There, as in a greenhouse, he draws together images from all seasons of the year:

> She will bring, in spite of frost,
> Beauties that the earth hath lost;
> She will bring thee, all together,
> All delights of summer weather;
> All buds and bells of May,
> From the dewy sward or thorny spray;
> All the heaped Autumn's wealth,
> With a still, mysterious stealth:
> She will mix these pleasures up
> Like three fit wines in a cup,
> And thou shalt quaff it.
>
> (lines 29–39)

Cameron clarifies the temporal concept that Keats presents as "heaped . . . wealth":

Although lyric verbs often record temporal change, they also collapse their progressions so that movement is not consecutive but is rather heaped or layered. This stacking up of movement, temporal forays cut off from linear progression and treated instead as if they were vertically additive . . . , is quite opposite to the way in which meaning "unfolds" in novels or in the drama. The least mimetic of all art forms, the lyric compresses rather than imitates life; it will withstand the outrage of any complexity for the sake of being able to present sequence as if it were a unity.[52]

Keats's Fancy, who compresses pleasure into the glassy hothouse of lyric, requires that her acolyte quaff seasonal progression. Inversely, in Hunt's parable, the mighty host that issues forth from the tiny nutshell must do so consecutively and in time. Contemplation of the nut's unfolding contents introduces temporality into a scene which, compressed within the circumference of the nut, would otherwise exist synchronously. Hunt's parable of the bangeater illuminates yet a different aspect of lyric temporality. In this case, the bangeater and his opium exist as a quintessence from which all extraneous elements have been husked away. The bangeater retreats within the moment of subjectivity in order to discover paradise. Coleridge captures such an opiate moment when he notes, "I should much wish, like the Indian Vishna, . . . to float about along an infinite ocean cradled in the flower of the Lotos, & wake once in a million years for a few minutes – just to know that I was going to sleep a million years more."[53] As these extraordinary images suggest, lyric, and especially minor lyric, operates on the principle of extraction from an external context and expansion from within, a point we are familiar with from Blake's augury, "a World in a Grain of Sand / And a Heaven in a Wild Flower."[54] Lyric does not plot time in the manner of epic poetry, which presumes a narrative, nor of georgic poetry, which follows roughly the seasons of the year or periods of the day; rather, lyric quaffs time, often through the expedient of extracting a moment from an unspoken context which it intensifies or essentializes.[55]

Sappho was the poet thought best to exemplify this aspect of lyricality, in part because her poetry was preserved in marvelous and elusive fragments that set the terms of temporal diffusion which the lyric moment purveys. A comment made by Young is especially illuminating since he not only suggests the sublime potential of lyric temporality, but also transmutes his own words into a metaphor for that principle:

Sapho's [sic] Muse like Lady _____ is passionately tender, and glowing; like Oyl set on fire, she is *soft*, and *warm*, in excess. *Sapho* has left us a few fragments only; Time has swallow'd the rest; But that little which remains like the remaining Jewel of *Cleopatra*, after the other was dissolv'd at her banquet, may be esteem'd (as was that Jewel) a sufficient Ornament for the Goddess of Beauty herself.[56]

In these few sentences, Young captures the essence of lyric, which produces excess through fragmentation. As Young's reference to an unnamed Lady suggests, this art is embodied and thereby thoroughly sensualized. Furthermore, excess and sensuality are especially palpable because "Time has swallow'd the rest." The fragments of Sappho's genius constitute the genius of the form that she consigned to the monstrous appetite of Time, which is itself transformed. The province of lyric thus becomes the isolated moment, the jewel esteemed because it has been extracted from its context as a fragment of a larger and lost ornament. Although Anna Seward's images are not as appetitive as Young's or Keats's, she captures the idea of the extracted moment when, commenting on two sonnets sent to her by an admirer, she invokes the common wisdom that the sonnet should focus on a single idea or emotion: "It is said to be an excellence in a sonnet, to have but one thought. These same sonnets appear to me as a couple of beautiful rings, – one a cluster of sapphires, amethysts, and diamonds, – the other, a large single brilliant, of the first water."[57] The "single brilliant," a gem extracted from a context, refers only to itself for its contracted yet sublime luster. What begins as a spatial metaphor becomes a metaphor for temporality. Time in such a form is conceived as both bounded and infinite.[58] Lyric space thus reorganizes sequentiality into simultaneity and discontinuity, a temporal order that is also figured in the formal technique of the sonnet's volta. Such images map space onto time, exposing lyric's power to control time and open internal space. The bounded, well-delineated space is the purchase from which eternity is perceived.

AUTHENTICITY

The three principles governing the contained space cited above – artifice, sublime affect, and temporality – would not have had the power to capture public attention in the last portion of the eighteenth century were it not for the impulse to invest such spaces with an indigenous tradition. As with any other representational form, it was necessary to submit the contained space to a process of authentication that would make it fully legitimate. Legitimation had not proved difficult in the case of the great ode, with its classical precedent in Pindar, its biblical model in the Psalms of David, and its status as an elevated form. Critics were pressed over the course of the century, however, to legitimate lyric form, especially lesser types, in terms of English precedents. In 1709 Henry Felton had defended English as a language intrinsically suitable for poetry. "Perhaps," he argues,

our tongue is not so musical to the Ear, nor so abundant in Multiplicity of Words; but its Strength is real, and its Words are therefore the more expressive: The peculiar Character of our Language is, that it is close, compact, and full . . . Let us not envy others, that they are more soft, diffused, and rarified; be it our Commendation to write as we pay in true Sterling; if we want Supplies, we had better revive *old* Words, than create *new* ones.[59]

Defenses of the rightness of English for a variety of poetic forms, especially the sonnet and lesser lyric, accumulated over the course of the century. While some argued that the rough Teutonic language ill-matched the mellifluousness of forms derived from Greek and Latin, it became possible in later decades of the century to take the position that the Saxon simplicity of English made it especially suitable to lyric utterance – or, as Coleridge would caustically and elliptically remark, "Pity that we dare not saxonize as boldly as our Forefathers by unfortunate preference latinized."[60] Just as the great ode was believed to be the aboriginal antecedent of poetry that arose spontaneously out of unaffected emotion, so lesser lyric, in its association with the lyrical qualities of the great ode, could be tied to a simplicity that was nevertheless artful. For much of the century classical poets were believed to be the unchallenged practitioners of this art. After the American War and especially during the Regency decade, however, the lesser lyrics of Chaucer, Spenser, Shakespeare, and Milton, which had fallen into disregard after the Restoration, provided an indigenous precedent. Like Felton, critics drew from these poets for a vernacular tradition. In 1815 Wordsworth looked to Spenser, "scarcely known beyond the limits of the British Isles"; to Shakespeare, by whom "[t]he People were delighted" and whose sonnets, omitted from eighteenth-century editions, he singles out for special praise; to Milton, with special commendation for his early "small poems."[61] Drawing on this enthusiasm for English diction and verse forms, Hunt writes, "All the merit I claim is that of having made an attempt to describe natural things in a language becoming them, and to do something towards the revival of what appears to me a proper English versification."[62] *The Story of Rimini*, which this comment prefaces, is a sequence of lyric moments – bright images, embowered recesses, a simple tale, and uncomplicated poetic language dominated by consciously English diction. Despite its fanciful Italianate subject, its debt to the revolution in ordinary language is profound. Keats suggests as much in a letter criticizing Wordsworth and Hunt, which testifies to the authenticating process in which they had been influential: "I don't mean to deny Wordsworth's grandeur & Hunt's merit," he writes to Reynolds, "but I mean to say we need not be teazed with grandeur & merit – when we can have them uncontaminated & unobtrusive. Let us have the old Poets, & robin Hood."[63] Keats's comment, like Wordsworth's and Hunt's, documents the legitimation of lyric practice in an English tradition which had become resoundingly nationalized. Similarly, the contained garden found a prototype in ancient English practice in the messuage or kitchen garden which was reconceived in the nineteenth century as the most English of all gardens – an historical interpretation so conducive to the English version of liberty after the Regency period that it found a venue in the invention of the tradition of the English cottage garden.

CHAPTER 8

The kitchen-garden manual

It is natural for a mind unacquainted with the powers of art, to suppose that professional assistance can effect little in laying out small
gardens or places of a few acres; but this is to infere, that nothing
can be beautiful that is not also extensive. Beauty or expression
depend no more on dimension than on expence, but are the result
of a combination of parts forming a whole, calculated by its fitness
and utility to gratify the mind, and by its effect to charm the eye.
The rules for the formation of such combinations in rural scenery,
constitute the art of laying out grounds; in the application of which,
to a small place, the artist will often meet with difficulties unknown
in places of greater extent; since these, by their magnitude, naturally possess a certain greatness of character; while a small spot is a
blank, depending for its effect wholly on the skill and ingenuity of
him who undertakes to fill it up.

J. C. Loudon
Hints on the Formation of Gardens and Pleasure Grounds (1812)

I wish to have a good walled garden.

James Boswell
Life of Johnson (1791)

In his *Spectator* series on the Pleasures of the Imagination (1712), Addison
promoted ideals not only for the unbounded prospect, but the kitchen
garden: "for besides the wholesome Luxury which that Place abounds
with," he says, "I have always thought a Kitchin-garden a more pleasant
Sight, than the finest Orangerie, or artificial Green-house." His description of this spot exhibits all the infectious delight that authors of garden
manuals characteristically display:

I love to see every thing in its Perfection, and am more pleased to survey my Rows
of Coleworts and Cabbages, with a thousand nameless Pot-herbs, springing up
in their full Fragrancy and Verdure, than to see the tender Plants of Foreign
Countries kept alive by artificial Heats, or withering in an Air and Soil that are
not adapted to them.[1]

Addison's idealization of the kitchen garden was aesthetic and patriotic rather than practical: he engagingly admits that he values his garden "more for being full of Blackbirds than Cherries, and very frankly give them Fruit for their Songs."[2] Read in hindsight through conventions solidified by manual writers in the eighteenth century, however, one can see that he captures principles governing contained space designed not primarily for beauty but for use. The aesthetic of this garden is achieved in heaping together discordant elements: cabbages mingle (licentiously, Johnson would surely remonstrate) with herbs and flowers, the fragrance and luxuriance of the latter forming bold transitions from the resolute practicality of the former, the whole sublimely profligate. And while Addison does not produce a sense of temporal expansion and diffusion as would later writers, he does link the kitchen garden to an indigenous, authentically English tradition. Rejecting the foreign exotics of the greenhouse, he finds beauty in the common produce of an ancient English tradition of gardening.

Addison's kitchen garden is subsumed by his pleasure garden. Visually eclectic, it fits the pattern of controlled havoc that permeates his aesthetic and would become the hallmark of the English cottage garden. Horticultural interest at this point in history was not yet destined, however, to fix upon the pleasures of such a confined space. Despite an evidently thriving practice of urban gardening, critical neglect of the small, decorative garden was so pronounced in the middle decades of the century that Kames could confidently say in his *Elements of Criticism* (1762), "gardening is now improved into a fine art; and when we talk of a garden without any epithet, a pleasure-garden, by way of eminence, is understood." Landscape aesthetic was so incontrovertibly associated with the great park that he could continue in the same breath, "The garden of Alcinoous, in modern language, was but a kitchen-garden."[3] Kames's comment reveals a disposition toward the open prospect that distorts the implications of his thought, for in fact, as we have seen, he deliberately theorizes the pleasures associated with utility, even claiming that "a kitchen-garden or an orchard is susceptible of intrinsic beauty."[4] He also implicitly endorses the idea that the small space cannot be designed simply as a miniature of the large park and espouses the common opinion of literary critics that a narrow form (such as the town garden or the sonnet) should express one emotion: a "small garden," he states, "comprehended at one view, ought to be confined to one expression; it may be gay, it may be sweet, it may be gloomy; but an attempt to mix these, would create a jumble of emotions not a little unpleasant."[5]

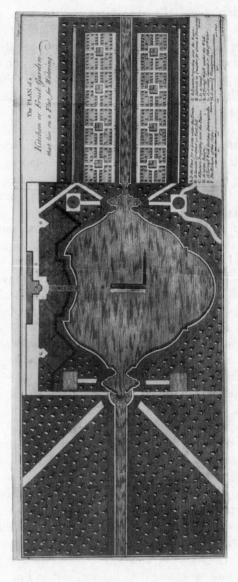

Figure 12 In this design, the garden is laid out like a park with fruit trees planted in quincunxes. The area on the right depicts "cabinets" enclosed within borders of evergreens and flowering shrubs. "Plan of a Kitchen or Fruit-Garden," Stephen Switzer, *Practical Fruit-Gardener* (1724), between pages 306/307, RB130938.

Contributing to the competing thoughts Kames expresses concerning the kitchen garden is his belief that "Those who depend for food on bodily labour, are totally void of taste; of such a taste at least as can be of use in the fine arts."[6] Given the association of the word labor with both art and toil, the depiction of labor in the kitchen garden was problematic, and authors of manuals walk a fine line between suggesting that the owner is merely a manual laborer and recommending garden labor as a redemptive art, healthful to persons of all social ranks, and perhaps most so to rulers – as Cincinnatus was to agriculture, so Diocletian was to the kitchen garden. The kitchen garden is thus widely depicted as a site in which labor is associated not merely with toil but with art. Not least, one of its products is beauty. Authors of garden manuals mine the possibilities of its delights by drawing lyric form and expression into the framework of didactic prose.

From the early years of concerted fruit and vegetable gardening, writers of garden manuals were intellectually engaged in plotting the intersection of garden design and productivity. Switzer, who popularized the open prospect, was also keenly interested in raising produce, expanding his efforts beyond *Ichnographia Rustica* (which includes agricultural advice) to *The Practical Fruit-Gardener* in 1724 and *The Practical Kitchen Gardiner* in 1727. The subtitle of the latter indicates its peculiar debt to the market gardens that sprang up from the grounds of London's neathouses in the seventeenth century and captures the relatively new English appetite for vegetables and fruit. Amplifying the possibilities inherent in the title, it reads,

Or, a new and entire system of directions for his employment in the melonry, kitchen-garden, and potagery, in the several seasons of the year. Being chiefly the observations of a person train'd up in the Neat-Houses or Kitchen-Gardens about London . . . To which is added, by way of supplement, the method of raising cucumbers and melons, mushrooms, borecole, broccoli, potatoes, and other curious and useful plants, as practised in France, Italy, Holland and Ireland . . . in a method never yet attempted.[7]

Glorious in its specificity, adamant about its originality, Switzer's subtitle suggests the riot of vegetables tempting the palates of urban dwellers. His plans for kitchen gardens, which combine the orchard with vegetables and herbs, closely resemble those for the wooded portions of his formal gardens with their carefully staggered trees, and suggest that the aesthetic he found so suitable for revealing prospects from the park also provided a rational system for ordering fruit trees and vegetables.

Although a critic of Switzer's overly conservative designs, Batty Langley also combined his dictates for pleasure gardens with an enthusiasm for fruits and vegetables. Not only did he write a treatise on the design of town gardens, but also *New Principles of Gardening* (1728). His garden manual is testimony to the porous boundaries between notions of design (which promote pleasure) and the cultivation of fruits and vegetables (which promote utility and profit) that existed throughout the century, but which have been obscured to modern readers by the flood of treatises describing great parks or, in the last quarter of the century, regulating the taste for the picturesque. In Langley's manual, principles of design indebted to Addison infiltrate and abet principles of cultivation. "The End and Design of a good Garden," he says, "is to be both profitable and delightful; wherein should be observed, that its Parts should be always presenting new Objects, which is a continual Entertainment to the Eye, and raises a Pleasure of the Imagination."[8] Unlike the town garden, Langley's ideal garden is a tumult of components, an

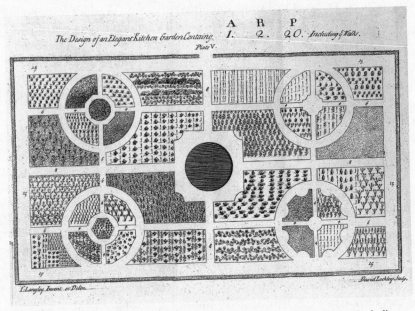

Figure 13 Langley's design incorporates parterres of stylized vegetables (including cabbages, asparagus, and cucumbers) and flowers. Walks around the parterres are highly formal, including four around circular, quartered parterres. "Design of an Elegant Kitchen Garden," Batty Langley, *New Principles of Gardening* (1728), fourth folded plan, RB 406726.

entire world in which pleasure and utility jostle together. Likewise, Philip Miller, editions of whose *Gardeners Dictionary* spanned the century, prefaced his encyclopedic manual with a series of rhetorical questions that advance the kitchen garden's claims for delight and use:

What can be more *delightful*, than in the *Spring-time*, to behold the Infant Plants putting forth their verdant Heads, from the Bosom of their fostering Mother the earth? In the *Summer Months*, the Flowers ting'd with a Variety of the most charming Dyes, seeming, as it were, to vie with each other, which shall most allure the Beholder's eye with their splendid Gaiety, and entertain the Nostrils with their enlivening Fragrancy? and in *Autumn*, to view the bending Boughs, as it were submissively offering their delicious Fruit, and courting the Gatherer's Acceptance?[9]

Finally, Repton, modifying ideals of the English landscape garden, espoused the kitchen-garden principle that beauty is one of the products of use. In his Red Book on Blenden Hall, excerpted in his *Fragments* (1816), he disparages the fashion for vast lawns and, more unexpectedly, for agriculture, advocating instead the produce of the garden:

It is surprising how tenacious every gentleman is of grass land, and with what reluctance he increases his garden, or contracts his farm; as if land were only given to produce hay, or to fatten cattle. He forgets the difference in value betwixt an acre of pasture and an acre of fruit garden; or the quantity of surface required to grow a load of hay or a load of currants, cauliflowers, or asparagus, with the prodigious difference in the value of each. For this reason, the Gardens of a Villa should be the principal object of attention; and at Blenden Hall, the ground betwixt the fruit trees in the orchard, which produces hay, small in quantity and bad in quality, might be turned to more advantage by planting currant bushes, or sowing garden crops; which even if sent to market, will yield five times the value of the feed for cattle. There is a clipt quickset-hedge, which forms the south boundary of the garden; this is as secure as a wall, and therefore worth preserving. I must also advise retaining the lofty wall to the west, as the greatest protection against the west winds: but a skreen of trees, or rather filberts and fruit trees, should be planted, to hide the wall from the approach, and to secure a slip on the outside, and make both sides of this lofty wall productive. If more walls be required, they may be added as described on the map, so as to shelter each other from blights; for it is not necessary that the garden should be a square area within four walls. A fruit garden may be so blended with flowers and vegetables, as to be interesting in all seasons; and the delight of a garden highly cultivated, and neatly kept, is amongst the purest pleasures which man can enjoy on earth.[10]

Although more restrained in his language than either Langley or Switzer and more designed in his writing and overt concerns than Miller, Repton encourages an Edenic ideal at the same time that he whets the appetite. Beauty and productivity are met together in a visual metaphor of taste which is both aesthetic and appetitive in the kind of garden which these writers believe is truly English. Treatises on parks, by contrast, even such lively and amusing histories as Walpole's "On Modern Gardening" or Sir William Chambers's outrageous *Dissertation on Oriental Gardening*, appealed almost exclusively to sight and the psychological effects of the categories of the landscape. The gustatory temptation proffered by garden manuals produces a didactic mode that joins the pleasures of the body with those of the mind. Artifice, sublime profusion, and temporal diffusion meet in a delimited, contrived space that, among its precedents, looks to British poetry.

In the kitchen-garden manual, lyric principles are separable only arbitrarily. To examine one is to open a window on each of the others. The role of the gardener demonstrates particularly well how interinvolved these principles become. It had been a conceit since Francis Bacon's essay "Of Gardens" that "God almighty first planted a Garden" and that Adam was therefore, in Philip Miller's words, a "Master Gardener."[11] The role of the gardener is therefore consistently defined as "recreative," even when the owner and actual gardener are not clearly distinguished. In calendar entries, especially, the gardener is portrayed as both regulator and genius of the garden. Under his tutelage, the garden is a product of artifice in which design, although everywhere apparent, produces sublime disorder. Thus Switzer, following Evelyn's translation of a garden manual by Jean de la Quintinye, director of the royal gardens in France, describes the garden in June as though it were a parterre in a park:

All the squares of the garden are now cover'd with green herbs, which compleats that natural tapestry with which the ground is or ought to be adorn'd; we gather, in all parts of the garden, such things as are ready and proper for it; and at the same time, with an agreeable profusion, distribute all those plants that are become so beautiful and accomplish'd as to fill up other places, which we now do, so that there hardly ever remains any part of space of our garden void.[12]

Purposeful art is essential to the kitchen garden's productivity since Nature is inadequate to these productions, either withdrawing her aid or hampered by England's "variable and uncertain" climate.[13] As Richard Bradley put it in his entry for December, "indeed 'tis now an ingenious Gardener will shew his Skill, in helping Nature by Artifice, to produce such Fruits and Herbs as she is not capable of bringing forth without very extraordinary Assistance."[14] Within the kitchen garden the effects of the

Fall, especially the withdrawal of Nature's *desire* to assist humankind, can be reversed by the diligence of an artful gardener, and the moral attributes which led to the Fall can be redefined through ingenuity.

Switzer reveals the intertwined discursive traditions of poetry and garden manuals when he compares the fruit garden to our original paradise, presuming reader familiarity with *Paradise Lost*:

And indeed, if Fruit-Trees had no other Advantage attending them than to look upon them, how pleasurable would *that* be? Since there is no flowering Shrub excells, if equals, that of a Peach or Apple-Tree in Bloom. The tender enammell'd Blossoms, verdant Foliage, with such a glorious Embroider of Festoons and Fruitages, wafting their Odours on every Blast of Wind: And at last bowing down their laden Branches, ready to yield their pregnant Offspring into the Hands of their laborious Planter and Owner. Indeed a well contriv'd Fruit-Garden is an Epitomy of Paradise it self, where the Mind of Man is in its highest Raptures, and where the Souls of the Virtuous enjoy the utmost Pleasures they are susceptible of in this sublunary State. For there the happy Planter is cooling and refreshing himself with *Scooping the brimming Stream* of those nectarous Juices, and the philosophizing thereon, as Mr. Milton has it in that excellent Description, Book iv.l.327. of *Paradise Lost*; also Mr. *Philips* very rapturously describes it in his Poem on *Cyder*.[15]

Switzer's passage begins with a rhetorical question that suggests that the purpose of the fruit tree is not its beauty; he nevertheless proceeds to the scene of productivity by describing the beauties of orchard flowers in the highly suggestive language of romance. In the most familiar terms of that tradition, Englished by Spenser, polished by Sidney, and domesticated by Milton, the language of the garden is both artful and sexual. Strewn with enameled blossoms and embroideries of flowers and fruits, its space is explicitly the product of contrivance, and for Switzer it follows that it is therefore the epitome of paradise. The scene is sensualized by images of tender blossoms, verdant foliage, wafting odors, pregnant offspring, mental raptures, and utmost pleasures assisted by brimming streams and nectarous juices. Significantly, Switzer substitutes *ingen*iousness for Genius, warden of Spenser's Garden of Adonis. In this garden one eats the fruit of the tree grown through the knowledge not only of good but of art.

The goal of artifice in garden manuals is to recreate within the narrow compass of garden walls or even narrower confines of the greenhouse a world replete not only with innumerable indigenous fruits and vegetables, but also with artificially cultivated produce of every latitude. This goal redirects the hope expressed by agriculturists that England would become the Garden of the World through a system of self-contained plots. In the latter view, England would radiate principles of agricultural practice onto less progressive nations. The image is expressive. In the kitchen garden, the garden is a world in itself. The image is centripetal, of attraction toward a well-defined center from "outlandish" regions. In the English garden the outlandish or exotic are "endenizon'd," to use Switzer's word, making foods safe and healthful which might otherwise poison the social body.[16] Switzer provides a graphic narrative of the process in his account of the virtue of peaches. Ancient authors, he tells us, claimed "that the *Persians* from whence they were first brought, and from whence they deriv'd their Names, dar'd not eat of them by Reason of their Malignity." He informs us that even now,

in *Persia* those Fruits have some malignant and over purgative Dispositions; but since those Trees were transported into *Egypt*, from thence replanted in *Italy*, and since that cultivated in *France* and other *European* Countries, they have lost those pernicious Qualities, and retain nothing but those that are purely purgative; and for this Virtue it is that they are esteem'd by the lovers of Health, who had rather eat a few Peaches in a Morning than take a Dose of Physick.

The progress of the peach through a series of countries presented as increasingly enlightened and, not incidentally, ever more proximate to England, filters the poisons out of the fruit. It thus reaches the apex of its healthful powers in England, where "the Art and Industry of our Gardeners have render'd [it] so commendable."[17] The kitchen garden parallels in efficacy an imperial foreign policy in which alien peoples, like pineapples and oranges, melons or peaches could, carefully managed, be productively nurtured and safely absorbed within a recognizably British order. This idea is, of course, expressed throughout Jago's history of Warwickshire, in which conquerors are always naturalized, or "endenizoned," in English soil. The wholly assimilated foreigner, like the ancient conquerors of England, *is* English, having improved the native stock, while becoming, in the process, improved. The authors of these treatises thus reveal the sense of native exuberance associated with bringing the world into the garden, as well as the concomitant fear so clearly expressed by Goldsmith and Cowper of the risks involved in the importation of foreignness within domestic boundaries.

The idea that the world could be brought into a garden is one filament in a web of discourses which support a view of England as Edenic because of its indigenous virtue and imperial success. The image is inseparable from Milton's depiction of Eden, in which we find "To all delight of human sense expos'd / In narrow room Nature's whole wealth, yea more, / A Heaven on Earth" (*Paradise Lost*, IV. 206–08). Rather than infinite space, heaven is emblematized as a walled garden planted with "All Trees of noblest kind for sight, smell, taste" (IV. 217). Its interior, like Blake's grain of sand, is larger than its exterior. But whereas Milton claimed that Eden was born from "not nice Art / . . . but Nature" (IV. 241–42), the kitchen garden required artifice of the highest sort, and celebrated contrivance in the production of its fruits and vegetables. In fact, while the idea of the world contained in the garden is given authority by its Miltonic precedent, it takes hold primarily because the arts of the garden assist and are assisted by commerce.

Productivity, created by compression and motivated by the systolic impetus of commerce, drove descriptions of the contents of the kitchen garden and greenhouse. These display profuse growth and productive power within a contracted and sharply defined area, and utility that generates extravagant beauty. For an audience schooled in didactic literature and still delighted by the georgic poem, garden manuals depicted the dizzying bounty of England's soil as both profligate and sensual. Within the contained space of the garden, one encounters sublime profusion. Although subject to the governance and ministration of a gardener, fruits and vegetables are depicted as lively, growing things:

Here we see artichokes rising as it were from the dead; and there asparagus piercing the ground in a thousand places; here we should with pleasure observe cabbage lettuces wind themselves up into round balls; and there multitudes of legumes and green herbs, so different in colour, and so various in their shape, that a contemplative man can't but stand still with wonder and amazement; these! these! are the innocent and natural dainties, where they present themselves and grow for the nourishment and delicious entertainment of human kind.[18]

As this passage indicates, a small garden is the site of vast productivity. Containing walls and divisions abet its productivity, since it bursts with pears from every wall, cabbages and artichokes from every parterre. Descriptions of great parks, thin by comparison, are psychologically rather than viscerally oriented. Garden calendars, especially, established a pattern of heaping fruits and vegetables in lists that by their sheer magnitude suggest the potentiality of English soil. Such lists, with dozens of varieties contained within specific kinds, like epic catalogues combine excess with purposeful order.

Manuals and calendars take such techniques to marvelous ends, conjuring images of Edenic gardens that provide endless fruit, vegetables, and flowers. Some lists jumble all three together, especially within the confines of the hothouse. Kidney beans, for example, rub shoulders with early dwarf peas, large lettuce plants and strawberries in John Abercrombie's *The Hot-House Gardener*; these give way to pots of mint, tarragon, and tansey, which are followed in abrupt transition by dwarf tulips, hyacinths, jonquils, irises, anemones, pinks, roses, hypericum, and Persian lilacs.[19] Other lists produce a slightly different effect by cataloguing many varieties of single fruits. A catalogue of the twenty different kinds of "oranges" available by 1769 does more than provide a rational typology of plants. The English names crowded together conjure exotic fruits through which the mythologized countries of their origins materialize. Gnarled picturesque plants are embedded between more elegant specimens; and the hothouse is pervaded by its own strangely vegetative form of eros. Thus are listed "common Seville, sweet Seville, China, curl-leaved, striped curled-leaved, horned, common striped, hermaphrodite, willow-leaved or Turkey, striped Turkey, Pumpelmoes or shaddock, double flowered, common dwarf or nutmeg, dwarf striped, dwarf China, childing, distorted, large-warted, starry, sweet rinded."[20] Similarly teeming lists of varietals appear for lemons, citrons, pears, peaches, nectarines, plums, and of course England's own fruit, the apple. Repeatedly inserted *etceteras* (*&c.*) in such lists suggest a plenitude which the manual can strive to call forth, but which it can only intimate. The form of the manual, constricted in space and time, must always fail to capture the profligacy of nature assisted by art. Rhetorically, the compression of proliferated images, evocation of taste, odor, and form, and radical turns from one kind of produce to another, generate an effect which, while predominantly didactic, is also decidedly lyrical. Use becomes the foundation of beauty, a subtle shift in the relationship between the two that William Mason captures in his Horatian georgic, "The English Garden," when he proclaims, "*Beauty* scorns to dwell / Where *Use* is exil'd."[21] Pure didacticism – useful discourse from which every extraneous element has been boiled away – reveals itself as essentially lyrical and sublime.

As in the minor lyric, therefore, expansion from within is the paradoxical metaphor for temporality within containment. The anchoring image is Eden: a place extracted from its larger context; a world compressed within the secure confines of the wall or hedge; a space within which fruit trees blossom and ripen and vegetables grow and reach maturity simultaneously. Blake provides a provocative figure of its collapsed time in his prologue to the third chapter of *Jerusalem*, with the epigraph:

I give you the end of a golden string,
Only wind it into a ball:
It will lead you in at Heavens gate,
Built in Jerusalems wall.[22]

Like Hunt's image of the army issuing out of a nutshell, Blake's image indicates that time can be perceived in two ways: sequentially, in which case it is a series of points disbursed along a length of unrolled string; or simultaneously and layered, as when the string is rolled into a ball so that the points over- and underlie each other. In the garden manual both times obtain: in the sequential structure which follows the seasons of the year and in the synchronic structure, the product of artifice. Time in the kitchen garden is a contained and rational infinitude, for by bringing the world into the garden, the gardener announces his power to control time by limiting space. The process of mapping time onto space is especially vivid in the garden calendar. In these pocket-sized manuals the progress of time has a logical yet arbitrary linearity. The author begins with January and ends with December. Reading from beginning to end, however, the reader becomes aware that the experience of gardeners is quite different, since they encounter time as ritually circular – January and December the neap tide in a seasonal cycle that achieves a plenum in July, August, and September. Even such a reordering of the calendar however does not catch the quality of continuous production effected through the agency of the hothouse. In the "glassary compartments" of this world-within-a-world, seedtime and harvest occur simultaneously: cucumbers are plucked in December; pineapples and oranges ripen as the first asparagus and salad are ready for the table.[23] In Cowper's metaphrase of this popular image,

The spiry myrtle with unwith'ring leaf
Shines there and flourishes. The golden boast
Of Portugal and western India there,
The ruddier orange and the paler lime
Peep through their polish'd foliage at the storm,
And seem to smile at what they need not fear.
Th' amomum there with intermingling flow'rs
And cherries hangs her twigs. Geranium boasts
Her crimson honors, and the spangled beau
Ficoides, glitters bright the winter long.
All plants of ev'ry leaf that can endure
The winter's frown if screen'd from his shrewd bite,
Live there and prosper. Those Ausonia claims,
Levantine regions these; th' Azores send

Their jessamine, her jessamine remote
Caffraia; foreigners from many lands
They form one social shade, as if convened
By magic summons of th' Orphean lyre.
(*The Task*, III. 570–87)

The greenhouse redeems time, preserving summer throughout winter's darkest months. In the kitchen garden, therefore, time is subject to artful design and mapped onto carefully functional forms, the end result of which is profuse beauty, sublime profligacy. Cowper's scene, like Switzer's narrative of the progress of the peach from Persia to England, leads inexorably to the parable that, deftly transplanted from their own fiery lands, "foreigners" may be absorbed safely into England's benign shades.

Although the kitchen garden was supplied with its own historic antecedent in the ancient English messuage, garden manuals before the eighteenth century do not draw on this English heritage. Rather, authors locate gardening precedent in Eden, as Bacon's too-frequently quoted beginning to "Of Gardens" suggests. Versions of his opening sally, "God Almighty first planted a garden," provide the starting point for many manuals, and become a voluntary for garden histories. Later, however, even when authors use Bacon as their starting point, emphasis shifts from the idea that gardening is innocent, healthful, profitable, and delightful because of its Edenic antecedent, to proofs that the English are particularly adept at the art.[24] Thus, in the first release of his *Gardeners Dictionary* (1724), Philip Miller could admit, "It is true the *Art* never arrived to any considerable *Pitch* in *England*, till within about thirty Years last past," but go on to extol the advances made by patrons of the art:

But of late years many *Persons* of Fortune and Ingenuity have bent their Genius to the Study of it, and by that *Means* have not only set the professed *Gardeners* an Example, but also have generously given Encouragement to *Artists* to labour to trace Nature more closely in the *Propagation* of *Vegetables*, either *Trees, Plants, Flowers, Fruits*, &c. both for *Profit* and *Pleasure*, for *Use* and *Ornament*; so that of late Years, to their Praise be it spoken, it has been highly improved and brought to a considerable *Pitch*.[25]

There is an incipient sense of the national importance of the horticultural endeavor in this statement, particularly since Miller proceeds to anoint "Persons of Fortune and Ingenuity" as "*Patriots* of horticulture" – a clear rejoinder to Evelyn's canonization of "Paradisean and Hortulan saints" the century before.[26] Miller's 1724 preface does not, however, address a uniquely English tradition. As the century progressed, national endeavor was linked to English history in order to emphasize the innate productivity of the *English* kitchen garden and its distinctive attributes. In the process, the link to the biblical narrative of Eden became important primarily because England's soil offered a redemptive site in which the effects of the Fall could be reversed. By 1829 William Cobbett could retort, "I will not, with Lord Bacon, praise pursuits like these, because 'God Almighty first planted a garden;' nor with Cowley, because 'a Garden is like Heaven;' nor with Addison, because a 'Garden was the habitation of our first parents before their fall;'"[27] In the intervening years there grew a conviction, somewhat inflated, that kitchen and fruit gardens brought values of England's ancient past into the present. The messuage, a modern version of which would be nostalgically depicted in Constable's painting of his father's kitchen garden in 1815, fed into a conservative aesthetic in which private property, independence, and the productive leisure of ordinary people who were the frugal, hardworking, modern counterparts of Saxon yeomen were given an indigenously English cast.

The nationalist tendency of garden manuals is visualized in the evolving editions of Philip Miller's *Gardeners Dictionary*. The modest 1724 octavo set gave way in 1731 to a large folio edition to which Miller appended a belated second volume in 1740. The first volume in this edition is handsomely introduced by a frontispiece depicting a garden designed similarly to those recommended by Switzer in his kitchen- and fruit-garden treatises. (See figure 12.) In one of the enclosures stands a Palladian conservatory fronted by potted orange trees. The rest of the park is partitioned into orchard plots and a kitchen garden, while the background is a wilderness of trees arranged in quincunxes. A broad canal bisects the plate from fore to background. Overhead, clouds support a pantheon of deities. This frontispiece was reprinted through the fifth edition of 1748. In the sixth edition of 1752, however, the frontispiece was dramatically changed. The plate of the country estate was replaced by a highly emblematic scene. In the center sits Britannia crowned with oak leaves and sitting beneath an oak tree holding the scepter of dominion in the crook of her left arm, while a shield embossed with the crosses of St. George and St. Andrew, the symbol of union between England and Scotland, leans against her left side. A large folio volume lies open leaning on another, giving a distinct impression of the enormous folio edition into which Miller's own dictionary had expanded. A hale older man presents Britannia with a cornucopia overflowing with hothouse fruits. In the shade of the oak tree a female figure, at the apex of a triangle completed

Figure 14 The 1731 frontispiece depicts a formal park divided into several different gardens, including an orchard, an orangery, and a kitchen garden. In the background a wilderness of trees is arranged in quincunxes. Frontispiece, Philip Miller, *Gardeners Dictionary* (1731), RB 27293.

Figure 15 The frontispiece chosen to replace that of 1731 depicts Britannia seated under an oak tree surrounded by Science, Industry, and Nature. Frontispiece, Philip Miller, *Gardeners Dictionary* (1752), Private Collection.

by the old man and Britannia, holds a large thermometer. Meanwhile another female figure, to the right of Britannia with her back to the viewer and her face turned, withholds a half-hidden cornucopia almost as long as her body, but containing only a scanty tribute. Implements of the gardener's trade litter the scene: watering can, spade, the woven basket used for cucumber and melon transplants, pruning hook and knife, wheelbarrow, and roller for keeping paths smooth and well-tamped. An elegant conservatory in the Palladian style with an attached greenhouse forms a distinctive architectural sidescreen to the left. A verse caption added to later editions helps to identify the cast of characters:

> What NATURE sparing gives, or half denies –
> See! healthfull INDUSTRY at large supplies –
> See! in BRITANNIA's Lap profusely pours –
> While heaven-born SCIENCE swells th' increasing Stores.

The emblematic scene would have been completely legible to an audience schooled by political cartoons, handbills, and illustrated moral pamphlets. Britannia, unifying the island of Britain, is paid willing tribute not by Nature, but by Industry with the support of Science. Rather than the homely georgic produce of the field which Nature half-denies, he offers the exotic harvest of the hothouse, the product of art and ingenuity.

The change in Miller's frontispieces illustrates the increasing sense of nationalistic purpose that the horticultural garden would come to affirm. Britannia recalls an ancient English past at the same time that she confirms the solidity of a British present within the beautifully delineated borders of her island. She replaces gods and goddesses, thereby providing a garden narrative that looks neither to Eden nor to the classics for its authenticity, but to England itself. Furthermore, the central grouping of figures is brought close to the viewer. Whereas in the first frontispiece, the classical gods dominate the scene, looking down on the minuscule inhabitants of the park, in the second, the emblematic figures *are* the garden's inhabitants, and bring its workings into proximity with the viewer. Rather than drawing the eye through the stately park to the distant prospect that surrounds it, Miller's second frontispiece focuses on the lively plenum of a narrow space enclosed by a greenhouse so high on one side and foliage so thick at the rear, that the prospect is completely excluded. The viewer stands outside the frame and rather than looking outward and down, occupies the same plane as the roller, the wheelbarrow, and the woven basket, looking inward and slightly upward at the figures acting out this emblematic drama. This is a scene that prophesies the turn to the enclosed site. It focuses not on the wider horizon, but on a space replete with the products of its own artifice.

THE THEMATICS OF SEXUALITY

A key reason for the deep suspicion of minor lyric that surfaces in literary criticism in the eighteenth century is the connection it asserts between artifice and sexuality. Following in the tradition of Petrarch and the ancients, the province of lyric was defined as love and seduction (or perhaps a good bout at the pub, which carried its own bawdy connotations). The rich imagery of lyric poetry provided a precedent for linking verbal sensuousness with sensuality, so that the one, etymologically linked to the senses, achieves intelligibility as a result of its close homonymic and semantic relationship with the other, linked to eros.[28] As appropriations of phraseology from lyric verse prove, these discourses present a familiar body of literature which provided manuals on the enclosed, luxurious space of the kitchen garden with a strong sexual sensibility. At the same time, the confluence of the two bodies of literature succeed in making sexuality in the garden appear to be inherent. This occurs in part simply because, as in lyric poetry, the *sensuous* language of garden manuals, which heaps the produce of the soil in a confined space, produces a distinctly *sensual* import. Deploring the adoption by essayists of lyric compression and disjunction that produced this effect, Johnson writes,

A writer of later times has, by the vivacity of his essays, reconciled mankind to the same licentiousness in short dissertations; and he therefore who wants skill to form a plan, or diligence to pursue it, needs only entitle his performance an essay, to acquire the right of heaping together the collections of half his life, without order, coherence, or propriety.[29]

Although the "licentiousness" to which Johnson refers is more strictly formal than moral, the word clearly implies that incontinence in compositional technique is homologous with sexual incontinence.

Despite Milton's powerful reinvention of the sonnet along political and meditative themes, the more conventional association between minor lyric and seduction remained strong during the eighteenth century. Thus, while shorter forms may have been thought more congenial to female intellectual capacities than georgic, the great ode, or epic, such subject matter could hardly recommend lyric poetry in an age when the definition of femininity was being moored to a maternal, nominally nonsexual image. Charlotte Smith's elegiac and domestic focus in her sonnets helped her audience to imagine different themes for the form, especially the social expectation that educated women reproduce normative family relationships. Smith thus helped to turn the sonnet from a Petrarchan semantics of unrequitable desire toward the more bitter loss of the paternal home. Second only to the loss of her father is that of her daughter through childbirth. The normative structure of desire that her sonnets invoke is thus familial and reproductive rather than erotic. The contained space, however, remained heavily freighted with erotic associations. Epic episodes, as in Spenser's Bower of Bliss, and conventional lyric contents form part of a discursive tradition in which contained spaces are both sexualized and feminized – a tradition that was cemented by Milton's erotic depiction of both Eden and Eve in *Paradise Lost.* This idea of the contained space obtained across the literary spectrum. As Johnson feared, it was not limited to minor lyric forms or even the great ode, but spilled over into expository forms such as the essay, and even the more empirical diction of the garden manual. The sexualization of this horticultural site intensified through the eighteenth century in part due to a strong tradition linking enclosed sites to female sexuality that provided a cultural memory for such an identification. The increasing tendency over the course of the eighteenth century to revalue women's sexuality as fundamentally maternal rather than erotic may seem alien to this impulse, yet the two are allied. The wholesale adoption of Linnaeus's sexual system of botanical classification in the late 1750s, which made requisite an increasingly specific sexual language in garden manuals, focused attention in the case of plants as that of women on reproductive function, and assisted in the clarification of sexual behavior while naturalizing distinctions between the sexes.[30] Though the Linnaean system may seem to be an adventitious factor in the history of the eros of contained space, this is not the case. In a century dazzled by classification schemes, Linnaeus's botanical taxonomy was one of several available systems. Botanists and horticulturists adopted it over other possibilities primarily, they argued, because of the simplicity of the method. This should not obscure the fact, however, that the sexual system was successful not merely because it was simple to apply, but because it seemed common-sensical, feeding into an already existing notion that garden space was erotic while confirming a developing logic of human sexual difference that focused on maternity and productivity.

In theory, for a sexual plant taxonomy to function scientifically, it should filter out aspects of sexuality, such as desire, that are not reproductive. But while Linnaeus made some attempt to isolate reproduction from other aspects of sexuality, he could not resist analogies to human sexual behavior that brought desire within the compass of the scientific discussion of reproduction.[31] Thus while the "sexual" classification system is manifestly about reproduction, it was impossible to isolate reproduction in plants as a discrete and purely empirical aspect of sexuality. As the connotative language of garden manuals demonstrates, sexuality cannot be contained by the limiting concept of reproduction, but is inevitably caught in the larger realm of the erotic. Each instruction for how to produce fruits and vegetables in such a system has the potential to bring with it other meanings. This penchant was abetted by the lyrical tendency in garden manuals to describe plants as active: twining, embracing, creeping, springing, catching hold of, clasping. So analogies between people and plants that energized the erotic quality of the garden supported emerging notions of sexual relations among people, providing visual images that quietly reified the continuities between sex, gender, and desire.

The discourse of sexuality in the botanical realm thus converged in the eighteenth century with other discursive practices that mutually supported each other and rationalized public understanding of the kitchen garden, manuals for which promoted the new classification method while paving the way for the representational status of the contained space. The sexual tradition in plant classification handed down from earlier centuries, the science of human reproduction brought to a fore the previous century by William Harvey, and the erotic impulse in lyrical verse, which authors of garden manuals delight in quoting, together provided an analogical framework within which reproduction could be understood. Even economic assumptions gendered labor in the garden, thus contributing to the sexual framework of reproduction. Richard Weston's treatises, geared toward trade, illustrate the material gendering of garden labor. He advocated that in order to secure maximum profits from the family garden, women and their daughters were ideally suited as nurturers of silk worms, while children (with whom women were typically classified) could tend the flowers grown for the urban market.[32]

Myths also contributed. Samuel Collins concluded his manual, *Paradise Retriev'd* (1717), with the prurient claim that for the protection of melon beds,

Ladies should not be invited to this Place, lest Nature should at that time prove in it's Venereall discharge, which has not only an Imaginary, but so real an Influence on Mellons newly set, that they will most of them drop off: I have found the consequence of this so fatal, that for many years last past (tho' they have been welcome to walk the rest of the Garden) I have been oblig'd at that time of fruiting, to deny their entrance into the Mellonry.[33]

Collins's superstition may seem fantastic, but had an ancient precedent in garden literature. Thomas Hyll advertized the idea in his discussion of cucumbers and gourds in 1563 and embroidered the notion over successive editions of his kitchen-garden manual, citing his authorities as the Roman treatise writers, Columella and Florentius.[34] Conventional assumptions concerning the inherent eros of near-Eastern fruits gave the idea validity, as Marvell's familiar poem, "The Garden," illustrates. The sensual fifth verse reads:

> What wond'rous Life in this I lead!
> Ripe Apples drop about my head;
> The Luscious Clusters of the Vine
> Upon my Mouth do crush their Wine;
> The Nectaren, and curious Peach,
> Into my hands themselves do reach;
> Stumbling on Melons, as I pass,
> Insnar'd with Flow'rs, I fall on Grass.
>   (lines 33–40)[35]

In Marvell's version of this idea the apple, like the more erotic Persian fruits, is willingly fallen. Thus while Collins's conjecture was at worst rejected as an outright piece of villainy and at best quizzically received, response to it succeeded in circulating a titillating and familiar notion.[36] In recounting such a superstition, regardless of motive, gardeners and botanists open a window on a tradition in which ties between the fertility of the kitchen garden and sexuality by way of the female body were mythicized. Linnaeus's sexual system of classification reinforced the inherent sexuality in the garden that these discourses foster.

Linnaeus's sexual system achieved popular currency in England in part through Erasmus Darwin's *Loves of the Plants*, published in 1789. This four-book, quasi-georgic poem exemplifies the sexual assumptions I have outlined above, working out the logical conclusions of the Linnaean system as a presentation of gendered relationships. Though the poem does not truly illustrate "the lascivious delight of a male-centered sexual fantasy,"[37] as has been charged, it mischievously exposes the sexual analogies between humans and plants that are such an important part of Linnaeus's premise. Thus, tongue-in-cheek, Darwin succeeds in making the continuities between sex, gender, and desire intelligible. His humanized accounts of gendered relationships in the plant world, even when they may seem perverse according to Western cultural practice, all support a sexual system in which the male is active and dominant, the female is passive and receptive, domesticity is central, and heterosexuality is relentless. This is reinforced by the fact that the regulative structure of the system which Darwin's poem exposes is homosocial: all plants are defined by the male stamen if possible, especially in its relation to other

Figure 16 "Flora at Play with Cupid," Frontispiece, Erasmus Darwin, *The Loves of the Plants* (1789), *The Botanic Garden*, vol. II, RB 387423.

stamens. The pistils (female) are defined only in relation to the male reproductive components. Contrary to what the objections of some of his critics may imply, Darwin also maintains cultural codes for chaste behavior, as the titillating prospect of a description for Cerea, a flower characterized by twenty male components and one female, proves. In the face of obvious and more stimulating possibilities, Cerea is described as a virtuous damsel surrounded by lovesick but well-behaved suitors:

> In crowds around thee gaze the admiring swains,
> And guard in silence the enchanted plains;
> Drop the still tear, or breathe the impassion'd sigh,
> And drink inebriate rapture from thine eye.
> (*Loves of the Plants*, IV. 29–32.)[38]

Other flowers with arrangements of stamens and pistils posing equally inventive possibilities are turned into sisters and brothers or, as in the case of Cyclamen, a maternal figure watching over her brood of sons. Nevertheless, it is significant that consistent with Linnaeus's system, the poem begins with Canna (*Monandria monogynia*), one male, one female. "The virtuous Pair" (I. 41) thus forms the implicit standard against which all other flowers can be construed as variants. Somewhat perplexingly, and with droll results, Darwin never explains how generation takes place among his masses of siblings, virtuous maids, and well-behaved suitors.

Anna Seward defended Darwin's compositions at least in part as a matter of local patriotism; nevertheless, her points regarding the sexual content of the poem are well taken. In the cause of both his *Temple of Nature* and *The Loves of the Plants*, she protests that

Young women who could be endangered by such descriptions, must have a temperament so unfortunately combustible as to render it unsafe to trust them with the writings of our best poets, whenever love is the theme. Paradise Lost presents more highly-coloured scenes than any which pass in the floral harems; so does the Song of Solomon, in which the language and images are infinitely more luxurious than the muse of botany ever exhibits.[39]

Seward's remark on the erotic language of *Paradise Lost* and *Song of Solomon* is shrewd. More to the point, however, each of her examples reinforces cultural sexual norms. Darwin's *Loves of the Plants*, in which even sexually anomalous orders such as the cryptogams are ingeniously brought under the standard of compulsory heterosexuality and appropriate female behavior, is equally assiduous. Indeed, one could argue that bowdlerizers of the Linnaean system were unsuccessful in their efforts to purge it of its erotic connotations not merely because their versions were less scientifically astute, but because the sexual relationships which Darwin so colorfully brought to life *were* what made the system commonsensical. As Darwin amply reveals, Linnaeus provided a unified system in which sex is oppositional and desire is natural because it arises out of that opposition. The gender roles that were being so closely delineated throughout the last four decades of the century were thus overwhelmingly confirmed in his poem.[40]

This is nowhere more apparent than in evolving descriptions in kitchen-garden manuals for methods of growing cucumbers, a salad vegetable that had been an object of horticultural diversification since at least the sixteenth century despite the ill humor ascribed to its coolness and dampness. Descriptions of cucumbers and instructions for growing them reveal the transformation of botanical classification from morphology to reproduction, which provided a means of classifying plants by clearly delineated sexual functions. In the 1720s and early 1730s, prior to the introduction of the Linnaean system, Richard Bradley, Regius Professor of Botany at Oxford, was the prime English apologist for a theory of plant sexuality. Fruits and vegetables, in his view, were sexual organisms, a thought that he stoutly and falsely claimed "is entirely new, and seems reasonable."[41] Bradley's treatises are also, however, an example of the way empirical language gives license to erotic diction. Thus he claims concerning the function of bees in fertilizing flowers,

Now, that the *Farina Foecundus* or *Male Dust* has a Magnetick Virtue, is evident; for it is that only which gather and lodge in the Cavities of their hind Legs to make their *Wax* with; and it is well known, that Wax, when it is warm, will attract to it any light Body. But again, if the Particles of this *Powder* should be required by Nature to pass into the Ovaries of the Plant, and even into the several *Eggs* or *Seeds* there contain'd, we may easily perceive, if we split the *Pistillum* of a *Flower*, that Nature has provided a sufficient Passage for it into the *Uterus*.[42]

While this description may seem almost clinical to a modern reader, Bradley's diction was ridiculed by contemporary gardeners as overly sensual and anthropomorphized.[43] Bradley's sexual theory could be espoused, however, without an offensive sensualizing of the process of plant reproduction, as Philip Miller's descriptions of cucumbers demonstrated in the early editions of his *Gardeners Dictionary*. The restrained language of this gardener who was viewed as the foremost horticultural expert of his day provided a corrective to Bradley's human analogies. While adopting Bradley's theory of plant generation, Miller ignored his erotic implications in the first edition of *The Gardeners Dictionary* (1724),

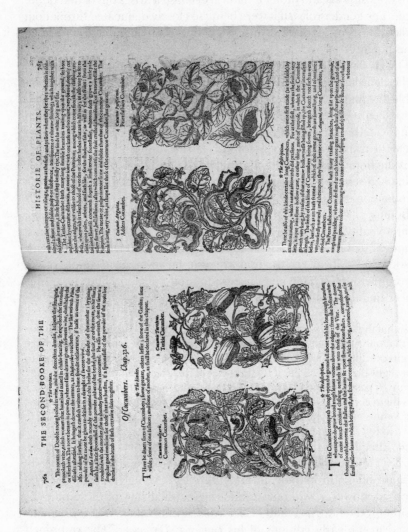

Figure 17 Four of the varieties of cucumbers already available in the sixteenth century. John Gerarde, *Herball* (1597), pages 762 and 763, RB 61079.

simply distinguishing the flowers as male or barren and female or fruiting. Successive editions between 1731 and the posthumous edition of 1807, however, follow a significant pattern.[44] First, Miller adds "Characters" – precise botanical descriptions – to each entry. The Character is set off as a separate, italicized paragraph at the beginning of the entry, thus clearly distinguishing it from instructions for growing and cultivating the plants. In the first folio editions the Characters of cucumbers are mildly sexual. For example, in the edition of 1731 under *Cucumis* we find:

It hath a Flower consisting of one single leaf, which is Bell-shap'd, and expanded towards the Top, and cut into many Segments, of which some are Male or Barren, having no Embryo, but only a large Style in the Middle, which is charg'd with the Farina; others are Female or Fruitful, being fasten'd to an Embryo, which is afterwards changed into a fleshy Fruit for the most part oblong, and turbinated, which is divided into three or four Cells inclosing many oblong Seeds.

By the seventh edition of 1759, however, when Miller reluctantly gave in to pressure to adopt Linnaeus's sexual taxonomy, he had tightened the Characters into an increasingly restrained and scientific diction. In the four lavishly illustrated folio volumes of the final, posthumous edition the Character of the cucumber has been brought completely under the rule of science. Its sexual properties have been concealed in a diction that succeeds in providing full authority for the sexuality of plants while removing all traces of an erotic and lyrical language. The description, too long to reproduce in its entirety, is now organized as a series of clipped phrases, replete with abbreviations and Latin terms. The section on male blossoms alone reads:

*Male flowers.
Cal. Perianth one-leafed, bell-shaped, the margin terminated by five subulate teeth.
Cor. five-parted, growing to the calyx, bell-shaped: divisions ovate, veiny-wrinkled.
Stam. Filaments three, very short, inserted into the calyx, converging, of which two are bifid at the tip. The anthers are lines creeping upwards and downwards, outwardly adnate.
Receptacle three-cornered, truncated, in the centre of the flower.[45]

The instructions for tending cucumbers in successive editions between 1724 and 1807 follow an inverse pattern. Beginning in 1724, Miller, by comparison to Bradley, had allowed barely a hint of sexual language but, with his adoption of the Linnaean system in the seventh edition, he overtly eroticizes the instructions:

When the Fruit appears upon the Plants, there will also appear many male Flowers on different Parts of the Plant, these may at first Sight be distinguished; for the female Flowers have the young Fruit situated under the Flowers, but the male have none, but these have three Stamina in their Center with their Summits which are loaded with a golden Powder, this is designed to impregnate the female Flowers; and when the Plants are fully exposed to the open Air, the soft Breezes of Wind convey this Farina or male Powder from the male to the female Flowers, but in the Frames, where the Air is frequently too much excluded at this Season, the Fruit often drops off for Want of it: And I have often observed that Bees that have crept into the Frames when the Glasses have been raised to admit the Air, have supplied the Want of those gentle Breezes of Wind; by carrying the Farina of the male Flowers on their hind Legs into the female Flowers, where a sufficient Quantity of it has been left to impregnate them. For as the Bees make their Wax of the Farina or male Powder of Flowers, so they search all the Flowers indifferently to find it; and I have observed them come out of some Flowers with their hind Legs loaded with it, and going immediately into other Flowers which have none, they have scattered a sufficient Quantity of this Farina about the Style of the female Flowers to impregnate and render them prolifick. These Insects have taught the Gardeners a Method to supply the Want of free Air, which is so necessary for the Performance of this in the natural Way; this is done by carefully gathering the male Flowers, at the Time when this Farina is fully formed, and carrying them to the female Flowers, turning them down over them, and with the Nail of one Finger gently striking the Outside of the male, so as to cause the Powder on the Summits to scatter into the female Flowers, and this is found to be sufficient to impregnate them, so that by practising this Method, the Gardeners have now arrived at a much greater Certainty than formerly to procure an early Crop of Cucumbers and Melons, and by this Method the new Varieties of Flowers from Seeds, which is done by the mixing of the Farina of different Flowers into each other.[46]

In this edition, Miller's bees have become promiscuous fellows, creeping into the cucumber's greenhouse home with their tribute carried on their hind legs to perform the fructifying office when breezes are denied. Furthermore, rather than merely perform their office, they instruct the gardener in his art. Augmenting the erotic content, the gardener's finger becomes the means by which the male flower's potency can be restored. The lyricism of the instructions has also deepened. Golden powder, soft breezes, and scattering pollen provide rich mental images, while activity itself has been theatricalized. The breezes, the bees, and the gardener all play a part in a delightful performance, the end result of which is fruition. Notably, Miller repeats Bradley's conclusion, now fortified by Linnaeus's work, that it is thus that the astonishing variety of vegetables or fruits within a given kind has been produced.

In this context, Cowper's metaphrase of Miller's instructions in the third book of *The Task* is instructive. Cowper preserves Miller's instructions while sanitizing them of their erotic content. His version, while retaining the vivid, active language of kitchen garden manuals, is nevertheless chaste. On the cultivation of his beloved cucumbers he merely comments,

> These have their sexes, and when summer shines
> The bee transports the fertilizing meal
> From flow'r to flow'r, and ev'n the breathing air
> Wafts the rich prize to its appointed use.
> Not so when winter scowls. Assistant art
> Then acts in nature's office, brings to pass
> The glad espousals and insures the crop.
>
> (*The Task*, III. 537–43)

Cowper's reluctance to displace the sexual into the erotic suggests the options that authors of kitchen-garden manuals were free to choose or reject. Indeed, in contrast to Cowper, Abercrombie elected to increase the erotic effect of Miller's instructions. Taking full advantage of the gardener's role in assisting the cucumber to fruition, he advises,

Likewise, when the plants are in blossom take care to impregnate the female flower with the *anthera* of the male, which you will pluck for that purpose the same day that both flowers first expand; pulling away the flower, leaf or petal of the male blossom, then holding the shank betwixt the finger and thumb, introduce the anthera into the center of the female flower, touching the stigmata thereof, twirl it about so as to leave some of the male powder upon the female organ, then throw it away, this completes the business, renders the flowers fertile, and the fruit sets freely.[47]

Significantly, by 1807 the role of the gardener in reproducing cucumbers had been qualified. The editor of the posthumous edition of Miller's *Gardeners Dictionary*, Thomas Martyn, notes, "it is probably less necessary to carry the males to [the female flowers], as practised by some gardeners, though nature having provided male flowers, it is most likely that the pollen in the anthers of the others is frequently defective."[48] Despite his reservations, however, he leaves intact the lyric residue of Miller's instructions, thus, as in the case of georgic error, indicating the power of convention to define practice even in the face of new data: soft breezes still carry the golden, inseminating powder to receptive female flowers; in their absence, the promiscuous bee fulfills his potentizing office; and, more reliably, despite Martyn's expressed reservations, the gardener supplies what the greenhouse wants, bringing the male flower to the female and facilitating the act of impregnation with a gentle tap of his finger. The telos of the reproductive system is revealed in the cucumber's prolific varieties, which, we are told, now includes the "gourd, globe cucumber, round prickly-fruited cucumber, African cucumber, acute-angled cucumber, common or musk melon, apple-shaped cucumber, hairy cucumber, common cucumber, serpent cucumber or melon, flex-uose cucumber or melon." The category of common cucumber alone may be distinguished by eight different sub-species.

The inverse relationship between the increasing restraint of the *Dictionary*'s Characters and intensifying sensual and lyric language in the instructions of successive editions has a subtle logic. The Linnaean tax-onomy, which systematized and regulated botany over the course of the eighteenth century, brought scientific legitimation to the sexual organiza-tion of plants. Darwin's theatricalization of plant sexuality and Linnaeus's anthropomorphisms simultaneously sanctioned broad parallels between plant and human sexuality. Thus botany achieved explanatory power in the realm of human behavior, even as human behavior was used to illuminate the secret life of plants. Overt sexual parallels were eventu-ally, however, erased. A neutral, elisionary scientific language naturalized these parallels even as it cloaked the sexual and erotic vocabulary that had given them power in the first place. Botany thus helped to legitimate emerging sexual distinctions as a part of the nature of things, not least since it was used as a tool in the education of girls. In the pursuit of taxonomy, notions of sexuality that formed the core of this system were absorbed along with the scientific language that sanitized them. The sex-ualization and desexualization of the cucumber in the *Gardeners Dictionary* contributed to the public logic in which women in the eighteenth century were transformed from problematically sexual beings, whose reproduc-tive capacities were a part of their erotic capacities, into maternal beings. The regulatory principle of the kitchen garden that plants be brought to fruit epitomized the transformation in the cultural realm whereby women were brought under the rule of maternity, with its suppressed erotic connotations. The kitchen garden thus provides a component of a larger signifying system that was used to elaborate normative human distinctions.

Linnaeus's sexual classification of plants may seem to have taken us far from John Abercrombie's "glassary compartments" teeming with veg-etables, flowers, and fruits, and even further from the literary world of the lesser lyric. Yet Abercrombie's marvelously lyrical phrase epitomizes the enigmatic relationship between private sentiment and public domain which lyric verse presumes. Patricia Fumerton has analyzed the relationship between private and public in the renaissance sonnet. She concludes, "However much we may need to define the concepts as separate (or envision a culture *all* one or the other), 'private' and 'public' can only be conceived as a split unity divided along a constantly resewn seam that can never be wholly closed or absolutely parted."[49] The discourse of the kitchen garden, which finds its distillation in the hothouse or greenhouse, reveals just this tenuousness. While the walls of the greenhouse are transparent for the modern scientific purpose of exposing plants to heat and sunlight, they also, in the most ancient purposes of the wall, command an exclusionary function. As the word "compartment" suggests, the greenhouse is a world set apart that functions according to its own laws. It connects to the discourse of lyric and of the female body in this salient way, providing the illusion of openness when it is, in actuality, compartmentalized and guarded. Like the female body, which was enlightened as science revealed its reproductive depths, yet more guarded as it was set apart by the ideology of domesticity, the kitchen garden revealed its horticultural contents while presenting itself as the most guarded of topographical spaces. In the historically specific circumstances of the late eighteenth century, compartmentalization and guardedness became linked, naturally it would seem, to productivity. The discourses of the female body and the kitchen garden that I have documented here thus epitomize the problem of lyric verse with its riddle of private sentiment that nevertheless assumes productivity in that it demands to be published. As this riddle affirms, despite the social and political attractions of the unbounded view which governed the aesthetic of landscapes and poetic forms for the majority of the eighteenth century, shifts in public perception made requisite a realignment between productivity and enclosure along a continuum of aesthetic, functional, and sexual forms.

CHAPTER 9

The poetics of the bower: Keats, Coleridge, and Hemans

> Still in the garden let me watch their pranks,
> And see in Dian's vest between the ranks
> Of the trim vines, some maid that half believes
> The vestal fires, of which her lover grieves,
> With that sly satyr peeping through the leaves.
>
> S. T. Coleridge
> "The Garden of Boccaccio" (1828)

> Oh! never did thine eye
> Through the green haunts of happy infancy
> Wander again, Joanne! Too much of fame
> Had shed its radiance on thy peasant name;
> And bought alone by gifts beyond all price –
> The trusting heart's repose, the paradise
> Of home, with all its loves – doth fate allow
> The crown of glory unto woman's brow.
>
> Felicia Hemans
> *Joan of Arc in Rheims* (1828)

Forms that expressed the trend towards containment after the American War were not confined to the material spaces of kitchen and town gardens, nor to the forms of minor lyric verse. They were also represented by the poetic topos of the bower poem, a form with an ancient lineage that proliferated in the final decades of the century. Bower poetry in its most conventional aspect locates an enclosed green space as the site of a tryst between a man who enters it and a female character or feminine object (like Keats's nightingale) which is an integral part of its terrain. By the end of the eighteenth century its conventions were braided from traditions as diverse as the classical bucolics, Christian *hortus conclusus*, and Italian romance epic. From the bucolic tradition was adapted the pleasance, a locus not necessarily enclosed but characterized by cool breezes, bird song, murmuring streams, and an isolated poet. From the *hortus conclusus* (the garden of the Virgin Mary) was adapted enclosed boundaries infused with a strong sexual and feminine sensibility. From the romance epic was adapted the figure of the lone knight/hero whose dynastic quest is punctuated by digressive interludes of embowered, sexualized encounters with maids, sorceresses, or divine female figures. As this suggests, bower poetry is highly conventional in that its primary reference is not to gardens but to the world of poetry. The differences between bower poems and gardens are therefore instrumental and should be acknowledged. The enclosed green space, the female inhabitant, richly ornamented environs, and gendered encounter may have resemblances to the garden's space, but they do not represent it. In the garden, herbaceous plants are grown for pleasure and for use, while activity centers on the gardener's careful governance and ritual pleasures. Though natural cycles such as the seasons may comprise elements in a symbolic system, they also form a constitutive set of circumstances tending toward the produce of flowers, vegetables, herbs, and fruits.

The bower poem, then, is a highly self-conscious, conceptual form by contrast to which the garden – visceral in its representation and designed and grown for pleasure, provision, or to confirm social status – seems relatively straightforward. During the romantic period especially, the conventions of the bower were used to anatomize the process of poetic productivity. The solitary quester and the bower's female inhabitant became emblems for the generative conditions of inspiration and composition, specifically for the complex and contested relationship between poet and muse. The motivations that govern the creation of gardens and poems may thus appear startlingly different. Even the sexual element inherent to these spaces supplies different significations. Sex in the garden is biological, the material source of its productivity, and the natural means to a pragmatic end. It is not an effect of style or poetic anecdote, but central to the garden's purpose. The eros of the bower, by contrast, is part of a poetic tradition dealing with a subset of very specifically defined gendered relations within the conventions of poetry, relationships that represent artistic processes in culturally accessible ways. The eros of the bower thus draws from a highly conventional system of signs.

Despite differences in form, motivation, and purpose, however, the experience of the real space of the garden is necessarily mediated by discursive traditions, including those of the bower. We cannot talk about topographical forms except through the intervention of materials such as instructional manuals and designs. Since discursive systems are themselves constructed through conventions, the natural signs that regulate the garden are transformed through them into conventions of specific discursive practices. In addition, though the discursive systems that shape gardens and bower poetry are generically different – one didactic and expository, the other metaphoric and poetic – both express and help to define contemporary concerns. In particular, they share assumptions about the nature of enclosed herbaceous sites, whether in the overtly symbolic system of signs that we associate with poetry or the practical one associated with instructional literature. While poets draw on familiar elements of the kitchen garden and its cousin the cottage garden to heighten the appeal of the bower, writers of instructional manuals draw on a poetic tradition in order to represent the garden in terms that are both intelligible and compelling. By demonstrating connections between kitchen gardens and the delights of Milton's Eden, Spenser's embowered recesses, or Sidney's enameled shades, they legitimate the kitchen garden as part of an ancient poetic inheritance. Cultural assumptions about the nature of enclosed sites thus cross and recross the intellectual boundaries that separate their symbolic domains. Indeed, the cultural intelligibility of these sites is determined, in part, *by* such crossings. Manuals translate gardens into a system that recalls the self-referential system of bower poetry; bower poetry is authenticated because it incorporates familiar components from kitchen and cottage gardens. Poems and manuals both look toward a poetic tradition that regulates the forms of their discourses. Their shared discursive conventions assume that the enclosed space is embodied, feminine, productive, and shaped by artifice. In the best bower poetry we discern the vernacular scene of England's gardens, even as poets use bower conventions as frameworks for aesthetic, metaphysical, and social concerns. These two sites, one literary and one topographical, thus share constituent, historically specific elements and produce similar social weight, although they differ in material form. In addition, they share an aesthetic of exuberance, which is simultaneously highly designed and sensual, and an association between containment and productivity.

As the preceding chapter shows, the kitchen garden was one expression of an emerging sense that containment, productivity, and female sexuality are connected. During this period, bower poetry was freighted with related social meaning. Keats's "Ode to a Nightingale" illustrates this point. His ode is regular, an experiment in imposing the rhyme scheme of a sonnet on strophic form. Each verse thus consists of a Shakespearean quatrain and Petrarchan sestet. Balancing this regularity, the poem is shot through with an intricate aural pattern which softens the rhyme scheme by means of closely interwoven sounds. Composed in Charles Brown's suburban Hampstead garden, the ode draws several images (eglantine, violets, musk roses) from Shakespeare's description of Titania's bower. One can imagine, therefore, and critics have, that Keats perceived Brown's garden through the lens of bower conventions.[1] Not least, like most bower poems of the period, Keats uses the ode to analyze the process of artistic production, questioning the relationship between inspiration and presence (the female figure in the bower) and, linking it instead to deferral and absence (the nightingale's fading song). In order to explore this possibility he inverts the machinery of the bower, especially the sensory hierarchy in which sight (the body of the female inhabitant) is privileged over sound (especially birdsong). In this ode, the speaker quests blindly, pursuing secondary qualities of sound and scent. Yet these images are not owed entirely to literary allusion. The poem also evokes elements of a kitchen garden: mossy ways and grass, flowering fruit trees, even the seemingly self-referential bower elements of eglantine, violets, and musk-roses. The garden is heaped with images imported from the intersecting worlds of literature and gardening. Eglantine, violets, and musk roses, for instance, were common in the cottage messuage. There, violets and musk roses were grown not only for their charm but as herbs having medicinal and cosmetic uses, while eglantine was cherished for the scent of its leaves and flowers. The nightingale's bower is thus rhetorical in its use of conventional literary setpieces and referential in its description of a real garden. The rhetorical and the referential fuse seamlessly because bower poetry and descriptions of real gardens are mediated by discursive traditions which poach on each other's territories.

Keats's ode is one in a proliferation of bower poems after the American War that supports the idealization of contained vernacular sites that we find in the landscape treatises of Repton and Loudon. His bowers illustrate the convergence particularly well. Many of his poems draw on highly stylized conventions, but while they are furnished with ancient setpieces of the topos – grass, flowers, trees, embowering shade, elusive female figures – they also incorporate modern elements drawn from the highly domestic, suburban back yards of Hampstead's professional middle class.[2] The trellises, casement windows embraced by vines, and fruit trees which load the rifts of his poetry correspond with recommendations made in architectural pattern books for the cottages of both laborers and gentry. John Papworth points out, for example, that the gardener's cottage may beautify the owner's park, since "he has the means of embowering it with shrubs, creepers, and flowering plants . . ."; similarly, the gentleman's cottage *ornée* should sport trellis work "for the purpose of receiving ornamental foliage, which may be entwined about it: indeed, the construction of this cottage would allow so extensive an application of plants, that the lower apartments of the garden front might be completely embowered."[3] Edmund Bartell, who recommends using vines to provide the effect of stained glass, finds that in the laborer's case "beauty and emolument should go hand-in-hand, and be kept constantly in view: therefore, instead of the ivy or the honey-suckle, let the apricot, the pear, the plumb, or any other productive wall-fruit, be placed as a substitute."[4] Architects thus expose the fantastic crossing between literary convention and current architectural designs for domestic sites (themselves inspired by imaginary gardens) that infiltrate many of Keats's poems. The description of the bower Lamia creates within her urban palace, for instance, parallels recommendations for ways to decorate one's home for a fête:

> Fresh carved cedar, mimicking a glade
> Of palm and plantain, met from either side,
> High in the midst, in honour of the bride:
> Two palms and then two plantains, and so on,
> From either side their stems branch'd one to one
> All down the aisled place; and beneath all
> There ran a stream of lamps straight on from wall to wall.
> . . .
> Between the tree-stems, marbled plain at first,
> Came jasper pannels; then, anon, there burst
> Forth creeping imagery of slighter trees,
> And with the larger wove in small intricacies.
>
> (*Lamia*, ii. 125–31 and 138–41)

Loudon's recommendations for decorations suitable for "routs," or parties, echoes Keats's, in that nature is arranged in intricate and highly artificial bowers. In fact, Keats and Loudon both echo Spenser, in whose Bower of Bliss art and nature strive to undermine each other:

During dinner a few pots of fruit-bearing shrubs, or trees with their fruit ripe, are arranged along the centre of the table, from which, during the dessert, the fruit is gathered by the company. Sometimes a row of orange trees, or standard peach trees, or cherries, or all of them, in fruit, surround the table of the guests; one plant being placed exactly behind each chair, leaving room for the servants to approach between . . . The drawing-room is sometimes lade out like an orange-grove by distributing tall orange trees all over it in regular quincunx, so that the heads of the trees may be higher than those of the company . . . One or two cages with nightingales and canary-birds are distributed among the branches, and where there is a want of real fruit, that is supplied by art. Sometimes also art supplies the entire tree, which during artificial illumination is hardly recognised as a work of art, and a very few real trees and flowers interspersed with these made ones, will keep up the odor and the illusion to nature.[5]

Architecturalized bowers such as these are governed by conventions fostered in the incessant dialogue between poets and writers of garden manuals over the course of centuries. As Loudon's description demonstrates, these conventions assume that the enclosed space is both sumptuous and highly designed. Though Loudon's instructions conceal the material purpose of routs to provide a setting within which courtship rituals could be conducted, Keats's bowers make explicit their association with eros and femininity. This association made bower conventions an especially advantageous means of exploring the nature of poetic productivity within confined space. The bower's enclosed yet accessible green space was identified with female sexuality and the questing subject who entered the garden with masculinity. This association was so common that in slang terminology the word "bower" became a graphic euphemism for female sex. Keats jokingly exploits the euphemism in a letter in which he congratulates Benjamin Bailey for obtaining a curacy. Punning on the slang terms "chair" for male sexuality and "bower" for female, he promises Bailey, "When you are settled I will come and take a peep at your Church – your house – try whether I shall have grow[n] two lusty for my chair – by the fire side – and take a peep at my cordials Bower."[6] This slang usage was in keeping with the word's architectural association with the internal, private rooms of a building as opposed to its public rooms or halls, and finds its French counterpart in the word "boudoir," an internal room specifically occupied by a woman. Perpetuating this popular understanding of the word's meaning, George Mason traces the word to the Saxon word *bur* or *bure: "the* characteristic mark of the Saxon word was *privacy*, and *bur* . . . signified an erection for private use, whether the whole of a building, or only an apartment."[7] In popular usage, the word "bower" was not even a particularly subtle metaphor, but presumed a common association between enclosed, interior spaces and the female body, and linked that presumption to a heterosexual imperative.

After the American War especially, when sex and gender were being rigidly defined, the set of conventions supplied by the bower provided poets with ways of troping models for the process of inspiration and poetic production that historically had been naturalized as sexual. Since the ancients, the relation between the composer and artistic power had been identified as gendered and sexual, an erotic encounter between the poet and the muse. Keats was only one of a proliferation of romantic poets who entered its rich environs in order to anatomize poetic subjectivity. In the rest of this chapter I focus on the poetry of Coleridge and Hemans in order to exemplify the diverse ways that poets use the enclosed environs of the bower to confront subjective concerns about poetic production. The selection of these two poets is in one respect deeply ironic: Hemans, as a female poet, should perhaps document her sense of exclusion from the embowered space of poetic production – as poets such as Barrett Browning certainly did. For Barrett Browning the sought-for bower vanishes when the figure of the quester-poet collapses into that of the embowered lady. Hemans, by contrast, employs its conventions to claim her authorial place and secure her authenticity as a specifically British female poet, while Coleridge is uncertain about his natural right to step into that patrilineage. His repeated return to the scene of the bower is driven by need and characterized by hesitation concerning the vocation of poetry. He cannot wholly subscribe to the "natural" relation with inspiration that gender relations in the bower proffer. At his most poignant, Coleridge demonstrates that male poets, like female poets, may feel excluded from the embowered space of poetry and explore connections between poetics and subjectivity that all poets experience in differing degrees. Whether poets challenge the poetic and sexual implications of the form or accept or redefine its strictures, they express through bower conventions their own problematic status as writing subjects. Their appropriation of this topos signals the renewed power of containment to figure forth the poetics of artistic potency in the context of changing sexual values. It also exposes the effect of those changes on private systems of meaning.

S. T. COLERIDGE: ABSTRUSE PHILOSOPHY

Coleridge's sense that he might well be excluded from the vocation of poetry is most clearly evident in his manipulation of the solitary figure whose interlude in the bower epitomizes the process of poetic production. In the trio of bower poems that he wrote from 1795 to 1797 – "The Eolian Harp," "Reflections on Having Left a Place of Retirement," and "This Lime-Tree Bower my Prison" – the moment of fullest being is described as sense of absolute solitude. "It was a luxury," he says in "Reflections," " – to be!" Coleridge would later take this solitary figure and transform it into a concept that enabled him to schematize the affect of loneliness. In his poetry, loneliness sets the condition for longing and is constituted as an element in his dynamic system. The backdrop for loneliness is typically a landscape or some mediation of a landscape. Coleridge's aesthetic classi-fication of landscapes has been carefully documented, yet it is sometimes in his less remarked comments about vegetables and kitchen gardens that he lays bare his habit of slipping from landscape to abstruse thought. Coleridge read widely among horticultural texts, from John Parkinson's *Theatrum Botanicum* to Erasmus Darwin's *Botanical Garden*, and sought to bring the natural world under the rule of a rigorous dynamic system in his foreshortened *Survey of the Natural World*. He was fascinated by the idea of productivity in the kitchen garden and imagined himself engag-ing in energetic labor or, preferably, invented projects for Wordsworth and Southey. He records recipes for vegetables, buys seeds for friends, and is entranced by the common flower of the potato. He sees beauty and productivity in the most vernacular scenes and ruminates on concepts by way of common images of farming and horticulture which allow him to imagine philosophic thought in counterintuitive ways. Considering the nature of mental abstraction, for instance, he produces the following set of ratios: "Abstruse Reasoning: the inductions of common sense: reaping: delving." The ratio suggests a new way of looking at the process of thought, and he continues, "But the Implements with which we reap, how are they gained? By Delving. – Besides what is common sense – it was abstruse Reasoning with earlier Ages."[8] He thus considers cultivation clichés that were commonly used to explain human thought, but goes behind them, as did Jago, to the iron tools that make cultivation possible.

He comments on this tendency in a notebook entry: "For a Thing at the moment is but a Thing of the moment / it must be taken up into the mind, diffuse itself thro' the whole multitude of Shapes & Thoughts, not one of which it leaves untinged – between each w^ch & it some new Thought is not engendered / this a work of Time / but the Body feels it quicken with me."[9] Whether observing the dance of flies or the tick of a clock, Coleridge notes, his mind metamorphoses things into abstract concep-tual shapes. The process is not arrested at this point, however, since these shapes are themselves altered by the impress of phenomenal form. Mind and body collude in reshaping things perceived into concepts and concepts are altered by their collision with things, a continuous process that ultimately gives the body its sense of life and brings phenomena into dynamic self-knowledge. This propensity for abstraction leaves its mark on Coleridge's bower poems. I have already spoken to the elements in "This Lime-Tree Bower my Prison" that depict the kitchen garden that lay behind his home – a garden that falls away before the imagination of the mental traveler, only to return in the end transformed and transformative. The same is true in "The Eolian Harp," also grounded in the recess of the cottage garden where the scent of bean flowers is accorded the same aesthetic status as jasmine and myrtle. He thus captures the effect of the nascent English cottage garden, as he does in his notebooks when he lists "Marygolds, yellow Lillies, lofti*est* Peas in Blossom, Beans, Onions, Cabbages" in the same breath.[10] Most importantly for his articulation of the bower, he incorporates into the strophes of the ode an affect, the feeling of loneliness, which governs the contents of his bower poems and which, in his extra-poetic writings, he raises into a constitutive aspect of poetic production. He puts into play a dialectic of poetic productivity within the confines of the bower which reveals that absence and loss form the primal conditions of poetry.

Coleridge first alludes to a poetics of loneliness in the preface to his anthology, *Sonnets from Various Authors* (1796): "In a Sonnet then we require a development of some lonely feeling, by whatever cause it may have been excited; but those Sonnets appear to me the most exquisite, in which moral Sentiments, Affections, or Feelings, are deduced from, and associated with, the scenery of Nature."[11] Although this definition excludes the majority of Coleridge's own sonnets, he did transfer the affective structure of loneliness grounded in a natural scene to the more capacious form of the lesser ode. It is true that loneliness was not restricted to a specific form in Coleridge's works any more than it was exclusive to him as a late eighteenth- and early nineteenth-century poet, but what is remarkable about Coleridge's use of this affect in his bower poetry is his ability to transform it from simple feeling to an abstract component of his dynamic system, and to impose that system on the bower's content. We can trace the outlines of the process of abstraction in early notebook entries. In 1803 he notes, "Passed a Cottage, not only the Roof but all the walls overgrown like a Hill with weeds & grass – Why not a Crop of Peas on the Roof – & Sallad on the walls."[12] Like a Gainsborough painting, Coleridge's initial description suggests the power of the solitary, empirical eye to locate a ruined cottage at the point of its reversion to nature. A connoisseur of landscape aesthetics, the solitary walker isolates and preserves the liminal moment between cultivation and decomposition. Coleridge's own yearning for vegetables, however whimsical, transforms the cottage from what it was to what it could be. It thus separates the impression of the moment from the object of imagination by means of a journey from past time into imagined space. The phenomenal object is characterized as a thing that can exist only in loss and reconstituted only as longing. Similarly, Coleridge's record of a visceral pleasure, "Very fond of Vegetables, particularly Bacon & Peas. – Bacon & Broad Beans," is couched as a genial longing.[13] Like many of his comments on vegetables this one is droll, yet it documents both a loss – the immediate pleasure of eating peas or broad beans with bacon – and the anticipation of a pleasure not yet present. The desultory writer is suspended in the linguistic space between these moments, present in neither. Coleridge repeatedly documents his absence from an anticipated or remembered moment of pleasure and builds that pleasure in the solitude of his mind. Initially humorous, as in his enthusiastic notes on vegetables or projected garden tasks, this tendency is recorded increasingly poignantly, as in a note of 1802 when, excluded from a visit to the Hutchinsons', he records the Wordsworths' and Hutchinsons' names, but not his own.[14] The entry subsequent to this list of beloved names notes, "Fear of Parting gives a yearning so like Absence, as at moments to turn your presence into absence."[15] The prospect of separation isolates the observing, sublimating mind and marks a division on which a poetics of loneliness and its contingent affect, yearning, depends.

Some of Coleridge's earliest poems evince a residual version of the longing which delineates the most consistent components of his bowers. Even his earliest bowers thus include a chaste lady, an indolent male figure, voyeuristic gaze, and filial relationship with the father which he later will draw into a dynamic structure. In these poems, longing is embodied in a fleeing or absent female figure who can be discerned in the traces of footprints or glancing of eyes caught in half light; or it can be evoked in half-heard fragments of music, elusive scents, and the slant light of evening. It is not surprising that Coleridge, himself deeply lonely, should seek to transform the condition of loneliness into terms that make it philosophically coherent but also safely distant. In his bowers, longing structures the activity of poetic composition itself, for there, where loneliness is most keenly felt, the poet is most productive. Coleridge begins to elaborate the structure of loneliness in 1808, when he defines it as pothos or its Latin counterpart, desiderium. In the context of the imagination, pothos is described as a negative yet productive creative condition, a perpetual search "signifying hunger, and thence capacity."[16] He indicates that pothos is the ground condition out of which creative genius is expressed. In a poetic legerdemain familiar in the lyric tradition at least from Petrarch, the negative state of pothos transmutes into artistic potency, since depth of longing reveals the capacity of the one who longs.[17] The conditions that ground poetry are parallel to those out of which Coleridge believed all phenomena proceed, and he carefully defined the abstract form that action took. He thus locates pothos as an affect of the process of symbol-making itself:

All minds must think by some *symbols* – the strongest minds possess the most vivid Symbols in the Imagination – yet this ingenerates a *want*, πόθον, *desiderium*, for vividness of Symbol: which something that is *without*, that has the property of *Outness* (a word which Berkley preferred to "Externality") can alone fully gratify/even that indeed not fully – for the utmost is only an approximation to that absolute *Union*, which the soul sensible of its imperfection in itself, of its *Halfness*, yearns after, whenever it exists free from meaner passions, as Lust, Avarice, love of worldly power . . . [18]

Coleridge's ideas concerning both the symbol and individuality as incomplete without an act of self-consciousness originate in painful personal experiences. His loneliness thus generated many of his abstruse musings on the constitution of the individual and the operation of the imagination. Bower conventions were apt vehicles for expressing these conditions, since concepts in the bower are articulated through the medium of love and erotic desire.

Coleridge's anatomy of pothos closely follows the dynamic schema proposed by naturphilosophers such as Schelling and Steffens, who argued that phenomena are the manifestation of the invisible, dynamic activity of nature.[19] In Schelling's schema nature's force brings phenomena, or appearances, into existence through three moments that occur in order of logic, not time. The founding moment comprises a ground of being (the Absolute) in which subject and object are undifferentiated. In this moment, the process of differentiation is potential but unexpressed: it is held in solution. The second comprises an act of self-consciousness in which potentiality in the ground is polarized into subject and object. The third is the manifestation of this act of self-differentiation in which the invisible, cyclic forces of nature manifest themselves as phenomena. In working out a dynamic logic that could bring human conditions such as love and artistic potency into one consistent intellectual system, Coleridge identifies pothos as the emotion associated with the ground, or first moment of dynamic activity. Following Socrates in *Cratylus*, he carefully differentiates pothos from affects related to love, such as lust or desire.[20] In his account, love is a form of the godhead's yearning to achieve self-consciousness. As he put it in his lecture "On the Prometheus of Aeschylus" delivered to the Royal Society of Literature in 1825,

As an idea, it [the ground, or "sub-position of all positions"] must be interpreted as a striving of the mind to distinguish *being* from *existence*, or *potential* being, the ground of being containing the possibility of existence, from being *actualised*. In the language of the Mysteries, it was the Esurience, the πόθος, or desiderium, the unfueled fire, the Ceres, the ever-seeking maternal goddess, the origin and interpretation of whose name is found in the Hebrew root signifying hunger, and thence capacity. It was, in short, an effort to represent the universal ground of all differences, distinct or opposite, but in relation to which all antithesis, as well as all antitheta, existed only potentially.[21]

In this scheme, pothos is not merely desire, but a hunger for self-consciousness on the finite level of human existence.

One can discern the outlines of this system in each of Coleridge's bower poems, even the Dejection Ode which may not initially appear to adopt the architecture of the bower. Yet even in the Dejection Ode, Coleridge adapts the constitutive elements of his bowers – green half-light, longing mood, an indolent male figure, and elusive or virtuous female figure – to the dialectical process of this dynamic system. Premised on the failure of the poet's "genial spirits," it carries with it the residue of the bower's machinery. The green and leafy space is replaced by abstract counterparts – evening's strange green light and the poet's metaphor for himself in a former time as an arbor of hope and creative capacity: "For hope grew round me, like the twining vine, / And fruits and foliage, not my own, seemed mine" (lines 80–81). The bower is further represented by its antithesis, the "dark brown gardens" (line 105) of winter. Thus only the vestiges of a kitchen garden remain in the fruit, vines, and foliage of the poet's former self. The failure of genial spirits yields, as critics have noted, one of the most startling instances of creative capacity in the language.[22] The confinement of the poet's power, "Which finds no natural outlet, no relief" (line 23), is the condition out of which sublimity is produced. The silent emotional structure of pothos informs the images and methodizes the wild logic of the ode. Yearning – a longing for intelligibility which the poet describes as the soul sending out from itself "A sweet and potent voice, of its own birth" (line 57) – measures the poet's "hunger and therefore capacity."

"The Garden of Boccaccio" responds directly to the problems presented in the Dejection Ode. Published in *The Keepsake* for 1829, it is a bower poem in the mode of Coleridge's conversation poems; yet it plainly participates in a dialogue with the Dejection Ode, and nowhere more so than its valuation of nature. The poem begins in the precise trajectory of the earlier ode and toys with the inference that the secret springs of poetic power derive from the interchange or eddying of the living soul with the natural world. But the "natural" world of "The Garden of Boccaccio" differs decisively from that of the Dejection Ode. Although Coleridge reduces the natural world of the latter into an abstraction, "The Garden of Boccaccio" transmutes nature into artifice. Not many years before Coleridge undertook this poem he could mention his neighbor's kitchen garden, a site that would in his early days have been the subject of affection and enthusiastic projects, as a mere stepping-off point for more abstruse musings. Too long to quote in its entirety, the linked set of thoughts leads from the merest acknowledgment of the kitchen garden, to grammar, to the Christian life of "*Grace by Faith*," to the question, "If so, what shall I think of a *such* a Woman *as Mrs Gillman?*" From thence Coleridge refers back to the natural scene in terms reminiscent of "This Lime-Tree Bower my Prison":

At this moment my eyes were dwelling on the lovely Lace-work of those fair fair Elm-trees, so richly so softly black between me and the deep red Clouds & Light of the Horizon, with their interstices of twilight *Air* made visible – and I received the solution of my difficulty, flashlike, in the word, Beauty!

He closes with a reflection that attaches this set of thoughts to longing: for the "refined Sensualist, the pure Toutos-kosmos Man, received from a fine Landscape – for him it is what a fine specimen of Calligraphy would be to a R an unalphabeted Rustic – To a spiritual Woman it is Music – the intelligible Language of Memory, Hope, Desiderium/the *rhythm* of the Soul's movements."[23] Thus the scene of his early bower poems – the kitchen garden at evening – leads, via the figure of Mrs. Gillman, to pothos. The external landscape is the tenuous phenomenal manifestation to which abstruse thought is tethered. As Coleridge comments in 1804 in a figure not uncommon among late eighteenth- and early nineteenth-century poets, "Like the Gossamer Spider, we may float upon air and seem to fly in mid heaven, but we have spun the slender Thread out of our fane own fancies, & it is always fastened to something below."[24] In "The Garden of Boccaccio," that slender thread is anchored not to nature but to artifice. Artifice rescues him from loneliness, which has "emptied" him "of all genial powers" and isolated him within his own abstruse thought. "I sate," he remarks, in a variation of the figure reclining midway on a slope, "and cow'r'd o'er my own vacancy!" (line 8). But a turn of events, a volta, ensues. Mrs. Gillman's silent, muse-like hand slips before his eyes an engraving: "An Idyll, with Boccaccio's spirit warm, / Framed in the silent poesy of form" (lines 17–18). Although Coleridge invokes images in this poem that echo the Dejection Ode, he uses them to chart a different course. Rather than gaze on nature with a blank mechanical eye, the poet

gazes with "silent might" (line 23) and describes an organic response to
the engraving:

> A tremulous warmth crept gradual o'er my chest,
> As though an infant's finger touch'd my breast.
> And one by one (I know not whence) were brought
> All spirits of power that most had stirr'd my thought
> In selfless boyhood, on a new world tost
> Of wonder, and in its own fancies lost.
>
> (lines 25–30)

In contrast to the Dejection Ode, in which the poet's "genial spirits
fail / . . . To lift the smothering weight from off my breast" (lines 39 and
41), the engraving touches him with the infant finger of absolute potentiality, warms his breast, and provides him access to those spirits that had
inspired his youthful genius.

The plate that inspired Coleridge was engraved after a watercolor by
Thomas Stothard which illustrates a scene from *The Decameron*. It depicts
a formal garden in which nine girls and three lads picnic, so an allusion
to the muses would not have seemed extraordinary. The enclosed site
is foreshortened by a high enarched hedge which architecturalizes the
embowered scene. A lute-playing lad is the central figure of the scene,
and spiralling around and outward from him are the nine girls dressed
in empire fashion and two lads in vaguely renaissance attire. The eye is
drawn through the figures to a ruined tower behind the central arch in the
hedge, while the formal centerpiece is a three-tiered fountain. Coleridge
provides the following ekphrasis of the scene, in which he joins in spirit
the activities of the figures:

> Thanks, gentle artist! now I can descry
> Thy fair creation with a mastering eye,
> And all awake! And now in fix'd gaze stand,
> Now wander through the Eden of thy hand;
> Praise the green arches, on the fountain clear
> See fragment shadows of the crossing deer;
> And with that serviceable nymph I stoop,
> The crystal, from its restless pool, to scoop.
> I see no longer! I myself am there,
> Sit on the ground-sward, and the banquet share.
> 'Tis I, that sweep that lute's love-echoing strings,
> And gaze upon the maid who gazing sings:
> Or pause and listen to the tinkling bells
> From the high tower, and think that there she dwells.
>
> (lines 57–70)

Figure 18 "The Garden of Boccaccio," engraving by Engelhart after Thomas
Stothard, *The Keepsake* (1829), between pages 232/233, RB 224377.

Seizing the scene of inspiration from the hand of the designing artist,
Coleridge infuses the engraving with a depth of feeling that it would
elicit from few modern viewers. Morton Paley suggests that despite the
fact that Coleridge saw in Stothard's work a "tendency to affectation,"
he would have found in this engraving a particular grace.[25] Clearly,
however, the fair interchange between nature and the human mind
which failed Coleridge in the Dejection Ode is here achieved between

imagination and artifice, and not, perhaps, artifice of the first water. The effect is palpable, and the initial lines of the poem, in which the poet describes the engraving as infused "with Boccaccio's spirit warm" (line 17), invite a physiological version of inspiration: "With old Boccaccio's soul I stand possest, / And breathe an air like life, that swells my chest" (lines 71–72). Ironically, the inspiring moment provides impetus for a peroration on the Tuscan countryside which modern readers, without benefit of the engraving, are likely to imagine as the engraving's actual subject. Mimicking the scene of the picnic, the poet Boccaccio sits with a volume of Homer on his knee and Ovid in his pocket encircled by Greek heroes, demigods, and goddesses. Stothard's charming engraving is thus transformed first when the poet insinuates himself into the scene and again when that scene is transmuted into the activity of Boccaccio and his Greek divinities. Ultimately, the figures of the lute-playing lad, the poet, and Boccaccio slide into one.

The conflation of creative figures in these scenes underscores the dynamic sequence of events that make composition possible. The embowered scene, while a poor cousin of the kitchen garden that lay outside Coleridge's window, is regenerated into one that produces poetry by means of a dynamic dialectic. Confinement in the scene of artifice is poetically productive. When the engraving is placed before Coleridge, a relationship between subject and object, poet and visual design is established. This relationship is placed within the context of the founding affect of the poem – the poet's yearning for "genial powers" (line 2). It thus shares a family resemblance with Coleridge's earlier conversation poems. The image of the Eolian harp is especially important. The sensual and passive instrument in "The Eolian Harp," whose "delicious surges sink and rise" (line 19), is rechristened in the Dejection Ode as an Eolian lute. There, an image of loss and yearning, it reverberates throughout the poem in increasingly distressful tones. The engraving, whose languorous youth strums an ordinary lute, provides an occasion for revisiting this image. Unlike the Eolian lute, the instrument in Stothard's scene requires human agency. Thus, in a verbal echo of "The Eolian Harp," whose strings are "Boldlier swept" by "the desultory breeze" (lines 18 and 14), the poet depicts himself as an agent who "sweep[s]" the lute's strings (line 67). The depiction of Boccaccio in the ensuing apostrophe to Florence forms a verbal parallel to this scene. Seated like the lute-playing youth and, implicitly, the poet amid a bevy of romantic figures, Boccaccio holds his own best instrument, the poetry of Homer and Ovid. The poet gazes on this scene, simultaneously external to it and central to it, an agent of the imagination who brings the scene to life and a figure self-cast in a drama of poetic productivity.

The poet is also, however, an abstraction, one of the terms in an antithesis between the active imagination and artifice. The grounding condition in this garden's embowered space is intense yearning and its action depends on the externalization of yearning into differential poles. The engraving forms one of these poles. Like the Lady in the Dejection Ode, it acts as an ideal object that provides the means for a necessary act of *self*-consciousness. The other pole is the "mastering eye," or con-sciousness made visible in its subjective form. These poles have additional correspondences in Coleridge's dynamic system. In his notes toward his *Survey of the Natural World* he indicates that the differential poles of the dynamic system may be transposed onto natural categories, including the sensible qualities of light and warmth. He associates light with vision "in the outness and splendor of Colors" and warmth with the secondary senses "in the inwardness and sweetness of Fragrance."[26] He incorpo-rates these qualities into the poem. The "mastering eye," as one might expect, is associated with his vision of Florence, which is dominated by images of light and color: "brightest star of star-bright Italy!," Florence is characterized by "The golden corn, the olive, and the vine," fountains, gardens, spangled beds of flowers, and fountains weeping "liquid gems" (lines 77–92 *passim*). The engraving, on the other hand, is associated with the quality of warmth; inspired by Boccaccio's warm spirit, it is the source of "tremulous warmth" which restores the poet to sentience. Boccaccio himself embodies an undisguised moment of synthesis in this idyll. He is the point of indifference, the "all-blending sage" (line 101) in whom antitheses sustain their active powers, but are changed and modified.

Coleridge concludes "The Garden of Boccaccio" by imagining himself as an inhabitant of Boccaccio's garden, yet excluded from the bower's enclosed, erotic center:

> Still in thy garden let me watch their pranks,
> And see in Dian's vest between the ranks
> Of the trim vines, some maid that half believes
> The vestal fires, of which her lover grieves,
> With that sly satyr peeping through the leaves!
>
> (lines 105–09)

The conclusion is self-proscriptive, and thus characteristic of Coleridge's poignant response to his sense of his poetic vocation, yet it is also filled with humor, an emotion related to joy in that it presumes a connection to the external world. The poet may be excluded, but he is also beguiled and amused by the erotic games of the satyr and maid and his own artful location as voyeur. Yearning, differentiated into the ideal object and the mastering eye, yields, on the level of affect, self-consciousness devoid of self-importance. On the level of artifice, however, it yields poetry, the realization of creative capacity. Thus "Yearning," as Coleridge says in his *Survey of the Natural World*, "offers up – resigns itself – passes wholly into another" – is wholly transmuted into the body of art.[27]

FELICIA HEMANS: REGULATED PASSIONS

Productivity within the bower's confined space was not limited to the emblematic constitution of the writing subject, although this remained central to its meaning. Felicia Hemans manipulated bower conventions to position herself as a writing subject, but she also used those conventions to articulate emerging social values for middle-class women. Although most of her bowers are informed by accounts of Persian, Moorish, and American gardens derived from her reading of travel literature and poetry, Hemans drew also on the scenes of her youth and domestic, ma- ternal present. She repeatedly describes her experience, first as a child in her father's home and then, estranged from her husband but surrounded by her children, as an embowered scene, one that she actively creates. Thus in 1825, in a letter to a friend, she places her domestic activity of creating an embowered garden beside the alien scene of an imag- ined East: "Whilst you have been hearing new languages spoken, amidst scenes of barbaric magnificence, as well as almost uncivilized rudeness, we have been quietly settling down into our new residence, planting roses, training honeysuckles, and keeping our grass-plots in order – very delightful occupations certainly, but such as afford few materials where- with to amuse our correspondents."[28] The exotic East, outlandish and therefore fascinating, and her own familiar scene merge in her poetry in an aesthetic characterized by formality and luxuriance, and it is this site that she impulsively seeks both in daily experience and in her tales. Thus, when visiting the Wordsworths in the summer of 1830, she describes a garden passing into ruin:

The ground is laid out in rather an antiquated style, which, now that nature is beginning to reclaim it from art, I do not at all dislike: there is a little grassy terrace immediately under the window, descending to a small court with a circular grass plot, on which grows one tall white rose-tree; you cannot imagine how I delight in that fair, solitary, neglected-looking tree. I am writing to you from an old-fashioned alcove in the little garden round which the sweet-briar and moss rose-tree have completely run wild. . . . It is quite a place in which to hear Mr. Wordsworth read poetry.[29]

The scene Hemans describes, although not the exotic one she favors in much of her verse, contains the crucial element of controlled havoc that characterize her bowers. Formal but prolific, it is occupied by herself – a sober, domestic, female figure, her own best pattern for her bower's inhabitants. As that figure, she is also a writer, although here female writing is epistolary, a quintessentially domestic art. Finally, characteristic of the bower in its most traditional form, it is completed by a male wanderer who will enter it – not to initiate a scene of seduction, but to recite his verse. As listener, Hemans is not excluded from the bower's productive center; rather, as composer and listener, her claims for its space have both public and private ramifications.

Hemans's ability to speak from the bower as a woman was crucial to the wide reception of her work. In his *Memorials*, published in 1836, Henry Chorley makes a point of commenting on this reason for her popularity:

An eloquent modern critic (Mrs. Jameson) has rightly said that Mrs. Hemans' poems 'could not have been written by a man.' Their love is without selfishness – their passion pure from sensual coarseness – their high heroism . . . unsullied by any base alloy of ambition. In their religion, too, she is essentially womanly – fervent, trustful, unquestioning, 'hoping on, hoping ever' – in spite of a painfully acute consciousness of the peculiar trials of her sex . . . [30]

The close identification of Hemans's life and character with her work has unlooked for consequences. Unlike similarly influential women poets such as Charlotte Smith and Elizabeth Barrett Browning, Hemans always assumes traditional roles for female figures, whether in narrators whose sympathies and intrusions intimate their femininity or through the clearly feminine first person voice in her lyrics.[31] Her affinity with female figures within the bower runs counter to the normal identification between the reader and errant male subject who is either, as in "The Garden of Boccaccio," a voyeur of the garden's inhabitants, or, more typically, a partner in an erotic encounter. As in the scene she describes when visiting the Wordsworths, Hemans rejects traditional arrangements of authorial potency (or impotency) and disturbs the naturalized continuity between authorial presence and the male wanderer. Her distinctively feminine voice dramatizes a different kind of continuity, since the virtuous inhabitants of her bowers embody and enunciate powerful contemporary ideals. The causal connection she creates between her sex and the gender of the bower's inhabitant gives the tropological arrangements in the bower a consistency that authenticates her social message, while her development of the domestic potential of the bower places her in the line of Spenser and Milton. In particular, as Chorley makes plain, Hemans's heroines reinforce the contemporary sexual regulative ideal of the passionless female. Adopting the voice of the bower's inhabitant, Hemans provides a version of artistic potency that is specifically feminine, thus forming an unexpected association between authorial power and the regulated female character.

One of the paradoxes of social history is that though women have been traditionally identified with nature, emotion, and lack of restraint, they assumed during the latter part of the eighteenth century the socially consistent public role of managing sexual passion. Women could exercise this authority when it became possible to imagine them as biologically passionless.[32] So, while political cartoons satirizing the Terror of 1792 to 1794 often depicted the French mob as a hysterical female figure, women were simultaneously viewed as the repositories and instructors of moral values. No one spoke more sharply for this public role than women reformers themselves, from conservatives such as Hannah More and Catherine Macaulay to radicals such as Mary Wollstonecraft. The social ideal of the passionless female was theorized and given broad cultural legitimacy by virtually every major political and social theorist, from Rousseau to the physician Elizabeth Blackwell. This ideal had a parallel movement in horticulture, as botanists who theorized plant generation abandoned the sexual classification scheme of Linnaeus and increasingly asserted, in Charles Darwin's words, that "sexual and asexual generation are fundamentally the same."[33] In his history of sexual theories of generation in plants, John Farley reflects, "In a curious way, nineteenth-century biological views on sexual reproduction mirrored nineteenth-century social views on sex. Socially and biologically, sex was denied. Indeed, one wonders whether biological theories of sex were at least partially determined by the social views these naturalists shared."[34] The passionless female regulator of the household, a component in the trend toward asexualization, would later find an encomium in Isabella Beeton's popular household manual, *Beeton's Book of Household Management* (1859):

A good wife is Heaven's last best gift to man, – his angel and minister of graces innumerable, – his gem of many virtues, – his casket of jewels – her voice is sweet music – her smiles his brightest day; her kiss, the guardian of his innocence; her arms, the pale of his safety, the balm of his health, the balsam of his life; – her industry, his surest wealth; – her economy, his safest steward; – her lips, his faithful counsellors – her bosom, the softest pillow of his cares; and her prayers, the ablest advocates of Heaven's blessings on his head."[35]

Hemans helped to produce the ideal that Beeton extols and through this ideal provided a distinctive role for the woman poet. Publishing in the literary form most suited for the evocation of the passions, the woman poet had always potentially been marked as a transgressor of social codes. By manipulating poetic conventions, Hemans could map a course for poetry that celebrated the passionless female as the center of progressive sexual codes. Hemans does precisely this in her subtle revision of the content of the bower poem.

In her poetry, the image of sexual purity is sustained by the eros of the bower, an irony that owes much to the influence of the *hortus conclusus* over bower conventions. The authenticity of the sober female bower inhabitant in Hemans's poetry is cemented not only by the legibility given it by Hemans herself, mother and champion of domesticity, but by this tradition deriving from the Song of Songs, which, read as an allegory for the body of the Virgin Mary, provided legitimation for the bower's erotic content. Each element of the Virgin's garden accrued moral significance so complete that even shade, which excluded the "heats of concupiscence," provided an emblem for her sexual virtue.[36] Yet the distinctive convention adapted by bower poets, and that which is most visible in Hemans's verse, was an identification of the enclosed space with the Virgin's body such that figure and ground became interchangeable. Gervase Markham makes this transposition especially clear when he assures the reader of the garden's intact state:

> All closely wall'd about, inviolate it stayes,
> No serpent can get in, nor shal for evermore,
> All goodly flowers and frutes, here in perfection grow,
> Vertue on stocks of grace, hath them engraffed so.[37]

Even when other elements – such as the wall itself – were not adapted, this identification was sustained. Furthermore, as Markham's lines ironically reveal, the radical assertion of the Virgin's purity intensifies the sexuality of the scene, so that she is simultaneously constituted as inviolate and an essentially erotic body. Similarly, Hemans's female characters are associated with the erotic not in spite of their virtue but because of it. Her poetry is characterized by the persistent working and reworking of this topos. Like Wordsworth's *Prelude*, her long narrative poems consist of a series of lyric moments; unlike *The Prelude*, virtually every scene is a bower in the tradition of the *hortus conclusus*. Rather than centering on plot, her narrative poems patiently explore the bower's numerous variations and her lush descriptions of these poetic spaces overwhelm the story. Repeatedly, at the heart of these lush bowers we find a passionless female figure.

"The Abencerrage" is typical. A version of *Romeo and Juliet*, it tells the tale of the Zegri maid, Zayda, daughter of the last Moorish king of Granada, whose lover Hamet, an Aben-Zurrah, successfully rebels against her father's rule. Their tragedy takes them from the opulent internal spaces and gardens of the Alhambra to the mountainous "citadel" of the "wild Alpuxarras."[38] There, in a cave, Zayda throws herself between Hamet and the fatal blow of a Zegri defender, leaving him to survive her comfortless and alone. The poem brings together most of the themes Hemans uses to define the passionless female. Zayda's moral behavior is set off by the voluptuous, erotic landscape of Moorish Spain; the implicitly sexual nature of her love for Hamet is contrasted with her childish love for her father; and the poem concludes with her death, which enables her to keep intact not only her maidenhood, but also her filial allegiance. Perhaps the only bower from Hemans's works that this early narrative poem does not include is that which warns against the consequences of female passion. Hemans illustrates such a situation in "The Indian City," published in *Records of Woman* in 1828, in which the murder of the son of a Moslem princess by Brahmins becomes the occasion for the princess's revenge. Her unrestrained passion catalyzes a devastating retaliation that leaves the Indian city in ruins. The poem closes with the line, "This was the work of one deep heart wrung!" (page 180). This anecdote, however, is rare in Hemans's poetry. Generally, she draws on a cultural storehouse of images that eroticize the components of the bower while allowing her to maintain the passionlessness of her heroine. The Alhambra in "The Abencerrage" provides the architectural form of a bower supplied with the mystery and enchantment of the East. It is reminiscent of the illusionary palace raised by Keats's Lamia:

> Wild, wondrous, brilliant, all – a mingling glow
> Of rainbow-tints, above, around, below;
> Bright streaming from the many-tinctured veins
> Of precious marble, and the vivid stains
> Of rich mosaics o'er the light arcade,
> In gay festoons and fairy knots displayed.
> On through the enchanted realm, that only seems

Meet for the radiant creatures of our dreams,
The royal conquerors pass – while still their sight
On some new wonder dwells with fresh delight.
Here the eye roves through slender colonnades,
O'er bowery terraces and myrtle shades;
Dark olive-woods beyond, and far on high
The vast sierra mingling with the sky.
There, scattering far around their diamond spray,
Clear streams from founts of alabaster play,
Through pillared halls, where exquisitely wrought,
Rich arabesques, with glittering foliage fraught,
Surmount each fretted arch, and lend the scene
A wild romantic, Oriental mien:
While many a verse, from Eastern bards of old,
Borders the walls in characters of gold.
Here Moslem luxury, in her own domain,
Hath held for ages her voluptuous reign
'Midst gorgeous domes, where soon shall silence brood
And all be lone – a splendid solitude.

(page 86)

The sensual, seductive, languorous, and feminine scene of the architectural bowers through which the conquerors pass is matched by its
garden counterpart. Elements of Zayda's garden are dispersed in the
poem, tracing Hemans's ritual recitations of the bower's components:
flowering myrtle, enchanted ground, deep repose (page 64); the fragrance of rose and citron (page 65); balmy dew, soft breeze, and deep
luxurious shade (page 72). The erotic Moorish scene is countered, however, by Zayda's virtue. Significantly, she is differentiated from her lover
not by the opposition between sexual passion and sexual purity, but by the
difference between the passions associated with the public and private
realms. Unrestrained political passions in the public realm are countered
and softened by the regulated passions in the private realm, which have
an instructive and social purpose. The latter are enduring, since Hamet
can internalize and retain Zayda's image as a sign of the civilized and
civilizing forces of feminine influence even in her absence. As he lovingly
observes, when he contrasts her passionlessness with his own political
fervor:

Zayda, thou tremblest – and thy gentle breast
Shrinks from the passions that destroy my rest;
Yet shall thy form, in many a stormy hour,
Pass brightly o'er my soul with softening power,

And, oft recalled, thy voice beguile my lot,
Like some sweet lay, once heard, and ne'er forgot.
(page 72)

The "stormy hour," which metaphorically counters the soft breeze of the bower, signals the external world of men's political (implicitly sexual) and potentially destabilizing passions. The bower's frequently invoked soft breezes, traditionally a part of its erotic furnishings, are transformed into a sign of feminine self-regulation.

Self-regulation is an outgrowth and development of the girl's place in the family home, with father and/or mother and siblings. This childhood site substitutes the power of innocent filial relationships for sexual passion. In "The Breeze from Shore," the present echoes with a past imbued with the memory of "green places" associated with passionless domestic relationships:

Their power is from the brighter clime
That in our birth hath part;
Their tones are of the world, which time
Sears not within the heart
They tell us of the living light
In its green places ever bright.   (page 364)

These places are illuminated by the soft or dim "green light" of an embowered childhood, and are furnished with distinctively British (specifically Welsh) features. Yet they also reveal an aspect of Hemans's adaptation of the *hortus conclusus*, her separation of the innocent bowers of childhood from those of adult sexuality. Structured as a pure There and Then to the Here and Now of adult passions, the ratio of childhood to adulthood is both geographical and temporal: equated with the temperate British clime of an ideal past and contrasted with the fierce, oriental heat of tropical or semitropical zones and masculine adulthood.[39]

Hemans graphs this ratio most vividly in "A Tale of the Fourteenth Century," the fragmentary story of a maid, Bertha, who leaves "Britannia" in order to be with her lover, Osbert. Bertha leaves a green land of glens and vales for the alien bowers of sexual love with Osbert located in the "bright Arcadian scenes" of "blooming Italy," and "Far from the frown of stern control, / That vainly would subdue the soul" (page 278). Despite Osbert's delightful description of their future marital bower, Bertha sighs for the bowers which she associates with a lost childhood:

There, in the dayspring of thy years,
Undimmed by passions or by tears,
Oft, while thy bright, enraptured eye
Wandered o'er ocean, earth, or sky.
While the wild breeze that round thee blew,
Tinged thy warm cheek with richer hue;
Pure as the skies that o'er thy head
Their clear and cloudless azure spread;
Pure as that gale, whose light wing drew
Its freshness from the mountain dew;
Glowed thy young heart with feelings high,
A heaven of hallowed ecstasy!
Such days were thine! ere love had drawn
A cloud o'er that celestial dawn!
As the clear dews in morning's beam,
With soft reflected coloring stream,
Catch every tint of eastern gem,
To form the rose's diadem;
But vanish when the noontide hour
Glows fiercely on the shrinking flower;
Thus in thy soul each calm delight,
Like morn's first dewdrops, pure and bright,
Fled swift from passion's blighting fire,
Or lingered only to expire!

                                                            (page 276)

All the elements of this landscape conspire to recall Bertha's childhood purity and contrast it with the scorching, deathly landscape of sexuality associated with Osbert. Loosed from her father's "stern control," she is impelled into the dubious freedom of indulged passion. Real power is associated with parental restraint, which permits intense yet sexually untainted emotion, the "feelings high" and "hallowed ecstasy" of youth. As a later passage suggests, the Italian bowers described by Osbert as Arcadian, are to Bertha merely the painted mimicry of passionless yet exuberant British bowers:

          – Oh! bitter to the youthful heart,
               That scarce a pang, a care has known,
          The hour when first from scenes we part,
               Where life's bright spring has flown!
          Forsaking, o'er the world to roam,
          That little shrine of peace – our home
          E'en if delighted fancy throw
          O'er that cold world, her brightest glow,

Painting its untried paths with flowers,
That will not live in earthly bowers
(Too frail, too exquisite, to bear
One breath of life's ungenial air).

(page 277)

The narrator in this poem, caught in the liminal moment between child-hood and adulthood represented geographically by the ocean, writes in an implied feminine, suggesting that the "we" of the poem refers to fem-inine experience. The promised recompense for this loss is to recreate the "little shrine of peace" for one's children – a home that reproduces the high-spirited yet controlled environment which channels feminine passions into the appropriate ones of "Fear, duty, love" (page 273).

Unlike bower poems by authors male or female, which may, like many of hers, entail the death or loss of a female figure, Hemans's implicit identification with her female characters, her championing of passion-lessness, and her idealization of the home as the site of pure feeling which it is the mother's task to reproduce, revisualizes the bower's con-tents. Rather than figuring the poet as a wanderer whose entry into the bower signals the process of poetic production – a scene women poets generally question and seek to disturb – Hemans conflates the scene of poetic production with the production of female domestic values. In doing so, she disturbs the bower's gendered terms, and nowhere more so than when she exoticizes the scene. Through her Persian and Moorish heroines, especially, she presents all the erotic expectations of a sensual and languorous bower, but fails to deliver the anticipated erotic female inhabitant. As in the *hortus conclusus*, the reader must negotiate the dis-crepancy between the scene, which invites the imagination's voyeuristic gaze, and the anecdote, with its firm delineation of the regulated passions associated with feminine domestic virtue.

PART FOUR

Conclusion

CHAPTER 10

Conclusion

Nuns fret not at their Convent's narrow room;
And hermits are contented with their Cells;
And Students with their pensive Citadels;
Maids at the Wheel, the Weaver at his Loom,
Sit blithe and happy; Bees that soar for bloom,
High as the highest Peak of Furness fells,
Will murmur by the hour in Foxglove bells:
In truth the prison, unto which we doom
Ourselves, no prison is: and hence to me,
In sundry moods, 'twas pastime to be bound
Within the Sonnet's scanty plot of ground:
Pleased if some Souls (for such there needs must be)
Who have felt the weight of too much liberty,
Should find short solace there, as I have found.
                              William Wordsworth
                              (Composed 1802–04)

This book charts the sea change in topographical and poetic forms in England's long eighteenth century. When the walled aristocratic gardens of Stuart monarchs gave way to the ideal of unrestrained views in the georgic decades, the kind of space that represented English national aspirations was radically altered, yet that alteration contained within itself the potential for imagining contained space in a revolutionized way. In both georgic poetry and the broad prospects of landscaped parks, the boundless view put into play a dialectic between containment and unrestrained space that ultimately provided containment with new symbolic possibilities. Rather than the power to control privacy, containment could be visualized anew as the means by which England could be made the Garden of the World; rather than mere exclusion, confinement of prospects could be provided with valences for ordinary people. Wordsworth's sonnet sets forth the complexities of that alteration, which did not come without

253

cost. He suggests that confinement of form is a recompense for broader possibilities. His poem thus embodies the sense of nostalgia and loss that accompanied changes in the forms and practices of eighteenth-century life. Written during the period when containment was being revalued as an aesthetic and representational space in its own right, the sonnet also demonstrates the association between containment and productivity that was most emblematically expressed in the parliamentary enclosure movement. Rather than linked with deprivation, nuns in their narrow rooms, hermits in their cells, and students in their citadels are linked to an intellectual and spiritual yield which cannot otherwise be achieved. In a radical revision of eighteenth-century poetic hierarchy, visual confinement produces intellectual breadth.

Images of maids spinning thread and the weaver weaving fabric, although idealized like the nuns, hermits, and students, also suggest the vernacular possibilities of the association between containment and productivity. The poet connects himself with these working figures, and like them is an ingenious, skillful and laborious artist whose product illustrates the role of contrivance in the narrow breadth of form. Containment is linked to productivity; beauty is a function of use. The central image of the sonnet, however, is drawn from nature: the bee, which eschews the eminence of Furness Fells for the rarified air of the foxglove bell, locates the heart of the sonnet in a space that is both geographical and temporal, and there realizes its most intense labor and its most intense delight. In this central image, nature is not narrowly defined by vertiginous heights, but by an inner expanse. Concentration, intensity, and immediacy set the conditions under which boundaries dissolve and the wide world is transformed into inner depth. As in Milton's image of the fallen angels, gigantic in form, who abruptly shrink by means of epic simile to the size of bees, a sublime diminution takes place suddenly at the heart of this poem. Furness Fells contracts within the narrow space of the flower; human figures telescope into the image of the murmuring bee. Bound within this space, the artist too is compressed, shrunk like Milton's angels into the hive of the intellect. Indeed, as Kames might suggest, too much liberty cancels the apprehension of the sublime. Verticality is transposed from height into the combustive potential of compressed space. As if to emphasize this point Wordsworth contracts the traditional octave into seven lines. The sonnet's argument turns to reflection not at the architecturally perfect balance point of the ninth line, but the wise proportion of the eighth. Equal weight is given the empiricist's catalogue of figures and the poet's self-altering eye.

Even in his epic composition, *The Prelude*, Wordsworth repeatedly, like the bee, confines himself to the self-imposed lyric moment. Thus, although the dialectic between expansion and containment which characterized the long poems of the eighteenth century is retained, it is weighted not toward boundlessness, but toward the economy of lyric vision. Strategies of digression and description that distinguish georgic form give way to the encapsulated moment. Although in this sonnet Wordsworth suggests that containment is temporary, in his most sustained work bounded space gives way to bounded space and each lyric moment provides its own inward infinitude; the spot of time grows larger the further into it we proceed. The progression between these delimited, temporally expansive sites is replicated in the diminutive but not diminished form of the sonnet. Similarly, the figures in the first seven lines unfold in time, yet collapse temporal sequence into an inner infinitude.

Containment was, of course, not merely visionary. It had its material counterpart: an enthusiasm for tiny things waxed in the decades after the Regency when containment continued to be associated with ingenuity, contrivance, and productivity. Neither were the implications of containment limited to the idealized labor of those who manufacture intellectual and material goods, as in the space of Wordsworth's sonnet. The language of enclosure and productivity reached into even the most domestic and private corners of ordinary English life. During the last quarter of the eighteenth century the growing usage of the word "confinement" for the intense period attending labor and childbirth provides a signal material instance of an epistemology that linked containment with productivity and associated that linkage with female sexuality. Female form was thus drawn into the nexus of meanings refracted by the fantasized correlation between these concepts, while female sexuality remained an intrinsic but suppressed element of confined space.

It was within the boundaries of such contracted sites as the sonnet and vernacular garden that the sublime and the sensuous would, counter to intuition, take root. These sites subverted from within notions of what constituted representative English space and within these boundaries craftsmanship, ingenuity, and contrivance produced a space that could be construed as the seminary of true English virtue. The writers of garden manuals and literary criticism explicitly sought to identify an aesthetic with ancient roots that could bring forth new social meanings. They found within the confines of the garden wall and the sonnet's scanty plot of ground a sublime expanse within which time, leisure, and female sexuality could be redeemed by productivity.

Notes

PART ONE

I INTRODUCTION: EXPANSION AND CONTRACTION

1 Throughout this study I differentiate the terms "England" and "Britain," drawing on Benedict Anderson's distinction between the heterogeneous character of "Britishness" and the more prestigious, parochial character of "Englishness" in the nineteenth century. *Imagined Communities: Reflections on the Origin and Spread of Nationalism* (London: Verso, 1983) 93–94. For critiques of Anderson's hypothesis see Elizabeth K. Helsinger, "Introduction: Land and Nation," *Rural Scenes and National Representation: Britain, 1815–1850* (Princeton University Press, 1997) 11 and Edward Said, *Culture and Imperialism* (New York: Knopf, 1993) 232. Even Anderson's critics acknowledge his distinction between the privileged, homogeneous metropole and heterogeneous colonial "dependencies."

2 The general discourse of expansionism is ubiquitous in critical texts on the eighteenth century. Thus Clifford Siskin comments, "Back then and there, everything appeared to rise: capitalism and the middle class, nationalism and imperialism, population and literacy, the novel and the author," before proceeding to question this persuasively expansionist image. *The Work of Writing: Literature and Social Change in Britain, 1700–1830* (Baltimore: Johns Hopkins University Press, 1998) 158.

3 C. A. Bayly, *Imperial Meridian: the British Empire and the World 1780–1830* (London: Longman, 1989) 3 and 10.

4 Linda Colley, "The Apotheosis of George III: Loyalty, Royalty and the British Nation 1760–1820," *Past and Present* 102 (1984): 94–129; Bayly, *Imperial Meridian*, 110 and 161.

5 Bayly, *Imperial Meridian*, 2 and 115.

6 I borrow the term from G. F. Leckie's 1808 treatise, *An Historical Survey of the Foreign Affairs of Great Britain*, in which he counsels, "We must therefore Britannize every part of insular Europe which suits our purpose" (quoted by Bayly, *Imperial Meridian*, 103).

7 Stephen Switzer, *Ichnographia Rustica: or, the Nobleman, Gentleman, and Gardener's Recreation*, 2nd edn., 3 vols. (1715; London: D. Browne, et al., 1718) xiv–xv; first published under the subtitle.

8 Stephen Daniels, *Fields of Vision: Landscape Imagery and National Identity in England and the United States* (Cambridge: Polity Press, 1993) 99–101.

9 Susan Stewart, *On Longing: Narratives of the Miniature, the Gigantic, the Souvenir, the Collection* (Durham: Duke University Press, 1993) 6.

10 Leigh Hunt and S. Adams Lee, eds., *The Book of the Sonnet* (London: Sampson, Low, et al., 1867) xiii–xiv.

11 Joseph Addison and Sir Richard Steele, *The Spectator*, ed. Donald F. Bond, 5 vols. (Oxford: Clarendon Press, 1965) 4: 190–91. Written as a letter from a correspondent, the number is strongly attributed to Addison.

12 William Chambers, *A Dissertation on Oriental Gardening* (London: W. Griffin, et al., 1772) 19.

13 William Marshall, *A Review of the Landscape, a Didactic Poem: also of An Essay on the Picturesque: Together with Practical Remarks on Rural Ornament* (London: G. Nicol, et al., 1795) 254.

14 John Ogilvie, *Poems on Several Subjects. To Which Is Prefix'd, An Essay on the Lyric Poetry of the Ancients* (London: n.p., 1762) xli.

15 John Aikin, *Essays on Song-Writing: With A Collection Of Such English Songs As Are Most Eminent For Poetical Merit* (London: J. Johnson, 1772) 1–2.

16 Samuel Taylor Coleridge, *The Notebooks of Samuel Taylor Coleridge*, ed. Kathleen Coburn, 4 vols. to date, Bollingen Series 50 (Princeton University Press, 1957–) 3: 4313.

17 Leigh Hunt, *Bacchus in Tuscany, a Dithyrambic Poem, from the Italian of Francesco Redi, with Notes Original and Select* (London: John and H. L. Hunt, 1825) 80.

18 Philip Miller, *The Gardeners and Florists Dictionary, or a Complete System of Horticulture, &c.* (London: Charles Rivington, 1724) ix; hereafter I have included the year of the appropriate edition in all references.

19 Joseph Warton, "Three Essays on Pastoral, Didactic, and Epic Poetry," *The Works of Virgil in Latin and English in Four Volumes*, ed. Joseph Warton (London: R. Dodsley, 1753) 1: 405 and 410.

20 Anna Seward, *Letters of Anna Seward: Written between the years 1784 and 1807*, 6 vols. (Edinburgh: Archibald Constable, et al., 1811) 6: 256.

21 John Keats, *The Letters of John Keats 1814–1821*, ed. Hyder Edward Rollins, 2 vols. (Cambridge: Harvard University Press, 1958) 1: 231.

22 Miller, *Dictionary* (1724), ix.

23 Oliver Goldsmith, "The Deserted Village," *Collected Works of Oliver Goldsmith*, ed. Arthur Friedman, 5 vols. (Oxford: Clarendon Press, 1966) 4: 285–304, line 55.

24 My discussions of space in both this and the following chapter, have been influenced by Henri Lefebvre's *The Production of Space*, trans. Donald Nicholson-Smith (Oxford: Blackwell, 1991; reprint 1992).

25 See Raymond Williams, *The Country and the City* (New York: Oxford University Press, 1973) 9–12.

26 Christopher Hussey, *English Gardens and Landscapes 1700–1750* (London: Country Life Limited, 1967) 16.

27 Humphry Repton, *Designs for the Pavillon at Brighton* (London: J. C. Stadler, 1808) iii.
28 For the provenance of the haha, see Miles Hadfield, "History of the Ha-Ha," *Country Life* (30 May 1963): 1261–62, and Hussey, *English Gardens*, 35–36.
29 John Barrell, *English Literature in History 1730–1780: an Equal, Wide Survey* (New York: St. Martin's Press, 1983) 51 and 76.
30 Kathleen Wilson, *The Sense of the People: Politics, Culture and Imperialism in England, 1715–1785* (Cambridge University Press, 1995) 206–37.
31 Bayly, *Imperial Meridian*, 116.
32 Wilson, *Sense of the People*, 211.
33 Paul Langford, *A Polite and Commercial People, England 1727–1783* (Oxford University Press, 1989) 94–95. On natural histories, see G. S. Rousseau, "Science Books and their Readers in the Eighteenth Century," *Books and their Readers In Eighteenth-Century England*, ed. Isabel Rivers (New York: St. Martin's Press, 1982) 203–24.
34 Langford, *Polite People*, 199–202; Linda Colley, *Britons: Forging the Nation 1707–1837* (New Haven: Yale University Press, 1992) 88; Michael W. Flinn (assisted by David Stoker), *The History of the British Coal Industry, vol. 2: 1700–1830: the Industrial Revolution* (Oxford: Clarendon Press, 1984) 426–29.
35 Langford, *Polite People*, 66.
36 William Cobbett, *Rural Rides*, eds. G. D. H. and Margaret Cole, 3 vols. (London: Peter Davies, 1930) 1: 276–77.
37 My interpretation of Cobbett's manipulation of cultural images is indebted to Leonora Nattrass, who shows that Cobbett's arguments were made less in the interests of intellectual purity than to mobilize his readers. *William Cobbett: the Politics of Style* (Cambridge University Press, 1995) 21.
38 Thorstein Veblen, *The Theory of the Leisure Class: an Economic Study of Institutions* (1899; New York: Modern Library, 1931) 59.
39 John Sekora, *Luxury: the Concept in Western Thought, Eden to Smollett* (Baltimore: Johns Hopkins University Press, 1977) 57–58 and 61–62.
40 Thomas Fairchild, *The City Gardener* (London: T. Woodward and J. Peele, 1722) 7.
41 Patrick Goode, "The Picturesque Controversy," *Humphry Repton Landscape Gardener 1752–1818*, eds. George Carter, Patrick Goode, and Kedrun Lauri (Norwich: Sainsbury Centre for Visual Arts, 1982) 38.
42 Veblen, *Leisure Class*, 84 and 85.
43 I derive my use of tactics from Michel de Certeau, who distinguishes tactics from strategies. The latter "are actions which, thanks to the establishment of a place of power (the property of a proper), elaborate theoretical places (systems and totalizing discourses) capable of articulating an ensemble of physical places in which forces are distributed." By contrast: "The space of a tactic is the space of the other. Thus it must play on and with a terrain imposed on it and organized by the law of a foreign power . . . In short, a tactic is an art of the weak." *The Practice of Everyday Life*, trans. Steven F. Rendall (Berkeley: University of California Press, 1984) 38 and 36–37.

44 Ibid., 26.

45 W. H. B. Court, *The Rise of the Midland Industries 1600–1838* (Oxford University Press, 1938) 141.

46 Donald Grove Barnes, *A History of the English Corn Laws 1660–1846* (New York: F. S. Crofts, 1930) 35–37.

47 Sekora, *Luxury*, 32.

48 Ibid., 104–05.

49 David Hume, *Essays Moral, Political, and Literary*, eds. T. H. Green and T. H. Grose, 2 vols. (1882; London: Scientia Verlag Aalen, 1964) 1: 299.

50 Ibid., 302–03.

51 Ibid., 306.

52 Sekora, *Luxury*, 18.

53 Sidney Mintz, "The Changing Roles of Food in the Study of Consumption," *Consumption and the World of Goods*, eds. John Brewer and Roy Porter (London: Routledge, 1993) 265.

54 Mintz, *Sweetness and Power: the Place of Sugar in Modern History* (New York: Viking, 1985) 122–23.

55 Mintz, "Changing Roles of Food," 266.

56 William Cowper, *The Task, a Poem in Six Books, The Poems of William Cowper*, eds. John D. Baird and Charles Ryskamp, 2 vols. (Oxford: Clarendon Press, 1995) IV. 39–40.

57 On aristocratic bias see Barrell's argument in *The Idea of Landscape and the Sense of Place 1730–1840: an Approach to the Poetry of John Clare* (Cambridge University Press, 1972) and *English Literature in History*; Williams, *Country and City*; John Chalker, *The English Georgic, a Study in the Development of a Form* (London: Routledge and Kegan Paul, 1969).

58 On painterly aspects of locodescription see Barrell, *Idea of Landscape*, 19–20.

59 Lefebvre, *Space*, 38–39.

60 John Claudius Loudon, *An Encyclopaedia of Gardening* (London: Longman, et al., 1835) 1225.

61 Todd Longstaffe-Gowan, "Gardening and the Middle Classes 1700–1830," *London's Pride: the Glorious History of the Capital's Gardens*, ed. Mireille Galinou (London: Anaya Publishers Ltd., 1990) 123.

62 Richard Bradley, *A General Treatise of Husbandry and Gardening*, 2 vols. (London: T. Woodward and J. Peele, 1726) 2: 92.

63 Fairchild, *City Gardener*, 8.

64 Longstaffe-Gowan, "Gardening and the Middle Classes," 128–33. On coal smoke see John Evelyn, *Fumifugium, or the Inconveniencie of the Aer and Smoak of London Dissipated* (London: Gabriel Bedel and Thomas Collins, 1661) and Fairchild, *City Gardener*, 11.

65 Fairchild, *City Gardener*, 6.

66 The long eighteenth century housed conceptions of nature, which could be viewed simultaneously as conventional, constructed, and constitutive. The English had a strong political sense of the natural; thus the Chartists could appeal to Nature as the provider of food for all, a conception which supported

their claims for the naturalism of a domestic cottage system. David Worrall, "Agrarians against the Picturesque: Ultra-Radicalism and the Revolutionary Politics of Land," *The Politics of the Picturesque: Literature, Landscape and Aesthetics since 1770*, eds. Stephen Copley and Peter Garside (Cambridge University Press, 1994) 246. The Chartist interpretation of nature derives from the idea that nature is the product of indigenous conventions, a notion that made possible the persuasion that Gothic architecture was a natural form. Blackstone applied this notion to English Common Law, which could thus by inference be viewed as England's natural legal system. Sir William Blackstone, *Commentaries on the Laws of England*, notes and additions by Edward Christian, 15th edn., 4 vols. (London: Cadell and Davies, 1809) 3: 268. Finally, as I discuss here, nature could be viewed either as wilderness uncorrupted by human intervention or as the product of artifice.

67 Leigh Hunt, *Foliage; Or Poems Original and Translated* (London: C. and J. Ollier, 1818) cxxvii.

68 Lefebvre, *Space*, 154.

69 Edmund Bartell, Jr. *Hints for Picturesque Improvements in Ornamented Cottages, and their Scenery* (London: J. Taylor, 1804) 9.

70 Isaac Ware, *A Complete Body of Architecture* (London: T. Osborne and J. Shipton, et al., 1756) 346.

2 CODIFYING CONTAINMENT: THE PARLIAMENTARY ENCLOSURES

1 Anonymous, *The Great Improvement of Commons that are Enclosed for the Advantage of the Lords of Manors, the Poor, and the Publick* (London: J. Roberts, 1732).

2 Thomas Wright, *A Short Address to the Public on the Monopoly of Small Farms, a Great Cause of the Present Scarcity and Dearness of Provisions. With the Plan of an Institution to Remedy the Evil: and for the Purpose of Increasing Small Farms throughout the Kingdom* (London: H. L. Galabin, 1795) 6–7.

3 Ibid., 10, 12, 11, and 14.

4 The idea of the cottage system is common among architectural pattern-book writers: Edmund Bartell, Jr., James Malton, John B. Papworth, W. F. Pocock, Joseph Gandy, and John Plaw, among others, advocate forms of the cottage system, including allocations of tenant properties located on great estates or village homes with gardens attached. Agriculturists who did so include Nathaniel Kent, Coke of Norfolk, and, surprisingly, Arthur Young. Picturesque theorist Uvedale Price also advocated such a system. Stephen Daniels and Charles Watkins, "Picturesque Landscaping and Estate Management: Uvedale Price and Nathaniel Kent at Foxley," *The Politics of the Picturesque: Literature, Landscape and Aesthetics since 1770*, eds. Stephen Copley and Peter Garside (Cambridge University Press, 1994) 24–31. The Chartists envisioned an uprising that would end in the equal redistribution of property. Worrall, "Agrarians against the Picturesque," 240–59 and Anne Janowitz, "The Chartist Picturesque," *The Politics of the Picturesque: Literature,*

Landscape and Aesthetics since 1770, eds. Stephen Copley and Peter Garside (Cambridge University Press, 1994) 261–81.

5 For most of his life Arthur Young did not oppose engrossment despite his endorsement of small properties for laborers. Nathaniel Kent, who believed that the value of commons for cottagers' welfare was overrated and who supported the enclosure of timber and wastelands, also advocated a cottage system. *Hints to Gentlemen of Landed Property. To which are now first added Supplementary Hints* (London: J. Dodsley, 1793) 187. Erasmus Darwin, who opposed the enclosure of arable land, did not object to the enclosure of commons. *Phytologia* (London: J. Johnson, 1800) 466. Cobbett's view was perhaps the broadest, and he detected in the politicians of the 1820s and 1830s a desire on the one hand to have laborers prosper in a cottage system, but on the other to "be dependent upon the élite for wages, politics and values." Ian Dyck, *William Cobbett and Rural Popular Culture* (Cambridge University Press, 1992) 202. For an analysis of farm sizes during the period see J. V. Beckett, "The Debate over Farm Sizes in Eighteenth- and Nineteenth-Century England," *Agricultural History* 57 (1983): 312–17. He shows, contrary to the claims of many historians since Engels, that in the period prior to 1851 small farms (less than fifty acres) remained the norm. Beckett reiterates his findings in "The Decline of the Small Landowner in England and Wales 1660–1900," *Landowners, Capitalists, and Entrepreneurs: Essays for Sir John Habakkuk*, ed. F. M. L. Thompson (Oxford: Clarendon Press, 1994) 89–112.

6 Richard Price, *Observations on Reversionary Payments*, 3rd edn. (London: T. Cadell, 1773) 388–92.

7 Ibid., 390–91.

8 David H. Solkin, "The Battle of the Ciceros: Richard Wilson and the Politics of Landscape in the Age of John Wilkes," *Reading Landscape: Country–City–Capital*, ed. Simon Pugh (Manchester University Press, 1990) 47.

9 Price, *Reversionary Payments*, 381 and 392. Other advocates of such a measure are mentioned by Barnes, *Corn Laws*, 79–81.

10 Arthur Young, ed., *Annals of Agriculture and other Useful Arts*, 46 vols. (Bury St. Edmunds: J. Rackham, et al., 1784–1815) 1: 54.

11 Ibid., 30: 3–4.

12 Goldsmith, *Works*, 3: 198.

13 J. M. Neeson, *Commoners: Common Right, Enclosure and Social Change in England 1700–1820* (Cambridge University Press, 1993) 41.

14 Price, *Reversionary Payments*, 380.

15 Mavis Batey, "Oliver Goldsmith: an Indictment of Landscape Gardening," *Furor Hortensis: Essays on the History of the English Landscape Garden in memory of H. F. Clark*, ed. Peter Willis (Edinburgh: Elysium Press, 1974) 57–71.

16 Anti-enclosure literature of the eighteenth century hypothesizes most of these correlations and many twentieth-century studies continue to do so even in light of conflicting evidence. For example, Ann Bermingham commences her study of the art of the rustic landscape with the parallelism "[i]t is a fact of history that in the eighteenth century, enclosure radically altered the

English countryside, suiting it to the needs of the expanding city market. It is a fact of art history that in the eighteenth century, with the 'discovery of Britain,' the English saw their landscape as a cultural and aesthetic object." *Landscape and Ideology: the English Rustic Tradition, 1740–1860* (Berkeley: University of California Press, 1986) 9. Neeson bases her investigation of the lives of commoners on the syllogism that "enclosure meant the extinction of common right and the extinction of common right meant the decline of small farms..." (Neeson, *Commoners*, 15). Bermingham and Neeson both echo the Hammonds, whose pioneering study of the social effects of parliamentary enclosure set a precedent for *post hoc ergo propter hoc* arguments. Statements with broad rhetorical appeal inform the Hammonds' argument. For example, they begin their chapter describing village life before the parliamentary enclosures with the misleading but eminently quotable assertion that "[a]t the time of the great Whig Revolution, England was in the main a country of commons and of common fields; at the time of the Reform Bill, England was in the main a country of individualist agriculture and of large enclosed farms." J. L. Hammond and Barbara Hammond, *The Village Labourer 1760–1832: a Study in the Government of England before the Reform Bill* (New York: Longmans, Green, and Co., 1912) 26. Such studies ignore regional differences. To give only two examples, some of the worst poverty among laborers occurred not in the newly enclosed Midlands, but in old enclosed regions such as Sussex and Kent, which were changed very little by parliamentary enclosure. In the industrial city of Birmingham, located in Warwickshire – a southwest Midland county of mixed enclosures – poor rates in the 1790s were driven not by the forcible enclosure of fields but by a change in the fashion of shoes which replaced buckles with slippers and laces, thus reducing 20,000 bucklemakers into abject poverty. E. M. Hewitt, "Industries," *The Victoria History of the County of Warwick*, ed. William Page, 8 vols. (London: Archibald Constable, 1908) 2: 241. The correlation between parliamentary enclosure and the misery of the poor, both rural and urban, is thus complex and inexact.

17 Bayly, *Imperial Meridian*, 27.
18 Ibid., 28.
19 Joan Thirsk, "The Common Fields," *Past and Present* 29 (1964) 3.
20 C. S. and C. S. Orwin, *The Open Fields* (Oxford: Clarendon Press, 1967) 42.
21 Ibid., 3.
22 William Langland provides a record of such small thefts in *The Vision of Piers Plowman*, trans. H. W. Wells (New York: Sheed and Ward, 1945) XIII. lines 390–96.
23 James R. Siemon, "Landlord Not King: Agrarian Change and Interarticulation," *Enclosure Acts: Sexuality, Property, and Culture in Early Modern England*, eds. Richard Burt and John Michael Archer (Ithaca: Cornell University Press, 1994) 22–28.
24 J. A. Yelling, *Common Field and Enclosure in England 1450–1850* (London: Macmillan, 1977) 22.

25 In *Common Field and Enclosure*, Yelling discusses the general history of different types of enclosure (16–23), provides an analysis of the Tudor Acts (20–21), and discusses the problem of linking enclosure directly to depopulation (23–24). In *Reversionary Payments*, Richard Price quotes Bacon when he refers to the fact that the Tudors did not, as some modern historians have claimed, forbid enclosure altogether: "*Inclosures* they would not forbid; and tillage they would not compel; but they took a course to take away *depopulating inclosures*, and *depopulating pasturage* by consequence" (391).

26 Thirsk, "Common Fields," 23–24.

27 J. R. Wordie, "The Chronology of English Enclosure, 1500–1914," *The Economic History Review*, 2nd series, 36.4 (1983): 494.

28 For glossaries of old agricultural words see T. W. Beastall, *The Agricultural Revolution in Lincolnshire* (Lincoln: History of Lincolnshire Committee, 1978) 236–39; Orwin and Orwin, *Open Fields*, 189–91; and W. E. Tate, *The English Village Community and the Enclosure Movements* (London: Camelot Press, 1967) 185–92. For a regionally specific listing see James Britten, *Old Country and Farming Words* (London: English Dialect Society, 1880).

29 Wordie, "Chronology," 494–95.

30 I follow Yelling's distinctions between kinds of enclosure (*Common Field and Enclosure*, 6–7).

31 J. V. Beckett, *The Agricultural Revolution* (Oxford: Basil Blackwell, 1990) 37.

32 Anthony Low, "Agricultural Reform and the Love Poems of Thomas Carew; with an Instance from Lovelace," *Culture and Cultivation in Early Modern England: Writing and the Land*, eds. Michael Leslie and Timothy Raylor (Leicester University Press, 1992) 68.

33 Neeson, *Commoners*, 64–71.

34 Those counties less than 5 percent enclosed by parliamentary act included Kent, Cornwall, Devon, Sussex, and Essex. For a rationalization of the figures, see Wordie, "Chronology," 498. I have rounded the decimals.

35 Beckett, *Agricultural Revolution*, 38.

36 See Michael Turner, *Enclosures in Britain, 1750–1830* (London: Macmillan, 1984) 16, and Beckett, *Agricultural Revolution*, 35–37.

37 See Andrew McRae, "Husbandry Manuals and the Language of Agrarian Improvement," *Culture and Cultivation in Early Modern England: Writing and the Land*, eds. Michael Leslie and Timothy Raylor (Leicester University Press, 1992) 37.

38 Quoted by Beckett, *Agricultural Revolution*, 39.

39 Barnes, *Corn Laws*, 32–36 and 81–82.

40 I draw my example from Valerie Ahl and T. F. H. Allen, *Hierarchy Theory: a Vision, Vocabulary, and Epistemology* (New York: Columbia University Press, 1996) 147–62. They suggest a broader cultural application of such surfaces, 150–53.

41 Bartell, *Picturesque Improvements*, 102–03.

42 For the latter, see Gilbert Slater, *The English Peasantry and the Enclosure of Common Fields* (1907; New York: A. M. Kelley, 1968), Hammond and Hammond,

Village Labourer (1912), and George Bourne (pseud. for Sturt), *Change in the Village* (1912; New York: A. M. Kelley, 1969).

43 Alistair M. Duckworth, "Fiction and Some Uses of the Country House Setting from Richardson to Scott," *Landscape in the Gardens and the Literature of Eighteenth-Century England: Papers Read at a Clark Library Seminar 18 March 1978* (read by David C. Streatfield and Alistair M. Duckworth) (Los Angeles: William Andrews Clark Memorial Library, 1981) 95.

44 Yelling, *Common Field and Enclosure*, 3. See also Eric Kerridge, *The Agricultural Revolution* (New York: Augustus M. Kelley, 1968) 16 and Thirsk, "Common Fields," 23–24.

45 Lefebvre, *Space*, 124.

46 Ibid., 185.

47 Ibid., 186.

48 Arthur Young was an influential proponent of this view. See Neeson for others (*Commoners*, 32–34).

49 Bartell, *Picturesque Improvements*, 114.

50 William Atkinson, *Views of Picturesque Cottages with Plans Selected from a Collection of Drawings taken in Different Parts of England* (London: T. Gardiner, 1805) v.

51 Jane Austen, *Mansfield Park* (Oxford University Press, 1990) 50. Michael Drayton, *The Poly-Olbion: a Chorographicall Description of Great Britain* (1622; Manchester: Spenser Society, 1889) 127. Switzer, *Ichnographia*, 1: xxvii.

52 Stewart, *On Longing*, 23.

53 These four elements of nostalgia are adapted from Bryan S. Turner's categories in "A Note on Nostalgia," *Theory, Culture and Society* 4.1 (1987): 150–51.

54 Stewart, *On Longing*, 23.

55 Neeson, *Commoners*, 2–3.

56 David Lowenthal, *The Past is a Foreign Country* (Cambridge University Press, 1985) 263.

57 Orwin and Orwin, *Open Fields*, 1.

3 ALTERING THE PROSPECTS: SWITZER, WHATELY, AND REPTON

1 For details concerning Repton's life and commissions I rely on Dorothy Stroud, *Humphry Repton* (London: Country Life Limited, 1962).

2 Humphry Repton, *Fragments on the Theory and Practice of Landscape Gardening* (London: J. Taylor, 1816) 179–80.

3 Ibid., 137.

4 Ibid., 139.

5 J. C. Loudon, *Hints on the Formation of Gardens and Pleasure Grounds* (London: John Harding, 1812) vii.

6 Daniels, *Fields of Vision*, 83.

7 Andrew Ashfield and Peter de Bolla, *The Sublime: a Reader in British Eighteenth-Century Aesthetic Theory* (Cambridge University Press, 1996) 14.

8 Henry Home, Lord Kames, *Elements of Criticism*, 3rd edn., 2 vols. (Edinburgh: A. Millar, A. Kincaid, and J. Bell, 1765) 1: 186 and 188.
9 Ibid., 2: 442.
10 Ashfield and de Bolla, *The Sublime*, 15.
11 Switzer, *Ichnographia*, 1: xxxv–xxxvi. For an assessment of early eighteenth-century attitudes toward gardening see William Alvis Brogden, "Stephen Switzer: '*La Grand Manier*,'" *Furor Hortensis: Essays on the History of the English Landscape Garden in Memory of H. F. Clark*, ed. Peter Willis (Edinburgh: Elysium Press Ltd., 1974) 21–30.
12 Switzer, *Ichnographia*, 1: xxxvi, 3: 48 and 82.
13 Ibid., 1: xvii and 82.
14 Addison and Steele, *Spectator*, 3: 551–52.
15 Switzer, *Ichnographia*, 3: 49.
16 Ibid., 1: xxxvi.
17 J. G. Zimmermann, *Solitude*, trans. J. B. Bercier (Dublin: J. Stockdale, 1792) 213.
18 Switzer, *Ichnographia*, 1: xviii and 3: 84.
19 Ibid., 2: 185.
20 See John Brewer, *Party Ideology and Popular Politics at the Accession of George III* (Cambridge University Press, 1976) 163–200. See also Solkin, "Battle of the Ciceros," 50–51.
21 Wilson, *Sense of the People*, 274.
22 Anderson, *Imagined Communities*, 110–11; on Scots, see Colley, *Britons*, 123–30.
23 For the absorption of the Gothic ideal into English culture and its association with liberty, see Samuel Kliger, *The Goths in England: a Study in Seventeenth- and Eighteenth-Century Thought* (Cambridge: Harvard University Press, 1952) 26.
24 [Thomas Whately], *Observations on Modern Gardening, Illustrated by Descriptions* (London: T. Payne, 1770), 8.
25 Ibid., 8.
26 Ibid., 10.
27 Kames, *Elements of Criticism*, 2: 453.
28 Whately, *Observations*, 10–11.
29 J. C. Loudon, *The Green-House Companion* (London: Harding, Triphook, and Lepard, 1824) 135.
30 Stephen Bending, "Re-Reading the English Landscape Garden," *English Arcadia: Landscape and Architecture in Britain and America*, ed. Guilland Sutherland (San Marino: Huntington Library, 1992) 393. See also Virginia C. Kenny, *The Country-House Ethos in English Literature 1688–1750: Themes of Personal Retreat and National Expansion* (New York: St. Martin's Press, 1984).
31 William Marshall, *Planting and Ornamental Gardening: a Practical Treatise* (London: J. Dodsley, 1785) 480–81 and 487.
32 Young, *Annals*, 1: 19.
33 Austen, *Mansfield Park*, 89–90.
34 Kames, *Elements of Criticism*, 1: 215.
35 Whately, *Observations*, 13.

36 Ibid., 12–13.
37 Emmanuel Kant, *Critique of Judgment*, trans. J. H. Bernard (New York: Macmillan, 1951) 88.
38 Whately, *Observations*, 66–67.
39 Quotations are from the Authorized Version, Genesis 1: 2 and 6 and Genesis 8: 8–9.
40 Whately, *Observations*, 93; Kames, *Elements of Criticism*, 2: 433–34.
41 Whately, *Observations*, 21.
42 Ibid., 21.
43 William Wordsworth, *The Prelude*, *The Oxford Authors: William Wordsworth*, ed. Stephen Gill (Oxford University Press, 1984) IV. 530–42; hereafter cited in the text by line number.
44 John Milton, *"Il Penseroso," with the paintings by William Blake* (New York: Heritage Press, 1954) 37 and 44.
45 On utility see Kedrun Laurie, "The Repton Park: Walks and Drives," *Humphry Repton Landscape Gardener 1752–1818*, eds. George Carter, Patrick Goode, and Kedrun Laurie (Norwich: Sainsbury Centre for Visual Arts, 1982) 62; on diminishing the view see Stephen Daniels, *Humphry Repton: Landscape Gardening and the Geography of Georgian England* (New Haven: Yale University Press, 1999) 25.
46 At one time the site of the Prince's liaison with Mrs. Fitzherbert, the Marine Pavilion had subsequently been given to Princess Caroline. Repton was called in to propose a plan for refurbishing the property in 1797, the year of Caroline's eviction from the place. At the time of the publication of the *Designs*, the Prince, who was insolvent, had not yet determined his architect. The contract was ultimately given to John Nash, whose faux East Indian design was viewed as an extravagant joke. As the Reverend Sydney Smith quipped, "the Dome of St. Paul's must have come down to Brighton and pupped." Henry D. Roberts, *A History of the Royal Pavilion at Brighton with an Account of its Original Furniture and Decoration* (London: Country Life Limited, 1939) 89.
47 Repton, *Fragments*, 40–48.
48 Daniels, *Fields of Vision*, 99.
49 Repton, *Fragments*, 235.
50 See Goode, "Picturesque Controversy," 34, Daniels, *Fields of Vision*, 88, and Worrall, "Agrarians against the Picturesque," 249–50.
51 Robert S. Nelson, "Appropriation," *Critical Terms for Art History*, eds. Robert S. Nelson and Robert Shiff (University of Chicago Press, 1996) 119.
52 Ibid., 119.
53 Daniels, *Fields of Vision*, 88.
54 Repton, *Fragments*, 233.
55 Ibid., 234.
56 Worrall, "Agrarians against the Picturesque," 249–50.
57 Repton, *Fragments*, 235.

58 Repton lived in his home at Hare Street in Essex for the rest of his life, while he and his wife raised seven children. (Nine died in infancy.) Much has been made of the fact that he redesigned this property to conceal the butcher shop and the busy village streets outside the front door – less of the fact that the family of nine and (as was necessary in the days before domestic technology) servants occupied six smallish bedrooms, or of the fact that Repton grew so attached to this place which he originally looked on as a temporary home that he remained there for over thirty years. The "common" Repton depicts in his before illustration, which was granted him by permission of the village, is a tiny triangle which he depicts covered with geese. The geese would have signified a widely known agricultural fact, that highly acidic fresh geese droppings ruined grassy ground making it unfit for other grazing animals. Repton was not unwittingly depicting the conversion of a piece of useful ground into pleasurable ground, but making the point (for good or for ill) that the triangle of grass surrounded by busy roads was poor public property. (For the alternate view see Worrall, "Agrarians against the Picturesque," 149.)

59 Repton, *Fragments*, 237.

60 Ibid., 146.

61 Ibid., 142.

62 Humphry Repton, *Sketches and Hints on Landscape Gardening* (London: W. Bulmer, 1794) 171.

63 Repton, *Fragments*, 53.

64 Repton, *Designs*, iii.

65 John Keats, *Lamia*, *The Poems of John Keats*, ed. Jack Stillinger (Cambridge: Harvard University Press, 1978) ii. 125–31; hereafter cited in the text by line number.

66 Repton, *Designs*, 2.

PART TWO

4 ENGLISH GEORGIC AND BRITISH NATIONHOOD

1 Arthur Young, *The Autobiography of Arthur Young with Selections from His Correspondence*, ed. M. Betham-Edwards (London: Smith, Elder, and Co., 1898) 173.

2 John Dryden, trans., *The Works of Virgil in English, 1697*, eds. William Frost and Vinton A. Dearing, vol. 5 of *The California Edition of the Works of John Dryden*, gen. ed. Vinton A. Dearing, 20 vols. (Berkeley: University of California Press, 1988) 137.

3 For an alternate opinion see G. E. Mingay, *Arthur Young and his Times* (London: Macmillan, 1975) Chapter 1.

4 Anthony Low, *The Georgic Revolution* (Princeton University Press, 1985) 12.

5 Jago is the final subject of John Chalker's study, *English Georgic, a Study in the Development of a form* (London: Routledge and Kegan Paul, 1969) 36–46.

John Barrell places the end of the genre at "1770 or so" in *The Dark Side of the Landscape: the Rural Poor in English Painting 1730–1840* (1980; Cambridge University Press, 1992) 37. Kurt Heinzelman also locates the end of the genre at about 1770 in "Roman Georgic in the Georgian Age: a Theory of Romantic Genre," *TSLL* 33 (1991): 199. The assumption that georgic died out in the final decades of the century is sometimes expressed in terms of its exclusion from romantic generic categories, as in the case of Stuart Curran's excellent genre study, *Poetic Form and British Romanticism* (Oxford University Press, 1986).

6 In the group of "true" georgics are generally included John Philips's *Cyder* (1708), John Gay's *Rural Sports* (1713; revised 1720), James Thomson's *The Seasons* (the collected edition in 1730), William Somervile's *The Chace* (1735), Christopher Smart's *The Hop-Garden* (1752), John Dyer's *The Fleece* (1757), James Grainger's *The Sugar-Cane* (1764), and Richard Jago's *Edge-Hill* (1767).

7 Critics have not, on the whole, been attuned to the impact of the Act of Union on the sudden appreciation for georgic poetry. Dwight L. Durling charts the gradual growth of its various manifestations. *Georgic Tradition in English Poetry* (New York: Columbia University Press, 1935). L. P. Wilkinson also marks 1697 as the beginning point of the georgic fashion, although he concludes that "the heyday of georgic poetry coincided with her [England's] meteoric rise in world prestige, the period that began with the union with Scotland, Marlborough's victories and the Treaty of Utrecht, and lasted into the reign of George III . . . " *The Georgics of Virgil, a Critical Survey* (Cambridge University Press, 1969) 299 and 301. John Chalker and Anthony Low argue that the popularity of English georgic is due to the parallel political situation, following the Restoration, of England with Virgil's Rome (Chalker, *English Georgic*, 10; Low, *Georgic Revolution*, 124). Kurt Heinzelman notes that Philips's *Cyder* may be a response to the Act of Union, although he links the epistemological forces underlying the popularity of the form to the "georgic" monarchs, George I, II, and III ("Roman Georgic," 203).

8 Bertrand H. Bronson speaks for this view when he notes, "if the epic surpassed [georgic], the epic was forbidding by comparison" in "The Trough of the Wave," *England in the Restoration and Early Eighteenth Century*, ed. H. T. Swedenberg, Jr. (Berkeley: University of California Press, 1972) 208.

9 Linda Colley, *Britons: forging the Nation 1707–1837* (New Heaven: Yale University Press, 1992) 11.

10 On Boswell, see Janet Adam Smith, "Some Eighteenth-Century Ideas of Scotland," *Scotland in the Age of Improvement: Essays in Scottish History in the Eighteenth Century*, eds. N. T. Phillipson and Rosalind Mitchison (Edinburgh University Press, 1970) 113. On Hume, see John Clive, "The Social Background of the Scottish Renaissance," *Scotland in the Age of Improvement: Essays in Scottish History in the Eighteenth Century*, eds. N. T. Phillipson and Rosalind Mitchison (Edinburgh: University Press, 1970) 239.

11 See Donald J. Withrington's description of the adaptation of the Scottish Universities in response to competition from the Academy Movement in

"Education and Society in the Eighteenth Century," *Scotland in the Age of Improvement: Essays in Scottish History in the Eighteenth Century*, eds. N. T. Phillipson and Rosalind Mitchison (Edinburgh University Press, 1970)169–99.

12 James William Johnson, "The Classics and John Bull, 1660–1714," *England in the Restoration and Early Eighteenth Century*, ed. H. T. Swedenberg, Jr. (Berkeley: University of California Press) 1–26, especially 24. See also G. S. Rousseau, "Science Books and their Readers in the Eighteenth Century," *Books and their Readers in Eighteenth-Century England*, ed. Isabel Rivers (New York: St. Martin's Press, 1982) 203–14.

13 Quoted by Withrington, "Education and Society," 172, who discusses this episode in a different context.

14 T. C. Smout, *A History of the Scottish People 1560–1830* (New York: Scribner's, 1969) 505.

15 Low, *Georgic Revolution*, 6. Eric Kerridge, *The Agricultural Revolution* (New York: Augustus M. Kelley, 1968) 15.

16 According to Sir E. John Russell, the Royal Society's Georgical Committee "functioned so well that early numbers of the Society's journal, the *Philosophical Transactions of the Royal Society*, contain numerous articles relating to agricultural science and practice" (21–22); so well, in fact, that when Christopher Wren reorganized the Society in 1681, the Georgical Committee was one of only two that were retained. *A History of Agricultural Science in Great Britain 1620–1954* (London: Allen and Unwin, 1966) 21–26.

17 Joseph Addison, "An Essay on Virgil's *Georgics*," *The Works of the Right Honourable Joseph Addison, Esq.*, 4 vols. (London: J. Tonson) 1: 256.

18 Young, *Autobiography*, 144.

19 Arthur Young, ed., *Annals of Agriculture and other Useful Arts*, 46 vols. (Bury St. Edmunds: J. Rackham, et al., 1784–1815) 1: 10.

20 Penelope Wilson, "Classical Poetry and the Eighteenth-Century Reader," *Books and their Readers in Eighteenth-Century England*, ed. Isabel Rivers (New York: St. Martin's Press) 80 and 81.

21 Heinzelman, "Roman Georgic," 199.

22 G. E. Fussell notes that *The Gentleman's Magazine and Historical Chronicle* began publishing articles pertaining to agriculture in 1739. *Chronological List of Early Agricultural Works in the Library of the Ministry of Agriculture and Fisheries* (London: His Majesty's Stationery Office, n.d.). More accurately, the first such article, "Considerations on Distilling, Husbandry, Trade, &c.," appeared in February 1732, little more than a year after publication began. *The Gentleman's Magazine* also published the *Philosophical Transactions* of the Royal Society every two months until well after the middle of the century. Its monthly listings of newly published books included agricultural entries from the magazine's inception; and natural histories, such as that of Norway in 1755, incorporated lengthy observations on agriculture. Coverage of agriculture in the popular press appeared much earlier than *The Gentleman's Magazine*, however. The first agricultural "newspaper," John Houghton's *A Collection of Letters for the Improvement of Husbandry and Trade* predates the first

weekly in England (John Dunton's *The Athenian Mercury*, first circulated in 1691), was published in two successful series, the first from 1681–83 and the second from 1692 to about 1702, and was reprinted in 1727. See G. E. Fussell, *The Old English Farming Books from Fitzherbert to Tull, 1523 to 1730* (London: Crosby Lockwood, 1947) 81–84. Finally, periodicals were important for advertising books and treatises on agricultural subjects as well as premiums for agricultural endeavors.

23 Young, *Autobiography*, 111–12; Terry Belanger, "Publishers and Writers in Eighteenth-Century England," *Books and their Readers in Eighteenth-Century England*, ed. Isabel Rivers (New York: St. Martin's Press. 1982) 5.

24 Sarah Wilmot notes that "[f]orty-four per cent of the first Proprietors of the Royal Institution were also members of the Board of Agriculture: of a total of nineteen governors of the Institution, fourteen belonged to the Board of Agriculture." *"The Business of Improvement": Agriculture and Scientific Culture in Britain, c.1770–c.1870*, Historical Geography Research Series 24 (Bristol: Historical Geography Research Group, 1990) 23.

25 Ibid., 11.

26 Ibid., 9.

27 See ibid., 11; Colley, *Britons*, 88.

28 John Dyer, *The Fleece: a Poem in Four Books* (London: R. and J. Dodsley, 1757) 3. 234–39 and 247–58.

29 Heinzelman, "Roman Georgic," 200.

30 Ben Jonson, "To Penshurst," *Ben Jonson: the Complete Poems*, ed. George Parfitt (New Haven: Yale University Press, 1975) lines 54 and 55–56.

31 Heinzelman, "Roman Georgic," 200.

32 Although the king's first farming efforts began at Richmond Park in 1771 with the transformation of a deer park into a sheep farm, his real efforts at experimental farming began at Windsor after 1790. Arthur Young records having been invited to visit Windsor twice, but makes no substantive comment (*Autobiography*, 224 and 322–23). Nathaniel Kent provides a sketchy description of the King's Norfolk and Flemish farms at Windsor Great Park, which suggests that the King approved of some variations on methods that had been developed in Norfolk and Gloucestershire, but describes no true innovations. *Transactions of the Society for the Encouragement of Arts, Manufactures, and Commerce* 17 (1799): 119–39. Kent has an extended piece on the King's farms in 1799, but he is absorbed in accounting for the failed performance of a plough developed by Lord Somerville that the king had commissioned for use on his farms (Young, *Annals*, 32: 154–73). Although throughout the *Annals*, Young and others write resolutions for creating experimental farms, the king's Norfolk and Flemish farms at Windsor are never mentioned as such, even in 1796 at the height of the king's efforts (27: 204). An entry of Young's in 1802 suggests that rather than improver the king's role is more accurately that of patron. In an obituary for Mr. Ducket, the farmer made famous by the king's pseudonymous letters to the *Annals* (under the name of his chief shepherd, Ralph Robinson), Young refers to "the BOARD OF AGRICULTURE (an establishment that forms one of the glories of GEORGE THE THIRD)." He

acknowledges three men, Arbuthnot, Ducket, and Bakewell as the foremost agricultural improvers of the age: "Let the three men whose labours did so much to promote the agriculture so nobly patronized, and so ably practised by our illustrious Sovereign, – long live in the remembrance of a grateful people" (38: 630). The king, as the chief shepherd of his people, is distinguished as patron and practitioner, the traditional paternalistic figurehead rather than radical improver.

33 John Galt, *George the Third, His Court, and Family*, 2 vols. (1820; London: Henry Colburn, 1824) 1: 7.

34 Young, *Autobiography*, 190–91.

35 Galt, *George the Third*, note 1: 75–76.

36 Ibid., 2: 157.

37 Ibid., 1: 468.

38 Ibid., 2: 125.

39 Charles Eisinger defines the freehold concept as the notion "that every man had a natural right to productive landed property" in "Land and Loyalty: Literary Expressions of Agrarian Nationalism in the Seventeenth and Eighteenth Centuries," *American Literature* 21 (1949): 165. For idealized labor, see Sister Eugenia, "Coleridge's Scheme of Pantisocracy and American Travel Accounts," *PMLA* 45 (1930): 1072.

40 Sister Eugenia, "Coleridge's Scheme of Pantisocracy," 1080–82.

41 G. Melvin Herndon, "Agriculture in America in the 1790s: an Englishman's View," *Agricultural History* 49 (1975): 506.

42 Carole Shammas, "The Rise of the Colonial Tenant," *Reviews in American History* 6 (1978): 490 and 494–95. See also Lucy Simler, "Tenancy in Colonial Pennsylvania: the Case of Chester County," *The William and Mary Quarterly* 43 (1986): 542–69.

43 Timothy Sweet, "American Pastoralism and the Marketplace. Eighteenth-Century Ideologies of Farming," *Early American Literature* 29 (1994): 66–69.

44 Myra Jehlen, *American Incarnation. The Individual, the Nation, and the Continent*, (Cambridge: Harvard University Press, 1986) 9.

45 Eisinger, "Land and Loyalty," 176.

46 Jehlen, *American Incarnation*, 14.

47 Joyce Appleby, "Commercial Farming and the 'Agrarian Myth' in the Early Republic," *The Journal of American History* 68 (1982): 840–41; Young, *Annals*, 1: 13.

48 Appleby, "Commercial Farming," 839–40.

49 I adapt the terms "variant" and "innovation" from Ralph Cohen, "Innovation and Variation: Literary Change and Georgic Poetry," *Literature and History: Papers Read at a Clark Library Seminar, March 3, 1973* (UCLA: William Andrews Clark Memorial Library, 1974) 3–42.

50 George Washington, *Letters from His Excellency George Washington to Arthur Young, Esq. F.R.S. and Sir John Sinclair, Bart. M.P*, ed. Arthur Young (Alexandria: Cotton and Stewart, 1803) 6.

51 Washington, *Letters*, 95.

52 Samuel Taylor Coleridge, *Essays on His Times in* The Morning Post *and* The Courier, 3 vols., ed. David V. Erdman, vol. 3 of *The Collected Works of Samuel Taylor Coleridge*, 16 vols. gen. ed. Kathleen Coburn, Bollingen Series 75 (Princeton University Press, 1978) 1: 32 and 2: 235.

53 Young's conversion appeared as "The Example of France a Warning to Britain" in 1793. In his review of "The Question of Scarcity Plainly Stated . . ." Coleridge attributes Young's changed sentiments to receiving a government sinecure in the form of Secretary of the Board of Agriculture in 1793 and a pension in 1797 (*Essays on His Times*, 1: 233–34).

54 Young, *Annals*, 18: 162.

55 Coleridge confers this title on Washington in his obituary for him in *The Morning Post*, 25 March 1800 (*Essays on His Times*, 1: 231).

56 Washington, *Letters*, 16.

57 Ibid., 128.

5 PHILIPS'S *CYDER*: ENGLISHING THE APPLE

1 H[arold] V[ictor] Taylor, *The Apples of England*, 3rd edn. (London: Crosby Lockwood and Son, 1948) epigraph.

2 Richard Sax, *Classic Home Desserts: a Treasury of Heirloom and Contemporary Recipes from Around the World* (Shelburne: Chapters Publishing, 1994) 496 and 497.

3 George Johnson, *A History of English Gardening Chronological, Biographical, Literary, and Critical* (London: Baldwin and Cradock, et al., 1829) 33.

4 I rely on Joan Thirsk's definition of the southwest Midlands in "The South-West Midlands: Warwickshire, Worcestershire, Gloucestershire, and Herefordshire," *1640–1750: Regional Farming Systems*, ed. Joan Thirsk, vol. 5.i of *The Agrarian History of England and Wales*, gen. ed. Joan Thirsk, 7 vols. (Cambridge University Press, 1967–92) 160. Some economic and industrial histories include Warwickshire in the west Midlands or simply the Midlands. More westerly than Warwickshire, Herefordshire is also often included within the ancient, shifting boundaries of Siluria. As Thirsk makes clear, however, the two counties share regional economic and political developments over the course of the seventeenth and eighteenth centuries, in particular, the sense of an ancient history – Herefordshire's linked to the ancient Britons, Warwickshire's to the Romans – and the sense of remoteness, due not to their distance from the political center of England but their inaccessibility as landlocked counties before the era of passable roads.

5 John Philips, *Cyder, The Poems of John Philips*, ed. M. G. Lloyd Thomas (Oxford: Basil Blackwell, 1927) 1. lines 1–6; hereafter cited by line number in the text.

6 John Milton, *Paradise Lost, Complete Poems and Major Prose*, ed. Merritt Y. Hughes (Indianapolis: Odyssey Press, 1957) 1. lines 1–2.

7 For definitions of Siluria see John Goodridge, *Rural Life in Eighteenth-Century English Poetry* (Cambridge University Press, 1995) 139, and Barrell, *Dark Side*, note 99, 173–74.

8 E. W. Brayley and J. Britton, *The Beauties of England and Wales: or Delineations Topographical, Historical and Descriptive*, 25 vols. (London: Vernor and Hood, et al., 1805) 4: 401.

9 Thirsk, "South-West Midlands," 160.

10 Ibid., 169; see also Joan Thirsk, "Agricultural Innovations and their Diffusion," *1640–1750: Agrarian Change*, ed. Joan Thirsk, vol. V.ii, of *The Agrarian History of England and Wales*, gen. ed. Joan Thirsk, 7 vols. (Cambridge University Press, 1967–92) 581–87.

11 Thirsk, "South-West Midlands," 181–82.

12 Celia Fiennes, *The Journeys of Celia Fiennes*, ed. Christopher Morris (London: Cresset Press, 1949) 43.

13 John Evelyn, *Sylva, or, A discourse of forest-trees, and the propagation of timber in His Majesties dominions . . . to which is annexed Pomona . . .*, 2nd edn. (London: John Martyn and James Allestry, 1670) 2.

14 John Beale, *Herefordshire Orchards, a Pattern for all England*. A 1730 edition bound with Richard Bradley, *New Improvements of Planting and Gardening, both Philosophical and Practical*, 6th edn. (London: J. and J. Knapton, et al., 1731) 504.

15 William Marshall, *The Rural Economy of Glocestershire*, 2 vols. (London: G. Nicol, 1789) 2: 240. Batty Langley early disputed Herefordshire's claim to the apple in *Pomona: or, the Fruit-Garden Illustrated* (London: G. Strahan, et al., 1729) 134.

16 Marshall, *Glocestershire*, 2: 221.

17 John Clark, *General View of the Agriculture of the County of Hereford* (London: Colin Macrae, 1794) 8.

18 Ibid., 8–9.

19 J. C. Loudon, *An Encyclopaedia of Agriculture* (London: Longman, et al., 1825) 597.

20 T[homas] A[ndrew] Knight, *A Treatise on the Culture of the Apple & Pear, and on the Manufacture of Cider & Perry* (Ludlow: H. Procter, 1797) 24–26.

21 For a useful discussion of this painting see Barrell, *Dark Side*, 115–17.

22 John Hill (pseud. Thomas Hale), *A Compleat Body of Husbandry* (London: T. Osborne, et al., 1756) 612.

23 Clark, *View of Hereford*, 38.

24 Ibid., 38–39.

25 Charles Dunster, notes, *John Philips's Cider, a Poem in two Books. With Notes Provincial, Historical, and Classical by Charles Dunster* (London: T. Cadell, 1791) 49–50.

26 The OED places this meaning under definition II: "A group or class of persons, animals, or things, having some common feature or features." Race as applied to the flavor of wine is the tenth entry: "A particular class of wine, or the characteristic flavor of this, supposed to be due to the soil." An entry occurs as late as 1835 from Tait's *Edinborough Magazine* II. 350–51: "Like certain wines and fruits . . . in removal, much of the *race*, or peculiar flavour of the soil, is sure to be lost."

27 Samuel Taylor Coleridge, *The Notebooks of Samuel Taylor Coleridge*, ed. Kathleen Coburn, 4 vols., Bollingen Series 50 (Princeton University Press, 1957–) 2: 2087.

28 For an alternative view, see Chris Mounsey, "Christopher Smart's *The Hop-garden* and John Philips's *Cyder*: a Battle of the Georgics? Mid-Eighteenth-Century Poetic Discussions of Authority, Science and Experience," *British Journal for Eighteenth-Century Studies* 22.1 (1999): 74–75.

29 [Samuel Hartlib], preface "To the Reader," *A Designe for Plentie, By an Universall Planting of Fruit-Trees: Tendred by some Wel-wishers to the Publick* (London: Richard Wodenothe, n.d.) n.p.

30 Gillian R. Overing, "Of Apples, Eve, and *Genesis B*: Contemporary Theory and Old English Practice," *ANQ* 3:2, New Series (1990): 87–90.

31 Thomas Browne, *Pseudodoxia Epidemica Books I–VII*, *The Works of Sir Thomas Browne*, ed. Geoffrey Keynes, 4 vols. (University of Chicago Press, 1964) 2: 486.

32 For an earlier literary example of such a reversal, see Margaret E. Goldsmith, "Piers' Apples: Some Bernardine Echoes in Piers Plowman," *Leeds Studies in English* 16, New Series (1985): 309–21.

33 Beale, *Herefordshire Orchards*, 502.

34 Dunster, *Cider*, 48. Marshall confirms the similarity to champagne (*Glocestershire*, II: 246).

35 Ra[lph] Austen, preface, *A Treatise of Fruit-Trees* (Oxford: Thomas Robinson, 1653) n.p.

36 Austen, preface, *The Spirituall Use of an Orchard* (bound with *A Treatise of Fruit-Trees*), n.p.

37 Austen, *A Treatise of Fruit-Trees*, 72. Walter Blith similarly makes no qualitative distinction between apples and pears in *The English Improver Improved or the Survey of Husbandry Surveyed*, third impression (London: John Wright, 1652) 265 [mispaginated as 752].

38 Stephen C. A. Pincus, "From Butterboxes to Wooden Shoes: the Shift in English Popular Sentiment from Anti-Dutch to Anti-French in the 1670s," *The Historical Journal* 38.2 (1995): 333–61.

39 Quoted by Pincus, "Butterboxes," 336.

40 Beale, *Herefordshire Orchards*, 522.

41 On Evelyn's contribution to the debate see Pincus, "Butterboxes," 336.

42 Browne, *Works*, 2: 530.

43 Evelyn, *Pomona*, 4.

44 In 1812 an American writer, William Coxe, suggests that the project of nation-alizing apples and pears was an Anglo-American concern when he points out, "[t]he writers on France are almost silent on this subject: in comparison with their favourite object, the vineyard, it is by them believed to be of little national importance; they are however full and correct on the management of the garden fruits." *A View of the Cultivation of Fruit Trees and the Management of Orchards and Cider* (Philadelphia: M. Carey and Son, 1817) 7.

45 Reverend George Turner, in comments included by Hale, *Husbandry*, 616.

46 Hale, *Husbandry*, 610.

47 Loudon, *Encyclopaedia of Gardening*, 887–88.

48 James P. Carley, *The Chronical of Glastonbury Abbey: an Edition, Translation and Study of John of Glastonbury's Cronica sive Antiquitates Glastoniensis Ecclesie*, trans. David Townsend (Woodbridge: Boydell Press, 1985) 11. For the etymology of Avalon see *The Oxford Companion to the Literature of Wales*, ed. Meic Stephens, (Oxford University Press, 1986) 671.

49 Carley, *Chronical*, quoting from the *Life of Merlin*, lines 908–15. He points out that the final lines are spurious.

6 JAGO'S *EDGE-HILL*: SIMULATION AND REPRESENTATION

1 Cowper's *The Task*, divided like Lucretius's *On the Nature of the Universe* into six books, was far more popular than Jago's. Its wide readership suggests that didactic poetry could achieve a brief renascence even after the form as a whole had lost its generic authority. Importantly, with the exception of Book III, "The Garden," Cowper's poem is not metaphrastic, and is devoted primarily to ethical and moral dilemmas which, like Jago's poem, redistribute georgic values. As Tim Fulford points out, Cowper refigures the authority of the landscape and clears a new location for georgic authority, even as the English georgic form was being emptied of its authoritative status. See *Landscape, Liberty and Authority: Poetry, Criticism and Politics from Thomson to Wordsworth* (Cambridge University Press, 1996) 38. For an earlier argument in favor of defining *The Task* as georgic in its structure and sensibility, see Dustin Griffin, "Redefining Georgic: Cowper's *Task*," *ELH* 57 (1990): 865–79.

2 Nathan Drake, *Literary Hours or Sketches Critical and Narrative* (Sudbury: T. Cadell and W. Davies, 1798) 137.

3 John Aikin, *An Essay on the Application of Natural History to Poetry* (London: J. Johnson, 1777) 58.

4 Joseph Warton, ed., *The Works of Virgil in Latin and English*, 4 vols. (London: R. Dodsley, 1753) 1: 394.

5 Aikin, *Essay*, 57–58.

6 James Grainger, *The Sugar-Cane: a Poem in Four Books* (London: R. and J. Dodsley, 1764) vii.

7 John Barrell, *The Idea of Landscape and the Sense of Place 1730–1840: an Approach to the Poetry of John Clare* (Cambridge University Press, 1972) 1–27.

8 Murray Krieger, *Ekphrasis: the Illusion of the Natural Sign* (Baltimore: Johns Hopkins University Press, 1992) 7.

9 Ibid., 85.

10 Barrell, *Idea of Landscape*, 24.

11 John Dryden, "Preface to Ovid's Epistles, " *Poems, 1649–1680*, eds. Edward Niles Hooker and H. T. Swedenberg, Jr. (Berkeley: University of California Press, 1988) vol. 1 of *The California Edition of the Works of John Dryden*, gen. ed. Vinton A. Dearing, 20 vols. to date, 1956–, 1: 114.

12 Warton, *Virgil*, 1: 397.

13 Aikin, *Essay*, 58–59.

14 John Aikin, Preface, John Armstrong, *The Art of Preserving Health* (London: T. Cadell and W. Davies, 1796) 1.

15 Hugh Blair, *Lectures on Rhetoric and Belles Lettres*, 2 vols. (London: W. Strahan et al., 1783) 2: 371.

16 Ibid., 2: 365.

17 For further discussion of the detachment of georgic images of labor from agriculture to mining see Stephen Copley, "William Gilpin and the Black-Lead Mine," *The Politics of the Picturesque: Literature, Landscape and Aesthetics since 1770*, eds. Stephen Copley and Peter Garside (Cambridge University Press, 1994) 42–61.

18 Thomas Southcliffe Ashton, *Iron and Steel in the Industrial Revolution* (University of Manchester Press, 1924) 5.

19 W[illiam] Hutton, *An History of Birmingham*, 3rd edn. (1781; Birmingham: Thomas Pearson, 1795) 102.

20 Ibid., 85.

21 Even in the case of the country-house poem, as G. R. Hibbard shows in the case of Jonson's *Sir Robert Wroth*, these qualities may be expressed "despite the lack of references to architecture . . . " "The Country House Poem of the Seventeenth Century," *Journal of the Warburg and Courtauld Institutes* 19 (1956): 166. Of central importance "is the value of traditional ways of living and of building, and the place of the great house in the life of the community" (167).

22 Ironically, Chandos was widely identified as Timon in Pope's *Epistle to Burlington*; Ibid. 162.

23 William Dugdale, *The Antiquities of Warwickshire Illustrated; From Records, Leiger-Books, Manuscripts, Charters, Evidences, Tombes, and Armes*, 2nd edn., 2 vols. (1656; London: John Osborn and Thomas Longman, 1730) 134.

24 Richard Jago, *Edge-Hill, or the Rural Prospect Delineated and Moralized. A Poem in Four Books* (London: J. Dodsley, 1767) vi–vii.

25 Quoted by Eric Hopkins, *Birmingham: the First Manufacturing Town in the World 1760–1840* (London: Weidenfeld and Nicolson, 1989) 26. Soho is discussed in every history of Warwickshire.

26 Myles Swinney, *Birmingham Directory*, 1774; quoted by Samuel Timmins, *The Resources, Products, and Industrial History of Birmingham and the Midland Hardware District* (London: Robert Hardwicke, 1866) 218.

27 There was labor abuse, especially appalling when it affected children; nevertheless, conditions were different than those in the textile cities. Though work conditions were harsh by modern (presumably legislative) standards, Birmingham industry was rooted in workshops rather than factories. As a result, workplace standards were determined largely by customary workshop practices rather than the new regimen of the large factory (Hopkins, *Birmingham*, 102–17). The main exception seems to have been pin making, used by Adam Smith as the prototype of industrial division of labor. Hopkins observes that

"[t]he worst job of all for children appears to have been pin-heading…, where only children of the very poorest were employed. Pin-makers were regarded as the most wretched part of the population, no decent mechanic (it was said) allowing his children to go to this work. Mr Phipson himself [the owner] described pin-heading as 'the refuge for the destitute'" (Hopkins, *Birmingham*, 107). Factory conditions in Birmingham overall, however, developed a different pattern than that outlined by Engels, with its specific application to the textile industry.

28 William West, *The History, Topography and Directory of Warwickshire* (Birmingham: R. Wrightson, 1830) 299.

29 Hutton, *History of Birmingham*, 24.

30 See Goodridge, *Rural Life*, 130 and 141–43.

31 The OED records that the term coal was used either for carbonized wood or mineral coal until the nineteenth century. Early references usually distinguish between the two, sometimes indicating the kind of wood that was used or referring to mineral coal with a variety of modifiers: earth coal, sea coal, stone coal, pit coal, or black stone. When not distinguished by modifiers, the context of the statement demonstrates the source of the coal.

32 Flinn cites J. C., *The Compleat Collier* (London: G. Conyers, 1708) and John Curr, *The Coal Viewer and Engine Builder's Practical Companion* (Sheffield: for the author by John Northall, 1797); Michael W. Flinn (assisted by David Stoker), *The History of the British Coal Industry*, vol. 2: *1700–1830: the Industrial Revolution* (Oxford: Clarendon Press, 1984) 3.

33 Hutton, *History of Birmingham*, 24.

34 The first furnaces in England were built in the oldest iron-making district, the Weald, which included Sussex, Kent, Surrey, and Hampshire. Charles K. Hyde, *Technological Change and the British Iron Industry 1700–1870* (Princeton University Press, 1977) 13–14. Charcoal, which is produced through a "smothered" combustion process, was used in smelting, refining, and chafing. For a history of the change from charcoal smelting to coke smelting, see 7–51.

35 Ibid., 56–57.

36 Pig iron made from charcoal also had a high carbon content, which made it suitable only for casting. Carbon could be reduced through the refining process, however, to produce a more malleable metal (ibid., 7). For a technical explanation of the importance of height of charge to the quality of smelted iron, see Dennis Kaegi, et al., "Coal Conversion Processes," *Encyclopedia of Chemical Technology*, ed. Mary Howe-Grant, 4th edn., 25 vols. (New York: John Wiley and Sons, 1993) 6: 504.

37 Abraham Darby discovered the coke-smelting process, although he was not the first to produce carbonized coal (coke). He was using coke exclusively at his Coalbrookedale furnace by 1718. Hyde argues that in spite of England's historic problem with fuel, coke smelting was not adopted by other iron-masters in the first half of the eighteenth century because of the overall cost

of producing coke-smelted iron (*British Iron Industry*, 56). Darby was able to profit from coke smelting because he produced cast rather than smithied articles.

38 Kaegi, et al., "Coal Conversion Processes," 6: 504.

39 Flinn, *British Coal Industry*, 15.

40 Ashton, *Iron and Steel*, 104.

41 Developed in the 1760s, the potting process was used for only a few decades before it was replaced by the even more efficient technique of "puddling" in the 1780s. Exposure of iron to coal (even coke) introduced sulphur contamination that made the metal red-short, or brittle when hot. The potting process circumvented this problem. Rather than exposing pig iron directly to the fuel, pigs were placed in earthenware pots which were heated indirectly by coal (Hyde, *British Iron Industry*, 83–84).

42 Hopkins convincingly disputes the traditional assumption that Birmingham's guild status was the cause of its vibrant trade (*Birmingham*, 5). This was, nevertheless, a central tenet of histories of Birmingham until well into the twentieth century.

43 Quoted by West, *History of Warwickshire*, 294.

44 W. H. B. Court, *The Rise of the Midland Industries 1600–1838* (Oxford University Press, 1994) 247.

45 Hopkins, *Birmingham*, 50.

46 Court, *Midland Industries*, 247.

47 Hutton, *History of Birmingham*, 39; Court, *Midland Industries*, 245.

48 Hewitt, "Industries," 303.

49 Ibid., 199.

50 Court, *Midland Industries*, 140.

51 Timmins, *Industrial History of Birmingham*, 214.

52 Hewitt, "Industries," 205.

53 Timmins, *Industrial History of Birmingham*, 220.

54 My discussion of simulation is indebted to Jean Baudrillard, "The Precession of Simulacra," *Simulacra and Simulation*, trans. Sheila Faria Glaser (Ann Arbor: University of Michigan Press, 1994) 1–42.

55 Timmins, *Industrial History of Birmingham*, 216.

56 Ibid., 215.

57 Dunster, *Cider*, 6.

PART THREE

7 LYRIC ART

1 J. C. Loudon, *An Encyclopaedia of Gardening* (London: Longman, Rees, et al., 1835) 1225.

2 Joseph Addison and Richard Steele, *The Spectator*, ed. Donald F. bond. 5 vols. (Oxford: Clarendon Press, 1965) 4: 190–91.

3 For discussions of the great ode, see Norman Maclean, "From Action to Image: Theories of the Lyric in the Eighteenth Century," *Critics and*

Criticism: Ancient and Modern, ed. R. S. Crane (1952; University of Chicago Press, 1961) 408–60; Paul Fry, *The Poet's Calling in the English Ode* (New Haven: Yale University Press, 1980); Stuart Curran, *Poetic Form and British Romanticism* (Oxford University Press, 1986) 56–84; Paul D. Sheats, "Keats, the Greater Ode, and the Trial of Imagination," *Coleridge, Keats, and the Imagination: Essays in Honor of Walter Jackson Bate*, eds. J. Robert Barth, S. J. and John L. Mahoney (Columbia: University of Missouri Press, 1990) 174–200.

4 Samuel H. Monk, *The Sublime: a Study of Critical Theories in Eighteenth-Century England* (New York: Modern Language Association, 1935) 19.

5 See Maclean, "From Action to Image," 423–28.

6 Addison and Steele, *Spectator*, 3: 541.

7 See Richard Feingold's discussion of the relationship between public purpose and lyric inwardness in *Moralized Song: the Character of Augustan Lyricism* (New Brunswick: Rutgers University Press, 1989) 1–22.

8 Clifford Siskin, *The Historicity of Romantic Discourse* (New York: Oxford University Press, 1988) 12.

9 Ibid., 12.

10 Edward Young, *Ocean. An Ode* (London: Thomas Worrall, 1728) 19.

11 Curran, *Poetic Form*, 29 and 224, note 1.

12 Thomas Warton (quoting John Harington), *The History of English Poetry, from the Close of the Eleventh to the Commencement of the Eighteenth Century*, 4 vols. (London: J. Dodsley, et al., 1774–81; Index, 1806) 4: 88.

13 Anna Seward, *Letters of Anna Seward: Written between the years 1784 and 1807*, 6 vols. (Edinburgh: Archibald Constable, et al., 1811) 2: 377.

14 John Keats, *Letters of John Keats*, ed. Hyder Edward Rollins, 2 vols. (Cambridge: Harvard University Press, 1958) 1: 303.

15 Alan Bewell implies Keats's lyric reading habit when he points out that "[t]he early Keats, especially, read poetry with the eye of a poet-nurseryman, someone who makes it his business to find, produce, and sell flowers – the flowers found either in nature or in literary texts." "Keats's 'Realm of Flora,'" *Studies in Romanticism* 31 (Spring 1992) 74.

16 John Keats, "On Seeing the Elgin Marbles," *The Poems of John Keats*, ed. Jack Stillinger (Cambridge: Harvard University Press, Belknap Press, 1978).

17 Margaret Doody, *The Daring Muse: Augustan Poetry Reconsidered* (Cambridge University Press, 1985) 61.

18 Some georgic poems have been written in three books, a variation on the less influential six-book precedent set by Lucretius. Richard Payne Knight's *The Landscape*, while importing Virgilian topoi, is divided into three books; similarly, John Evans's *The Bees*, though written in four books, was published in only three.

19 Feingold, *Moralized Song*, 2–3.

20 Samuel Taylor Coleridge, *Coleridge's Miscellaneous Criticism*, ed. Thomas Middleton Raysor (London: Constable, 1936) 25.

21 Felix E. Schelling, *The English Lyric* (Boston: Houghton Mifflin, 1913) 1.

22 Tilottama Rajan, "Romanticism and the Death of Lyric Consciousness," *Lyric Poetry: Beyond New Criticism,* eds. Chaviva Hošek and Patricia Parker (Ithaca: Cornell University Press, 1985) 196.

23 Two critics, especially, have reintroduced ways of reading lyric which connect it to its form, its history, and its public purpose. See Curran, *Poetic Form,* and Annabel Patterson, "Lyric and Society in Jonson's Under-wood," *Lyric Poetry,* eds. Hošek and Parker, 148–63.

24 Curran, *Poetic Form,* 10. See also C. S. Lewis's relevant comments in *A Preface to Paradise Lost* (1942; London: Oxford University Press, 1982) 1–2.

25 Anne Williams, *Prophetic Strain: the Greater Lyric in the Eighteenth Century* (University of Chicago Press, 1984) 15.

26 Patterson, "Lyric and Society," 151.

27 J. B. Harley, "Maps, Knowledge, and Power," *The Iconography of Landscape,* eds. Denis Cosgrove and Stephen Daniels (Cambridge University Press, 1988) 292.

28 Loudon, *Encyclopedia of Gardening,* 1225; on coalminers' gardens, see Michael W. Flinn (assisted by David Stoker), *The History of the British Coal Industry,* vol 2: *1700–1830: the Industrial Revolution* (Oxford: Clarendon Press, 1984) 440.

29 Richard Bradley, *A General Treatise of Husbandry and Gardening,* 2 vols. (London: T. Woodward and J. Peele, 1726) 2: 246.

30 George Mason, *An Essay on Design in Gardening* (Dublin: John Exshaw, 1770) 25. Loudon quotes Mason's comment, with minor changes, in *Observations on the Formation and Management of Useful and Ornamental Plantations* (Edinburgh: Achibald Constable, 1804) 217.

31 Humphry Repton, *Fragments on the Theory and Practice of Landscape Gardening* (London: J. Taylor, 1816) 180.

32 Richard Weston, *Tracts on Practical Agriculture and Gardening* (London: S. Hooper, 1769) 42–43.

33 W. R. Johnson, *The Idea of Lyric: Lyric Modes in Ancient and Modern Poetry* (Berkeley: University of California Press, 1982) 82.

34 Refer to Chapter 1, note 65 for a summary of interpretations of nature in the eighteenth century.

35 William Marshall, *Planting and Ornamental Gardening; a Practical Treatise* (London: J. Dodsley, 1785) 585 and 586–87.

36 Ibid., 603.

37 Leigh Hunt, quoting Tasso in *Stories from the Italian Poets: with Lives of the Writers,* 2 vols. (London: Chapman and Hall, 1846) 1: 453.

38 Hunt and Lee, *Sonnet,* 75.

39 Anna Laetitia Barbauld, "Prefatory Essay," *The Poetical Works of Mr. William Collins. With a Prefatory Essay, by Mrs. Barbauld,* by William Collins (London: T. Cadell and W. Davies, 1797) v.

40 Ibid., vi.

41 See W. R. Johnson on the recovery of the function of lyric *vates* by Pindar, *Idea of Lyric,* 59–60.

42 John Aikin, *Essays on Song-Writing: with a Collection of Such English Songs As Are Most Eminent For Poetical Merit* (London: J. Johnson, 1772) ix.

43 Barbauld, "Prefatory Essay," vi–vii.

44 Leigh Hunt, *Bacchus in Tuscany, a Dithyrambic Poem, from the Italian of Francesco Redi, with Notes Original and Select* (London: John and H. L. Hunt, 1825) 165.

45 Sharon Cameron, *Lyric Time: Dickinson and the Limits of Genre* (Baltimore: Johns Hopkins University Press, 1979) 248.

46 Samuel Johnson, *The Rambler*, eds. W. J. Bate and Albrecht B. Strauss, vol. 5 of *The Yale Edition of the Works of Samuel Johnson*, 16 vols. to date (New Haven: Yale University Press, 1958–) 5: 78.

47 John Ogilvie, *Poems On Several Subjects. To Which is Prefix'd, An Essay on the Lyric Poetry of the Ancients* (London: n.p., 1762) xxx–xxxi.

48 John Pinkerton [pseud. Robert Heron, Esq.], *Letters of Literature* (London: G. G. J. and J. Robinson, 1785) 34–35.

49 Hunt, *Bacchus*, xix.

50 ibid., 225–26.

51 Johnson, *Rambler*, 5: 77.

52 Cameron, *Lyric Time*, 24–41.

53 Samuel Taylor Coleridge, *Collected Letters*, ed. Earl Leslie Griggs, 6 vols. (Oxford: Clarendon Press, 1956–1971) 1: 350. See also 1: 394: "Laudanum gave me repose, not sleep: but YOU, I believe, know how divine that repose is – what a spot of inchantment, a green spot of fountains, & flowers & trees, in the very heart of a waste of Sands!"

54 William Blake, *The Complete Poetry and Prose of William Blake*, ed. David V. Erdman (Garden City: Anchor Press, 1982) 490.

55 Thomas G. Rosenmeyer traces this quality back to ancient lyric poetry, in which "extended descriptions of landscapes . . . occur in the form of enclaves, sealed capsules set aside from the larger action, to be enjoyed for their own sake." *The Green Cabinet: Theocritus and the European Pastoral Lyric* (Berkeley: University of California Press, 1969) 192.

56 Young, *Ocean*, 23–24.

57 Seward, *Letters*, 2: 207.

58 For further discussion of this aspect of lyric time, see Cameron, *Lyric Time*, 204.

59 Henry Felton, *A Dissertation on Reading the Classics, And Forming a Just Style*, 2nd edn. (1709; London: Jonah Bowyer, 1715) 89–90.

60 Samuel Taylor Coleridge, *The Notebooks of Samuel Taylor Coleridge*, ed. Kathleen Coburn, 4 vols., Bollingen Series 50 (Princeton University Press, 1957–) 2: 3113.

61 William Wordsworth, "Essay Supplementary to the Preface (1815)," *The Oxford Authors: William Wordsworth*, ed. Stephen Gill (Oxford University Press, 1984) 645, 646, and 648.

62 Leigh Hunt, *The Story of Rimini, a Poem* (London: J. Murray, 1816) xviii.

63 Keats, *Letters*, 1: 225.

8 THE KITCHEN-GARDEN MANUAL

1 Addison and Steele, *Spectator*, 4: 189.
2 Ibid., 189–90.
3 Kames, *Elements of Criticism*, 2: 425.
4 Ibid., 442.
5 Ibid., 427.
6 Ibid., 493–94.
7 Stephen Switzer, *The Practical Kitchen Gardiner* (London: Thomas Woodward, 1727) title page.
8 Batty Langley, *New Principles of Gardening* (London: A. Bettesworth, et al., 1728) 193.
9 Philip Miller, *The Gardeners and Florists Dictionary, or a Complete System of Horticulture, &c.* (1731; London: Charles Rivington, 1724) v.
10 Repton, *Fragments*, 27–28.
11 Francis Bacon, "Of Gardens," *The Works of Francis Bacon*, eds. James Spedding, Robert Leslie Ellis, and Douglas Denon Heath, 12 vols. (Boston: Brown and Taggard, 1860) 12: 235; Miller, *Dictionary* (1724), vii.
12 Switzer, *Kitchen Gardiner*, 396–97. Jean de la Quintinye, *The Compleat Gard'ner*, trans. John Evelyn (London: Matthew Gillyflower and James Partridge, 1693) VI. 179.
13 Richard Weston, *The Universal Botanist and Nurseryman*, 2nd edn., 4 vols. (London: J. Bell, 1777) I: iv.
14 Richard Bradley, *The Gentleman and Gardener's Kalendar*, 4th edn. (London: W. Mears, 1724) 50.
15 Stephen Switzer, *The Practical Fruit-Gardener* (London: Thomas Woodward, 1724) 3–4.
16 Ibid., 81.
17 Ibid., 78–80.
18 Switzer, *Kitchen Gardiner*, xx. He quotes from Evelyn's translation of Quintinye's calendar entry for April (*Compleat Gard'ner* VI. 179).
19 John Abercrombie, *The Hot-House Gardener* (London: John Stockdale, 1789) 127–28.
20 Weston, *Tracts*, 194–95.
21 William Mason, *The English Garden: a Poem*, 4 books (London: J. Dodsley, et al., 1778–81) II. 21–22.
22 William Blake, *Jerusalem, Blake*, 231.
23 The term "glassary apartments" is Abercrombie's (*Hot-House Gardener*, 123, 128, 185).
24 George Johnson, *A History of English Gardening Chronological, Biographical, Literary and Critical* (London: Baldwin and Craddock, et al., 1829) 1.
25 Miller, *Dictionary* (1724), 9.
26 Ibid., xii; John Evelyn, "Garden Letters," *Sir William Temple upon the Gardens of Epicurus, with other seventeenth-century garden essays*, ed. Albert Forbes Sieveking (London, n.p., 1908) 176.

27 William Cobbett, *The English Gardener* (London: n.p., 1829) paragraph 58.

28 As the OED indicates, Milton invented the distinction between the words "sensuous" and "sensual," but it was not until Coleridge put the word "sensuous" into use that the distinction was commonly made. See Coleridge, *Notebooks*, 2: 2442. Although this precise vocabulary may not have been common in the intervening century, comments of literary critics, especially Samuel Johnson, indicate the erotic associations of richly sensuous lyric diction.

29 Johnson, *Rambler*, 77.

30 Ann B. Shteir provides an analysis of the cultural contexts and effects of Linnaeus's classification system in her study of women in botany in *Cultivating Women Cultivating Science: Flora's Daughters and Botany in England 1760 to 1860* (Baltimore: Johns Hopkins University Press, 1996) 9–32.

31 John Farley quotes a suggestive example. In an extended metaphor, Linnaeus imagines that "[t]he *calyx* then is the marriage bed, the *corolla* the curtains, the filaments the spermatic vessels, the *antherae* the testicles, the dust the male sperm, the *stigma* the extremity of the female organ, the *style* the *vagina*, the *germen* the ovary, the *pericardium* the ovary impregnated, the seeds the *ovula* or eggs." *Gametes and Spores: Ideas about Sexual Reproduction, 1750–1914* (Baltimore: Johns Hopkins University Press, 1982) 7.

32 Weston, *Tracts*, 28 and 62.

33 Samuel Collins, *Paradise Retriev'd* (London: John Collins, 1717) 106. Collins was not considered simply a crackpot: his methods for raising cucumbers served as a source for Miller's *Dictionary*.

34 Thomas Hyll, *First Garden Book: Being a Faithful Reprint of A Most Briefe and Pleasaunt Treatvse, Teaching howe to Dress, Sowe, and Set a Garden*, eds. Violet and Hal W. Trovillion (Londyner, 1563; this edition n.d.) n.p. The superstition is repeated in editions of 1568, titled *The Proffitable Arte of Gardening* (3rd edn. p. 178v.), and 1608, titled *The Arte of Gardening*, 151.

35 Andrew Marvell, *The Poems and Letters of Andrew Marvell*, ed. H. M. Margoliouth, 3rd edn. rev. by Pierre Legouis with E. E. Duncan-Jones, 2 vols. (Oxford: Clarendon Press, 1971) 1: 52.

36 An anonymous pamphlet published shortly after Collins's singles out this theory as indecent. *A Letter from a Gentleman in the Country to his Friend in Town: concerning two Books lately published by Mr. Bradley, and Mr. Collins* (London: Bernard Lintot, 1717) 33–34. Bradley, while quizzical, does not deny the notion's credibility. *New Improvements of Planting and Gardening, Both Philosophical and Practical*, 6th edn. (London: J. and J. Knapton, 1731) 265. Informal discussions I have had with a variety of people indicate that the superstition is still alive.

37 Shteir, *Cultivating Women*, 27.

38 Erasmus Darwin, *The Loves of the Plants, The Botanic Garden, A Poem. In Two Parts. Part I. Containing The Economy of Vegetation. Part II. The Loves of the Plants. With Philosophical Notes*, 4th edn., 2 vols. (1789; London: J. Johnson, 1799).

39 Seward, *Letters*, 6: 142.

40 As Erasmus Darwin points out in his treatise on education for girls, "I forbear to mention the Botanic garden; as some ladies have intimated to me, that the Loves of the Plants are described in too glowing colours; but as the descriptions are in general of female forms in graceful attitudes, the objection is less forceable in respect to female readers." *A Plan for the Conduct of Female Education in Boarding Schools* (Derby: J. Johnson, 1797) 38.

41 Bradley, *Husbandry and Gardening*, 1: 333. Although Bradley's notion of plant sexuality was not new, he does seem to have formulated a theory that both pollen and seed contribute characteristics to the new plant well before Linnaeus's work became known in England.

42 Richard Bradley, *Improvements of Planting and Gardening*, 11.

43 Both Switzer and Langley reject Bradley's insinuations. Switzer, *Kitchen Gardiner*, 112; Langley, *New Principles of Gardening*, 38.

44 Miller's instructions for planting melons are from the beginning more sexualized than those of cucumbers, despite the fact that the characters are very similar. In the case of melons, Miller describes the importance of "impregnat[ing] the Ovary of the fruitful Flowers: Which when done, the Fruit will soon swell and grow large." Completing the image, he claims that if his instructions are heeded, "there is no Danger of miscarrying." *Dictionary* (1731), "Melo," arranged alphabetically. This is not surprising given the erotic associations of melons as exotic oriental fruits in the lyric tradition. In later editions of the *Dictionary*, Miller's instructions for tending melons replicate those for tending cucumbers.

45 Philip Miller, *The Gardener's and Botanist's Dictionary*, ed. Thomas Martyn, 4 vols. (London: F. C. and J. Rivington, et al., 1807) alphabetical.

46 Miller's description amplifies the method for fertilizing flowers described by Linnaeus in a prize-winning lecture at the Imperial Academy at Petersburg in 1760. Carl Linnaeus, *A Dissertation on the Sexes of Plants*, trans. James Edward Smith (London: George Nicol, 1786) 36–39.

47 John Abercrombie, *The Complete Forcing-Gardener* (London: Lockyer Davis, 1781) 66–67.

48 Miller, *Gardener's and Botanist's Dictionary*, alphabetical.

49 Patricia Fumerton, *Cultural Aesthetics: Renaissance Literature and the Practice of Social Ornament* (University of Chicago Press, 1991) 109–10.

9 THE POETICS OF THE BOWER: KEATS, COLERIDGE, AND HEMANS

1 Helen Vendler, *The Odes of John Keats* (Cambridge: Belknap Press, 1983) 84–85.

2 For Keats's suburban images, see Bewell, "Keats's 'Realm of Flora,'" 71–98 and Elizabeth Jones, "Keats in the Suburbs," *Keats-Shelley Journal* 45 (1996): 23–43.

3 W. F. Pocock, *Architectural Designs for Rustic Cottages, Picturesque Dwellings, Villas, &c.* (London: Taylor, 1807) 13 and 31.

4 Edmund Bartell, Jr. *Hints for Picturesque Improvements in Ornamental Cottages, and their Scenery* (London: J. Taylor, 1804) 55.

5 J. C. Loudon, *The Green-House Companion* (London: Harding, Triphook, and Lepard, 1824) 249–51.

6 Keats, *Letters*, 1: 175. I use Gittings's redaction of "cordials." Gittings notes that "[a]ll editors, including Rollins, print the unknown word 'cardials'. Keats's *o*'s and *a*'s in this letter are very irregular, and 'cordials' makes sense in the context. It is the Regency slang word for semen. As 'chair' is slang for male sex and 'Bower' for female, the sentence is a sexual joke." John Keats, *Letters of John Keats*, ed. Robert Gittings (Oxford University Press, 1970) 401.

7 George Mason, *An Essay on Design in Gardening (Greatly Augmented)*, 2nd edn. (1768; London: C. Roworth, 1795) 175–76.

8 Coleridge, *Notebooks*, 1: 1700.

9 Ibid., 1597.

10 Ibid., 1211.

11 Samuel Taylor Coleridge, *Sonnets from Various Authors*, bound with Rev. W. L. Bowles's "Sonnets," annotated by Paul M. Zall (1796; Glendale: La Siesta Press, 1968) 1.

12 Coleridge, *Notebooks*, 1: 1489.

13 Ibid., 163.

14 Ibid., 1333.

15 Ibid., 1334.

16 Samuel Taylor Coleridge, "On the Prometheus of Aeschylus," *Shorter Works and Fragments*, 2 vols., eds. H. J. Jackson and J. R. de J. Jackson, vol. 11 of *The Collected Works of Samuel Taylor Coleridge*, 16 vols. gen. ed. Kathleen Coburn, Bollingen Series 75 (Princeton University Press, 1995) 2: 1270.

17 For a more detailed discussion of the surprise reversal of authorial impotency in the history of bower poetry see Rachel Crawford, "Troping the Subject: Behn, Smith, Hemans and the Poetics of the Bower," *Studies in Romanticism* 38.2 (Summer 1999): 249–79.

18 Coleridge, *Notebooks*, 3: 3325.

19 For studies of Coleridge's adaptation of the dynamic system see Raimonda Modiano, *Coleridge and the Concept of Nature* (Tallahassee: Florida State University Press, 1985) 138–206; Trevor Levere, *Poetry Realized in Nature: Samuel Taylor Coleridge and Early Nineteenth-Century Science* (Cambridge University Press, 1981) 64–69; and Thomas McFarland, *Romanticism and the Forms of Ruin* (Princeton University Press, 1981) 289–341.

20 Plato, "Cratylus," *The Dialogues of Plato*, trans. B. Jowett, 2 vols. (New York: Random House, 1937) 1: 209. Coleridge classified many of the terms related to love and longing. For examples, see *Notebook* entries 1: 448, 2: 2739, 2: 2984, 3: 4335, and 4: 4885.

21 Coleridge, "On the Prometheus of Aeschylus," *Shorter Works and Fragments*, eds. H. J. Jackson and J. R. de J. Jackson, 2 vols., vol. 11 of *The Collected Works of Samuel Taylor Coleridge*, gen. ed. Kathleen Coburn, 16 vols., Bollingen Series 75 (Princeton University Press, 1995) 2: 1269–70.

22 See especially M. H. Abrams, "Structure and Style in the Greater Romantic Lyric," *The Correspondent Breeze: Essays on English Romanticism* (New York: W. W. Norton, 1984) 101.

23 Coleridge, *Notebooks*, 4: 5428.

24 Ibid., 2: 2166.

25 Morton Paley, "Coleridge and the Annuals," *The Huntington Library Quarterly* 57 (1994): 12.

26 Coleridge, "Survey of the Natural World," *Shorter Works*, 2: 1454.

27 Ibid.

28 Henry F. Chorley, *Memorials of Mrs. Hemans, with Illustrations of her Literary Character from her Private Correspondence*, 2 vols. (New York: Saunders and Otley, 1836) 1: 88.

29 Ibid., 2: 103–04.

30 Ibid., 1: 112.

31 See Dorothy Mermin, "The Damsel, the Knight, and the Victorian Woman Poet," *Critical Inquiry* 13 (1986): 64–80 and Rachel Crawford, "Troping the Subject," 263–69.

32 Thomas Laqueur, *Making Sex: Body and Gender from the Greeks to Freud* (Cambridge: Harvard University Press, 1990) 161.

33 Quoted by Farley, *Gametes and Spores*, 111.

34 Ibid., 111.

35 Ibid., 115.

36 Quoted by Stanley Stewart, *The Enclosed Garden: the Tradition and the Image in Seventeenth-Century Poetry* (Madison: University of Wisconsin Press, 1966) 45. My discussion of the *hortus conclusus* is indebted to Stewart's work.

37 Quoted in ibid., 42.

38 Felicia Hemans, *The Poetical Works of Mrs. Hemans*, ed. W. M. Rossetti (New York: Thomas Y. Crowell, n.d.) 88. The lines in this edition are not numbered; hereafter referred to in the text by page number.

39 I am indebted for insight into the categories of Here and Now and There and Then to Anne Pippin Burnett's discussion of longing in Sappho's fragments: *Three Archaic Poets: Archilochus, Alcaeus, Sappho* (Cambridge: Harvard University Press, 1983) 303.

Bibliography

Abercrombie, John. *The Complete Forcing-Gardner*. London: Lockyer Davis, 1781.
The Hot-House Gardener. London: John Stockdale, 1789.

Abrams, M. H. "Structure and Style in the Greater Romantic Lyric." *The Correspondent Breeze: Essays on English Romanticism*. New York: W. W. Norton, 1984, 76–108.

Addison, Joseph. "An Essay on Virgil's Georgics." *The Works of the Right Honourable Joseph Addison, Esq.* 4 vols. London: J. Tonson, 1721, 248–58.

Addison, Joseph and Sir Richard Steele. *The Spectator*. Ed. Donald F. Bond. 5 vols. Oxford: Clarendon Press, 1965.

Ahl, Valerie and T. F. H Allen. *Hierarchy Theory: a Vision, Vocabulary, and Epistemology*. New York: Columbia University Press, 1996.

Aikin, John. *Essays on Song-Writing: With A Collection Of Such English Songs As Are Most Eminent For Poetical Merit*. London: J. Johnson, 1772.
An Essay on the Application of Natural History to Poetry. London: J. Johnson, 1777.
Preface, John Armstrong. *The Art of Preserving Health*. London: T. Cadell and W. Davies, 1796.

Anderson, Benedict. *Imagined Communities: Reflections on the Origin and Spread of Nationalism*. London: Verso, 1983.

Anonymous. *A Letter from a Gentleman in the Country to his Friend in Town: concerning two Books lately published by Mr. Bradley, and Mr. Collins*. London: Bernard Lintot, 1717.
The Great Improvement of Commons that are Enclosed for the Advantage of the Lords of Manors, the Poor, and the Publick. London: J. Roberts, 1732.

Appleby, Joyce. "Commercial Farming and the 'Agrarian Myth' in the Early Republic." *The Journal of American History* 68 (1982): 833–49.

Ashfield, Andrew and Peter de Bolla, eds. *The Sublime: a Reader in British Eighteenth-Century Aesthetic Theory*. Cambridge University Press, 1996.

Ashton, Thomas Southcliffe. *Iron and Steel in the Industrial Revolution*. University of Manchester Press, 1924.

Atkinson, William. *Views of Picturesque Cottages with Plans Selected from a Collection of Drawings taken in Different Parts of England*. London: T. Gardiner, 1805.

Austen, Jane. *Mansfield Park*. Oxford University Press, World's Classics, 1990.

Austen, Ra[lph]. *A Treatise of Fruit-Trees* bound with *The Spirituall Use of an Orchard*. Oxford: Thomas Robinson, 1653.

Bacon, Francis. "Of Gardens," *The Works of Francis Bacon*. Ed. James Spedding, Robert Leslie Ellis, and Douglas Denon Heath. 12 vols. Boston: Brown and Taggard, 1860, 12: 235–45.

Barbauld, Anna Laetitia. "Prefatory Essay." *The Poetical Works of Mr. William Collins. With a Prefatory Essay, by Mrs. [Anna Laetitia] Barbauld.* By William Collins. London: Cadell and Davies, 1797.

Barnes, Donald Grove. *A History of the English Corn Laws 1660–1846*. New York: F. S. Crofts, 1930.

Barrell, John. *The Idea of Landscape and the Sense of Place 1730–1840: an Approach to the Poetry of John Clare.* Cambridge University Press, 1972.

English Literature in History 1730–1780: an Equal, Wide Survey. New York: St. Martin's Press, 1983.

The Dark Side of the Landscape: the Rural Poor in English Painting 1730–1840. 1980. Cambridge University Press, 1992.

Bartell, Edmund, Jr. *Hints for Picturesque Improvements in Ornamented Cottages, and their Scenery.* London: J. Taylor, 1804.

Barth, J. Robert, S. J. and John L. Mahoney, eds. *Coleridge, Keats, and the Imagination: Essays in Honor of Walter Jackson Bate.* Columbia: University of Missouri Press, 1990.

Batey, Mavis. "Oliver Goldsmith: an Indictment of Landscape Gardening." *Furor Hortensis: Essays on the History of the English Landscape Garden in Memory of H. F. Clark.* Ed. Peter Willis. Edinburgh: Elysium Press, 1974, 57–71.

Baudrillard, Jean. "The Precession of Simulacra." *Simulacra and Simulation.* Trans. Sheila Faria Glaser. Ann Arbor: University of Michigan Press, 1994, 1–42.

Bayly, C. A. *Imperial Meridian: the British Empire and the World 1780–1830*. London: Longman, 1989.

Beale, John. *Herefordshire Orchards, a Pattern for all England.* A 1730 edition bound with Richard Bradley, *New Improvements of Planting and Gardening, both Philosophical and Practical.* 6th edn. London: J. and J. Knapton, et al., 1731.

Beastall, T. W. *The Agricultural Revolution in Lincolnshire.* Lincoln: History of Lincolnshire Committee, 1978.

Beckett, J. V. "The Debate over Farm Sizes in Eighteenth- and Nineteenth-Century England." *Agricultural History* 57 (1983): 308–25.

The Agricultural Revolution. Oxford: Basil Blackwell, 1990.

"The Decline of the Small Landowner in England and Wales 1660–1900." *Landowners, Capitalists, and Entrepreneurs: Essays for Sir John Habakkuk.* Ed. F. M. L. Thompson. Oxford: Clarendon Press, 1994, 89–112.

Belanger, Terry. "Publishers and Writers in Eighteenth-Century England." Ed. Isabel Rivers. *Books and their Readers in Eighteenth-Century England.* New York: St. Martin's Press, 1982, 5–26.

Bending, Stephen. "Re-Reading the English Landscape Garden." *English Arcadia: Landscape and Architecture in Britain and America.* Ed. Guilland Sutherland. San Marino: Huntington Library, 1992, 379–99.

Bermingham, Ann. *Landscape and Ideology: the English Rustic Tradition, 1740–1860*. Berkeley: University of California Press, 1986.

Bewell, Alan. "Keats's 'Realm of Flora.'" *Studies in Romanticism* 31 (Spring 1992): 71–98.

Blackstone, Sir William. *Commentaries on the Laws of England*. Notes and additions by Edward Christian. 15th edn. 4 vols. London: Cadell and Davies, 1809.

Blair, Hugh. *Lectures on Rhetoric and Belles Lettres*. 2 vols. London: W. Strahan et al., 1783.

Blake, William, *The Complete Poetry and Prose of William Blake*. Ed. David V. Erdman. Garden City: Anchor Press, 1982.

Blith, Walter. *The English Improver Improved or the Svrvey of Hvsbandry Svrveyed*. Third impression. London: John Wright, 1652.

Bourne (pseud. for Sturt), George. *Change in the Village*. New York: A. M. Kelley, 1969; reprint of the 1912 edn.

Bradley, Richard. *The Gentleman and Gardener's Kalendar*. 4th edn. London: W. Mears, 1724.

A General Treatise of Husbandry and Gardening. 2 vols. London: T. Woodward and J. Peele, 1726.

New Improvements of Planting and Gardening, both Philosophical and Practical. 6th edn. London: J. and J. Knapton, 1731.

Brayley, E. W. and J. Britton. *The Beauties of England and Wales: or Delineations Topographical, Historical and Descriptive*. 25 vols. London: Vernor and Hood, et al., 1805.

Brewer, John. *Party Ideology and Popular Politics at the Accession of George III*. Cambridge University Press, 1976.

Brewer, John and Roy Porter, eds. *Consumption and the World of Goods*. London: Routledge, 1993.

Britten, James. *Old Country and Farming Words*. London: English Dialect Society, 1880.

Brogden, William Alvis. "Stephen Switzer: '*La Grand Manier.*'" Furor Hortensis: *Essays on the History of the English Landscape Garden in Memory of H. F. Clark*. Ed. Peter Willis. Edinburgh: Elysium Press Limited, 1974, 21–30.

Bronson, Bertrand H. "The Trough of the Wave." *England in the Restoration and Early Eighteenth Century*. Ed. H. T. Swedenberg, Jr. Berkeley: University of California Press, 1972, 197–226.

Browne, Thomas. *The Works of Sir Thomas Browne*. Ed. Geoffrey Keynes. 4 vols. University of Chicago Press, 1964.

Burnett, Anne Pippin. *Three Archaic Poets: Archilochus, Alcaeus, Sappho*. Cambridge: Harvard University Press, 1983.

Burt, Richard and John Michael Archer, eds. *Enclosure Acts: Sexuality, Property, and Culture in Early Modern England*. Ithaca: Cornell University Press, 1994.

Cameron, Sharon. *Lyric Time: Dickinson and the Limits of Genre*. Baltimore: Johns Hopkins University Press, 1979.

Carley, James P. *The Chronical of Glastonbury Abbey: an Edition, Translation and Study of John of Glastonbury's Cronica sive Antiquitates Glastoniensis Ecclesie.* Trans. David Townsend. Woodbridge: Boydell Press, 1985.

Carter, George, Patrick Goode, and Kedrun Lauri, eds. *Humphry Repton Landscape Gardener 1752–1818.* Norwich: Sainsbury Centre for Visual Arts, 1982.

Certeau, Michel de. *The Practice of Everyday Life.* Trans. Steven F. Rendall. Berkeley: University of California Press, 1984.

Chalker, John. *The English Georgic, a Study in the Development of a Form.* London: Routledge and Kegan Paul, 1969.

Chambers, William. *A Dissertation on Oriental Gardening.* London: W. Griffin, et al., 1772.

Chorley, Henry F. *Memorials of Mrs. Hemans, with Illustrations of her Literary Character from her Private Correspondence.* 2 vols. New York: Saunders and Otley, 1836.

Clark, John. *General View of the Agriculture of the County of Hereford.* London: Colin Macrae, 1794.

Clive, John. "The Social Background of the Scottish Renaissance." *Scotland in the Age of Improvement: Essays in Scottish History in the Eighteenth Century,* Eds. N. T. Phillipson and Rosalind Mitchison. Edinburgh: University Press, 1970, 225–44.

Cobbett, William. *The English Gardener.* London: n.p., 1829.

Rural Rides. Eds. G. D. H. and Margaret Cole. 3 vols. London: Peter Davies, 1930.

Cohen, Ralph. "Innovation and Variation: Literary Change and Georgic Poetry." *Literature and History: Papers Read at a Clark Library Seminar, March 3, 1973.* UCLA: William Andrews Clark Memorial Library, 1974, 3–42.

Coleridge, Samuel Taylor. *Coleridge's Miscellaneous Criticism.* Ed. Thomas Middleton Raysor. London: Constable, 1936.

Collected Letters. 6 vols. Ed. Earl Leslie Griggs. Oxford: Clarendon Press, 1956–1971.

The Notebooks of Samuel Taylor Coleridge. Ed. Kathleen Coburn. Bollingen Series 50. 4 vols to date. Princeton University Press, 1957–.

Sonnets from Various Authors. Bound with Rev. W. L. Bowles's "Sonnets." Annotated by Paul M. Zall. 1796. Glendale: La Siesta Press, 1968.

Essays on His Times in The Morning Post *and* The Courier. 3 vols. Ed. David V. Erdman. Princeton: Princeton University Press, 1978. Vol. 3 of *The Collected Works of Samuel Taylor Coleridge.* Gen. Ed. Kathleen Coburn. 16 vols. Bollingen Series 75. 1971–2001.

"On the Prometheus of Aeschylus." *Shorter Works and Fragments.* 2 vols. Eds. H. J. Jackson and J. R. de J. Jackson. Princeton University Press, 1995, 2: 1251–1301. Vol. 11 of *The Collected Works of Samuel Taylor Coleridge.* Gen. Ed. Kathleen Coburn. 16 vols. Bollingen Series 75. 1971–2001.

Shorter Works and Fragments. 2 vols. Eds. H. J. Jackson and J. R. de J. Jackson. Princeton University Press, 1995. Vol. 11 of *The Collected Works of Samuel*

Taylor Coleridge. Gen. Ed. Kathleen Coburn. 16 vols. Bollingen Series 75. 1971–2001.

"Survey of the Natural World." *Shorter Works and Fragments.* 2 vols. Ed. H. J. Jackson and J. R. de J. Jackson. Princeton University Press, 1995, 2: 1453–56. Vol. 11 of *The Collected Works of Samuel Taylor Coleridge.* Gen. Ed. Kathleen Coburn. 16 vols. Bollingen Series 75. 1971–2001.

The Collected Works of Samuel Taylor Coleridge. 16 vols. Gen. Ed. Kathleen Coburn. Bollingen Series 75. Princeton: Princeton University Press, 1971–2001.

Colley, Linda. "The Apotheosis of George III: Loyalty, Royalty and the British Nation 1760–1820." *Past and Present* 102 (1984): 94–129.

Britons: Forging the Nation 1707–1837. New Haven: Yale University Press, 1992.

Collins, Samuel. *Paradise Retriev'd.* London: John Collins, 1717.

Collins, William. *The Poetical Works of Mr. William Collins. With a Prefatory Essay, by Mrs. [Anna Laetitia] Barbauld.* London: T. Cadell and W. Davies, 1797.

Copley, Stephen. "William Gilpin and the Black-Lead Mine." Eds. Stephen Copley and Peter Garside. *The Politics of the Picturesque: Literature, Landscape and Aesthetics since 1770.* Cambridge University Press, 1994, 42–61.

Copley, Stephen and Peter Garside, eds. *The Politics of the Picturesque: Literature, Landscape and Aesthetics since 1770.* Cambridge University Press, 1994.

Court, W. H. B. *The Rise of the Midland Industries 1600–1838.* Oxford University Press, 1938.

Cowper, William. *The Task, a Poem in Six Books, The Poems of William Cowper.* Eds. John D. Baird and Charles Ryskamp. 2 vols. Oxford: Clarendon Press, 1995.

Coxe, William. *A View of the Cultivation of Fruit Trees and the Management of Orchards and Cider.* Philadelphia: M. Carey and Son, 1817.

Crawford, Rachel. "Troping the Subject: Behn, Smith, Hemans and the Poetics of the Bower." *Studies in Romanticism* 38.2 (Summer 1999): 249–79.

Curr, John. *The Coal Viewer and the Engine Builder's Practical Companion.* Sheffield: John Northall, 1797.

Curran, Stuart. *Poetic Form and British Romanticism.* Oxford University Press, 1986.

Daniels, Stephen. *Fields of Vision: Landscape Imagery and National Identity in England and the United States.* Cambridge: Polity Press, 1993.

Humphry Repton: Landscape Gardening and the Geography of Georgian England. New Haven: Yale University Press, 1999.

Daniels, Stephen and Charles Watkins. "Picturesque Landscaping and Estate Management: Uvedale Price and Nathaniel Kent at Foxley." *The Politics of the Picturesque: Literature, Landscape and Aesthetics since 1770.* Eds. Stephen Copley and Peter Garside. Cambridge University Press, 1994, 13–31.

Darwin, Erasmus. *A Plan for the Conduct of Female Education in Boarding Schools.* Derby: J. Johnson, 1797.

The Loves of the Plants, The Botanic Garden. A Poem. In Two Parts. Part 1. Containing *The Economy of vegetation.* Part 11. *The Loves of the Plants. With Philosophical Notes.* 4th edn. 2 vols. (1789.) London: J. Johnson, 1799.

Phytologia. London: J. Johnson, 1800.

Doody, Margaret. *The Daring Muse: Augustan Poetry Reconsidered.* Cambridge University Press, 1985.

Drake, Nathan. *Literary Hours or Sketches Critical and Narrative.* Sudbury: T. Cadell and W. Davies, 1798.

Drayton, Michael. *The Poly-Olbion: a Chorographicall Description of Great Britain.* 1622. Manchester: Spenser Society, 1889.

Dryden, John, "Preface to Ovid's Epistles." *Poems, 1649–1680.* Eds. Edward Niles Hooker and H. T. Swedenberg, Jr. Berkeley: University of California Press, 1956. Vol. 1 of *The California Edition of the Works of John Dryden.* Gen. Ed. Vinton A. Dearing. 20 vols. to date. 1956–.

Dryden, John, trans. *The Works of Virgil in English,* 1697. Eds. William Frost and Vinton A. Dearing. Berkeley: University of California Press, 1988. Vol. 5 of *The California Edition of the Works of John Dryden.* Gen. Ed. Vinton A. Dearing. 20 vols. to date. 1956–.

Duckworth, Alistair M. "Fiction and Some Uses of the Country House Setting from Richardson to Scott." *Landscape in the Gardens and the Literature of Eighteenth-Century England: Papers read at a Clark Library Seminar 18 March 1978* (read by David C. Streatfield and Alistair M. Duckworth), Los Angeles: William Andrews Clark Memorial Library, 1981, 89–128.

Dugdale, William. *The Antiquities of Warwickshire Illustrated; From Records, Leiger-Books, Manuscripts, Charters, Evidences, Tombes, and Armes.* 2nd edn. 2 vols. London: John Osborn and Thomas Longman, 1730.

Dunster, Charles, ed. *John Philips's Cider, a Poem in two Books. With Notes Provincial, Historical, and Classical.* London: T. Cadell, 1791.

Durling, Dwight L. *Georgic Tradition in English Poetry.* New York: Columbia University Press, 1935.

Dyck, Ian. *William Cobbett and Rural Popular Culture.* Cambridge University Press, 1992.

Dyer, John. *The Fleece: a Poem in Four Books.* London: R. and J. Dodsley, 1757.

Eisinger, Charles. "Land and Loyalty: Literary Expressions of Agrarian Nationalism in the Seventeenth and Eighteenth Centuries." *American Literature* 21 (1949): 160–78.

Eugenia, Sister. "Coleridge's Scheme of Pantisocracy and American Travel Accounts." *PMLA* 45 (1930): 1069–84.

Evelyn, John. *Fumifugium, or the Inconveniencie of the Aer and Smoak of London dissipated.* London: Gabriel Bedel and Thomas Collins, 1661.

Sylva, or, A discourse of forest-trees, and the propagation of timber in His Majesties dominions . . . to which is annexed Pomona . . . 2nd edn. London: John Martyn and James Allestry, 1670.

"Garden Letters." *Sir William Temple upon the Gardens of Epicurus, with other seventeenth-century garden essays.* Ed. Albert Forbes Sieveking. London: n.p., 1908.

Fairchild, Thomas. *The City Gardener.* London: T. Woodward and J. Peele, 1722.

Farley, John. *Gametes and Spores: Ideas about Sexual Reproduction, 1750–1914.* Baltimore: Johns Hopkins University Press, 1982.

Feingold, Richard. *Moralized Song: the Character of Augustan Lyricism.* New Brunswick: Rutgers University Press, 1989.

Felton, Henry. *A Dissertation on Reading the Classics, And Forming a Just Style.* 2nd edn. 1709. London: Jonah Bowyer, 1715.

Fiennes, Celia. *The Journeys of Celia Fiennes.* Ed. Christopher Morris. London: Cresset Press, 1949.

Flinn, Michael W. (assisted by David Stoker). *The History of the British Coal Industry.* Vol. 2: *1700–1830: the Industrial Revolution.* Oxford: Clarendon Press, 1984.

Fry, Paul. *The Poet's Calling in the English Ode.* New Haven: Yale University Press, 1980.

Fulford, Tim. *Landscape, Liberty and Authority: Poetry, Criticism and Politics from Thomson to Wordsworth.* Cambridge University Press, 1996.

Fumerton, Patricia. *Cultural Aesthetics: Renaissance Literature and the Practice of Social Ornament.* University of Chicago Press, 1991.

Fussell, G. E., ed. *Chronological List of Early Agricultural Works in the Library of the Ministry of Agriculture and Fisheries.* London: His Majesty's Stationery Office, n.d. *The Old English Farming Books from Fitzherbert to Tull, 1523 to 1730.* London: Crosby Lockwood, 1947.

Galinou, Mireille, ed. *London's Pride: the Glorious History of the Capital's Gardens.* London: Anaya Publishers Ltd., 1990.

Galt, John. *George the Third, His Court, and Family.* 2 vols. London: Henry Colburn, 1824.

Gay, John. *Rural Sports.* 1713. London: J. Tonson, 1720.

Gerarde, John. *The Herball or Generall Historie of Plantes.* London: J. Norton, 1597.

Goldsmith, Margaret E. "Piers' Apples: Some Bernardine Echoes in Piers Plowman." *Leeds Studies in English* 16, New Series (1985): 309–21.

Goldsmith, Oliver. *Collected Works of Oliver Goldsmith.* Ed. Arthur Friedman. 5 vols. Oxford: Clarendon Press, 1966.

Goode, Patrick. "The Picturesque Controversy." *Humphry Repton Landscape Gardener 1752–1818.* Eds. George Carter, Patrick Goode, and Kedrun Lauri. Norwich: Sainsbury Centre for Visual Arts, 1982, 34–41.

Goodridge, John. *Rural Life in Eighteenth-Century English Poetry.* Cambridge University Press, 1995.

Grainger, James. *The Sugar-Cane: a Poem in Four Books.* London: R. and J. Dodsley, 1764.

Griffin, Dustin. "Redefining Georgic: Cowper's *Task.*" *ELH* 57 (1990): 865–79.

Hadfield, Miles. "History of the Ha-Ha." *Country Life* 30 May 1963: 1261–62.

Hale, Thomas: pseud. for John Hill. *A Compleat Body of Husbandry.* London: T. Osborne, et al., 1756.

Hammond, J. L. and Barbara Hammond. *The Village Labourer 1760–1832: a Study in the Government of England before the Reform Bill.* New York: Longmans, Green, and Co., 1912.

Harley, J. B. "Maps, Knowledge, and Power." *The Iconography of Landscape.* Eds. Denis Cosgrove and Stephen Daniels. Cambridge University Press, 1988, 277–312.

Hartlib, [Samuel]. "To the Reader." *A Designe for Plentie, By an Universall Plant-ing of Fruit-Trees: Tendred by some Wel-wishers to the Publick.* London: Richard Wodenothe, n.d.

Heinzelman, Kurt. "Roman Georgic in the Georgian Age: a Theory of Romantic Genre." *TSLL* 33 (1991): 182–214.

Helsinger, Elizabeth K. "Introduction: Land and Nation." *Rural Scenes and National Representation: Britain, 1815–1850.* Princeton University Press, 1997, 3–37.

Hemans, Felicia. *The Poetical Works of Mrs. Hemans.* Ed. W. M. Rossetti. New York: Thomas Y. Crowell, n.d.

Herndon, G. Melvin. "Agriculture in America in the 1790s: an Englishman's View." *Agricultural History* 49 (1975): 505–16.

Hewitt, E. M. "Industries." *The Victoria History of the County of Warwick.* 8 vols. Ed. William Page. London: Archibald Constable, 1908, 2: 193–268.

Hibbard, G. R. "The Country House Poem of the Seventeenth Century." *Journal of the Warburg and Courtauld Institutes* 19 (1956): 159–74.

Hopkins, Eric. *Birmingham: the First Manufacturing Town in the World 1760–1840.* London: Weidenfeld and Nicolson, 1989.

Hošek, Chaviva and Patricia Parker, eds. *Lyric Poetry: Beyond New Criticism.* Ithaca: Cornell University Press, 1985.

Hume, David. *Essays Moral, Political, and Literary.* Eds. T. H. Green and T. H. Grose. 2 vols. 1882. London: Scientia Verlag Aalen, 1964.

Hunt, Leigh. *The Story of Rimini, a Poem.* London: J. Murray, 1816.
   Foliage; Or Poems Original and Translated. London: C. and J. Ollier, 1818.
   Bacchus in Tuscany, a Dithyrambic Poem, from the Italian of Francesco Redi, with Notes Original and Select. London: John and H. L. Hunt, 1825.
   Stories from the Italian Poets: with Lives of the Writers. 2 vols. London: Chapman and Hall, 1846.

Hunt, Leigh and S. Adams Lee, eds. *The Book of the Sonnet.* London: Sampson, Low, et al., 1867.

Hussey, Christopher. *English Gardens and Landscapes 1700–1750.* London: Country Life Limited, 1967.

Hutton, W[illiam]. *An History of Birmingham.* 3rd edn. Birmingham: Thomas Pearson, 1795.

Hyde, Charles K. *Technological Change and the British Iron Industry 1700–1870.* Princeton University Press, 1977.

Hyll, Thomas. *First Garden Book: Being a Faithful Reprint of A Most Briefe and Pleasaunt Treatvse, Teaching howe to Dress, Sowe, and Set a Garden.* Eds. Violet and Hal W. Trovillion. 1563. Londyner: n.p. This edition n.d.

J. C. *The Compleat Collier.* London: G. Conyers, 1708.

Jago, Richard. *Edge-Hill, or the Rural Prospect Delineated and Moralized. A Poem in Four Books.* London: J. Dodsley, 1767.

Janowitz, Anne. "The Chartist Picturesque." *The Politics of the Picturesque: Literature, Landscape and Aesthetics since 1770.* Ed. Stephen Copley and Peter Garside. Cambridge University Press, 1994, 261–81.

Jehlen, Myra. *American Incarnation. The Individual, the Nation, and the Continent.* Cambridge: Harvard University Press, 1986.

Johnson, George. *A History of English Gardening Chronological, Biographical, Literary, and Critical.* London: Baldwin and Cradock, et al., 1829.

Johnson, James William. "The Classics and John Bull, 1660–1714." *England in the Restoration and Early Eighteenth Century.* Ed. H. T. Swedenberg Jr. Berkeley: University of California Press, 1972, 1–26.

Johnson, Samuel. *The Rambler.* Eds. W. J. Bate and Albrecht B. Strauss. New Haven: Yale University Press, 1969. Vol. 5 of *The Yale Edition of the Works of Samuel Johnson.* 16 vols. to date. 1958–.

Johnson, W. R. *The Idea of Lyric: Lyric Modes in Ancient and Modern Poetry.* Berkeley: University of California Press, 1982.

Jones, Elizabeth. "Keats in the Suburbs." *Keats-Shelley Journal* 45 (1996): 23–43.

Jonson, Ben. "To Penshurst." *Ben Jonson: the Complete Poems.* Ed. George Parfitt. New Haven: Yale University Press, 1975.

Kaegi, Dennis, Valery Addes, Hardarshan Valia, and Michael Grant. "Coal Conversion Processes," *Encyclopedia of Chemical Technology.* Ed. Mary Howe-Grant. 4th edn. 25 vols. New York: John Wiley and Sons; A Wiley-Interscience Publication, 1993. 6: 489–594.

Kames, Henry Home, Lord. *Elements of Criticism.* 3rd edn. 2 vols. Edinburgh: A. Millar, A. Kincaid, and J. Bell, 1765.

Kant, Emmanuel. *Critique of Judgment.* Trans. J. H. Bernard. New York: Macmillan, 1951.

Keats, John. *Letters of John Keats.* Ed. Robert Gittings. Oxford University Press, 1970.

  The Letters of John Keats 1814–1821. Ed. Hyder Edward Rollins. 2 vols. Cambridge: Harvard University Press, 1958.

  The Poems of John Keats. Ed. Jack Stillinger. Cambridge: Harvard University Press, 1978.

Keepsake, The. Ed. Frederic Mansel Reynolds (November, 1828).

Kenny, Virginia C. *The Country-House Ethos in English Literature 1688–1750: Themes of Personal Retreat and National Expansion.* New York: St. Martin's Press, 1984.

Kent, Nathaniel. *Hints to Gentlemen of Landed Property. To which are now first added Supplementary Hints.* London: J. Dodsley, 1793.

  Transactions of the Society for the Encouragement of Arts, Manufactures, and Commerce 17 (1799): 119–39.

Kerridge, Eric. *The Agricultural Revolution.* New York: Augustus M. Kelley, 1968.

Kip, Johannes and L. Knyff. *Britannia Illustrata.* London: n.p., 1714.

Kliger, Samuel. *The Goths in England: a Study in Seventeenth- and Eighteenth-Century Thought.* Cambridge: Harvard University Press, 1952.

Knight, T[homas] A[ndrew]. *A Treatise on the Culture of the Apple & Pear, and on the Manufacture of Cider & Perry.* Ludlow: H. Procter, 1797.

Krieger, Murray. *Ekphrasis: the Illusion of the Natural Sign.* Baltimore: Johns Hopkins University Press, 1992.

Langford, Paul. *A Polite and Commercial People: England 1727–1783*. Oxford University Press, 1989.

Langland, William. *The Vision of Piers Plowman*. Trans. H. W. Wells. New York: Sheed and Ward, 1945.

Langley, Batty. *New Principles of Gardening*. London: A. Bettesworth, et al., 1728. *Pomona: or, the Fruit-Garden Illustrated*. London: G. Strahan, et al., 1729.

Laqueur, Thomas. *Making Sex: Body and Gender from the Greeks to Freud*. Cambridge: Harvard University Press, 1990.

Laurie, Kedrun. "The Repton Park: Walks and Drives." *Humphry Repton Landscape Gardener 1752–1818*. Eds. George Carter, Patrick Goode, and Kedrun Lauri. Norwich: Sainsbury Centre for Visual Arts, 1982, pp. 62–63.

Lefebvre, Henri. *The Production of Space*. Trans. Donald Nicholson-Smith. Oxford: Blackwell, 1991.

Leslie, Michael and Timothy Raylor, eds. *Culture and Cultivation in Early Modern England: Writing and the Land*. Leicester University Press, 1992.

Levere, Trevor. *Poetry Realized in Nature: Samuel Taylor Coleridge and Early Nineteenth-Century Science*. Cambridge University Press, 1981.

Lewis, C. S. *A Preface to Paradise Lost*. London: Oxford University Press, 1942; reprint, 1982.

Linnaeus, Carl. *A Dissertation on the Sexes of Plants*. Trans. James Edward Smith. London: George Nicol, 1786.

Longstaffe-Gowan, Todd. "Gardening and the Middle Classes 1700–1830." *London's Pride: the Glorious History of the Capital's Gardens*. Ed. Mireille Galinou. London: Anaya Publishers Ltd., 1990, 122–33.

Louden J. C. *Observations on the Formation and Management of Useful and Ornamental Plantations*. Edinburgh: Archibald Constable, 1804.

Hints on the Formation of Gardens and Pleasure Grounds. London: John Harding, 1812.

The Green-House Companion. London: Harding, Triphook, and Lepard, 1824.

An Encyclopaedia of Agriculture. London: Longman, et al., 1825.

An Encyclopaedia of Gardening. London: Longman, Rees, et al., 1835.

Low, Anthony. *The Georgic Revolution*. Princeton University Press, 1985.

"Agricultural Reform and the Love Poems of Thomas Carew; with an Instance from Lovelace." *Culture and Cultivation in Early Modern England: Writing and the Land*. Eds. Michael Leslie and Timothy Raylor. Leicester University Press, 1992, 63–80.

Lowenthal, David. *The Past is a Foreign Country*. Cambridge University Press, 1985.

Maclean, Norman. "From Action to Image: Theories of the Lyric in the Eighteenth Century." *Critics and Criticism: Ancient and Modern*. Ed. R. S. Crane. University of Chicago Press, 1952; third impression, 1961, 408–60.

Marshall, William. *Planting and Ornamental Gardening; a Practical Treatise*. London: J. Dodsley, 1785.

The Rural Economy of Glocestershire. 2 vols. London: G. Nicol, 1789.

A Review of the Landscape, a Didactic Poem: also of An Essay on the Picturesque: together with Practical Remarks on Rural Ornament. London: G. Nicol, et al., 1795.

Marvell, Andrew. *The Poems and Letters of Andrew Marvell.* Ed. H. M. Margoliouth rev. by Pierre Legouis with E. E. Duncan Jones. 3rd edn. 2 vols. Oxford: Clarendon Press, 1971.

Mason, George. *An Essay on Design in Gardening.* Dublin: John Exshaw, 1770.

An Essay on Design in Gardening (Greatly Augmented). 1768. London: C. Roworth, 1795.

Mason, William. *The English Garden: a Poem.* 4 books. London: J. Dodsley, et al., 1778–81.

McFarland, Thomas. *Romanticism and the Forms of Ruin.* Princeton University Press, 1981.

McRae, Andrew. "Husbandry Manuals and the Language of Agrarian Improvement." *Culture and Cultivation in Early Modern England: Writing and the Land.* Eds. Michael Leslie and Timothy Raylor. Leicester University Press, 1992, 35–62.

Mermin, Dorothy. "The Damsel, the Knight, and the Victorian Woman Poet." *Critical Inquiry* 13 (1986): 64–80.

Miller, Philip. *The Gardeners and Florists Dictionary, or a Complete System of Horticulture, &c.* London: Charles Rivington, 1724–1768.

The Gardener's and Botanist's Dictionary. Ed. Thomas Martyn. 4 vols. London: F. C. and J. Rivington, et al., 1807.

Milton, John. *"Il Penseroso," with the paintings by William Blake.* New York: Heritage Press, 1954.

Paradise Lost, Complete Poems and Major Prose. Ed. Merritt Y. Hughes. Indianapolis: Odyssey Press, 1957.

Mingay, G. E. *Arthur Young and his Times.* London: Macmillan, 1975.

Mintz, Sidney. *Sweetness and Power: the Place of Sugar in Modern History.* New York: Viking, 1985.

"The Changing Roles of Food in the Study of Consumption." *Consumption and the World of Goods.* Eds. John Brewer and Roy Porter. London: Routledge, 1993, 261–73.

Modiano, Raimonda. *Coleridge and the Concept of Nature.* Tallahassee: Florida State University Press, 1985.

Monk, Samuel H. *The Sublime: a Study of Critical Theories in Eighteenth-Century England.* New York: Modern Language Association, 1935.

Mounsey, Chris. "Christopher's Smart's *The Hop-garden* and John Philips's *Cyder:* a Battle of the Georgics? Mid-Eighteenth-Century Poetic Discussions of Authority, Science and Experience." *British Journal for Eighteenth-Century Studies* 22.1 (1999): 67–84.

Nattrass, Leonora. *William Cobbett: the Politics of Style.* Cambridge University Press, 1995.

Neeson, J. M. *Commoners: Common Right, Enclosure and Social Change in England 1700–1820.* Cambridge University Press, 1993.

Nelson, Robert S. "Appropriation." *Critical Terms for Art History*. Eds. Robert S. Nelson and Robert Shiff. University of Chicago Press, 1996, 116–28.

Ogilvie, John. *Poems on Several Subjects. To Which is Prefix'd, An Essay on the Lyric Poetry of the Ancients*. London: n.p., 1762.

Orwin, C. S. and C. S. Orwin. *The Open Fields*. Oxford: Clarendon Press, 1967.

Overing, Gillian R. "Of Apples, Eve, and *Genesis B*: Contemporary Theory and Old English Practice." *ANQ* 3:2, New Series (1990): 87–90.

Page, William, ed. *The Victoria History of the County of Warwick*. 8 vols. London: Archibald Constable, 1908.

Paley, Morton. "Coleridge and the Annuals." *The Huntington Library Quarterly* 57 (1994): 1–24.

Patterson, Annabel. "Lyric and Society in Jonson's Under-wood." *Lyric Poetry: Beyond New Criticism*. Eds. Chaviva Hošek and Patricia Parker. Ithaca: Cornell University Press, 1985, 148–63.

Philips, John. *The Poems of John Philips*. Ed. M. G. Lloyd Thomas. Oxford: Basil Blackwell, 1927.

Phillipson, N. T. and Rosalind Mitchison, eds. *Scotland in the Age of Improvement: Essays in Scottish History in the Eighteenth Century*. Edinburgh: University Press, 1970.

Pincus, Stephen C. A. "From Butterboxes to Wooden Shoes: the Shift in English Popular Sentiment from Anti-Dutch to Anti-French in the 1670s." *The Historical Journal* 38.2 (1995): 333–61.

Pinkerton, John [pseud. Robert Heron, Esq.]. *Letters of Literature*. London: G. G. J. and J. Robinson, 1785.

Plato. "Cratylus." *The Dialogues of Plato*. Trans. B. Jowett. 2 vols. New York: Random House, 1937, 1:173–229.

Pocock, W. F. *Architectural Designs for Rustic Cottages, Picturesque Dwellings, Villas, &c.* London: Taylor, 1807.

Price, Richard. *Observations on Reversionary Payments*. 3rd edn. London: T. Cadell, 1773.

Pugh, Simon, ed. *Reading Landscape: Country–City–Capital*. Manchester University Press, 1990.

Quintinye, Jean de la. *The Compleat Gard'ner*. Trans. John Evelyn. London: Matthew Gillyflower and James Partridge, 1693.

Rajan, Tilottama. "Romanticism and the Death of Lyric Consciousness." *Lyric Poetry: Beyond New Criticism*. Eds. Chaviva Hošek and Patricia Parker. Ithaca: Cornell University Press, 1985, 194–207.

Repton, Humphry. *Sketches and Hints on Landscape Gardening*. London: W. Bulmer, 1794.
　Designs for the Pavillon at Brighton. London: J. C. Stadler, 1808.
　Fragments on the Theory and Practice of Landscape Gardening. London: J. Taylor, 1816.

Rivers, Isabel, ed. *Books and their Readers in Eighteenth-Century England*. New York: St. Martin's Press, 1982.

Roberts, Henry D. *A History of the Royal Pavilion at Brighton with an Account of its Original Furniture and Decoration*. London: Country Life Limited, 1939.

Rocque, J. *An exact Survey of the Cities of London and Westminster, Borough of Southwark, with the Country near ten Miles round.* London: W. Pratt, 1746.

Rosenmeyer, Thomas G. *The Green Cabinet: Theocritus and the European Pastoral Lyric.* Berkeley: University of California Press, 1969.

Rousseau, G. S. "Science Books and their Readers in the Eighteenth Century." *Books and their Readers in Eighteenth-Century England.* Ed. Isabel Rivers. New York: St. Martin's Press, 1982, 203–24.

Russell, Sir E. John. *A History of Agricultural Science in Great Britain 1620–1954.* London: Allen and Unwin, 1966.

Said, Edward. *Culture and Imperialism.* New York: Knopf, 1993.

Sax, Richard. *Classic Home Desserts: a Treasury of Heirloom and Contemporary Recipes from Around the World.* Shelburne: Chapters Publishing, 1994.

Schelling, Felix E. *The English Lyric.* Boston: Houghton Mifflin, 1913.

Sekora, John. *Luxury: the Concept in Western Thought, Eden to Smollett.* Baltimore: Johns Hopkins University Press, 1977.

Seward, Anna. *Letters of Anna Seward: Written between the years 1784 and 1807.* 6 vols. Edinburgh: Archibald Constable, et al., 1811.

Shammas, Carole. "The Rise of the Colonial Tenant." *Reviews in American History* 6 (1978): 490–95.

Sheats, Paul D. "Keats, the Greater Ode, and the Trial of Imagination." *Coleridge, Keats, and the Imagination: Essays in Honor of Walter Jackson Bate.* Eds. J. Robert Barth, S. J. and John L. Mahoney. Columbia: University of Missouri Press, 1990, 174–200.

Shteir, Ann B. *Cultivating Women Cultivating Science: Flora's Daughters and Botany in England 1760 to 1860.* Baltimore: Johns Hopkins University Press, 1996.

Siemon, James R. "Landlord Not King: Agrarian Change and Interarticulation." *Enclosure Acts: Sexuality, Property, and Culture in Early Modern England.* Eds. Richard Burt and John Michael Archer. Ithaca: Cornell University Press, 1994, 17–33.

Simler, Lucy. "Tenancy in Colonial Pennsylvania: the Case of Chester County." *The William and Mary Quarterly* 43 (1986): 542–69.

Siskin, Clifford. *The Historicity of Romantic Discourse.* New York: Oxford University Press, 1988.

The Work of Writing: Literature and Social Change in Britain, 1700–1830. Baltimore: Johns Hopkins University Press, 1998.

Slater, Gilbert. *The English Peasantry and the Enclosure of Common Fields.* 1907. New York: A. M. Kelley, 1968.

Smart, Christopher. *The Hop-Garden. Poems on Several Occasions.* London: W. Strahan, 1752.

Smith, Adam. *An Inquiry into the Nature and Causes of the Wealth of Nations.* Gen. Ed. R. H. Campbell and A. S. Skinner. Textual ed. W. B. Todd. Oxford: Clarendon Press, 1976.

Smith, Janet Adam. "Some Eighteenth-Century Ideas of Scotland." *Scotland in the Age of Improvement: Essays in Scottish History in the Eighteenth Century*, Eds.

N. T. Phillipson and Rosalind Mitchison. Edinburgh: University Press, 1970, 107–24.

Smout, T. C. *A History of the Scottish People 1560–1830.* New York: Scribner's, 1969.

Solkin, David H. "The Battle of the Ciceros: Richard Wilson and the Politics of Landscape in the Age of John Wilkes." *Reading Landscape: Country–City–Capital.* Ed. Simon Pugh. Manchester University Press, 1990, 41–65.

Somervile, William. *The Chace. A Poem.* London: G. Hawkins, 1735.

Spedding, James, Robert Leslie Ellis, and Douglas Denon Heath, eds. *The Works of Francis Bacon.* 12 vols. Boston: Brown and Taggard, 1860.

Stephens, Meic, ed. *The Oxford Companion to the Literature of Wales.* Oxford University Press, 1986.

Stewart, Stanley. *The Enclosed Garden: the Tradition and the Image in Seventeenth-Century Poetry.* Madison: University of Wisconsin Press, 1966.

Stewart, Susan. *On Longing: Narratives of the Miniature, the Gigantic, the Souvenir, the Collection.* Durham: Duke University Press, 1993.

Stroud, Dorothy. *Humphry Repton.* London: Country Life Limited, 1962.

Sutherland, Guilland, ed. *English Arcadia: Landscape and Architecture in Britain and America.* San Marino: Huntington Library, 1992.

Swedenberg, H. T. Jr., ed. *England in the Restoration and Early Eighteenth Century.* Berkeley: University of California Press, 1972.

Sweet, Timothy. "American Pastoralism and the Marketplace. Eighteenth-Century Ideologies of Farming." *Early American Literature* 29 (1994): 59–80.

Switzer, Stephen. *Ichnographia Rustica: or, the Nobleman, Gentleman, and Gardener's Recreation.* 2nd edn. 3 vols. London: D. Browne, et al., 1718.

The Practical Fruit-Gardener. London: Thomas Woodward, 1724.

The Practical Kitchen Gardiner. London: Thomas Woodward, 1727.

Tate, W. E. *The English Village Community and the Enclosure Movements.* London: Camelot Press, 1967.

Taylor, H[arold] V[ictor]. *The Apples of England.* 3rd edn. London: Crosby Lockwood and Son, 1948.

Thirsk, Joan. "The Common Fields." *Past and Present* 29 (1964): 3–25.

"The South-West Midlands: Warwickshire, Worcestershire, Gloucestershire, and Herefordshire." *1640–1750: Regional Farming Systems.* Cambridge University Press, 1984, 159–97. Vol 5.i of *The Agrarian History of England and Wales.* Gen. Ed. Joan Thirsk. 7 vols. 1967–92.

"Agricultural Innovations and Their Diffusion." *1640–1750: Agrarian Change.* Cambridge University Press, 1985, 533–89. Vol 5.ii of *The Agrarian History of England and Wales.* Gen. ed. Joan Thirsk. 7 vols. 1967–92.

Thirsk, Joan, gen. ed. *1640–1750: the Agrarian History of England and Wales.* 7 vols. Cambridge University Press, 1967–92.

Thomson, James. *The Seasons.* London: John Millar, 1730.

Timmins, Samuel. *The Resources, Products, and Industrial History of Birmingham and the Midland Hardware District.* London: Robert Hardwicke, 1866.

Turner, Bryan. "A Note on Nostalgia." *Theory, Culture and Society* 4.1 (1987), 147–56.

Turner, Michael. *Enclosures in Britain, 1750–1830.* London: Macmillan, 1984.

Veblen, Thorstein. *The Theory of the Leisure Class: an Economic Study of Institutions.* New York: Macmillan, 1899; reprint, New York: Modern Library, 1931.

Vendler, Helen. *The Odes of John Keats.* Cambridge: Belknap Press, 1983.

Ware, Isaac. *A Complete Body of Architecture.* London: T. Osborne and J. Shipton, et al., 1756.

Warton, Joseph, ed. *The Works of Virgil in Latin and English.* 4 vols. London: R. Dodsley, 1753.

Warton, Thomas. *The History of English Poetry, from the Close of the Eleventh to the Commencement of the Eighteenth Century.* 4 vols. London: J. Dodsley, et al., 1774–81.

Washington, George. *Letters from His Excellency George Washington to Arthur Young, Esq. F. R. S. and Sir John Sinclair, Bart. M.P.* Ed. Arthur Young. Alexandria: Cotton and Stewart, 1803.

West, William. *The History, Topography and Directory of Warwickshire.* Birmingham: R. Wrightson, 1830.

Weston, Richard. *Tracts on Practical Agriculture and Gardening.* London: S. Hooper, 1769.

The Universal Botanist and Nurseryman. 2nd edn. 4 vols. London: J. Bell, 1777.

[Whately, Thomas]. *Observations on Modern Gardening, Illustrated by Descriptions.* London: T. Payne, 1770.

Wilkinson, L. P. *The Georgics of Virgil, a Critical Survey.* Cambridge University Press, 1969.

Williams, Anne. *Prophetic Strain: the Greater Lyric in the Eighteenth Century.* University of Chicago Press, 1984.

Williams, Raymond. *The Country and the City.* New York: Oxford University Press, 1973.

Willis, Peter, ed. Furor Hortensis*: Essays on the History of the English Landscape Garden in Memory of H. F. Clark.* Edinburgh: Elysium Press Limited, 1974.

Wilmot, Sarah. *"The Business of Improvement": Agriculture and Scientific Culture in Britain, c.1770–c.1870.* Historical Geography Research Series 24. Bristol: Historical Geography Research Group, 1990.

Wilson, Kathleen. *The Sense of the People: Politics, Culture and Imperialism in England, 1715–1785.* Cambridge University Press, 1995.

Wilson, Penelope. "Classical Poetry and the Eighteenth-Century Reader." *Books and their Readers in Eighteenth-Century England.* Ed. Isabel Rivers. New York: St. Martin's Press, 1982, 69–96.

Withrington, Donald J. "Education and Society in the Eighteenth Century." *Scotland in the Age of Improvement: Essays in Scottish History in the Eighteenth Century.* Eds. N. T. Phillipson and Rosalind Mitchison. Edinburgh: University Press, 1970, 169–99.

Wordie, J. R. "The Chronology of English Enclosure, 1500–1914." *The Economic History Review*, 2nd series. 36.4 (1983), 483–505.

Wordsworth, William. *The Oxford Authors: William Wordsworth*. Ed. Stephen Gill. Oxford University Press, 1984.

Worrall, David. "Agrarians against the Picturesque: Ultra-Radicalism and the Revolutionary Politics of Land." *The Politics of the Picturesque: Literature, Landscape and Aesthetics since 1770*. Eds. Stephen Copley and Peter Garside. Cambridge University Press, 1994, 240–60.

Wright, Thomas. *A Short Address to the Public on the Monopoly of Small Farms, a Great Cause of the Present Scarcity and Dearness of Provisions. With the Plan of an Institution to Remedy the Evil: and for the Purpose of Increasing Small Farms throughout the Kingdom*. London: H. L. Galabin, 1795.

Yelling, J. A. *Common Field and Enclosure in England 1450–1850*. London: Macmillan, 1977.

Young, Arthur, ed. *Annals of Agriculture and other Useful Arts*. 46 vols. Bury St. Edmunds: J. Rackham, et al., 1784–1815.

Young, Arthur. *The Autobiography of Arthur Young with Selections from His Correspondence*. Ed. M. Betham-Edwards. London: Smith, Elder, and Co., 1898.

Young, Edward. *Ocean. An Ode*. London: Thomas Worrall, 1728.

Zimmermann, J. G. *Solitude*. Trans. J. B. Bercier. Dublin: J. Stockdale, 1792.

Index

Abercrombie, John, 222
  on cucumber reproduction, 221
  The Hot-House Gardener, 204
Act of Union (1707)
  and appreciation of georgic poetry, 92, 94
  and expansion, 3, 5
  Philips on, 126, 128, 129
Adam, as Master Gardener, 200
Addison, Joseph
  on kitchen garden, 194–95
  "The Pleasures of the Imagination," 67, 69,
    194–95
  on poetry and gardening, 7, 171–72
  on utility and beauty, 71
  on Virgil, 97
agricultural revolution, timing of, 95–96, 97
agricultural societies, 96–97, 99, 100–01
agricultural treatises, 97–98
  georgic poetry displaced by, 98–99
agriculture, *see* farming
Aikin, John
  on didactic poetry, 141
  on epic poetry, 8
  on georgic poetry vs. prose, 91, 138–39
  on minor lyric poetry, 187
America
  aesthetics of space and policies toward, 79
  agricultural potential of, fascination with,
    107–08
  apple pie in, symbolism of, 114
  and British national identity, 112–13
  Coleridge's description of, 111
  and enclosure, model for, 39, 109, 110
  and expansion, 110
  exports to Great Britain, 109
  georgic response to, 102, 103, 108
  idealization of, 53, 108–09
  productivity in, 109, 110–11
  space and history of, vs. Old World, 109–10
American War, loss of, 3–4
  and agricultural endeavor, 98

and concept of space, 5, 66, 109
and demise of georgic poetry, 93
Young's response to, 76
Anacreon, 187
Anderson, Benedict, 256n.1
Anne, Queen, 126, 128, 148
apple(s)
  best soil for, 120, 122
  and English national identity, 28, 114, 126,
    129–30, 133, 134
  etymology of word, 115, 130
  and evil, semantic connection between, 130
  in garden treatises, 115
  Hereford redstreak, 131, 137
  mythology surrounding, 136–37
  vs. pears, 132–33, 134–35
  symbolism of, 28, 130–31
  see also cider; orchard(s)
apple pie, in American symbolism, 114
Appleby, Joyce, 109
appropriation
  artistic, artifice as, 185–86
  Repton's notion of, 23–24, 83–84
  of views, 14–15, 70
  see also property
architecture
  garden designs mimicking, 33, *33*, 86,
    229–30
  Gothic, 26on.66
Arden, the, 155
Ariconium, 125
Aristotle, 10, 22
art
  containment and, 77
  labor and, 10, 11, 197
  nature and, 185, 229–30
  Sidney's notion of, 184
artifice, 184–86
  as artistic appropriation, 185–86
  in Coleridge's poetry, 237, 240
  in confined forms, 184

303

AEI-1362